ALSO BY THE EDITORS AT AMERICA'S TEST KITCHEN

PRAISE FOR OTHER AMERICA'S TEST KITCHEN TITLES

"Buy this gem for the foodie in your family, and spend the extra money to get yourself a copy, too."
THE MISSOURIAN ON *THE BEST OF AMERICA'S TEST KITCHEN 2015*

"An exceptional resource for novice canners, though preserving veterans will find plenty here to love as well."
THE NEW YORK TIMES ON *FOOLPROOF PRESERVING*

"Carnivores with an obsession for perfection will likely have found their new bible
in this comprehensive collection."
PUBLISHERS WEEKLY (STARRED REVIEW) ON *THE COOK'S ILLUSTRATED MEAT BOOK*

"A one-volume kitchen seminar, addressing in one smart chapter after another the sometimes
surprising whys behind a cook's best practices. . . . You get the myth, the theory, the science and
the proof, all rigorously interrogated as only America's Test Kitchen can do."
NPR ON *THE SCIENCE OF GOOD COOKING*

"The entire book is stuffed with recipes that will blow your dinner-table audience away
like leaves from a sidewalk in November."
SAN FRANCISCO BOOK REVIEW ON *THE COMPLETE COOK'S COUNTRY TV SHOW COOKBOOK*

"A terrifically accessible and useful guide to grilling in all its forms that sets a new bar for its competitors on the bookshelf. . . .
The book is packed with practical advice, simple tips, and approachable recipes."
PUBLISHER'S WEEKLY (STARRED REVIEW) ON *MASTER OF THE GRILL*

"This book upgrades slow cooking for discriminating, 21st-century palates—that is indeed revolutionary."
THE DALLAS MORNING NEWS ON *SLOW COOKER REVOLUTION*

"The 21st-century *Fannie Farmer Cookbook* or *The Joy of Cooking*. If you had to have
one cookbook and that's all you could have, this one would do it."
CBS SAN FRANCISCO ON *THE NEW FAMILY COOKBOOK*

"The sum total of exhaustive experimentation . . . anyone interested in gluten-free cookery simply shouldn't be without it."
NIGELLA LAWSON ON *THE HOW CAN IT BE GLUTEN-FREE COOKBOOK*

"The go-to gift book for newlyweds, small families, or empty nesters."
ORLANDO SENTINEL ON *THE COMPLETE COOKING FOR TWO COOKBOOK*

"This book is a comprehensive, no-nonsense guide . . . a well-thought-out,
clearly explained primer for every aspect of home baking."
THE WALL STREET JOURNAL ON *THE COOK'S ILLUSTRATED BAKING BOOK*

"Some 2,500 photos walk readers through 600 painstakingly tested recipes, leaving little room for error."
ASSOCIATED PRESS ON *THE AMERICA'S TEST KITCHEN COOKING SCHOOL COOKBOOK*

"Cook-friendly and kitchen-oriented, illuminating the process of preparing food instead
of mystifying it . . . the perfect kitchen home companion."
THE WALL STREET JOURNAL ON *THE COOK'S ILLUSTRATED COOKBOOK*

THE BEST OF

— AMERICA'S —

TEST KITCHEN

BEST RECIPES, EQUIPMENT REVIEWS, AND TASTINGS

2018

THE EDITORS AT
AMERICA'S TEST KITCHEN

AMERICA'S TEST KITCHEN
21 Drydock, Suite 210E, Boston, MA 02210

THE BEST OF AMERICA'S TEST KITCHEN 2018
Best Recipes, Equipment Reviews, and Tastings

1st Edition

ISBN: 978-1-945256-03-5
ISSN: 1940-3925

Manufactured in the United States of America

10 9 8 7 6 5 4 3 2 1

Distributed by Penguin Random House Publisher Services
Tel: 800-733-3000

CHIEF CREATIVE OFFICER: Jack Bishop
EDITORIAL DIRECTOR, BOOKS: Elizabeth Carduff
EXECUTIVE EDITOR: Adam Kowit
SENIOR MANAGING EDITOR: Debra Hudak
ASSOCIATE EDITOR: Melissa Drumm
ASSISTANT EDITOR: Samantha Ronan
DESIGN DIRECTOR: Carole Goodman
PRODUCTION DESIGNER: Reinaldo Cruz
PHOTOGRAPHY DIRECTOR: Julie Cote
PHOTOGRAPHY PRODUCER: Mary Ball
FRONT COVER PHOTOGRAPH: Keller + Keller
ASSOCIATE ART DIRECTOR, PHOTOGRAPHY: Steve Klise
STAFF PHOTOGRAPHER: Daniel J. van Ackere
ADDITIONAL PHOTOGRAPHY: Carl Tremblay
FOOD STYLING: Catrine Kelty and Marie Piraino
PHOTOSHOOT KITCHEN TEAM:
    ASSOCIATE EDITOR: Chris O'Connor
    TEST COOK: Daniel Cellucci
    ASSISTANT TEST COOK: Allison Berkey and Matthew Fairman
ILLUSTRATIONS: John Burgoyne
PRODUCTION DIRECTOR: Guy Rochford
SENIOR PRODUCTION MANAGER: Jessica Quirk
PRODUCTION MANAGER: Christine Walsh
IMAGING MANAGER: Lauren Robbins
PRODUCTION AND IMAGING SPECIALISTS: Heather Dube, Dennis Noble, and Jessica Voas
COPYEDITOR: Cheryl Redmond
PROOFREADER: Amanda Poulsen Dix
INDEXER: Elizabeth Parson

PICTURED ON FRONT COVER: Carrot–Honey Layer Cake (page 235)

CONTENTS

APPETIZERS

QUESO FUNDIDO

✓ **WHY THIS RECIPE WORKS:** This stringy, molten cheese dip is popular appetizer fare in Texas. To serve authentic *queso fundido* at home, we used a mixture of smooth-melting, spicy pepper Jack cheese and Colby Jack cheese for extra flavor. Microwaving proved the most efficient, cleanup-friendly melting method, and adding some water helped protect against hot spots for gentler melting. Adding just a teaspoon of cornstarch was enough to keep our melted cheese blend from breaking. For some extra spicy punch, we stirred in sautéed Mexican chorizo, chopped onion, and chopped poblano chile. After a few minutes in the microwave and a quick stir, our authentic queso fundido was piping hot, superstretchy, and begging to be scooped up with tortilla chips.

A clay-colored dish holding hot, bubbling cheese topped with strips of smoky poblano peppers and crumbles of meaty, spicy chorizo sausage—what could be better? In northern Mexico, *queso fundido* (literally "molten cheese") is appetizer fare often served in rolled tortillas. It has since become a mainstay in Mexican American restaurants as a dip; more than a few of us have finished a crockful on our own—washed down with a Mexican beer, of course.

To get started, I armed myself with a box grater and five existing queso fundido recipes I'd found in our massive cookbook library. While the queso fundido I'd eaten while in Texas was cohesive, most of the versions I made separated, leaving a plasticky ball of cheese bobbing in a pool of grease. But this test at least helped me choose a cheese. Unlike creamy chile con queso—the popular dip made with processed cheese and canned tomatoes and peppers—queso fundido is characterized by its gooey, string-like texture. In Mexico this is achieved by using cheeses such as *queso asadero* or *queso Chihuahua* (a cheese, not a dog). But most American recipes turn to mozzarella, cheddar, or the best melter in this initial test: Monterey Jack.

I started with a method I'd read about in a few recipes, whisking shredded Monterey Jack into boiling water. I topped the mixture with sautéed poblano chile, onion, and chorizo. But even after adjusting the amount of liquid, this felt more like a cheesy cream sauce than a thick-but-flowing, tortilla chip–coating queso.

A test kitchen colleague suggested I reference an uncommon offering in the Cook's Country arsenal: a recipe for steamed cheeseburgers. She mentioned that the steamed cheese topping was gooey and magma-like; in other words, it sounded a lot like the consistency and texture I was after for my queso fundido.

So I set a bowl of cheese atop a stovetop steamer that I'd positioned in a Dutch oven and covered it. When I opened the pot's lid 5 minutes later, I was met by clouds of steam and cheese that was perfectly soft and stringy. Our science editor confirmed that steaming heats cheese more gently and protects it from separating.

But bringing out a steamer to make cheese dip was awkward and ridiculous. To replicate the steamer's effect, I combined shredded Monterey Jack with ¼ cup of water, covered the mixture, and microwaved it. A few minutes later, I had a smooth and supple queso, identical to the one I'd made on the stovetop. For my next test, to add even more silkiness, I tossed the cheese with a teaspoon of cornstarch. This trick, one we use frequently in the test kitchen for cheese sauces and fondues, helps keep the cheese from breaking and leaving thick clumps of cheese swimming in oil.

What's more, microwaving the cheese directly in its serving vessel saved me from dirtying an extra dish. And this method also heated up that serving dish so the dip would stay nice and hot.

After all this testing, I circled back to my cheese choice. I loved the way the Monterey Jack melted into a silky dip, but was I getting enough flavor out of it? After experiments with several cheeses, I settled on a mixture of Colby Jack (a twofer cheese of cheddar-like Colby and Monterey Jack) and spicy pepper Jack.

It'd be so easy to make a batch of this smoky, spicy queso fundido next time I have a party. But then I'd have to share.

—MORGAN BOLLING, *Cook's Country*

MAKES 3 CUPS

To reheat, microwave the queso, covered, in 30-second intervals, whisking after each, until melted. Serve with tortilla chips. Our favorite pepper Jack cheese is Boar's Head Monterey Jack Cheese with Jalapeño. You can substitute ground pork for the Mexican-style chorizo sausage, if desired.

1 tablespoon vegetable oil

4 ounces fresh Mexican-style chorizo sausage, casings removed

1 small onion, chopped fine

1 poblano chile, stemmed, seeded, and chopped fine

8 ounces pepper Jack cheese, shredded (2 cups)

8 ounces Colby Jack cheese, shredded (2 cups)

1 teaspoon cornstarch

¼ cup water

1. Heat oil in 10-inch nonstick skillet over medium-high heat until shimmering. Add chorizo and cook, breaking up meat with wooden spoon, until browned, 3 to 5 minutes. Add onion and poblano and cook until vegetables are softened and lightly browned, 3 to 5 minutes. Transfer chorizo mixture to paper towel–lined plate.

2. Toss pepper Jack, Colby Jack, and cornstarch in 2-quart casserole dish until cornstarch lightly coats cheese. Stir in water and chorizo mixture until combined.

3. Cover with plate and microwave until cheese begins to melt around edges of dish, 1 to 2 minutes. Stir and continue to microwave, covered, until cheese is completely melted and just beginning to bubble around edges of dish, 1 to 3 minutes longer, whisking once halfway through microwaving (temperature of cheese should not exceed 180 degrees). Whisk and serve immediately.

NOTES FROM THE TEST KITCHEN

KEEPING DIP WARM
Warm dips are party favorites, but most cool and congeal within minutes. The **Elite Cuisine 1.5 Quart Mini Slow Cooker** kept Queso Fundido warm for 2-plus hours and its lid preserved moisture.

CLASSIC GUACAMOLE

✔ WHY THIS RECIPE WORKS: To make a guacamole with balanced flavor and even texture, we mimicked the coarse surface of a *molcajete*, a Mexican mortar, by mincing the onion and serrano chile with kosher salt. The crystals broke down the aromatics, releasing their juices and flavors and transforming them into a paste that was easily combined with the avocado. A bit of lime zest added further brightness without acidity. We used a whisk to mix and mash the avocado into the paste, creating a creamy but still chunky dip. Diced tomato and chopped cilantro added fruity flavor and freshness.

There's no consensus on what makes a good guacamole. Case in point: As soon as I set out different versions of the dip, the arguing began. Some of my colleagues pounced on a minimalist mash of avocados, salt, and onion as their favorite. Others cast their votes for batches featuring additional ingredients including chiles, fresh lime juice, garlic, diced tomato, fresh cilantro, and spices. Further debate ensued about what the texture should be: thick and chunky, creamy and smooth, or something in between.

That said, the favorite recipes did have one thing in common: In each, the aromatics were thoroughly incorporated into the mashed avocado so that every bite featured a cohesive balance of flavor—not just a bland, unseasoned bite of avocado here and a sharp pop of onion, garlic, and/or chile there.

To achieve this cohesive flavor, the traditional recipes I followed called for grinding the aromatics in a *molcajete*, a three-legged mortar made from volcanic rock, which you may be familiar with if you've ever seen guacamole prepared tableside in a restaurant. Its coarse surface is ideal for pulverizing the aromatic ingredients so that they thoroughly break down and release their flavors. Once that's done, the avocado and any other ingredients are mixed in the molcajete's wide, shallow bowl until the paste is fully incorporated and the chunks are broken down to the desired consistency.

Before I decided what, exactly, would go into my dip beyond the basics, I wanted to figure out the best way to achieve a paste without a molcajete, since most home cooks don't own one. Many recipes default to a food

CLASSIC GUACAMOLE

processor, but after a couple of tests I decided this was unreliable; the blades had a hard time grabbing and breaking down such a small quantity of aromatics (just a few tablespoons total), and it was impossible to blend in the avocado without pureeing it completely. I also tried to do all the preparation by hand, finely mincing some onion (a placeholder for now) and a serrano chile, tossing them in a bowl with salt, and then mashing three avocados (the nutty, buttery Hass variety was a must) into the aromatics with a fork. But the seasoning wasn't as evenly dispersed as the molcajete-made batch, and my arm was worn out.

What I needed was something abrasive like the molcajete to quickly and thoroughly break down the aromatics. Fortunately I had something right in the bowl: salt. In the test kitchen, we often use salt to help break down garlic into a creamy paste, since it grinds the particles and draws moisture out of the cells so that they quickly collapse and soften. Borrowing this idea, I piled together a finely chopped onion (I'd test it against garlic later), a minced chile, and ½ teaspoon of kosher salt. As I ran my knife through the pile, I could see that the salt was helping draw the juices from the onion and chile, and after less than a minute of chopping, I had the homogeneous, fragrant paste I was looking for. I transferred it to a bowl and looked around the kitchen for a better tool with which to incorporate the avocado.

Since my colleagues couldn't agree on the ideal texture, I stuck with my own preference: a creamy base with chunks scattered throughout. I needed a tool that would cut through the avocado but not break it down too much. That ruled out rubber spatulas, wooden spoons, and potato mashers (all too flat), but I paused when I saw a whisk. The top of the whisk, where the wires meet, can mash the avocado efficiently; the gaps between the wires along the body allow most of the avocado chunks to remain whole during mixing; and its rounded shape conforms to the bowl, allowing it to easily incorporate the aromatics. Just a couple of quick turns of the whisk yielded a guacamole that had the right ratio of chunks to mash.

Now for the hard part: getting consensus on the added flavors. Everyone agreed that lime juice was a must to balance the rich avocado, so I stirred in a couple of tablespoons. It wasn't quite enough, but adding more juice would make the dip too loose and acidic. Instead, I added lime zest, unlocking its flavor by working it into the onion-chile paste.

As for the other potential additions, everyone preferred onion to the sharper, hotter flavor of raw garlic. Cumin and black pepper didn't make the cut, but cilantro and tomato did; I seeded the tomato to prevent the jelly from diluting the finished guacamole. I also upped the salt to a full teaspoon, since we've found that rich ingredients often need more aggressive seasoning; doing so also helped the paste ingredients break down more quickly.

The end result was a perfect hybrid of buttery avocado chunks bound by the smooth, well-seasoned mash. My tasters asked me to whip up a few more batches—just so that we could be sure it was perfect.

—LAN LAM, *Cook's Illustrated*

Classic Guacamole

MAKES 2 CUPS

For a spicier version, mince the ribs and seeds from the chile with the other ingredients. A mortar and pestle can be used to process the aromatics.

  2 tablespoons finely chopped onion
  1 serrano chile, stemmed, seeded and minced
     Kosher salt
  ¼ teaspoon grated lime zest plus 1½–2 tablespoons juice
  3 ripe Hass avocados, halved, pitted, and cut into ½-inch pieces
  1 plum tomato, cored, seeded, and cut into ⅛-inch dice
  2 tablespoons chopped fresh cilantro

Place onion, chile, 1 teaspoon salt, and lime zest on cutting board and chop until very finely minced. Transfer onion mixture to medium bowl and stir in 1½ tablespoons lime juice. Add avocado and, using sturdy whisk, mash and stir mixture until well combined with some ¼- to ½-inch chunks remaining. Stir in tomato and cilantro. Season with salt and up to additional ½ tablespoon lime juice to taste. Serve.

PROVENÇAL-STYLE ANCHOVY DIP

✔ **WHY THIS RECIPE WORKS:** A Provençal favorite, *anchoïade* is a potently flavorful mixture of anchovies, olive oil, and garlic that can be spread on toast or used as a dip for vegetables. But many versions of this puree can be unappealingly oily or overrun with unnecessary ingredients that drown out the anchovy flavor. To make a smooth, anchovy-rich dip, we started by creating a creamy, neutral-flavored base with almonds. When boiled and pureed, the nuts took on a smooth consistency that helped to keep our dip cohesive and provided richness without being greasy. We processed anchovy fillets with the softened almonds, along with raisins for subtle sweetness and a few savory ingredients to round out the flavor. Extra-virgin olive oil can become bitter if overprocessed, so we waited until the dip was mostly smooth before slowly drizzling it in. Fresh chives and a final drizzle of olive oil were all this dip needed for a refined presentation.

I thought I knew everything about French cuisine—that is, until I started researching Mediterranean recipes. I quickly learned that Provençal cooking is completely distinct from the quintessential Parisian or Lyonnaise dishes I studied in culinary school. Because it borders the Mediterranean Sea, Provence's food bears a greater resemblance to Italian or Greek cuisine. During my research, one dish in particular caught my eye: *anchoïade*, a dip or spread starring anchovies, garlic, and olive oil. As much as I love anchovies, I wasn't sure I could handle this pungent combination, but I forged ahead anyhow, tracking down several anchoïade recipes and getting to work.

Off the bat, I was amazed at the wide array of ingredients, ranging from briny capers to sweet dried fruit. Like many regional specialties, anchoïades vary from village to village, even kitchen to kitchen, so I made sure to gather a range of styles. The first thing I noticed was the variety of textures. From thin and oily to coarse and clumpy, these recipes ran the gamut, but the one with a smoother, spreadable texture was favored by my tasters as the best option, perfect for serving with crudité or slices of crusty baguette. When it came to flavor, dips with dried fruit like figs and apricots were overly sweet

while those with raisins were more mellow; peppers and onions tasted far too vegetal. It became clear that balance would be key.

But back to texture: With minced anchovies, garlic, and olive oil as my key ingredients, I needed to look elsewhere to create a smooth, thick consistency. Some of the recipes I tried used bread to boost body, but those that used nuts won me over for their superior flavor. While dry crushed nuts yielded a grainy texture, I was wowed by the results when the nuts were soaked and softened in water. Soaked cashews yielded a beautiful whipped consistency, but their buttery flavor proved distracting and the texture was not quite dense enough. Almonds also take well to soaking and pureeing (plus they're a classic Provençal ingredient), so I gave them a shot. Bingo: Soaked overnight and pureed, these nuts lent just the right neutral, savory flavor while also lending plenty of body. Before moving ahead, I wanted to determine how much soaking time was really necessary to deliver these results, and I was pleased to discover that, while a 24-hour soak worked well, the almonds blended just as well following a 20-minute stint in boiling water.

On to flavor. I wanted to round out the distinct, powerful umami punch of the anchovies while still keeping them in the spotlight. A single clove of garlic was all that I needed to add garlic flavor without overwhelming the fish. I wanted a touch of sweetness to offset the intense anchovy flavor, but I still wanted the fish to stay in focus. Dried fruit is a common ingredient, and a few tests revealed that a couple tablespoons of raisins added just enough sweetness. Fresh lemon juice offered a pop of brightness and Dijon mustard added complexity.

Up until now, I had been using the food processor to combine my ingredients—it was fast, convenient, and produced a beautifully smooth dip. But overprocessing olive oil—an essential ingredient in any anchoïade—is a surefire way to turn its nutty, buttery taste unpleasantly bitter. Luckily, this was easily avoided by slowly drizzling in the oil toward the end, allowing it to fully emulsify into the already smooth mixture.

My dip was richly flavored with just a hint of sweetness and a velvety, smooth body. To give it some color and fresh, savory flavor, I folded in minced chives and

PROVENÇAL-STYLE ANCHOVY DIP

drizzled on more lemon juice and olive oil. Spread onto a crusty hunk of bread or, better yet, some crunchy homemade pita chips, this authentic Provençal spread was certainly not for the faint of heart, delivering just the intense, over-the-top savory anchovy flavor I wanted in one real eye-opener of a dip.

—LEAH COLINS, *America's Test Kitchen Books*

Provençal-Style Anchovy Dip

MAKES ABOUT 1½ CUPS

Our favorite brand of anchovies is King Oscar Anchovies—Flat Fillets in Olive Oil. Serve with Olive Oil–Sea Salt Pita Chips (recipe follows), slices of toasted baguette, or raw vegetables.

- ¾ cup whole blanched almonds
- 20 anchovy fillets (1½ ounces), rinsed, patted dry, and minced
- 2 tablespoons raisins
- 2 tablespoons lemon juice, plus extra for serving
- 1 garlic clove, minced
- 1 teaspoon Dijon mustard
  Salt and pepper
- ¼ cup extra-virgin olive oil, plus extra for serving
- 1 tablespoon minced fresh chives

1. Bring 4 cups water to boil in medium saucepan over medium-high heat. Add almonds and cook until softened, about 20 minutes. Drain and rinse well.

2. Process drained almonds, ¼ cup water, anchovies, raisins, lemon juice, garlic, mustard, ¼ teaspoon pepper, and ⅛ teaspoon salt in food processor to mostly smooth paste, about 2 minutes, scraping down sides of bowl as needed. With processor running, slowly add oil and process to smooth puree, about 2 minutes.

3. Transfer mixture to bowl, stir in 2 teaspoons chives, and season with salt and extra lemon juice to taste. (Dip can be refrigerated for up to 2 days; bring to room temperature before serving.) Sprinkle with remaining 1 teaspoon chives and drizzle with extra oil to taste before serving.

Olive Oil–Sea Salt Pita Chips

SERVES 8

Both white and whole-wheat pita breads will work well here. We prefer the larger crystal size of sea salt or kosher salt here; if using table salt, reduce the amount of salt by half.

- 4 (8-inch) pita breads
- ½ cup extra-virgin olive oil
- 1 teaspoon sea salt or kosher salt

1. Adjust oven racks to upper-middle and lower-middle positions and heat oven to 350 degrees. Using kitchen shears, cut around perimeter of each pita and separate into 2 thin rounds.

2. Working with 1 round at a time, brush rough side generously with oil and sprinkle with salt. Stack rounds on top of one another, rough side up, as you go. Using chef's knife, cut pita stack into 8 wedges. Spread wedges, rough side up and in single layer, on 2 rimmed baking sheets.

3. Bake until wedges are golden brown and crisp, about 15 minutes, switching and rotating sheets halfway through baking. Let cool before serving. (Pita chips can be stored at room temperature for up to 3 days.)

VARIATION

Rosemary-Parmesan Pita Chips

Reduce amount of salt to ½ teaspoon. Toss salt with ½ cup grated Parmesan and 2 tablespoons minced fresh rosemary before sprinkling over pitas.

NOTES FROM THE TEST KITCHEN

TASTING ANCHOVIES

All preserved anchovies have been cured in salt, but they come to the market in two forms: packed in olive oil or in salt. The salt-packed variety is the least processed, having only the heads and some entrails removed, leaving the filleting and rinsing to the home cook. Oil-packed anchovies have been filleted at the factory and are ready to use. Our favorite brand is **King Oscar Anchovies— Flat Fillets in Olive Oil**, which have a firm, meaty texture and pleasantly briny, savory flavor.

MOZZARELLA STICKS

✓ **WHY THIS RECIPE WORKS:** To make these crunchy, cheesy apps at home, we worked from the inside out. Whole-milk mozzarella tasted best and offered the stretchy consistency you expect from mozzarella sticks. Plain panko crumbs left gaps in the breading, so we pulsed the crumbs in a food processor (along with some dried oregano and garlic powder for added flavor) to create a cohesive coating. After dredging the sliced mozzarella in flour and egg, we rolled each stick in our seasoned breading and froze the sticks to prevent the cheese from oozing out during frying. Our mozzarella sticks needed only a minute in the hot oil to turn golden brown and supercrisp.

When word got out that I was working on a recipe for mozzarella sticks, a restaurant favorite that few people make at home, I quickly became the most popular cook in the test kitchen.

I started by testing five existing recipes. The results ranged from exploded sticks of cheese with barely any bread crumbs to chunky, bread-heavy spears with hardly any cheese. But while the results were disappointing, I learned a trick or two.

For one thing, a handful of these recipes called for freezing the coated mozzarella sticks before frying—frozen sticks proved less likely to explode during frying. And while some recipes call for string cheese, my tasters and I preferred sticks cut from a block of actual mozzarella. For the breading, standard bread crumbs proved dusty and prone to sogginess; panko-style crumbs provided the most rewarding crunch. I stitched together a working recipe and hit the kitchen.

I cut the mozzarella into ½-inch-wide planks and cut each plank into three "sticks." I coated each stick using our standard breading procedure (dredge in flour, dip in beaten egg, and press on bread crumbs) and placed the breaded sticks in the freezer. After an hour, I fried them. The panko, though pleasantly crunchy, was too coarse to make a solid coating and left gaps where the cheese could leak out. I decided to give the bread crumbs a spin in the food processor until they were finely ground, hoping they'd form a more cohesive coating. This did the trick.

I dropped one last batch of mozzarella sticks into the frying oil. After just 1 minute in the 400-degree oil, they were a lovely shade of golden brown. I used a spider to remove the sticks, set them on paper towels to let them cool slightly, called down my team, and waited for feedback. It was positive, and it came not in words but in smiles.

—ASHLEY MOORE, *Cook's Country*

Mozzarella Sticks

SERVES 4 TO 6

Do not use fresh or part-skim mozzarella in this recipe; their high moisture content can cause the sticks to rupture in the hot oil. This recipe was developed with Sorrento Galbani Whole Milk Mozzarella. We do not recommend using string cheese. Use a Dutch oven that holds 6 quarts or more for this recipe.

- 1 **pound whole-milk mozzarella cheese**
- ½ **cup all-purpose flour**
- 2 **large eggs**
- 2 **cups panko bread crumbs**
- ½ **teaspoon salt**
- ½ **teaspoon pepper**
- ¼ **teaspoon dried oregano**
- ¼ **teaspoon garlic powder**
- 2 **quarts peanut or vegetable oil**
- 1 **cup jarred marinara sauce, warmed**

1. Set wire rack in rimmed baking sheet and line half of rack with triple layer of paper towels. Slice mozzarella crosswise into six ½-inch-wide planks. Cut each plank lengthwise into 3 equal sticks. (You will have 18 pieces.)

2. Spread flour in shallow dish. Beat eggs in second shallow dish. Pulse panko, salt, pepper, oregano, and garlic powder in food processor until finely ground, about 10 pulses; transfer to third shallow dish.

3. Working with 1 piece at a time, coat sticks with flour, shaking to remove excess; dip in eggs, allowing excess to drip off; and dredge in panko mixture, pressing to adhere. Transfer to plate. Freeze sticks until firm, at least 1 hour or up to 2 hours.

4. Add oil to large Dutch oven until it measures about 1½ inches deep and heat over medium-high heat to 400 degrees. Add 6 sticks to hot oil and fry until deeply browned on all sides, about 1 minute. Adjust burner as necessary to maintain oil temperature between 375 and 400 degrees.

5. Transfer sticks to paper towel–lined side of prepared rack to drain for 30 seconds, then move to unlined side of rack. Return oil to 400 degrees and repeat frying in 2 more batches with remaining 12 sticks. Serve with marinara.

TO MAKE AHEAD: Mozzarella sticks can be prepared through step 3 and frozen in zipper-lock bag or airtight container for up to 1 month. After frying (do not thaw sticks), let sticks rest for 3 minutes before serving to allow residual heat to continue to melt centers.

BUFFALO CAULIFLOWER BITES

☑ **WHY THIS RECIPE WORKS:** These crunchy, tangy, spicy, and just plain addictive cauliflower bites will be the new star of your game day table. To make these vegan-friendly snacks, the key was to come up with a flavorful, crunchy coating that would hold up under the Buffalo sauce. A mixture of cornstarch and cornmeal gave us the ultracrisp exterior we wanted. Because cauliflower is not naturally moist (like chicken), we dunked the florets in canned coconut milk first, which had the right viscosity and helped the coating really cling. Frying the bites in hot oil guaranteed a crisp coating, and an herby, dairy-free ranch dressing offered a cooling foil to the kick of the bites.

Step aside potato skins and nachos: When it comes to bar snacks, I'm all about spicy, saucy Buffalo wings. Whether I'm watching the game at my neighborhood watering hole or hosting a laid-back get together, you'll find me camped out in front of a big platter of wings (and boasting the sauce-stained fingers to go with them). Buffalo wings are the ultimate crowd-pleaser, unless that crowd includes folks eliminating animal products from their diet. Rather than cut my vegan friends from my next party's invite list, I set out to see if I could bring the best of Buffalo chicken to a meatless, party-ready app.

Vegan snacks have slowly made their way into the mainstream in recent years, so I had little trouble finding some appealing recipes as I began my research. Across the board, cauliflower proved the go-to stand-in for chicken in poppable, dippable bites, but its treatment varied widely. To get the mild florets nice and crispy, recipes called for a whole host of vegan batters and coatings followed by deep frying or baking. I liked where these recipes were headed, but the end results were uniformly uninteresting. From overly delicate coatings to flat flavors to overcooked florets, these Buffalo bites were decidedly bland. I wanted addictive, finger-licking-good flavor, and these recipes were letting me down. I knew I could do better.

To turn plain cauliflower into a crispy, savory treat, I started with the coating. The liquids called for in my early tests—various vegan milks mixed with hot sauce—were simply too thin to create the coating I was after, so I set my sights on something more substantial. Since eggs were out of the question and the cauliflower lacked the natural moisture of uncooked chicken, I looked to a rich, creamy alternative that would cling to all of the florets' nooks and crannies: coconut milk. The mild, subtly sweet flavor would be a great match for the cauliflower and spicy sauce. I dunked a few florets in a mixture of coconut milk and hot sauce, tossed them with cornstarch, and lowered them into hot oil. This first batch was promising—the cauliflower emerged coated with a good amount of batter—but the texture was still too delicate, ill-suited to the requisite final coating of Buffalo sauce and a dunk in ranch dressing.

To improve the bites' crunch, I dug through my pantry looking for inspiration, and spotted my answer: cornmeal. I stirred some in with the cornstarch, seasoned the mixture with salt and pepper, and tried again. This time, the bites boasted a significant shattering crust, but it wasn't a home run; even with the perfect coating, the florets themselves were unevenly cooked. To make this recipe truly foolproof, I needed to standardize the size of my cauliflower bites and determine their ideal frying temperature. The first matter was simple: As soon as I got my hands on my next head of cauliflower, I carefully cut it into manageable 1½-inch florets. To nail the cooking temperature, I did some tinkering and discovered that I needed very hot oil—400 degrees—otherwise the cauliflower would turn mushy before the coating had a chance to crisp up. A mere 3 minutes in the oil was all the bites needed.

As a final fine-tuning, I streamlined my dredging process, making just enough of the coconut milk–hot sauce mixture and cornmeal-cornstarch mixture to eliminate any excess. This small tweak meant I could stir the florets into the wet ingredients, stir in the dry ingredients, and fry the bites in no time. A dunk in

BUFFALO CAULIFLOWER BITES

some cool, fresh-tasting vegan ranch dressing was the perfect finishing touch.

I gathered my vegan and non-vegan tasters, and my success was clear: Nobody could keep their hands off my crisp, spicy cauliflower bites (and they had the neon orange fingers to prove it).

—NICOLE KONSTANTINAKOS,
America's Test Kitchen Books

Buffalo Cauliflower Bites

SERVES 4 TO 6

We used Frank's RedHot Original Cayenne Pepper Sauce but other hot sauces can be used. Use a Dutch oven that holds 6 quarts or more for this recipe.

BUFFALO SAUCE

¼   cup coconut oil
½   cup hot sauce
1   tablespoon packed organic dark brown sugar
2   teaspoons cider vinegar

CAULIFLOWER

1–2   quarts peanut or vegetable oil
¾   cup cornstarch
¼   cup cornmeal
      Salt and pepper
⅔   cup canned coconut milk
1   tablespoon hot sauce
1   pound cauliflower florets, cut into 1½-inch pieces
1   recipe Vegan Ranch Dressing (recipe follows)

1. FOR THE BUFFALO SAUCE: Melt coconut oil in small saucepan over low heat. Whisk in hot sauce, brown sugar, and vinegar until combined. Remove from heat and cover to keep warm; set aside.

2. FOR THE CAULIFLOWER: Line platter with triple layer of paper towels. Add oil to large Dutch oven until it measures about 1½ inches deep and heat over medium-high heat to 400 degrees. While oil heats, combine cornstarch, cornmeal, ½ teaspoon salt, and ¼ teaspoon pepper in small bowl. Whisk coconut milk and hot sauce together in large bowl. Add cauliflower; toss to coat well. Sprinkle cornstarch mixture over cauliflower; fold with rubber spatula until thoroughly coated.

3. Fry half of cauliflower, adding 1 or 2 pieces to oil at a time, until golden and crisp, gently stirring as needed to prevent pieces from sticking together, about 3 minutes.

With slotted spoon, transfer fried cauliflower to prepared baking sheet.

4. Return oil to 400 degrees and repeat with remaining cauliflower. Transfer ½ cup sauce to clean large bowl, add fried cauliflower and gently toss to coat. Serve immediately with remaining sauce and Vegan Ranch Dressing.

Vegan Ranch Dressing

MAKES ABOUT ½ CUP

We strongly prefer our favorite vegan mayonnaise, Just Mayo.

½   cup vegan mayonnaise
2   tablespoons unsweetened plain coconut milk yogurt
1   teaspoon white wine vinegar
1½   teaspoons minced fresh chives
1½   teaspoons minced fresh dill
¼   teaspoon garlic powder
⅛   teaspoon salt
⅛   teaspoon pepper

Whisk all ingredients together in bowl until smooth. (Dressing can be refrigerated for up to 4 days.)

SCALLION PANCAKES WITH DIPPING SAUCE

✓ **WHY THIS RECIPE WORKS:** Great scallion pancakes are full of rich flavor and flaky, golden brown layers. The secret to perfect pancakes lies in the cooking method. Using boiling water helped keep the pancake dough firmer and less sticky than cold water, and it also made it easier to roll and shape the pancakes before frying. After coating the pancake dough with a mixture of vegetable oil, sesame oil, and flour to prevent sticking, we cooked it in a hot cast-iron skillet, first covered to cook the pancake through and then uncovered to crisp up the exterior. A simple slit cut in the center of each pancake allowed steam to escape and gave us more even browning and better crisping. The finishing touch was a quick sweet-salty dipping sauce.

Forget casinos and racetracks: I do my gambling at Chinese restaurants when I order scallion pancakes. Hitting the jackpot means digging into golden-brown flatbread wedges with crispy exteriors that break away in flaky shards to reveal paper-thin, scallion-studded layers within. But as luck more often has it, I usually end up with floppy, pallid triangles with doughy inner leaves that fuse to form a single dense, gummy layer.

I decided it was time to stop leaving good scallion pancakes to chance and develop my own recipe. A quick look at a few recipes was encouraging. Their ingredient lists included just flour, water, oil, scallions, and salt. And the way the layers were formed seemed clever and interesting: You coat the rolled-out dough with oil and sliced scallions and then fold it up and roll it out again in such a way that you produce multiple sheets of dough separated by fat. When you fry the pancakes, the water in the dough turns to steam, which is trapped between the layers and so forces them apart.

Scallion pancake dough is usually 2 parts flour to 1 part water by volume, but some recipes called for boiling water and others for cool. I tried it both ways, keeping all other variables the same. The cool-water dough proved noticeably stickier and forced me to use a lot of flour on the counter, which I knew would stick to the pancakes and burn in the pan during cooking. The cool-water dough also kept springing back when I tried to roll it out. The dough made with boiling water was not only firmer and less sticky but also more relaxed. Our science editor explained that hot water dissolves the flour's tightly packed starch molecules to a greater extent than cold water does, allowing the starch to absorb the free water that would otherwise make the dough overly sticky. It also decreases the elasticity of the gluten network, so the dough is less prone to snapping back.

Since the finished pancakes in each batch were comparable and the hot-water dough was much easier to work with, the choice was clear. I made another batch, mixing 1½ cups of flour and ¾ cup of boiling water with a wooden spoon and then kneading the dough by hand for a few minutes. I separated it into four pieces and let them rest for 30 minutes before rolling them out into thin rounds. Next I brushed each round with a mixture of vegetable oil and toasted sesame oil added for flavor, sprinkled on the scallions, and proceeded with the rolling into a cylinder, coiling, and second rolling steps, which sounds time-consuming but was actually quickly accomplished. Lastly, I heated 2 teaspoons of vegetable oil in a nonstick skillet and fried my four pancakes, replenishing the oil as needed.

These pancakes definitely had some issues. Steam built up under some of them as they fried, lifting large parts away from the skillet, so they didn't brown evenly. The exteriors were tough and chewy rather than crispy, and the inside was undercooked, verging on raw. And I wasn't wild about repeating the rolling, coiling, and frying steps four times.

Reducing the repetition was easy: I simply rolled out two larger pancakes instead of four smaller ones. I also realized that I might be able to increase the inner flakiness if I created a more distinct barrier between the folds to keep them separated, so I added a bit of flour to the oil that I brushed on the rounds. As for the exterior toughness, I suspected it might be because I had skimped on the oil in the frying step, so I tried the other extreme: deep frying, as many restaurants do. But while the interiors were a bit more cooked through (and the oil-flour mixture did make the pancakes more layered), the pancakes wouldn't stay submerged. I went back to a skillet, but this time I added 2 tablespoons of oil per pancake and switched out nonstick for the steadier, more even heat of cast iron.

The other tweak I made was to cut a slit in the center of each pancake before cooking, hoping that it would allow steam to escape from underneath so the pancake would lie flush against the skillet rather than ballooning in the center. Then, after placing the pancake in the skillet, I covered it, thinking that doing so might trap some heat and cook the interior more thoroughly while the exterior browned and crisped.

After about 1½ minutes, I brushed the top of the pancake with a bit more oil, flipped it (it had indeed remained flat) and covered it again to brown the second side. After another minute or so, both sides were nicely browned but not very crispy. Covering the skillet had trapped not only heat but also steam, which made the pancakes soggy. Another 40 seconds on each side with the skillet uncovered took care of that.

These pancakes were as crispy, as flaky, as layered, and as well cooked as the best I'd ever eaten, and they had been so easy to make that I had time to stir together a quick sauce for dipping. Now that I'm assured of hitting the jackpot every time, I know exactly where to place my bet.

—ANDREA GEARY, *Cook's Illustrated*

Scallion Pancakes with Dipping Sauce

SERVES 4 TO 6

For this recipe, we prefer the steady, even heat of a cast-iron skillet. A heavy stainless-steel skillet may be used, but you may have to increase the heat slightly.

DIPPING SAUCE

- 2 tablespoons soy sauce
- 1 scallion, sliced thin
- 1 tablespoon water
- 2 teaspoons rice vinegar
- 1 teaspoon honey
- 1 teaspoon toasted sesame oil
- Pinch red pepper flakes

PANCAKES

- 1½ cups (7½ ounces) plus 1 tablespoon all-purpose flour
- ¾ cup boiling water
- 7 tablespoons vegetable oil
- 1 tablespoon toasted sesame oil
- 1 teaspoon kosher salt
- 4 scallions, sliced thin

1. FOR THE DIPPING SAUCE: Whisk all ingredients together in small bowl; set aside.

2. FOR THE PANCAKES: Using wooden spoon, mix 1½ cups flour and boiling water in bowl to form rough dough. When cool enough to handle, transfer dough to lightly floured counter and knead until tacky (but not sticky) ball forms, about 4 minutes (dough will not be perfectly smooth). Cover loosely with plastic wrap and let rest for 30 minutes.

3. While dough is resting, stir together 1 tablespoon vegetable oil, sesame oil, and remaining 1 tablespoon flour. Set aside.

4. Place 10-inch cast-iron skillet over low heat to preheat. Divide dough in half. Cover 1 half of dough with plastic wrap and set aside. Roll remaining dough into 12-inch round on lightly floured counter. Drizzle with 1 tablespoon oil-flour mixture and use pastry brush to spread evenly over entire surface. Sprinkle with ½ teaspoon salt and half of scallions. Roll dough into cylinder. Coil cylinder into spiral, tuck end underneath, and flatten spiral with your palm. Cover with plastic and repeat with remaining dough, oil-flour mixture, salt, and scallions.

SHAPING SCALLION PANCAKES

1. After rolling dough into 12-inch round, brush with oil-flour mixture, sprinkle with salt and scallions, and roll round into cylinder.

2. Coil cylinder, tucking end underneath, then flatten.

3. Roll out flattened spiral into 9-inch round; cut ½-inch slit in center of pancake.

5. Roll first spiral into 9-inch round. Cut ½-inch slit in center of pancake. Cover with plastic. Roll and cut slit in second pancake. Place 2 tablespoons vegetable oil in skillet and increase heat to medium-low. Place 1 pancake in skillet (oil should sizzle). Cover and cook, shaking skillet occasionally, until pancake is slightly puffy and golden brown on underside, 1 to 1½ minutes. (If underside is not browned after 1 minute, turn heat up slightly. If it is browning too quickly, turn heat down slightly.) Drizzle 1 tablespoon vegetable oil over pancake. Use pastry brush to distribute over entire surface. Carefully flip pancake. Cover and cook, shaking skillet occasionally, until second side is golden brown, 1 to 1½ minutes. Uncover skillet and continue to cook until bottom is deep golden brown and crispy, 30 to 60 seconds longer. Flip and cook until deep golden brown and crispy, 30 to 60 seconds. Transfer to wire rack. Repeat with remaining 3 tablespoons vegetable oil and remaining pancake. Cut each pancake into 8 wedges and serve, passing dipping sauce separately.

TO MAKE AHEAD: Stack uncooked pancakes between layers of parchment paper, wrap tightly in plastic wrap, and refrigerate for up to 24 hours or freeze for up to 1 month. If frozen, thaw pancakes in single layer for 15 minutes before cooking.

KOREAN FRIED CHICKEN WINGS

✓ WHY THIS RECIPE WORKS: A thin, crispy exterior and a spicy-sweet-salty sauce are the hallmarks of Korean fried chicken. Hoping to make these addicting wings easy to prepare at home, we streamlined our procedure. After dunking the wings in a loose, clingy batter of flour, cornstarch, and water, we let the excess drip back into the bowl and dropped them right into a pot of hot oil. To help the coating withstand a wet sauce, we double-fried the wings, eliminating any excess moisture from the skin and making the coating extra crispy. After letting the coating set, we tossed the wings in a bold sauce that starred the spicy Korean chile paste known as *gochujang*.

I crave fried chicken as much as the next person, but I have never been partial to fried wings. To me, they're bar snacks—fine for occasionally sharing with friends over cold beers but not worth the trouble to make at home.

Or that's how I felt until I tasted the fried wings at a local Korean restaurant. The biggest selling point of this style is its crackly exterior that gives way to juicy meat with an audible crunch—an impressive trait considering that the surface of the chicken is doused with sauce. And unlike many styles of wings that are just sweet, salty, or fiery, these delivered a perfect balance of all those flavors.

That profile has made this style of fried chicken wildly popular as an accompaniment to beer and the pickled side dishes known as *banchan* in South Korean bars and restaurants. In fact, the fried chicken–beer combination is now a multibillion-dollar industry that has spawned the term *chimaek* (chi for "chicken" and maek for "maekju," the Korean word for beer), a South Korean festival, and worldwide restaurant chains like Bon Chon that are centered on this particular dish.

Needless to say, I was hooked and determined to make Korean fried chicken for myself. Once I started to research the recipe, I also learned a practical explanation for using wings: In Korea, where chickens are smaller, restaurants often cut up and fry the whole bird, but because the larger breasts and thighs on American birds are harder to cook evenly, wings are the easier choice. The more I thought about it, I realized I could even make a meal out of Korean fried chicken wings; their bold flavors would surely pair well with a bowl of rice and (in place of the banchan) a bright, fresh slaw.

Replicating the sauce would be easy enough once I figured out the ingredients. So I first focused on nailing the wings' delicate but substantial crunch, reviewing the coatings and frying methods I found in a handful of recipes. The coatings varied considerably—from a simple cornstarch dredge to a thick batter made with eggs, flour, and cornstarch—and I found methods for both single frying and double frying. Figuring I'd start with a minimalist approach, I tossed 3 pounds of wings (which would feed at least four people) in cornstarch before frying them once, for about 10 minutes, in a Dutch oven filled with 2 quarts of 350-degree oil.

The meat on these wings was a tad dry, but their worst flaw was the coating—or lack thereof. Most of the cornstarch fell off as soon as the wings hit the oil, so the crust was wimpy—nothing that could stand up to a sauce—and only lightly browned.

Thinking that the starch needed some moisture to help it cling to the chicken, I next tried a series of batter coatings. Not surprisingly, the shaggy mixture of flour, cornstarch, and egg fried up thick and craggy, more like the coating on American fried chicken. I also tried a combination of just cornstarch and water, but it was another bust: Adding enough liquid to make the mixture loose enough to coat the chicken also made it too runny to cling, but without enough water the mixture thickened up like liquid cement. Coating the wings with a creamy, loose slurry of flour and water yielded a nicely thin crust, though it was a bit tough and lacked the elusive shattery texture I was after. From there, I tried various ratios of flour and cornstarch and found that supplementing a flour-based batter with just 3 tablespoons of cornstarch helped the coating crisp up nicely. I understood why once I learned that flour and cornstarch play different but complementary roles in frying: The proteins in wheat flour help the batter bond to the meat and also brown deeply; cornstarch (a pure starch) doesn't cling or brown as well as flour, but it crisps up nicely. Why? Because pure starch releases more amylose, a starch molecule that fries up supercrispy. Cornstarch also can't form gluten, so it doesn't turn tough.

KOREAN FRIED CHICKEN WINGS

I dunked the wings in the batter and let the excess drip back into the bowl before adding them to the hot oil. When they emerged, I thought I'd finally nailed the crust, which was gorgeously crispy and brown. But when I slathered the wings with my placeholder sauce (a mixture of the spicy-sweet Korean chile-soybean paste *gochujang*, sugar, garlic, ginger, sesame oil, soy sauce, and a little water) and took a bite, I paused. They'd gone from supercrispy to soggy in minutes.

It was a setback that made me wonder if double frying might be worth a try, so I ran the obvious head-to-head test: one batch of wings fried continuously until done versus another fried partway, removed from the oil and allowed to rest briefly, and then fried again until cooked through. After draining, I would toss both batches in the same amount of sauce to see which one stayed crispier.

It wasn't even a contest: Whereas the wings that had been fried once and then sauced started to soften up almost instantly, the double-fried batch still delivered real crunch after being doused with the sauce. What's more, the double-fried wings were juicier than any batch I'd made before. Why? Chicken skin contains a lot of moisture, so producing crispy wings (which have a higher ratio of skin to meat than any other part of the chicken) means removing as much moisture as possible from the chicken skin before the meat overcooks. When you fry just once, the meat finishes cooking before all of the moisture is driven out of the chicken skin, and the remaining moisture migrates to the crust and turns it soggy. Covering the wings with sauce makes the sogginess even worse. But when you fry twice, the interruption of the cooking and the brief cooldown period slow the cooking of the meat; as a result, you can extend the overall cooking time and expel all the moisture from the skin without overcooking the chicken.

There was my proof that double frying was worth the time—and it wasn't the tediously long cooking process I expected. I had to do the first fry in two batches, for two reasons: The oil temperature would drop too much if I put all the chicken in at once because there would be so much moisture from the skin to cook off; plus, the wet coating would cause the wings to stick together if they were crowded in the pot. But the frying took only about 7 minutes per batch. As the parcooked wings rested, I brought the oil temperature up to 375 degrees. Then, following the lead of one of the more prominent Korean fried chicken recipes I'd found, I dumped all the wings back into the pot at once for the second stage.

After another 7 minutes, they were deeply golden and shatteringly crispy. All told, I'd produced 3 pounds of perfectly crispy wings in roughly half an hour. Not bad.

Back to my placeholder sauce, which was close but a tad sharp from the raw minced garlic and ginger. Instead, I placed the ginger and garlic in a large bowl with a tablespoon of sesame oil and microwaved the mixture for 1 minute, just long enough to take the edge off. Then I whisked in the remaining sauce ingredients. The sweet-savory-spicy balance was pitch-perfect.

Before tossing them in the sauce, I let the wings rest for 2 minutes so the coating could cool and set. When I did add them to the sauce, they were still so crispy that they clunked encouragingly against the sides of the bowl. In fact, the crust's staying power made me curious to see how long the crunch would last, so I set some wings aside and found that they stayed crispy for 2 hours. Impressive, though I knew they'd be gobbled up long before that.

—ANDREA GEARY, *Cook's Illustrated*

Korean Fried Chicken Wings

SERVES 8 TO 10

A rasp-style grater makes quick work of turning the garlic into a paste. Our favorite rasp-style grater is the Microplane Classic Zester Grater. *Gochujang*, a Korean chile-soybean paste, can be found in Asian markets and in some supermarkets. Tailor the heat level of your wings by adjusting its amount. If you can't find gochujang, substitute an equal amount of Sriracha sauce and add only 2 tablespoons of water to the sauce.

1	tablespoon toasted sesame oil
1	teaspoon garlic, minced to paste
1	teaspoon grated fresh ginger
1¾	cups water
3	tablespoons sugar
2–3	tablespoons gochujang
1	tablespoon soy sauce
2	quarts vegetable oil
1	cup all-purpose flour
3	tablespoons cornstarch
3	pounds chicken wings, cut at joints, wingtips discarded

1. Combine sesame oil, garlic, and ginger in large bowl and microwave until mixture is bubbly and garlic and ginger are fragrant but not browned, 40 to

60 seconds. Whisk in ¼ cup water, sugar, gochujang, and soy sauce until smooth; set aside.

2. Heat vegetable oil in large Dutch oven over medium-high heat to 350 degrees. While oil heats, whisk flour, cornstarch, and remaining 1½ cups water in second large bowl until smooth. Set wire rack in rimmed baking sheet and set aside.

3. Place half of wings in batter and stir to coat. Using tongs, remove wings from batter one at a time, allowing any excess batter to drip back into bowl, and add to hot oil. Increase heat to high and cook, stirring occasionally to prevent wings from sticking, until coating is light golden and beginning to crisp, about 7 minutes. (Oil temperature will drop sharply after adding wings.) Transfer wings to prepared rack. Return oil to 350 degrees and repeat with remaining wings. Reduce heat to medium and let second batch of wings rest for 5 minutes.

4. Heat oil to 375 degrees. Carefully return all wings to oil and cook, stirring occasionally, until deep golden brown and very crispy, about 7 minutes. Return wings to rack and let stand for 2 minutes. Transfer wings to reserved sauce and toss until coated. Return wings to rack and let stand for 2 minutes to allow coating to set. Transfer to platter and serve.

DEVILS ON HORSEBACK

✔ WHY THIS RECIPE WORKS: Devils on horseback are a cocktail hour favorite, uniting sweet dried dates, intense blue cheese, and salty bacon into a bite-sized morsel exploding with flavor. We set out to simplify assembly of this sometimes tedious appetizer. Pitted Deglet Noor dates proved the easiest to work with—we simply sliced them open and stuffed them with cheese. Freezing the cheese made it easier to work with. We wrapped just half a slice of bacon around each stuffed date to avoid a lot of overlap (and the resulting gumminess). Baking the devils on a wire rack set in a baking sheet ensured that the bacon crisped evenly as the fat dripped away.

Devils on horseback are dates or prunes stuffed with cheese and wrapped in bacon. Alone, each ingredient is capable of an intense cocktail-hour performance. But when they play together, they have the potential to be transformative. Or disastrous.

Making this appetizer can be tedious, time-consuming, and messy, and you run the risk of ending up with burnt or flabby bacon, grease-soaked dates, and cheese that oozes onto the pan to burn. I set out to create a quick and effective assembly process that would keep all the parts in the right places.

After trying a range of recipes, I found prunes too difficult to work with, and my tasters balked at the ropey texture of larger Medjool dates. I settled on more common pitted Deglet Noor dates for their manageable size, tender texture, and ample room for stuffing.

But stuffing cheese into the dates' small holes gave me a headache. Splitting the dates open with a paring knife proved to be the answer (their natural stickiness helped them seal back up nicely), but portioning the creamy blue cheese was a pain. Using a ¼-teaspoon measure to scoop portions of it left more on my fingers than in the dates, and trying to cut the wedge into pieces gunked up my knife and turned my cutting board into a sticky disaster zone. A coworker suggested freezing the cheese. Exasperated, I threw the chunk of cheese in the freezer and walked away. We both needed to chill out.

I returned a bit later to take another swing and, happily, found the fresh-out-of-the-freezer cheese much easier to work with. It was easy to crumble the cold cheese, and the crumbles fit perfectly in the dates.

Wrapping the filled dates in bacon slices and securing each with a toothpick, I placed them directly on a baking sheet and baked them at 450 degrees, assuming that the high temperature and direct contact with the hot sheet would quickly crisp the bacon. Reaching into a smoky oven to flip them, I found nothing but burnt devils swimming in grease.

I needed to slow the cooking and get the devils out of the grease. I reduced the oven temperature to 400 degrees and grabbed a wire rack, setting it in my baking sheet to elevate the devils and allow them to shed their grease. And rather than use a full slice of bacon for each date, I cut the slices in half crosswise. They overlapped just a bit but rendered beautifully nonetheless, with no residual gumminess. And with the rack in play, I didn't need to individually flip each devil over halfway through baking.

Since I was opening, stuffing, wrapping, and skewering 32 devils, I was looking for just one step fewer. Hopeful, I assembled another batch (omitting the toothpick skewering step) and positioned them seam side down on the rack. To my satisfaction, as the bacon cooked, it closed tightly around the dates, making the toothpicks superfluous. I instead placed toothpicks on the serving platter for my tasters to use to spear and eat the devils—which they devoured in mere minutes.

—CECELIA JENKINS, *Cook's Country*

Devils on Horseback

MAKES 32 PIECES

Use tender dates that measure at least 1¼ inches in length; smaller, drier dates are difficult to stuff. Do not use Medjool dates or thick-cut bacon in this recipe. Freezing the blue cheese for 20 minutes makes it easier to crumble. Our preferred supermarket blue cheese is Stella Blue.

   4   ounces blue cheese
  32   pitted Deglet Noor dates, about 1¼ inches long
  16   slices bacon

1. Adjust oven rack to middle position and heat oven to 400 degrees. Set wire rack in aluminum foil–lined rimmed baking sheet. Freeze blue cheese until firm, about 20 minutes.

2. Cut through 1 long side of each date and open like book. Crumble blue cheese and divide evenly among dates. Close dates around blue cheese and squeeze lightly to seal (dates should be full but not overflowing).

3. Lay bacon slices on cutting board and halve each slice crosswise. Working with 1 date at a time, place blue cheese–filled date on end of 1 halved bacon slice and roll to enclose date. Place wrapped dates seam side down on prepared rack.

4. Bake until bacon is browned, 27 to 30 minutes, rotating sheet halfway through baking. Let cool for 10 minutes. Serve with toothpicks.

TO MAKE AHEAD: Devils on Horseback can be assembled through step 3 and frozen seam side down on rimmed baking sheet. Frozen pieces can be transferred to zipper-lock bag and frozen for up to 1 month. Increase baking time by 8 to 10 minutes.

SHRIMP RÉMOULADE

✓ **WHY THIS RECIPE WORKS:** Shrimp rémoulade is a cool, creamy New Orleans specialty that pairs plump, juicy shrimp with a smooth, tangy sauce. We wanted to bring this elegant appetizer home but without the laundry list of ingredients that most recipes call for, so we set our sights on a streamlined version. For perfectly tender jumbo shrimp, we gently poached them in salty water. Our red rémoulade sauce came together with mayonnaise as its base. We mimicked hard-to-find Creole mustard's heat with spicy brown mustard, horseradish, and a touch of cayenne. Crunchy cornichons delivered bite and texture, scallions and lemon juice added a fresh pop, and ketchup and paprika delivered extra complexity and appealing color. Stirring the shrimp into our simple, pantry-friendly rémoulade and chilling it for an hour allowed the flavors to meld.

Roaming around the French Quarter in New Orleans, you're almost certain to come across Arnaud's Restaurant, a 19-room establishment spanning almost a full block and housing an extensive collection of Mardi Gras costumes alongside the main dining room. Arnaud's is legendary for many reasons, including its iconic version of one of the city's most beloved dishes: shrimp rémoulade, an appetizer of poached shrimp tossed with a creamy, zesty sauce and perched on a bed of lettuce.

But since I can't get to New Orleans as often as I'd like, I wanted an easy version to make at home. I started by trying out six recipes from a mix of New Orleans greats, including Paul Prudhomme and John Folse. They were delicious, but they had mile-long ingredient lists and time-consuming steps like making homemade mayonnaise. I wanted an easier way.

My research revealed just how varied rémoulade sauces are. There are two main types: white and red (really more pink than red). The former is similar to tartar sauce, with a mayonnaise base that's amped up with herbs and pickles or capers. The more common red kind gets its color from ketchup and/or paprika. Both are boldly seasoned with vinegar or citrus, Creole mustard (a vibrant, spicy Louisiana specialty), spices, and usually the "Cajun trinity" of bell peppers, celery, and onion. It often has a pleasant—but not overwhelming—kick.

I opted to go with a red rémoulade, deciding that its potent personality would pair well with the relatively mild shrimp. To keep things doable, I started with store-bought mayonnaise mixed with a few squirts of lemon juice; I found its citrusy punch preferable to vinegar. Since Creole mustard is hard to get outside of New Orleans, I substituted a mix of spicy brown mustard and potent horseradish. I also experimented with cayenne and hot sauce, eventually choosing the former since it contributed heat without extra acidity. In a nod to the Cajun trinity, a combo of chopped green bell pepper, scallions, and celery added vegetal crunch while ketchup and paprika contributed the traditional red color. A little Worcestershire and garlic offered savory depth while cornichons, though more common in white rémoulade, supplied a briny element that brought the sauce together.

To poach the shrimp, I borrowed a technique from the test kitchen's recipe for shrimp salad that eliminates any chance that the shellfish will turn tough. In that recipe, we start the shrimp in a pot of cold water with a handful of aromatics and bring the water to 170 degrees. Then we kill the heat and cover the pot until the shrimp turn pink and perfectly tender, which takes about 5 minutes. Finally, we shock the shrimp under cold water to stop the cooking. The result? Perfectly tender shrimp. After testing the method myself, I ditched the aromatics from the cooking liquid, finding that my vibrant rémoulade covered up any flavor they added.

I put a batch of my shrimp rémoulade into the fridge and sampled it again an hour later with a fresh palate. It tasted even better. A subsequent side-by-side matchup confirmed that letting the shrimp hang out for a while in the sauce was the right move. It gave the bright, authentic rémoulade sauce plenty of time to permeate the mild seafood, resulting in a more balanced flavor.

New Orleans, I'll see you soon. But in the meantime, I'll get my "remy" fix at home.

—MORGAN BOLLING, *Cook's Country*

Shrimp Rémoulade

SERVES 4

We prefer shrimp not treated with sodium or preservatives. Most frozen E-Z peel shrimp are treated (see the ingredient list). If using treated shrimp, reduce the salt in step 1 to ½ teaspoon.

SHRIMP

1½ pounds jumbo shrimp (16 to 20 per pound), peeled, deveined, and tails removed
    Salt and pepper

RÉMOULADE

⅔   cup mayonnaise
¼   cup finely chopped celery
¼   cup finely chopped green bell pepper
3   tablespoons minced cornichons
2   scallions, sliced thin
1   tablespoon lemon juice
1½ teaspoons prepared horseradish, drained
1   teaspoon spicy brown mustard
1   teaspoon ketchup
1   garlic clove, minced
½   teaspoon paprika
½   teaspoon Worcestershire sauce
¼   teaspoon salt
¼   teaspoon pepper
⅛   teaspoon cayenne pepper

½   head Bibb lettuce (4 ounces), leaves separated and torn
    Lemon wedges
    Hot sauce

1. FOR THE SHRIMP: Combine 3 cups cold water, shrimp, and 1½ teaspoons salt in Dutch oven. Set pot over medium-high heat and cook, stirring occasionally, until water registers 170 degrees and shrimp are just beginning to turn pink, 5 to 7 minutes.

2. Remove pot from heat, cover, and let sit until shrimp are completely pink and firm, about 5 minutes. Drain shrimp in colander. Rinse shrimp under cold water, then pat dry with paper towels. Transfer shrimp to large bowl and refrigerate until ready to use.

3. FOR THE RÉMOULADE: Combine all ingredients in bowl.

4. Fold rémoulade into shrimp until combined. Season with salt and pepper to taste. Cover and refrigerate for 1 hour. Serve over lettuce with lemon wedges and hot sauce.

SHRIMP RÉMOULADE

CHAPTER 2

SOUPS, STEWS, AND CURRIES

TURKISH TOMATO, BULGUR, AND RED PEPPER SOUP

☑ **WHY THIS RECIPE WORKS:** Turkish tomato and red pepper soups have countless variations, but all are full-flavored and enriched with grains. We started our soup with onion and red bell peppers, softening them before creating a solid flavor backbone with garlic, tomato paste, white wine, dried mint, smoked paprika, and red pepper flakes. Canned fire-roasted tomatoes added extra smokiness. For the grain, we turned to versatile, quick-cooking bulgur. As we stirred it into the soup, the bulgur absorbed the surrounding flavors, and gave off enough starch to create a silky texture. A sprinkle of fresh mint gave the soup a final punch of flavor.

From prepping the vegetables and carefully cooking each component to the extended simmering, home-made soups are a time-consuming pleasure I have always reserved for lazy weekends. When I began developing soups for a new collection of Mediterranean recipes, I expected much of the same: fresh, fragrant soups I would spend a laid-back Sunday perfecting. That is, until I learned more about the Mediterranean diet. This popular, healthful style of cookery puts its focus on vegetables first and foremost, using meat sparingly if at all and turning to rich, nutty olive oil in place of butter. Coming up with a meatless soup seemed easy enough, but I wondered if, in taking inspiration from the pared-down yet impactful ingredient lists used in many Mediterranean dishes, I could manage to make a weeknight-friendly soup that would still taste great.

I began with a trip to the test kitchen's extensive cookbook library. Flipping through books focused on Mediterranean cuisine, I encountered several recipes for a smoky Turkish soup made with fresh tomato and red bell pepper seasoned with mint, smoked paprika, and red pepper flakes. The simple flavor profile and quick cooking time seemed right up my alley, so I gathered the key ingredients and got to work.

I wanted this soup to be fresh-tasting but I also wanted to be able to prepare it well beyond tomato season, so I started out with a few pounds of year-round varieties as well as canned options. Most recipes included bulgur, a quick-cooking grain that promised to add some heft and heartiness to an otherwise thin soup. In my earliest attempts, fresh tomatoes were the first to go. They offered bright tomato flavor, but when stirred in with softened red bell peppers and broth, not even a heavy hand with the seasonings could give my soup life; it was taking a hard turn at simple and veering toward plain. Even the canned tomatoes (I tried whole and diced) made a lackluster soup. Revisiting my tomato options, I picked up some canned fire-roasted tomatoes and began again, upping the aromatics by softening chopped onion along with the red bell pepper and blooming smoked paprika, spicy red pepper flakes, and garlic. Mint was widely used in the recipes I encountered, and while my preference is usually for fresh mint, traditional Turkish cooking has a clear preference for dried. Crushed up and bloomed with the other aromatics, the dried mint added understated fresh flavor, and I later reinforced its taste by garnishing with chopped fresh mint. A tablespoon of tomato paste promised some extra depth and concentrated tomato taste.

Having nailed this nuanced base, I was hesitant to mute it with an overly rich broth. I started by adding a hit of dry white wine for brightness that complemented the smoky tomatoes. I allowed the wine to reduce before adding more liquid so my soup didn't taste boozy and the flavors had a chance to meld. Savory chicken broth cut with a good amount of water was just the thing to keep the soup robust without diminishing the key flavors. (Vegetable broth worked well, too.) Bulgur takes no time at all to turn tender, so I added it towards the end and let the pot simmer away. After 20 minutes or so, the grains had softened and released some starch, giving the broth some welcome body.

I served myself a bowl of this deep red soup, sprinkled on some fresh mint, and with one taste I was sold. Rich yet bright, loaded with fragrant, exotic spices yet made with pantry ingredients, deeply flavorful yet ready in well under an hour, this was exactly the simple soup I'd been looking for.

—RUSSELL SELANDER, *America's Test Kitchen Books*

Turkish Tomato, Bulgur, and Red Pepper Soup
SERVES 6 TO 8

You can use vegetable broth instead of chicken broth if desired. When shopping, don't confuse bulgur with cracked wheat, which has a much longer cooking time and will not work in this recipe.

2 tablespoons extra-virgin olive oil

1 onion, chopped

2 red bell peppers, stemmed, seeded, and chopped

Salt and pepper

3 garlic cloves, minced

1 teaspoon dried mint, crumbled

½ teaspoon smoked paprika

⅛ teaspoon red pepper flakes

1 tablespoon tomato paste

½ cup dry white wine

1 (28-ounce) can diced fire-roasted tomatoes

4 cups chicken broth

2 cups water

¾ cup medium-grind bulgur, rinsed

⅓ cup chopped fresh mint

1. Heat oil in Dutch oven over medium heat until shimmering. Add onion, bell peppers, ¾ teaspoon salt, and ¼ teaspoon pepper and cook until softened and lightly browned, 6 to 8 minutes. Stir in garlic, dried mint, smoked paprika, and pepper flakes and cook until fragrant, about 30 seconds. Stir in tomato paste and cook for 1 minute.

2. Stir in wine, scraping up any browned bits, and simmer until reduced by half, about 1 minute. Add tomatoes and their juice and cook, stirring occasionally, until tomatoes soften and begin to break apart, about 10 minutes.

3. Stir in broth, water, and bulgur and bring to simmer. Reduce heat to low, cover, and simmer gently until bulgur is tender, about 20 minutes. Season with salt and pepper to taste. Serve, sprinkling individual portions with fresh mint.

NOTES FROM THE TEST KITCHEN

TASTING FIRE-ROASTED TOMATOES

Boasting both sweet and smoky flavors in every can, fire-roasted tomatoes gave our Turkish Tomato, Bulgur, and Red Pepper Soup its signature intensity. The rich red color and deep roasted taste of **Delallo Fire-Roasted Diced Tomatoes** made it our favorite brand.

BUTTERNUT SQUASH AND WHITE BEAN SOUP

✔ WHY THIS RECIPE WORKS: Instead of the usual creamy, rich pureed style of butternut squash soup, we wanted a heartier version that could stand on its own as a meal. We opted to feature chunks of squash paired with creamy cannellini beans to give our soup some heft. Because the bulb portion of the squash is difficult to cut into cubes that will cook evenly, and because it naturally cooks faster than the dense neck portion, we cut the bulb into wedges, cooked them in the broth until they were soft, and then mashed them to make a "squash stock" that gave our soup base body and flavor. We then cooked the neck portion, cut into chunks, in this stock. Adding butter to the stock at the start of its simmering time allowed it to fully emulsify, giving the soup base richness and a more velvety texture. A swirl of sage pesto, which we quickly made in the food processor, lent the right bright, fresh finish.

A cup of pureed butternut squash soup is fine as a dinner starter or as a side to a sandwich, but this winter I wanted a heartier soup I could enjoy as a stand-alone meal. I've seen a few versions that pair chunks of squash with creamy cannellini beans, which sounded like just what I was after.

I sautéed sliced leeks, added diced squash and chicken broth, simmered it all for 10 minutes, added the beans, and simmered a little longer to warm them through. I wanted simple, but this was too simple, as the soup was thin in taste and texture. Furthermore, the squash had cooked unevenly.

There was one clear reason for the uneven cooking: It's easy to evenly dice the neck of a butternut squash but not the bulb end: I ended up with oddly shaped bits. I could cut the bulb into equal pieces if I made them larger, but tasters found these unwieldy to eat.

The flesh from the squash neck is also much more dense, and thus slower to cook, than that of the bulb, which tended to blow out and turn stringy. I tried cutting the neck into smaller pieces than the bulb to equalize their cooking times, but the oddly shaped bits of bulb nagged at me. Then a fellow test cook made a suggestion: Why not cut the bulb into wedges, cook these in the broth until they were completely soft, and then mash them to create a "squash stock" for the soup's base? Then I'd cook the diced neck pieces in

BUTTERNUT SQUASH AND WHITE BEAN SOUP WITH SAGE PESTO

the stock. Good idea—this gave my soup body and flavor and avoided the issue of uneven cooking.

But the soup had a one-note sweetness from the squash. Two of our favorite umami boosters, soy sauce and tomato paste (along with some minced garlic), lent needed depth. Sautéing tomato paste with the leeks deepened its flavor further.

My soup still tasted lean, though, so I tried drizzling it with olive oil. Unfortunately, the oil didn't provide the infusion of richness I was after. Cream was a poor fit in this brothy soup and muted the flavors. Then my mind drifted to the technique of enriching sauces by whisking in butter toward the end. Adding butter at the end would be difficult given everything in the pot, so I added it to the stock at the start of its cooking. The lengthy agitation of the simmer fully emulsified the butter, no fussy whisking required.

For a final touch I prepared a sage and walnut pesto to swirl into the soup at the table. This was just the satisfying, hearty main dish I'd set out to make.

—STEVE DUNN, *Cook's Illustrated*

Butternut Squash and White Bean Soup with Sage Pesto
SERVES 6 TO 8

For the best texture, it's important to remove the fibrous white flesh just below the squash's skin.

PESTO
- ½ cup walnuts, toasted
- 2 garlic cloves, minced
- 1 cup fresh parsley leaves
- ½ cup fresh sage leaves
- ¾ cup extra-virgin olive oil
- 1 ounce Parmesan cheese, grated (½ cup), plus extra for serving
- Salt and pepper

SOUP
- 1 (2- to 2½-pound) butternut squash
- 4 cups chicken broth
- 3 cups water
- 4 tablespoons unsalted butter
- 1 tablespoon soy sauce
- 1 tablespoon vegetable oil
- 1 pound leeks, white and light green parts only, halved lengthwise, sliced thin, and washed thoroughly
- 1 tablespoon tomato paste
- 2 garlic cloves, minced
- Salt and pepper
- 3 (15-ounce) cans cannellini beans
- 1 teaspoon white wine vinegar

1. FOR THE PESTO: Pulse walnuts and garlic in food processor until coarsely chopped, about 5 pulses. Add parsley and sage; with processor running, slowly add oil and process until smooth, about 1 minute. Transfer to bowl, stir in Parmesan, and season with salt and pepper to taste. Set aside.

2. FOR THE SOUP: Using sharp vegetable peeler or chef's knife, remove skin and fibrous threads just below skin from squash (peel until squash is completely orange with no white flesh remaining, roughly ⅛ inch deep). Cut round bulb section off squash and cut in half lengthwise. Scoop out and discard seeds; cut each bulb half into 4 wedges.

3. Bring squash wedges, broth, water, butter, and soy sauce to boil in medium saucepan over high heat. Reduce heat to medium, partially cover, and simmer vigorously until squash is very tender and starting to fall apart, about 20 minutes. Using potato masher, mash squash, still in broth, until completely broken down. Cover to keep warm; set aside.

4. While broth cooks, cut neck of squash into ⅓-inch pieces. Heat oil in large Dutch oven over medium heat until shimmering. Add leeks and tomato paste and cook, stirring occasionally, until leeks have softened and tomato paste has darkened, about 5 minutes. Add garlic and cook until fragrant, about 30 seconds. Add squash pieces, ¾ teaspoon salt, and ¼ teaspoon pepper and cook, stirring occasionally, for 5 minutes. Add squash broth and bring to simmer. Partially cover and cook for 10 minutes.

5. Add beans and their liquid, partially cover, and cook, stirring occasionally, until squash is just tender, 15 to 20 minutes. Stir in vinegar and season with salt and pepper to taste. Serve, passing pesto and extra Parmesan separately.

RISI E BISI

✓ WHY THIS RECIPE WORKS: *Risi e bisi* is a simple dish of rice and peas with a consistency that falls somewhere between risotto and soup. We wanted a clean-tasting bowl of risi e bisi with a velvety consistency, so we kept the flavorings simple, browning pancetta and then using its rendered fat to soften chopped onion and minced garlic. We briefly toasted arborio rice with the aromatics before pouring in warm chicken broth and water and bringing the pot to a boil. The rice was tender after just 15 minutes, and a vigorous whisking at the end of cooking released enough starch to thicken the broth, providing the dish with a light but satisfying consistency. We stirred in thawed frozen baby peas for bursts of sweetness, Parmesan for its nutty, savory taste, and parsley and fresh lemon juice for a bright finish.

Venetians have a centuries-old tradition of dishing up *risi e bisi* (rice and peas) every April 25, St. Mark's Day, to celebrate spring's first peas and to honor the importance of rice production in the Veneto region. Thinner than a traditional risotto yet thicker than soup, the dish's unique consistency and fresh flavors make it the ideal ambassador for the season: a light and vibrant—yet still satisfying—escape from heavier winter fare.

The classic version is made with Arborio rice and fresh spring peas along with onion, garlic, Parmesan cheese, and pancetta. Most recipes adhere to the long-established risotto method of vigorously stirring broth into the rice in multiple additions. Extra broth is then poured in at the end to create something looser than a creamy risotto.

Since my goal was not to create a rich, velvety consistency, I was fairly certain I could jettison the laborious stirring routine and simply cook the dish more like a soup. I was right. I sautéed finely chopped pancetta, onion, and garlic until the meat rendered its fat and the onion turned translucent; added the rice; poured in hot broth all at once; brought the mixture to a boil; and then let it simmer, adding the peas and Parmesan last.

I then focused on the peas. Since fresh pea season is fleeting at best, I'd have to rely on the frozen kind. Stirring them in thawed at the end of cooking, just to warm them through, was key for preserving their texture and verdant color. I also picked petite peas, which were noticeably sweeter and more tender than full-size peas.

As for the broth, recipes are divided on whether to use chicken or vegetable. I conducted a few tests, ultimately finding that chicken broth diluted with water struck just the right balance of savoriness and lightness. Unfortunately, the consistency of the broth itself was too thin. I tried adding a few pats of butter, but this masked the dish's delicate flavors.

I realized that my hands-off approach was freeing little starch from the rice. Maybe I needed to stir the rice after all? Indeed, aggressively whisking just before adding the peas and Parmesan loosened just enough starch to lightly thicken the broth.

And with that, I gave this simple supper a final nod to spring, adding a spritz of lemon juice and a sprinkle of minced fresh parsley.

—STEVE DUNN, *Cook's Illustrated*

Risi e Bisi

SERVES 4 TO 6

We use frozen petite peas here, but regular frozen peas can be substituted, if desired. For the proper consistency, make sure to cook the rice at a gentle boil. Our favorite Arborio rice is from RiceSelect.

- 4 cups chicken broth
- 1½ cups water
- 3 tablespoons extra-virgin olive oil
- 2 ounces pancetta, chopped fine
- 1 onion, chopped fine
- 2 garlic cloves, minced
- 1 cup Arborio rice
- 2 cups frozen petite peas, thawed
- 1 ounce Parmesan cheese, grated (½ cup), plus extra for serving
- 3 tablespoons minced fresh parsley
- 1 teaspoon lemon juice, plus lemon wedges for serving
  Salt and pepper

1. Bring broth and water to boil in large saucepan over high heat. Remove from heat and cover to keep warm.

2. Cook oil and pancetta in Dutch oven over medium-low heat until pancetta is browned and rendered, 5 to 7 minutes. Add onion and cook, stirring frequently, until softened, 4 to 5 minutes. Add garlic and cook until fragrant, about 30 seconds. Add rice and stir to coat, about 1 minute.

RISI E BISI

3. Add 5 cups broth mixture, increase heat to high, and bring to boil. Reduce heat to medium-low, cover, and boil gently until rice is tender but not mushy, about 15 minutes, stirring every 5 minutes to ensure rice is gently boiling.

4. Remove pot from heat and whisk rice vigorously until broth has thickened slightly, 15 seconds. Stir in peas, Parmesan, parsley, and lemon juice. Season with salt and pepper to taste. Adjust consistency with remaining ½ cup broth as needed. Serve, passing lemon wedges and extra Parmesan separately.

AVGOLEMONO

WHY THIS RECIPE WORKS: *Avgolemono*, or Greek chicken and rice soup, gets its name from the egg-lemon mixture that thickens and flavors it. To make a version that was hearty enough to serve as a meal, we decided to include shredded chicken as well. We started by building a nuanced broth, simmering a sachet of lemon zest strips, citrusy coriander seeds, fresh dill, black peppercorns, and a smashed garlic clove in savory chicken broth. We cooked the rice and chicken right in the broth, allowing each to cook perfectly while also boosting the broth's savory flavor and giving it some subtle thickening. When incorporating the eggs, we avoided curdling by pureeing them with lemon juice and some of the hot cooked rice in a blender; the addition of extra yolks boosted the soup's richness. A sprinkling of dill and a final drizzle of lemon juice freshened the flavors.

When beaten eggs and fresh lemon juice are whisked together with a little hot chicken broth, the duo is transformed into the classic Greek sauce known as *avgolemono* (egg-lemon). Increase the amount of broth (homemade if you've got it) and throw in a handful of rice, and avgolemono becomes a creamy, comforting first-course soup punctuated with lemony tang. The chicken from which the broth is made, along with an assortment of vegetables, typically follows as the main course.

As lovely as the classic version of avgolemono is, it's a more practical variation that interests me: Simply shredding the chicken and adding it to the soup, along with increasing the amount of rice, turns this starter into a light yet satisfying meal. I wanted a savory, citrusy soup, velvety with egg and studded with tender bites of chicken—all in a reasonable amount of time.

For the chicken, I chose boneless, skinless breasts. Their milder flavor would fit in better with the fresh, light nature of this soup than thighs would. As a bonus, the breasts would also cook faster than thighs.

Before poaching and shredding, I halved the chicken breasts lengthwise. The benefit of this small move was threefold: First, the extra surface area created helped salt penetrate more uniformly. Second, the smaller pieces of chicken cooked more quickly. Third, halving the muscle fibers ensured that the shreds of chicken would be short enough to fit neatly on a spoon. I let the salted meat sit while I got the soup going, giving the salt time to both season the chicken and change its protein structure, which would help it stay juicy when cooked.

My plan was to cook the chicken and rice in tandem to save time, but I knew that just dropping the chicken into simmering broth wouldn't work. That's because water simmers at approximately 190 degrees, and when a chicken breast hits this hot liquid, the exterior quickly overshoots the target doneness temperature of 160 degrees. The result? Dry, chalky meat.

The test kitchen's solution to this problem is to submerge the chicken in subsimmering water and then shut off the heat. The water drops in temperature when the chicken is added; the chicken then cooks very gently with no risk of overshooting the 160-degree mark.

I brought 8 cups of broth and 1 cup of rice to a boil and then let the pot simmer for just 5 minutes. In went the prepared breasts, at which point I put a lid on and shut off the heat. After 15 minutes, the chicken was almost—but not quite—cooked through and the rice was al dente. I removed the breasts from the broth, shredded them, and returned the pieces to the pot, where they quickly finished cooking. Just as I expected, the shreds remained supermoist and tender.

Having achieved perfectly poached chicken, I turned to avgolemono's namesake egg-lemon mixture, which thickens the soup. It's the egg proteins that do the work: They uncoil, entangle, and form an open mesh that prevents water molecules from moving freely, thus increasing viscosity. Before being whisked into the soup, the egg mixture is typically tempered, meaning it is combined with a portion of the hot broth to prevent the eggs from curdling when they make contact with the rest of the liquid in the pot. Some Greek cooks so fear a curdled soup that they are known to chant the "avgolemono prayer"—"please don't curdle, please don't curdle"—or make a kissing sound while adding the eggs to magically ensure smooth results. I saw no need for such extreme measures, but I was curious and felt that some testing was in order. I found that tempering worked not because it raised the temperature of the eggs but rather because it diluted the egg proteins.

The tempering step safeguarded against curdling, but I had another issue to deal with. As the proteins in egg whites unwind, they unleash hydrogen sulfide, a compound that can give off a lightly sulfurous aroma. To limit this smell while getting the same thickening power, I mixed lemon juice with two eggs and two yolks (diluted with a little broth) instead of three eggs. This mixture didn't provide quite as much body as I'd hoped, but I didn't want to add more eggs lest the soup become too rich. Luckily, there was another thickener present: amylose, a starch molecule in rice. Similar to egg proteins, it increases viscosity by entangling and forming a matrix that slows the movement of water. To put this starch to work, I needed to release it from the rice grains. And I knew just how to do it: I'd puree some of the rice.

I went back to the stove and prepared another batch of soup, this time using 1 cup of cooked rice from the soup to dilute the eggs. I put the rice into the blender jar along with the eggs, yolks, and lemon juice. After a minute of processing, I had a starchy egg-lemon-rice puree to stir into the broth. And there it was, a soup with exactly the luxurious creamy consistency I wanted.

But there was more. Reheating avgolemono is typically a no-no because the eggs will curdle when they are cooked a second time. In this version, though, because the rice had enough starchy bulk even after being pureed to physically interrupt the egg proteins from interacting with each other, the proteins had a hard time forming curds, even when the soup was reheated—a nice bonus.

NOTES FROM THE TEST KITCHEN

MAXIMIZING LEMON FLAVOR
A trio of ingredients brings multifaceted lemon flavor to our Avgolemono's broth: Lemon zest provides fruitiness, coriander seeds add herbal/citrus notes, and lemon juice offers tartness.

The sumptuous consistency of the soup was right where I wanted it, but its flavor needed attention. Although it was tart from the lemon juice, it needed some tweaking if it was to also boast more complexity. I chose garlic, black peppercorns, and lemony coriander seeds to add depth, along with dill for an herbal note. I also used a vegetable peeler to strip the zest from a couple of lemons. The intensely flavored oils in the zest would boost the fruity, citrusy notes without making the soup overly sour.

The complexity imparted by the herb bundle, in combination with the creamy soup and tender chicken, made this avgolemono outshine all the rest.

—LAN LAM, *Cook's Illustrated*

Greek Chicken and Rice Soup with Egg and Lemon (Avgolemono)
SERVES 4 TO 6

If you have homemade chicken broth such as our Classic Chicken Broth (recipe follows), we recommend using it in this recipe, as it gives the soup the best flavor and body. Our preferred commercial chicken broth is Swanson Chicken Stock. Use a vegetable peeler to remove strips of zest from the lemons.

1½ pounds boneless, skinless chicken breasts, trimmed
   Salt and pepper
12 (3-inch) strips lemon zest plus 6 tablespoons juice, plus extra juice for seasoning (3 lemons)
2 sprigs fresh dill, plus 2 teaspoons chopped
2 teaspoons coriander seeds
1 teaspoon black peppercorns
1 garlic clove, peeled and smashed
8 cups chicken broth
1 cup long-grain rice
2 large eggs plus 2 large yolks

1. Cut each chicken breast in half lengthwise. Toss with 1¾ teaspoons salt and let stand at room temperature for at least 15 minutes or up to 30 minutes. Cut 8-inch square of triple-thickness cheesecloth. Place lemon zest, dill sprigs, coriander seeds, peppercorns, and garlic in center of cheesecloth and tie into bundle with kitchen twine.

2. Bring broth, rice, and spice bundle to boil in large saucepan over high heat. Reduce heat to low, cover, and cook for 5 minutes. Turn off heat, add chicken, cover, and let stand for 15 minutes.

3. Transfer chicken to large plate and discard spice bundle. Using 2 forks, shred chicken into bite-size pieces. Using ladle, transfer 1 cup cooked rice to blender (leave any liquid in pot). Add lemon juice and eggs and yolks to blender and process until smooth, about 1 minute.

4. Return chicken and any accumulated juices to pot. Return soup to simmer over high heat. Remove pot from heat and stir in egg mixture until fully incorporated. Stir in chopped dill and season with salt, pepper, and extra lemon juice to taste. Serve.

Classic Chicken Broth

MAKES 8 CUPS

If you have a large pot (at least 12 quarts), you can easily double this recipe to make 1 gallon.

4 pounds chicken backs and wings
3½ quarts water
1 onion, chopped
2 bay leaves
2 teaspoons salt

1. Heat chicken and water in large stockpot or Dutch oven over medium-high heat until boiling, skimming off any scum that comes to the surface. Reduce heat to low and simmer gently for 3 hours.

2. Add onion, bay leaves, and salt and continue to simmer for another 2 hours.

3. Strain broth through fine-mesh strainer into large pot or container, pressing on solids to extract as much liquid as possible. Let broth settle for about 5 minutes, then skim off fat.

CHICKEN AND PASTRY

✓ **WHY THIS RECIPE WORKS:** This Lowcountry chicken soup features tender shreds of chicken and chewy bites of pastry in an ultrasavory stock. We prepared our own make-shift stock by browning meaty chicken thighs before pouring in chicken broth and water. Adding a halved onion and a celery rib and letting the pot simmer for 25 minutes infused the broth with rich, savory flavor. For the soup's trademark pastry, we prepared a quick dough of flour, butter, milk, and baking powder and rolled it out thin, slicing it into diamonds using a pizza cutter. Stirred in and gently simmered, the pastry cooked up soft and subtly thickened the soup.

It took me a few years of living in North Carolina before I fully understood the ubiquitous phrase "Bless her heart." While the saying can, on occasion, be heartfelt, it's just as often a roundabout way to soften an otherwise devastating blow: "Bless her heart, she's no beauty queen."

It's a colloquialism I tend to avoid for fear of sending an unintended message, but I found myself leaning on a version of it recently when describing comforting chicken and pastry to non-Southern friends. To them, the recipe's name, "chicken and pastry," conjured elegance and formality: lofty images of golden, flaky puff pastry surrounding carefully, fussily cooked chicken. But, bless its heart, true Southern chicken and pastry—tender shreds of chicken and slightly chewy pastry wading in a thickened, chicken-infused broth—is no looker. Still, I truly believed that this dish's beauty was within, and I hoped to develop a straightforward recipe that, would dazzle with its deep flavor.

To get started, I simmered my way through several existing recipes from Southern culinary icons Bill Neal and Edna Lewis, as well as a few Alabama home cooks.

I was delighted to discover that my best results came from the simplest recipes with the fewest ingredients. (Adding vegetables turned the dish into something more like chicken pot pie—tasty, but not my ultimate goal.)

Stewing chicken pieces in broth made a robust base; including celery and onion, which I would later remove once they'd given off their flavors, added even more depth without distracting. Lean breasts dried out in tests, but bone-in chicken thighs stayed tender and moist even after simmering longer to extract more flavor. Browning the thighs beforehand made for an even more savory stew.

Base completed, I now focused firmly on pastry. Some recipes called for leftover biscuit dough or uncooked canned biscuits. But the biscuit dough dissolved, and canned biscuits turned gummy. A simple homemade dough—a mixture of flour, fat (butter, naturally), milk, and leavener—made for the most flavorful pastry.

But which leavening agent was best? After some experiments, I found that baking soda made the dumplings too tender, causing them to swell until they disintegrated. So I chose baking powder, which kept them light while still allowing them to hold their shape. Rolling the pastry into a ⅛-inch-thick square gave me the ideal texture: more tender than a noodle but just chewy enough.

I took Edna Lewis's suggestion and cut the pastry into diamond shapes—a bit of flair for this homely dish—because why not? It's just as easy as cutting squares, and a dish this deeply satisfying deserves a flourish.

The homemade pastry had another benefit, too. Adding it to the boiling broth and stirring the pot occasionally released just enough starch into the liquid to thicken its consistency into something more like a stew.

The resulting supper—tender pieces of chicken and fluffy, soft pastry cloaked in a velvety chicken broth—is rich, comforting, and simply delicious. No Southern courtesy required.

—MORGAN BOLLING, *Cook's Country*

Chicken and Pastry

SERVES 4 TO 6

Keep the root ends of the onion halves intact so the petals don't separate during cooking and the onion is easy to remove from the pot.

1½ cups (7½ ounces) all-purpose flour
2 teaspoons baking powder
Salt and pepper
½ cup milk
2 tablespoons unsalted butter, melted, plus 1 tablespoon unsalted butter
2 pounds bone-in chicken thighs, trimmed
4 cups chicken broth
1 cup water
1 onion, peeled and halved through root end
1 celery rib, halved crosswise

1. Combine flour, baking powder, ½ teaspoon salt, and ½ teaspoon pepper in large bowl. Combine milk and melted butter in second bowl (butter may form clumps). Using rubber spatula, stir milk mixture into flour mixture until just incorporated. Turn dough out onto lightly floured counter and knead until no flour streaks remain, about 1 minute. Return dough to large bowl, cover with plastic wrap, and set aside.

NOTES FROM THE TEST KITCHEN

MAKING THE PASTRY
Here's how to turn a simple homemade dough into uniquely shaped pastry dumplings.

1. Roll dough into 12-inch square, about ⅛ inch thick.

2. Using pizza cutter or knife, cut dough lengthwise into 1-inch-wide strips, then cut diagonally into 1-inch-wide strips to form diamonds.

3. Add pastry to simmering broth and cook until tender and puffed.

2. Pat chicken dry with paper towels and season with pepper. Melt remaining 1 tablespoon butter in Dutch oven over medium-high heat. Add chicken, skin side down, and cook until golden brown, 3 to 5 minutes. Flip chicken and continue to cook until golden brown on second side, 3 to 5 minutes longer.

3. Add broth and water, scraping up any browned bits. Nestle onion and celery into pot and bring to boil. Reduce heat to low, cover, and simmer for 25 minutes.

4. Meanwhile, roll dough into 12-inch square, about ⅛ inch thick. Using pizza cutter or knife, cut dough lengthwise into 1-inch-wide strips, then cut diagonally into 1-inch-wide strips to form diamonds (pieces around edges will not be diamonds; this is OK).

5. Remove pot from heat. Transfer chicken to plate and let cool slightly. Discard onion and celery. Return broth to boil over medium-high heat and add pastry. Reduce heat to low, cover, and simmer, stirring occasionally, until pastry is tender and puffed, about 15 minutes. While pastry cooks, shred chicken into bite-size pieces, discarding skin and bones.

6. Stir chicken into stew and cook, uncovered, until warmed through and stew has thickened slightly, 2 to 4 minutes. Season with salt and pepper to taste. Serve.

CHICKEN AND SAUSAGE GUMBO

✔ **WHY THIS RECIPE WORKS:** Most recipes for Louisiana gumbo start with a wet roux, a cooked paste of flour and fat that can take an hour or more to make. To turn out a streamlined gumbo at home, we made a hands-off dry roux by toasting flour in the oven. To incorporate the roux and achieve the perfect consistency in our gumbo, we created a thick paste by gradually stirring broth into the toasted flour and then working that paste into the richly spiced broth. Using easy-to-work-with meaty boneless chicken thighs and spicy andouille sausage kept our gumbo simple yet flavorful, and stirring in white vinegar at the end added a pop of acidity that didn't distract from the dish's nuanced taste.

Like any folk recipe, gumbo has hundreds of variations. The flavor, texture, and even the provenance of this legendary soup—a symbol of melting-pot cooking—are all fodder for debate.

There are, however, some characteristics that all gumbos share. A pot typically holds seafood, poultry, or wild game, along with sausage or some type of cured smoked pork. The proteins are simmered with the Cajun "holy trinity" of celery, bell pepper, and onion while seasonings such as garlic, cayenne, paprika, thyme, and bay leaves provide complexity. All are thickened, sometimes with okra or ground dried sassafras leaves, known as *filé* (fee-LAY) powder. Last, but perhaps most important, is the roux—a slow-cooked mixture of flour and fat that gives the soup its deep brown color, a bit of body, and a toasty flavor. (Gumbo isn't brothy, but it's still too thin to be considered a stew.)

Inspired by the late Louisiana chef Paul Prudhomme's poultry-centric gumbo, I decided to develop my own recipe featuring chicken and andouille but no seafood or game. I also opted to omit okra and filé—okra is more typical of shrimp- and tomato-based gumbos, and filé's distinct, earthy flavor can be polarizing.

I started with the roux. In classic French cuisine, roux is cooked to a shade ranging from blondish white to the color of peanut butter. But Cajun and Creole chefs push the roux much further—to a deep, dark brown or even just short of black—to develop the toasty, nutty flavor that characterizes gumbo. To guard against burning, the roux is stirred constantly over low heat, meaning it can take an hour or more of hands-on attention to make.

That said, there are renegade techniques for making dark roux that don't require stirring at the stove for long (if at all). I found methods using the microwave or the oven, as well as a quick one that involved heating the oil on the stovetop until smoking and then adding the flour.

Working with the typical 1:1 ratio of all-purpose flour to vegetable oil—½ cup of each for now—I first tried the quick method of adding flour to smoking oil. This produced a superdark roux in a mere 10 minutes, but the flour ended up more burnt than deeply toasted. The microwave wasn't much more hands-off than the stove, as I had to stir the roux frequently between short bursts of heating. However, in the dry, even heat of a 425-degree oven, a roux required stirring just every 20 minutes. The downside was that it took 1¼ hours to reach the proper dark chocolate color.

Still, I pressed on. In the roux, I sautéed onion, celery, and green bell pepper. I then poured in 6 cups of chicken broth and added a couple of pounds of boneless, skinless chicken thighs and some sliced andouille.

CHICKEN AND SAUSAGE GUMBO

I kept the seasonings simple for now: cayenne, bay leaves, and thyme sprigs. I simmered the gumbo until the chicken was tender, at which point I removed it, shredded it for easy eating, and added it back to the pot. This version boasted just the right toastiness from the roux, but the seasonings needed tweaking.

I'd address those later. For now, I wanted to deal with the fact that the roux had taken more than an hour to make. Plus, my gumbo was thin, with a slick of grease that had to be skimmed off. That wasn't surprising: Fat coats the flour particles in a roux, making them easier to disperse in a hot liquid without forming lumps. As the soup cooks and the starch dissolves into the liquid, it becomes hydrated and thickens the liquid. But at some point, heating the flour causes it to lose some of its ability to hold on to the fat, which then separates out. This is where okra and filé powder, both of which add body, often come in, but I stuck to my decision to keep them out of the pot.

This is when I decided to consider a less-common approach that I had initially dismissed: a dry roux, where the flour is toasted without fat. The benefits were clear: no hot oil-flour paste to stand over, no skimming, and—while it hadn't been my original goal—a gumbo with less fat overall. What, if anything, would I be losing if I ditched the oil?

To find out, I would need to produce a dry roux comparable in color to the wet roux I'd been using. Dry roux can be made on the stovetop or in the microwave, but each method has the same challenges as a wet roux does, so I stuck with the oven. Conveniently, a hands-off dry roux cooked faster than the wet kind, clocking in at about 45 minutes. That's because a hot pan transfers heat more rapidly to dry flour than to oil-coated flour, as oil is a much poorer conductor of heat energy than hot metal is.

I moved forward, making two batches of gumbo: one with a dry roux and one with a wet one. Happily, the dry-roux gumbo boasted a dark color and rich flavor that compared favorably to the wet-roux gumbo. What's more, thanks to the dark-meat chicken and sausage, the dish wasn't wanting for fat, even though I'd cut out an entire ½ cup of oil. Satisfied, I shifted my focus to the gumbo's consistency.

The most obvious way to make the gumbo thicker was to increase the amount of roux. I gradually added more flour until I hit a full cup. It helped, but it wasn't enough. Rather than use even more flour, which might have overwhelmed the dish, I decided to compensate by decreasing the amount of broth. After a few tests, I found that using just 4 cups finally gave me the perfect ratio of liquid to dark roux, yielding a rich, glossy, emulsified gumbo with body that coated the back of a spoon.

My gumbo was coming along and, at this point, took just under 2 hours from start to finish. I wondered if I could speed things along by adding the roux at the end of cooking instead of the beginning. That way I could prep my other ingredients and start cooking while the flour toasted.

Whisking the roux directly into the simmering broth made it difficult to incorporate without clumping, so I decided to reserve half the broth used for cooking the chicken to make a paste with the flour, allowing me to break up any lumps beforehand. Bingo: The paste whisked seamlessly into the remaining broth. Now I had rich, dark, luscious gumbo in just under 90 minutes.

All that was left to do was enliven the flavors. I stirred in black pepper, paprika, and minced garlic to mimic and highlight the seasonings in the andouille. I also incorporated some sliced scallions, a common garnish. The gumbo needed acidity to lift its rich, meaty flavor, but rather than add hot sauce (the usual final flourish), I stirred in clean-tasting white vinegar, letting my guests choose whether to add hot sauce to their own portions.

As I ladled my gumbo over white rice, I felt comfort and satisfaction with my recipe, and as I watched it disappear from the pot, I knew everyone else did, too.

—ANNIE PETITO, *Cook's Illustrated*

Chicken and Sausage Gumbo

SERVES 6

This recipe is engineered for efficiency: Start the flour toasting in the oven and then prep the remaining ingredients and begin cooking. We strongly recommend using andouille, but in a pinch, kielbasa can be substituted. The salt level of the final dish may vary depending on the brand of andouille, so liberal seasoning with additional salt at the end may be necessary. Serve over white rice.

1   cup all-purpose flour
1   tablespoon vegetable oil
1   onion, chopped fine
1   green bell pepper, chopped fine
2   celery ribs, chopped fine

1 tablespoon minced fresh thyme

3 garlic cloves, minced

1 teaspoon paprika

2 bay leaves

½ teaspoon cayenne pepper

   Salt and pepper

4 cups chicken broth, room temperature

2 pounds boneless, skinless chicken thighs, trimmed

8 ounces andouille sausage, halved and sliced ¼ inch thick

6 scallions, sliced thin

1 teaspoon white vinegar

   Hot sauce

1. Adjust oven rack to middle position and heat oven to 425 degrees. Place flour in 12-inch skillet and bake, stirring occasionally, until color of ground cinnamon or dark brown sugar, 40 to 55 minutes. (As flour approaches desired color, it will take on very nutty aroma that will smell faintly of burnt popcorn, and it will need to be stirred more frequently.) Transfer flour to medium bowl and let cool. (Toasted flour can be stored for up to 1 week.)

2. Heat oil in Dutch oven over medium heat until shimmering. Add onion, bell pepper, and celery and cook, stirring frequently, until softened, 5 to 7 minutes. Stir in thyme, garlic, paprika, bay leaves, cayenne, ¼ teaspoon salt, and ¼ teaspoon pepper and cook until fragrant, about 1 minute. Stir in 2 cups broth. Add chicken in single layer (chicken will not be completely submerged in liquid) and bring to simmer. Reduce heat to medium-low, cover, and simmer until chicken is fork-tender, 15 to 17 minutes. Transfer chicken to plate.

3. Slowly whisk remaining 2 cups broth into toasted flour until thick, batter-like paste forms. (Add broth in small increments to prevent clumps from forming.) Increase heat to medium and slowly whisk paste into gumbo, making sure each addition is incorporated before adding next. Stir in andouille. Simmer, uncovered, until gumbo thickens slightly, 20 to 25 minutes.

4. Once cool enough to handle, shred chicken into bite-size pieces. Stir chicken and scallions into gumbo. Remove pot from heat, stir in vinegar, and season to taste with salt. Discard bay leaves. Serve, passing hot sauce separately. (Gumbo can be refrigerated for 1 day.)

ROASTED CORN AND POBLANO CHOWDER

✓ WHY THIS RECIPE WORKS: We wanted chowder with unquestionably sweet corn flavor paired with mildly spicy poblano chiles. Broiling fresh kernels and halved poblanos helped concentrate their contrasting flavors and brought in some tasty char. For a thick, complex chowder that supported the corn and poblanos, we crisped chopped bacon for a smoky, salty base and used its renderings to soften chopped onion and minced garlic. Chicken broth promised a rich, savory chowder, and hearty bites of red potato added texture and subtle thickening. After a 15-minute simmer, we added half-and-half for instant richness and then, to give the chowder even more body, we pureed a portion in the blender. Blending corn tortillas into the puree offered even more thickening and reinforced the corn flavor. We stirred this mixture back into the chowder and finished it off with fresh stir-ins like bright cilantro and mild queso fresco.

"We just don't taste the corn," my tasters said. "Or the poblanos." I was ready to throw in the towel. I had cooked a dozen batches of corn and poblano chowder using every trick I could think of, but the sweet flavor of the corn and the slightly spicy, earthy taste of the poblano chiles weren't coming through.

I was in search of a creamy, silky soup full of these contrasting flavors, shucking ears of corn to roast until browned alongside poblanos before stirring them into a soup—to lackluster results. No matter what I tried, the vegetables always turned soft, steamy, and flat.

I set to tinkering, and my first adjustment was promising: I switched from roasting to broiling. After stripping the corn kernels from the cob, I tossed them with oil, salt, and pepper; spread them over a baking sheet with halved poblanos on the side; and set the whole thing to broil. In just 10 minutes, I had beautiful charred vegetables.

Meanwhile, I sautéed some onion and garlic in a Dutch oven, poured in chicken broth, and then added the corn and poblanos along with some cut-up red potatoes. After 15 minutes of simmering, the potatoes were tender.

Things were finally moving in the right direction, but the chowder's flavor was still a bit flat. Bring on the bacon: I rendered some in the pot, using its fat to cook the onion and garlic before adding the other ingredients.

To add some body, I whirred a few ladles of the simmered soup in the blender and stirred this puree back into the pot. This helped, but the color was murky. For my next try, I kept the roasted poblanos out of the soup until the end, adding them to warm through when the soup was done. This soup had a better color, but even with a bit of half-and-half, it needed more thickness.

I considered a trick I'd seen in a few recipes: adding ground masa (corn flour) to the chowder for deeper corn flavor and some thickening. But I didn't want to hunt down a specialty ingredient, so I used a substitute that was just as flavorful and easier to find—corn tortillas. I tore a couple of tortillas into pieces and added them to the blender. The mixture was decidedly thicker, with even stronger corn flavor. Some fresh chopped cilantro and a few squirts of lime juice added a final flourish.

—ASHLEY MOORE, *Cook's Country*

Roasted Corn and Poblano Chowder

SERVES 6 TO 8

Don't substitute frozen corn for fresh. In addition to the usual garnishes, you can serve the chowder with our Fried Corn Tortilla Pieces (recipe follows), if desired.

- 2 poblano chiles, stemmed, halved lengthwise, and seeded
- 1 tablespoon vegetable oil
- 6 ears corn, kernels cut from cobs (5¼ cups)
  Salt and pepper
- 4 slices bacon, chopped fine
- 1 onion, chopped fine
- 2 garlic cloves, minced
- 7 cups chicken broth
- 1 pound red potatoes, unpeeled, cut into ½-inch chunks
- ¼ cup half-and-half
- 2 (6-inch) corn tortillas, torn into 1-inch pieces
- 1 tablespoon minced fresh cilantro, plus leaves for serving
- 1 tablespoon lime juice, plus lime wedges for serving
  Sour cream
  Crumbled queso fresco

1. Adjust oven rack 6 inches from broiler element and heat broiler. Line rimmed baking sheet with aluminum foil. Toss poblanos with 1 teaspoon oil in bowl. Arrange poblanos cut side down in single column flush against short side of sheet.

2. Toss corn, remaining 2 teaspoons oil, ½ teaspoon salt, and ½ teaspoon pepper together in now-empty bowl. Spread corn in even layer on remaining portion of sheet next to poblanos. Broil until poblanos are mostly blackened and corn is well browned and tender, 10 to 15 minutes, flipping poblanos and stirring corn halfway through broiling.

3. Place poblanos in bowl, cover with plastic wrap, and let cool for 5 minutes. Remove skins and chop poblanos into ½-inch pieces; transfer to clean bowl and set aside.

4. Meanwhile, cook bacon in Dutch oven over medium heat until crispy, 5 to 7 minutes. Using slotted spoon, transfer bacon to paper towel–lined plate. Add onion and ¼ teaspoon salt to fat left in pot and cook until onion is softened and beginning to brown, 5 to 7 minutes. Add garlic and cook until fragrant, about 30 seconds.

5. Add broth, potatoes, browned corn, and ½ teaspoon salt to Dutch oven and bring to simmer, scraping up any browned bits. Cook at vigorous simmer until potatoes are tender, 15 to 20 minutes. Remove from heat and stir in half-and-half.

6. Transfer 2 cups chowder to blender. Add tortillas and process until smooth, about 1 minute. Return pureed chowder to pot and stir in chopped poblanos. Return to medium heat and bring to simmer. Stir in minced cilantro, lime juice, ¾ teaspoon salt, and ¾ teaspoon pepper. Serve, passing bacon, cilantro leaves, lime wedges, sour cream, and queso fresco separately.

Fried Corn Tortilla Pieces

MAKES ABOUT 1 CUP

These fried pieces of tortilla make an excellent crispy accompaniment to soups and chowders, including our Roasted Corn and Poblano Chowder.

- ¾ cup vegetable oil
- 4 (6-inch) corn tortillas, cut into ½-inch pieces
  Salt

Heat oil in 10-inch skillet over medium-high heat until shimmering. Add tortillas and cook, stirring occasionally, until golden brown, 3 to 5 minutes. Using slotted spoon, transfer tortillas to paper towel–lined plate. Sprinkle with salt and let cool slightly to crisp.

TRANSYLVANIAN GOULASH

✓ **WHY THIS RECIPE WORKS:** This hearty, brick-colored stew—a close cousin to Hungarian goulash—uses rich, marbled pork butt as its base. Browning hearty chunks of pork in batches left a flavorful fond, which we enhanced with aromatic vegetables like onion, celery, and green bell pepper; a chopped plum tomato brightened the base. Paprika imparts this dish's trademark color and intense flavor, so we added a whopping 3 tablespoons to the vegetables along with caraway seeds and minced garlic, rounding out our deeply fragrant base. We preferred water over chicken broth here, as it encouraged the full range of flavors to shine through. Sauerkraut—another staple ingredient in Transylvanian goulash—added toward the end of cooking balanced the richness of the pork; rinsing the sauerkraut tamed its tang. Served with a dollop of cool sour cream and a sprinkling of dill, this goulash was loaded with meaty, invigorating flavors, making it our new cold-weather favorite.

Among the most popular dishes served at Alexander Bodnar's tiny restaurant in the Hazelwood neighborhood of Pittsburgh is his signature Transylvanian goulash. Like its Hungarian counterpart, Transylvanian goulash (named for the picturesque area in central Romania, Hungary's next door neighbor) is a flavorful stew made of browned meat, aromatic vegetables, and a heavy dose of paprika. But while most Hungarian goulash is made with beef, Bodnar's version features pork and tangy sauerkraut.

To re-create the dish, I started with a boneless pork butt roast that I cut into chunks. I knew that this cut has good marbling and was therefore well suited to a prolonged braise that would result in tender meat and deep flavor. Browning the pork in batches built up a flavorful fond in the bottom of the pot. I consulted Bodnar on the vegetables he uses to add complexity: onion, celery, green bell pepper, and a single tomato. I cooked these in the rendered pork fat for about 8 minutes to soften them before adding spices.

The dish's trademark red color and subtle earthy, slightly fruity flavor come from 3 tablespoons of sweet

Hungarian paprika (not to be confused with sweet smoked paprika—a different beast entirely). I loved the addition of caraway seeds, another staple in Eastern European cooking; though sharp and assertive in rye and pumpernickel breads, the seeds' flavor mellows over the long cooking time into a subtle, almost citrusy presence.

While we often add chicken stock in the test kitchen to boost savory depth in all sorts of stews, Bodnar insisted that water would better allow the complex flavors of the different ingredients to shine. Tasters agreed: The stew was intensely flavored and deeply savory, especially after the addition of sauerkraut two-thirds of the way through cooking. But the sauerkraut was too sour to all but one of my tasters—a professed sauerkraut lover. At Bodnar's suggestion, I rinsed the sauerkraut to remove some of the excess brine and soften the flavor before adding it to the stew.

Once the pork was fully cooked and the stew was ready to serve, I took another cue from Bodnar and served it with a dollop of tangy sour cream and a sprinkling of fresh minced dill (a family tradition inspired by its abundance in his mother's garden).

The textures and flavors were in sync: The pork was perfectly tender but still held its shape, its richness balanced by the sturdy backbone of paprika and the faintly sharp sauerkraut. I had a satisfying, entirely comforting stew, full of flavors from Pittsburgh—and Transylvania, too.

—CHRISTIE MORRISON, *Cook's Country*

NOTES FROM THE TEST KITCHEN

TASTING PAPRIKA
With its deep reddish hue and rich, earthy flavor, paprika is an essential element of Transylvanian Goulash. It's made by grinding dried sweet red chile peppers, a different variety than is used to make hot or smoked paprika. Our favorite sweet paprika—**The Spice House Hungarian Sweet Paprika**—has great earthy, fruity flavors.

TRANSYLVANIAN GOULASH

Transylvanian Goulash

SERVES 6 TO 8

Pork butt roast is often labeled Boston butt. Paprika is vital to the success of this recipe, so use a fresh bottle. Do not substitute hot or smoked Spanish paprika for the sweet paprika. Eden Organic jarred sauerkraut is the test kitchen's favorite sauerkraut. Rinsing the sauerkraut mellows its flavor. Serve with white rice, if desired.

- 1 (3½-pound) boneless pork butt roast, trimmed and cut into 1½-inch pieces
  Salt and pepper
- 1 tablespoon vegetable oil
- 1 onion, chopped fine
- 1 green bell pepper, stemmed, seeded, and chopped fine
- 2 celery ribs, chopped fine
- 1 plum tomato, chopped
- 3 tablespoons paprika
- 1 tablespoon caraway seeds
- 2 garlic cloves, minced
- 3 cups water
- 2 cups sauerkraut, rinsed and drained
  Sour cream
  Minced fresh dill

1. Adjust oven rack to lower-middle position and heat oven to 325 degrees. Pat pork dry with paper towels and sprinkle with 1 teaspoon salt and ½ teaspoon pepper.

2. Heat oil in Dutch oven over medium-high heat until just smoking. Add half of pork and cook, stirring occasionally, until brown on all sides, about 8 minutes; transfer to bowl. (Reduce heat if bottom of pot begins to scorch.) Repeat with remaining pork.

3. Reduce heat to medium. Add onion, bell pepper, celery, tomato, and ½ teaspoon salt to now-empty pot and cook until vegetables are softened and liquid has evaporated, 8 to 10 minutes, scraping up any browned bits.

4. Add paprika, caraway seeds, and garlic and cook until fragrant, about 1 minute. Stir in water and pork and any accumulated juices and bring to simmer, scraping up any browned bits. Cover, transfer to oven, and cook for 1 hour. Stir in sauerkraut, cover, return pot to oven, and continue to cook until pork is fully tender, about 30 minutes longer.

5. Using wide spoon, skim off any surface fat. Season with salt and pepper to taste. Serve, garnished with sour cream and dill.

EASTERN NORTH CAROLINA FISH STEW

✓ WHY THIS RECIPE WORKS: For authentic fish stew with a nuanced broth, tender potatoes, and perfectly cooked fish, we needed to work in stages. After crisping chopped strips of bacon in a Dutch oven, we softened chopped onion and bloomed spicy red pepper flakes in the rendered fat. We built our broth from this base, pouring in water to keep the flavors clear and scooping in a whole can of tomato paste to infuse the pot with intense tomato flavor. With the broth in place, we added in chunks of unpeeled red potatoes and brought the pot to a vigorous simmer to turn them tender. Using firm whitefish fillets meant our stew would boast hearty bites of fish that wouldn't disintegrate into the broth; we nestled thick chunks in among the potatoes where they gradually cooked through. Eggs are a traditional component, and we added them last, allowing them to cook up gently in the hot, flavorful broth.

When cast-iron stew pots come out in Lenoir County, North Carolina, the safe bet is that a fish stew is nigh.

Here's how it goes down: First, the host renders bacon or salt pork in a large pot. He or she then layers in sliced onions, sliced potatoes, and chunks of whitefish and adds water, tomato, and red pepper flakes—and then walks away for a bit (it's essential to not stir the stew as it cooks to keep the fish from breaking up). When the stew's nearly done, the cook cracks eggs into it to poach until just cooked through. The stew is served with sliced white bread to mop up the spicy broth.

Wait. Eggs?

Yes, eggs.

The origins of this egg addition are murky, so I reached out to Vivian Howard, a chef from Kinston, North Carolina. She speculated, "A frugal farmer probably went fishing and wanted to stretch the fish he got." Note to self: Next time I have a disappointing catch, stop by the grocery store for eggs.

To find a starting point for my own fish stew, I cooked five recipes—two authentic versions from born-and-bred Carolinians and three similar-but-different stews from acclaimed chefs like Craig Claiborne. What I found was this: The simplest stews were the best. Adding all sorts of vegetables and other spices distracted from the simple yet comforting and restorative flavor built from bacon, tomato, fish, and heat.

While most local recipes called for adding the uncooked potatoes, onions, and fish all at once to let them cook together, I found it more effective to do things in stages: After rendering the bacon, I cooked the onions and then added the tomato paste and potatoes. Adding the delicate fish last helped protect it and kept it from breaking down too much.

Most Carolinians use bone-in chunks of firm, flavorful, locally caught fish like striped bass, sheepshead, or redfish. I wanted a fish that was widely available at any time of year, so I tried cod, halibut, hake, and haddock. I was happy to learn that any mild, firm whitefish worked as long as it was cut into chunks of similar thickness.

I cracked eight eggs into several pots of stew—with mixed results. In one batch, gelatinous eggs floated atop the stew; in another, they boiled into rubber balls. The best approach turned out to be covering the pot and setting it over medium-low heat, which produced eggs with a silky texture. That frugal farmer was onto something.

NOTES FROM THE TEST KITCHEN

BUYING FISH FOR STEW

Eastern North Carolina Fish Stew calls for fillets that will hold their shape during cooking. Look for thick, mild whitefish fillets such as bass, rockfish, cod, hake, haddock, or halibut. Thin, flaky fish like flounder, catfish, and tilapia are not good choices.

USE THESE: THICK AND FIRM
Firm fillets such as bass, cod, and haddock will keep their shape.

NO-GO: THIN AND FLAKY
Thin fillets such as flounder, catfish, and tilapia will fall apart.

At a final test kitchen tasting on a very cold winter day, a coworker called it "a bouillabaisse with love from a Southern grandma." She was right.

—MORGAN BOLLING, *Cook's Country*

Eastern North Carolina Fish Stew
SERVES 8

Any mild, firm-fleshed whitefish, such as bass, rockfish, cod, hake, haddock, or halibut, will work well in this stew. Serve with soft white sandwich bread (Wonderbread is traditional) or saltines.

- 6 slices thick-cut bacon, cut into ½-inch-wide strips
- 2 onions, halved and sliced thin
  Salt
- ½ teaspoon red pepper flakes
- 6 cups water
- 1 (6-ounce) can tomato paste
- 1 pound red potatoes, unpeeled, sliced ¼ inch thick
- 1 bay leaf
- 1 teaspoon Tabasco sauce, plus extra for serving
- 2 pounds skinless whitefish fillets, 1 to 1½ inches thick, cut into 2-inch chunks
- 8 large eggs

1. Cook bacon in Dutch oven over medium heat until crispy, 9 to 11 minutes, stirring occasionally. Add onions, 1½ teaspoons salt, and pepper flakes and cook until onions begin to soften, about 5 minutes.

2. Stir in water and tomato paste, scraping up any browned bits. Add potatoes and bay leaf. Increase heat to medium-high and bring to boil. Reduce heat to medium and cook at vigorous simmer for 10 minutes.

3. Reduce heat to medium-low and stir in Tabasco. Nestle fish into stew but do not stir. Crack eggs into stew, spacing them evenly. Cover and cook until eggs are just set, 17 to 22 minutes. Season with salt to taste. Serve, passing extra Tabasco separately.

EASTERN NORTH CAROLINA FISH STEW

CLASSIC CHICKEN CURRY

CLASSIC CHICKEN CURRY

WHY THIS RECIPE WORKS: For a quick weeknight chicken curry that is a one-pot dish to boot, we began by blooming curry powder in butter to enliven its flavor. From there, we built a bold, spicy base with onion, garlic, ginger, and jalapeño. Staggering cooking times ensured that each element of the dish was cooked to perfection: We started by adding bone-in split chicken breasts and a moderate amount of water to the pot and simmering them, covered, flipping the chicken halfway through cooking. We plucked the breasts from the pot and replaced them with our vegetables, starting with hearty chunks of potato and later adding quicker-cooking cauliflower florets. We shredded the chicken while the vegetables cooked, adding the meat back to the pot at the end along with sweet frozen peas, leaving just enough time for both to warm through. Whole-milk yogurt, stirred in off the heat, contributed creaminess and tang, tying the fragrant, rich dish together in no time.

Curry has deep roots in America. It enjoyed its first stateside vogue during the 19th century, when East Coast seaports from Charleston to Portland found themselves suddenly favored with new spices from Asia. Many cookbooks from that era, including *Mrs. Rorer's Philadelphia Cook Book* and *Mrs. Lincoln's Boston Cook Book*, included recipes for chicken flavored with curry powder.

Curry powder was and still is a complex blend of spices. Many home cooks create their own blends, but we've had great success with store-bought mixes (our favorite is Penzeys Sweet Curry Powder). Simply tossing chicken with the stuff and cooking it off produces a good dish.

But good isn't good enough; I wanted something great. What's more, I wanted to round out my curry with traditional ingredients including potatoes, cauliflower, and peas to create a one-pot meal.

I started with the curry powder, which, as we know from many years of test kitchen work, benefits (as most spices do) from a quick cooking in fat to "bloom," or release its oils and aromas. Just 10 seconds in the bottom of a Dutch oven does the trick. Because I wanted savory onion flavor to infuse the entire dish, I tossed onions in next, cooking them until just soft. Garlic, ginger, and jalapeño, three curry staples, completed this flavor base.

I wanted my final curry to feature shredded chicken, but I also knew that cooking bone-in, skin-on chicken would give more flavor to the dish. So I added two split chicken breasts to the pot with the onions and curry, followed by a few cut-up Yukon Gold potatoes (tasters liked their flavor), half a head of cauliflower that I had cut into florets, and a couple of cups of water. I set everything to simmer and came back a while later to have a taste. But my hopes for an all-in-one method were dashed when I found rubbery chicken, mushy cauliflower, and underdone spuds. I'd have to use a staggered approach.

For the next go-round, I added chicken to the pot with 1½ cups of water (enough to braise it and then the potatoes). I brought the water to a simmer, covered the pot, and cooked the chicken for about 20 minutes before transferring it a plate. While the chicken cooled, I added the potatoes to the liquid in the pot and cooked them for 8 minutes before tossing in the cauliflower. Fifteen minutes later, the vegetables were tender. By now I'd taken the chicken off the bone and tossed the skin, and the meat was cool enough to tear into shreds. I stirred the meat (and the juices that had accumulated on the plate) back into the pot with a cup of frozen peas. Once everything was warmed through, it was ready to serve.

NOTES FROM THE TEST KITCHEN

TASTING CURRY POWDER

Curry powders come in two basic styles: mild (or sweet) and a hotter version called Madras. We call for a mild version in our Classic Chicken Curry; it contains as many as 20 ground spices, herbs, and seeds such as turmeric, coriander, cumin, black and red peppers, cinnamon, cloves, fennel seeds, cardamom, ginger, and fenugreek. Our favorite is **Penzeys Sweet Curry Powder**, which is vivid and well-rounded.

Or so I thought. While my curry was hearty and aromatic, it lacked a signature characteristic: tangy creaminess. A cup of whole-milk yogurt stirred in off the heat, plus a scattering of cilantro over the top, sealed the deal on this old-school classic.

—CECELIA JENKINS, *Cook's Country*

Classic Chicken Curry

SERVES 4

Do not substitute low-fat or nonfat yogurt for the whole-milk yogurt called for in this recipe or the finished dish will be much less creamy. The curry is best served with white rice.

- 3 tablespoons unsalted butter
- 2 tablespoons curry powder
- 2 onions, chopped
- 1 jalapeño chile, stemmed, seeded, and minced
  Salt and pepper
- 3 garlic cloves, minced
- 1 tablespoon minced fresh ginger
- 2 (10- to 12-ounce) bone-in split chicken breasts, trimmed
- 1½ cups water
- 8 ounces Yukon Gold potatoes, peeled and cut into ½-inch chunks
- ½ head cauliflower (1 pound), cored and cut into 1-inch florets
- 1 cup frozen peas
- ¼ cup minced fresh cilantro
- ¾ cup plain whole-milk yogurt

1. Melt butter in Dutch oven over medium heat. Add curry powder and cook until fragrant, about 10 seconds. Add onions, jalapeño, 1¼ teaspoons salt, and ¼ teaspoon pepper and cook until vegetables are softened, about 5 minutes. Stir in garlic and ginger and cook until fragrant, about 30 seconds.

2. Add chicken and water to pot. Increase heat to medium-high and bring mixture to boil. Reduce heat to low, cover, and simmer until chicken registers 160 degrees, 22 to 24 minutes, flipping chicken halfway through cooking. Transfer chicken to plate and let cool for 5 minutes. Once chicken has cooled, use two forks to shred meat into approximate 2-inch pieces; discard skin and bones.

3. Meanwhile, stir potatoes and ¼ teaspoon salt into curry, cover, and cook until potatoes are slightly tender, about 8 minutes. Stir in cauliflower and continue to cook, covered, until potatoes are fully cooked and cauliflower is tender, about 15 minutes longer, stirring occasionally.

4. Stir in peas, cilantro, and shredded chicken and cook until curry is warmed through, about 1 minute. Off heat, stir in yogurt. Season with salt and pepper to taste, and serve.

PANANG BEEF CURRY

WHY THIS RECIPE WORKS: For a *panang* curry that's just as rich and flavorful as traditional versions but quicker to make, we relied on two shortcuts: easy-to-prep beef and jarred red curry paste. Beef short ribs required no knifework and cooked up tender in about an hour. In order to keep the sauce's flavor distinct, we cooked the beef separately, simmering thin-sliced ribs in water. We turned storebought curry paste into an authentic panang sauce by blooming it in a skillet and then incorporating coconut milk, fish sauce, sugar, and a halved Thai red chile for spicy heat. Kaffir lime leaves gave this dish a pop of citrusy brightness, and they needed only a few minutes in the simmering sauce to unleash their zippy freshness. To finish, we stirred in the beef and allowed the sauce to thicken around it. Peanuts are a traditional element in this dish, and we preserved their crunch by sprinkling them on just before serving.

Savory, stew-like Thai curries are often categorized by the color of the spice paste used to flavor and thicken them. Green is hot and pungent, mild yellow is sweet-spiced, orange is pleasantly sour, and salty-sweet red features a lingering burn. And then there is *panang*—a sweeter, more unctuous derivative of red curry that's enriched with ground peanuts and seasoned with sugar, fish sauce, deeply fragrant kaffir lime leaves, and a touch of fiery Thai chile. Panang curries are typically made with beef—usually a flavorful but tough cut, such as chuck roast, shank, or brisket, that needs to cook for a long time to turn tender. And unlike those other, more familiar curries, which are typically very brothy, panang is a dry curry that contains a judicious amount of coconut milk, giving it a thick, velvety consistency that steadfastly clings to the pieces of meat.

For a cook who has time, making panang curry from scratch can be a rewarding labor of love: toasting and pounding spices and aromatics to make the paste; frying the paste in a little oil; adding the coconut milk, seasonings, and beef; and, finally, simmering it all to meld and concentrate the flavors. But even in Thailand, many cooks start with store-bought paste, which can make this dish just as easy as—and actually less work than—your typical stir-fry.

Most traditional panang curry recipes call for a tough, collagen-rich cut of beef for the same reason that Western stews do: The abundant collagen breaks down during the prolonged cooking time, so the beef turns silky and fall-apart tender. I came across a few modern panang curry recipes calling for quick-cooking cuts such as sirloin or flank steak, but they weren't nearly as nice to eat; cooked briefly, these cuts have a steak-like chew that's not right in Thai curry, while a lengthy simmer toughens them. I'd stick with traditional collagen-rich cuts.

However, unlike Western beef stews, which cook the meat directly in the braising liquid to maximize beefy flavor, most traditional panang curry recipes I found called for cutting the beef into chunks or slices and simmering them in plain water until tender, which takes 1 to 2 hours, depending on the cut. The water is then discarded, and the meat is combined with the sauce for the last few minutes of cooking to purposely limit the amount of beefy flavor so that it won't muddy the flavors of the spice paste. I proceeded with simmering the meat separately, but I planned to double back at the end of testing and try cooking the meat in the sauce.

But first: Which cut of beef should I use? For my early tests, I defaulted to chuck roast for three reasons: its good flavor, availability, and affordability. The

downsides were that trimming fat and gristle from the roast was time-consuming and generated a lot of waste, and even after when cut into thin slices, it needed 2 hours of simmering to turn tender. Looking for other options, I considered cuts such as shank and brisket, but these would require some trimming as well as a long simmering time. Ultimately, I ditched them all in favor of a cut we often turn to for braising: boneless short ribs. They're flavorful and well marbled, so they'd be sure to cook up moist. And even though they're a bit pricier than chuck, there'd be much less waste and knife work—a worthwhile trade-off. Sliced ¼ inch thick, the short ribs cooked up tender after just about an hour of simmering. On to the paste.

I usually wouldn't be so quick to endorse a prefab ingredient, but most commercial Thai curry pastes are nothing more than purees of the same herbs and spices I would have to seek out and grind myself—in this case dried red chiles, shallots, garlic, galangal, lemon grass, kaffir lime leaves, coriander root, white pepper, and salt. Plus, pastes are inexpensive and keep well in the refrigerator for about a month.

Unfortunately, panang curry paste isn't widely available in American markets, so I'd have to start with the more common red variety and doctor its flavor. That wouldn't be hard, though, since all I needed to do was add some form of peanut and work in plenty of kaffir lime leaves so that their bright, citrusy fragrance would stand out in the rich sauce.

Once I had another batch of beef ready to go, I sizzled a few tablespoons of red curry paste in a little vegetable oil to intensify its flavor and then added a can of coconut milk. Traditional recipes often call for frying the paste in the "cracked" coconut cream that rises to the top of a can of coconut milk, but we've found that coconut milks from different brands yield varying amounts of cream and that vegetable oil works just as well. To that mixture I added a few teaspoons of fish sauce and a touch of sugar for salty-sweet balance, followed by the cooked short ribs. I then simmered the curry until the liquid was reduced by roughly half and was thick enough to coat the meat. Finally, I stirred in a few tablespoons of peanut butter, an amount I'd seen

PANANG BEEF CURRY

called for in several recipes. The flavor and texture overwhelmed and overthickened the curry, so I reduced the amount of peanut butter in subsequent batches, but it never tasted quite right. The better option was to scatter finely chopped roasted peanuts over the top before serving, which lent the dish subtle nuttiness as well as a nice crunch.

Some recipes instruct you to simmer whole kaffir lime leaves in the sauce and remove them just before serving, as you would bay leaves in a soup or stew. Others called for slicing the stiff, shiny leaves into very thin slivers and adding them to the pot just before serving or even sprinkling them over the top as a garnish. After trying both approaches, I found that the latter delivered brighter, more vibrant citrus flavor in every bite. I also came up with an acceptable substitute: a 50-50 combination of lime and lemon zest strips.

I doubled back to the question of whether to cook the beef in water or in the sauce: A side-by-side test confirmed that tasters unanimously preferred the water method; the sauce in the other batch was not only muddy-tasting but also much too rich after reducing for such a long time.

With savory-sweet heat; lush, creamy body; nutty richness; and floral, citrusy tang, my version of panang curry was satisfying in a way that belied the ease of making it.

—ANNIE PETITO, *Cook's Illustrated*

Panang Beef Curry

SERVES 6

Red curry pastes from different brands vary in spiciness, so start by adding 2 tablespoons and then taste the sauce and add up to 2 tablespoons more. Kaffir lime leaves are well worth seeking out. If you can't find them, substitute three 3-inch strips each of lemon zest and lime zest, adding them to the sauce with the beef in step 2 (remove the zest strips before serving). Do not substitute light coconut milk. Serve this rich dish with rice and vegetables.

2	pounds boneless beef short ribs, trimmed
2	tablespoons vegetable oil
2–4	tablespoons red curry paste
1	(14 ounce) can unsweetened coconut milk
4	teaspoons fish sauce
2	teaspoons sugar
1	Thai red chile, halved lengthwise (optional)
6	kaffir lime leaves, middle vein removed, sliced thin
1/3	cup unsalted dry-roasted peanuts, chopped fine

1. Cut each rib crosswise with grain into 3 equal pieces. Slice each piece against grain 1/4 inch thick. Place beef in large saucepan and add water to cover. Bring to boil over high heat. Cover, reduce heat to low, and cook until beef is fork-tender, 1 to 1 1/4 hours. Using slotted spoon, transfer beef to bowl; discard water. (Beef can be refrigerated in airtight container for up to 24 hours; when ready to use, add it to curry as directed in step 2.)

2. Heat oil in 12-inch nonstick skillet over medium heat until shimmering. Add 2 tablespoons curry paste and cook, stirring frequently, until paste is fragrant and darkens in color to brick red, 5 to 8 minutes. Add coconut milk, fish sauce, sugar, and chile, if using; stir to combine and dissolve sugar. Taste sauce and add up to 2 tablespoons more red curry paste to achieve desired spiciness. Add beef, stir to coat with sauce, and bring to simmer.

3. Rapidly simmer, stirring occasionally, until sauce is thickened and reduced by half and coats beef, 12 to 15 minutes. (Sauce should be quite thick, and streaks of oil will appear. Sauce will continue to thicken as it cools.) Add kaffir lime leaves and simmer until fragrant, 1 to 2 minutes. Transfer to serving platter, sprinkle with peanuts, and serve.

CHAPTER 3

VEGETABLES AND SIDES

SPINACH AND STRAWBERRY SALAD

✔ **WHY THIS RECIPE WORKS:** We thought classic spinach and strawberry salad deserved a fresh reboot. First, we livened up the greens by pairing the tender baby spinach with crunchy romaine lettuce. Fresh strawberries need no embellishing, so we skipped salting or sugaring them and bumped up the total amount of berries to 1 pound. For a poppy seed dressing that actually tasted like its key component, we toasted the poppy seeds, coaxing out their nutty flavor. Before preparing the vinaigrette, we combined red wine vinegar, sugar, and some salt, microwaving a portion of it to create a quick pickling liquid for slices of red onion. We whisked the remaining vinegar mixture with oil and dry mustard for a savory edge and tossed in toasted almonds for some finishing crunch.

Spinach and strawberry salad has been popular for generations, served in various forms in high-end restaurants and fast food drive-throughs alike. But when I made a few versions in the test kitchen following existing published recipes, my tasters and I had a hard time understanding why. Baby spinach leaves and sliced strawberries on their own are just fine, of course, but once paired and tossed with a thick, viscous, sweet poppy seed dressing, the pairing becomes a clumpy, cloying mess. This dish needed a facelift.

To start my salad reboot, I decided to cut back on the spinach, which can verge on chalky when the leaves are eaten raw. Instead I swapped crisp, vibrant chopped romaine for half the spinach. I then looked at different ways to prepare the strawberries—quartered, halved, or sliced? Sugared or salted? I settled on quartered berries, which my tasters found easiest to eat, and no salt or sugar, since good strawberries don't need either. I bumped up the berries from the usual 1 or 2 cups to a full pound so that there'd be berries in every bite.

Many of the recipes I tried featured extra ingredients, including red onion, toasted nuts, and even cucumber. I decided to skip watery cucumber, but my tasters voted to keep nuts in the mix—specifically, toasted sliced almonds. And to temper the bite of raw onion, I opted to partially soften the slices in a bit of warmed-up vinegar mixed with sugar and salt.

The real work started when I began testing the poppy seed dressing. I wanted to honor the spirit of the original but tone down its sweetness. Starting from scratch, I whisked together a simple vinaigrette of red wine vinegar, salt, a bit of sugar, and vegetable oil, hoping the oil's neutral, mild flavor would allow the strawberries to shine. I just needed poppy seeds. But why? Whatever flavor they have—and it isn't much—was indiscernible in the salad. To see if I could coax some flavor out of the tiny seeds, I turned to a method we often use for sesame seeds: toasting them, lightly and quickly, in a skillet. It worked. The trick brought out a nutty, pleasant flavor that subtly permeated the salad dressing.

I tossed the sweet-sour dressing with the spinach, romaine, toasted almonds, pickled onions, and quartered strawberries and called my team over for a taste. The consensus: victory. My salad had a mix of crisp, vibrant greens; softly sweet berries; the faint bite of barely pickled onion; notes of deep toasted almond flavor; and a light but flavorful dressing.

—DIANE UNGER, *Cook's Country*

Spinach and Strawberry Salad with Poppy Seed Dressing
SERVES 4 TO 6

Since poppy seeds are dark and it's hard to tell when they're fully toasted, use your nose: They should smell nutty. The pickled onions can be made and refrigerated up to two days in advance of serving the salad.

½ cup red wine vinegar
⅓ cup sugar
  Salt and pepper
½ red onion, sliced thin
1 tablespoon poppy seeds
½ cup sliced almonds
¼ cup vegetable oil
1 teaspoon dry mustard
1 pound strawberries, hulled and quartered (2½ cups)
1 romaine lettuce heart (6 ounces), torn into bite-size pieces
5 ounces (5 cups) baby spinach

1. Whisk vinegar, sugar, and ¾ teaspoon salt together in bowl. Transfer ¼ cup vinegar mixture to small bowl and microwave until hot, about 1 minute. Add onion, stir to combine, and let sit for at least 30 minutes.

SPINACH AND STRAWBERRY SALAD WITH POPPY SEED DRESSING

2. Meanwhile, toast poppy seeds in 8-inch nonstick skillet over medium heat until fragrant and slightly darkened, 1 to 2 minutes; transfer to bowl and set aside. Add almonds to now-empty skillet, return to medium heat, and toast until fragrant and golden, 3 to 5 minutes.

3. Whisk oil, mustard, poppy seeds, and ½ teaspoon pepper into remaining vinegar mixture. Combine strawberries, romaine, spinach, and ¼ cup almonds in large bowl. Using fork, remove onions from vinegar mixture and add to salad. Add poppy seed dressing to salad and toss to combine. Season with salt and pepper to taste. Transfer salad to serving platter and top with remaining ¼ cup almonds. Serve.

GRAPEFRUIT-AVOCADO SALAD

✔ **WHY THIS RECIPE WORKS:** Grapefruit and avocado are the perfect starting place for a tart yet buttery wintertime salad. We began by segmenting the grapefruit to rid them of the bitter pith and hard-to-eat membranes and placed them atop a platter of thinly sliced avocado rather than tossing them together, keeping their textures intact. Whisking together a vinaigrette using some of the grapefruit's juices with sugar and buttery olive oil helped balance out the grapefruit's bite. We used a judicious amount of fresh herbs in place of traditional greens and sprinkled on toasted hazelnuts to finish off the salad with simple elegance.

Pale green avocado and vibrant pink grapefruit, both in season during winter's bleakest months, make a handsome couple. At the fruits' best, the buttery and nutty notes of the soft avocado play well with the grapefruit's invigorating tang. But if assembled carelessly, the combination can be bitter and wet. I wanted a salad that showcased the natural beauty and best flavors of each fruit.

Grapefruit peel is intensely bitter, as is the pith—the soft white layer between the fruit and its skin. I tried simply cutting away these two offending layers and then slicing the exposed fruit into rounds. This method was quick and easy, but the result still retained too much membrane and was tricky to eat. The better method was to cut each segment away from its membranes, leaving pure, sweet bites of grapefruit.

Tossing cut-up avocado with the other salad ingredients made for a muddy result, so I had to assemble this salad less roughly. I dispensed with the idea of arranging the components on a platter in an alternating pattern of green and pink—too fancy and precious. Instead, I arranged a single layer of grapefruit segments over the avocado slices. Attractive and simple.

I considered incorporating salad greens, but these obscured the colors of the avocado and grapefruit. Instead, I went for herbs: Whole cilantro leaves and torn mint leaves packed plenty of flavor without becoming overwhelming, and they looked pretty, too. Toasted hazelnuts added a little crunch.

I needed a carefully crafted dressing with a strong olive oil presence and a little sugar to enhance the grapefruit's sweetness and temper its tang. I used a shallot for its subtle onion flavor and some Dijon for both its zip and its emulsifying properties. For brightness, I added juice left over from segmenting the grapefruits, along with a teaspoon of white wine vinegar.

—KATIE LEAIRD, *Cook's Country*

Grapefruit-Avocado Salad
SERVES 4 TO 6

A ripe avocado will yield slightly to a gentle squeeze when held in the palm of your hand.

  3 **red grapefruits**
  2 **ripe avocados, halved, pitted, and sliced ¼ inch thick**
  ¼ **cup fresh mint leaves, torn**
  ¼ **cup fresh cilantro leaves**
  ¼ **cup blanched hazelnuts, toasted and chopped coarse**
  3 **tablespoons extra-virgin olive oil**
  1 **tablespoon minced shallot**
  1 **teaspoon white wine vinegar**
  1 **teaspoon Dijon mustard**
  1 **teaspoon sugar**
  ½ **teaspoon salt**

1. Cut away peel and pith from grapefruits. Holding fruit over bowl, use paring knife to slice between membranes to release segments. Reserve 2 tablespoons grapefruit juice.

2. Arrange avocado in single layer on large platter. Distribute grapefruit evenly over top. Sprinkle mint, cilantro, and hazelnuts over top.

3. Whisk oil, shallot, vinegar, mustard, sugar, salt, and reserved grapefruit juice together in bowl. Drizzle dressing over salad. Serve immediately.

PREPPING GRAPEFRUIT FOR SALAD

We keep grapefruit segments perfectly intact with a few careful prep steps.

1. Using a chef's or paring knife, trim away the peel and pith.

2. Cut toward the center between the pulp and the membrane to remove each segment.

BEET, ENDIVE, AND PEAR SLAW

✓ **WHY THIS RECIPE WORKS:** Hoping to create a bright, tangy slaw that we could make year-round, we looked to earthy-sweet beets. Grating the tough vegetables on a box grater produced a pile of evenly shredded beets, and tossing the shreds with salt and sugar helped soften them while drawing out any excess moisture. Subtly bitter Belgian endives and mildly sweet pears, all sliced thin, added some textural variety. Rather than turn to the standard mayo-based dressing, we tossed our crunchy slaw in a lively vinaigrette of sherry vinegar, Dijon mustard, and olive oil.

Cabbage may be the traditional choice for coleslaw, but it's not the only option. I suspected that root vegetables like beets, carrots, celery root, and kohlrabi would stay just as crisp once dressed, and their distinctive flavors would enliven a slaw. And while mayonnaise-based dressings are a common choice, I liked the idea of pairing my shredded root vegetables with a tangy vinaigrette.

With their deep, rich color and earthy-sweet flavor, beets seemed like a great starting place for my testing.

But unlike cabbage, which succumbs to a sharp knife with little effort, dense beets would take more elbow grease to turn them into shreds thin enough to be palatable raw. A mandoline could do the job, but I ruled it out since not everyone owns this tool. Fortunately, I found that both the shredding disk of a food processor and the large holes of a box grater made relatively quick work of the task. We typically call for pretreating cabbage to remove much of its abundant water; otherwise, you'd wind up with a waterlogged mess of a slaw. I had hoped I could skip this step for beets, but one test confirmed that they contain enough water to cause problems. Plus, while the shreds were thin, they were still too woody for tasters. Some sort of pretreatment was a must.

Tossing a vegetable with salt and letting it sit is a common way to pull out water. I worked my way up to using 1 teaspoon of salt with the beets before I had to put on the brakes—any more and the slaw was too salty. It also took an hour, which was too long to wait. Luckily, salt wasn't my only pretreatment option. Just as it does with fruit, sugar can extract liquid from vegetables. It isn't as effective as salt at the task—how quickly water gets pulled to the surface is determined by how many dissolved particles are in the solution, and sugar remains one molecule when dissolved whereas salt breaks down into two ions—but the combination of the two would speed up the process. And I liked the idea of the contrast that the sweetness would provide against the tangy vinaigrette.

I tossed a new batch of shredded beets with 1 teaspoon of salt plus ¼ cup of sugar and let the mixture sit. By the time I'd finished prepping my other ingredients (which took about 15 minutes), they were sufficiently wilted; I gave them a quick spin in a salad spinner, and they were ready to go.

Now I just needed a few complementary ingredients and a dressing. I settled on endive since its bitterness would make a nice foil to the sweet beets. For another layer of texture and some floral sweetness, I added some pears. And finally, for contrasting color and another layer of flavor, I tossed in some cilantro.

As for the vinaigrette, sherry vinegar offered an oaky complexity that complemented the beets, and adding plenty of Dijon mustard punched up the flavor and lent the dressing body.

BEET, ENDIVE, AND PEAR SLAW

From here, it was easy to create a few variations based on the formula. I paired earthy carrots with peppery radishes and sweet kohlrabi with bitter radicchio. Changing out the pear for apple and swapping in different vinegars—rice or white wine—and alternate herbs helped give each slaw a unique profile. And with so much texture, flavor, and alluring color, these slaws were sure to appear on my dinner table throughout the year.

—ANDREW JANJIGIAN, *Cook's Illustrated*

Beet, Endive, and Pear Slaw

SERVES 4 TO 6

To save time, we recommend shredding and treating the beets before prepping the remaining ingredients. Shred the beets on the large holes of a box grater or with the shredding disk of a food processor.

1½ pounds beets, trimmed, peeled, and shredded
¼ cup sugar, plus extra for seasoning
Salt and pepper
½ cup extra-virgin olive oil
3 tablespoons sherry vinegar, plus extra for seasoning
2 tablespoons Dijon mustard
2 heads Belgian endive (4 ounces each), cored and sliced thin on bias
2 pears, peeled, halved, cored, and cut into ⅛-inch matchsticks
1 cup fresh cilantro leaves

1. Toss beets with sugar and 1 teaspoon salt in large bowl and let sit until partially wilted and reduced in volume by one-third, about 15 minutes.

2. Meanwhile, whisk oil, vinegar, mustard, ½ teaspoon salt, and ½ teaspoon pepper in large bowl until combined.

3. Transfer beets to salad spinner and spin until excess water is removed, 10 to 20 seconds. Transfer beets to bowl with dressing. Add endive, pears, and cilantro to bowl with beets and toss to combine. Season with salt, pepper, extra sugar, and/or extra vinegar to taste. Serve immediately.

VARIATIONS

Carrot, Radish, and Asian Pear Slaw

Shred the carrots on the large holes of a box grater or with the shredding disk of a food processor.

Substitute carrots for beets and rice vinegar for sherry vinegar. Add 1 tablespoon toasted sesame oil to dressing in step 2. Substitute 12 ounces radishes, trimmed, halved, and sliced thin, for endive; Asian pears for pears; and 10 scallions, green parts only, sliced thin on bias, for cilantro.

Kohlrabi, Radicchio, and Apple Slaw

Shred the kohlrabi on the large holes of a box grater or with the shredding disk of a food processor.

Substitute kohlrabi for beets and white wine vinegar for sherry vinegar. Substitute 1 small head radicchio, halved, cored, and sliced ½ inch thick, for endive; Granny Smith apples for pears; and ½ cup coarsely chopped fresh mint for cilantro.

GRILLED ARTICHOKES WITH LEMON BUTTER

✓ **WHY THIS RECIPE WORKS:** Steaming is the most common cooking method for artichokes, but grilling is a better way to unlock their rich, nutty flavor. To ready our chokes for the grill, we trimmed away the tough outer leaves and spiked tips and parboiled them in water flavored with lemon juice, red pepper flakes, and salt; this step ensured they were completely tender and thoroughly seasoned. Brushing the artichokes with extra-virgin olive oil before grilling encouraged flavorful char. After giving each side enough time to take on some color, we served our full-flavored artichokes with a bright lemon-garlic butter.

The center of the artichoke universe is Monterey County, California, which produces millions of pounds of the vegetable each year. Locals love artichokes' delicate flavor, especially when grilled. Cooking them over an open fire brings out a nutty note.

Artichokes are part of the thistle family and are technically the bud of a flower; the spiky tips of the leaves evolved to protect the bud from predators—except for those with a sharp knife. After experimenting, I found it best to use a vegetable peeler to remove the fibrous outer skin of the stem before snapping off the bottom rows of the remaining tough leaves. Placing each artichoke on its side and lopping off the top quarter got rid of most of the spikes. I pruned the rest of the leaves with scissors.

Early tests proved that precooking the artichokes was essential; if done entirely on the grill, they'd burn before cooking through. Boiling them in a seasoned broth of water, lemon juice, and red pepper flakes softened them just enough. It was easy to cut them in half and scoop out the fuzzy, inedible chokes with a spoon.

Because my artichokes were mostly cooked through, all I needed from the fire was a solid char, which I achieved with just 2 to 4 minutes per side over hot coals.

NOTES FROM THE TEST KITCHEN

PREPPING ARTICHOKES FOR THE GRILL

1. Cut off bottom ¼ inch of stem and remove any leaves attached to stem. Using vegetable peeler, peel stem.

2. Pull bottom row of tough outer leaves downward toward stem and break off at base.

3. Cut off and discard top quarter. Use scissors to cut off sharp tips of remaining leaves.

I wanted a straightforward sauce to highlight the artichokes' flavor. A blend of lemon, garlic, and butter was the answer. It came together in minutes and was perfect for drizzling and dipping.

—MORGAN BOLLING, *Cook's Country*

Grilled Artichokes with Lemon Butter

SERVES 4 TO 6

Look for artichokes that are bright green, with tightly packed leaves; avoid soft artichokes or those with brown splotches. The leaves should not appear feathery or dried out. To eat, use your teeth to scrape the flesh from the inner part of the exterior leaves. The tender inner leaves, heart, and stem are entirely edible.

> 4   artichokes (8 to 10 ounces each)
>   Salt and pepper
> ½   teaspoon red pepper flakes
> 2   lemons
> 6   tablespoons unsalted butter
> 1   garlic clove, minced to paste
> 2   tablespoons olive oil

1. Cut off and discard bottom ¼ inch of each artichoke stem, and remove any leaves attached to stems. Using vegetable peeler, peel away outer layer of stems. Pull bottom row of tough outer leaves downward toward stems and break off at base. Cut off and discard top quarter of each artichoke. Using scissors, cut off sharp tips of remaining leaves all around artichokes.

2. Combine 3 quarts water, 3 tablespoons salt, and pepper flakes in Dutch oven. Cut 1 lemon in half; squeeze juice into pot, then add spent halves. Bring to boil over high heat. Add artichokes, cover, and reduce heat to medium-low. Simmer until tip of paring knife inserted into base of artichoke slips easily in and out, 25 to 28 minutes, stirring occasionally.

3. Meanwhile, grate 2 teaspoons zest from remaining lemon; combine with butter, garlic, ½ teaspoon salt, and ¼ teaspoon pepper in bowl. Microwave at 50 percent power until butter is melted and bubbling and garlic is fragrant, about 2 minutes, stirring occasionally. Squeeze 1½ tablespoons juice from zested lemon and stir into butter mixture. Season with salt and pepper to taste.

4. Set wire rack in rimmed baking sheet. Place artichokes stem side up on prepared rack and let drain for 10 minutes. Cut artichokes in half lengthwise. Using spoon, scoop out fuzzy choke, leaving small cavity in center of each half.

5A. FOR A CHARCOAL GRILL: Open bottom vent completely. Light large chimney starter filled with charcoal briquettes (6 quarts). When top coals are partially covered with ash, pour evenly over grill. Set cooking grate in place, cover, and open lid vent completely. Heat grill until hot, about 5 minutes.

5B. FOR A GAS GRILL: Turn all burners to high, cover, and heat grill until hot, about 15 minutes. Leave all burners on high.

6. Clean and oil cooking grate. Brush artichokes with oil. Place artichokes on grill and cook (covered if using gas) until lightly charred, 2 to 4 minutes per side. Transfer artichokes to platter and tent with aluminum foil. Briefly rewarm lemon butter in microwave, if necessary, and serve with artichokes.

BROILED BROCCOLI RABE

✔ **WHY THIS RECIPE WORKS:** Most recipes for broccoli rabe call for blanching and shocking the vegetable before cooking in order to tame its bitterness, but broiling is just as effective (and not nearly as fussy). On top of being quick, broiling also created deep caramelization on the pieces without overcooking them. We cut the stalks into bite-size pieces, leaving the leaves and florets intact, and kept the seasoning simple, drizzling the pieces with a mixture of oil, minced garlic, salt, and red pepper flakes to complement the rabe's toned-down bite. After broiling long enough to impart plenty of char, we served our broccoli rabe with a brightening squeeze of fresh lemon juice.

In the past I rarely, if ever, cooked broccoli rabe. (Rabe, or *rapini*, as it's known in Italy where the vegetable is a mainstay in the cuisine, is actually more closely related to spicy turnips than to regular, more mellow broccoli.) While I'm a fan of this green's bitter, mustardy bite, I seem to be in the minority on this. As a result, the majority of recipes you find jump through

hoops to subdue its characteristic flavor. One of the most popular approaches calls for chopping, blanching, shocking, draining, and sautéing the pieces with strong-flavored aromatics—a lengthy ordeal that wipes out just about any trace of the green's pungency and leaves you with a sink full of dirty dishes. At that point, why bother?

I've always thought that if you could temper rabe's bitterness but not eliminate it entirely, this green would offer much more character than most vegetables. As a bonus, it would need little or no dressing before it hit the plate. The trick would be figuring out the most efficient way to do this.

I made some headway by researching where broccoli rabe gets it bitter flavor. The technical explanation is that when the plant is cut or chewed and its cells thus damaged, two components stored mainly in its florets—the enzyme myrosinase and a bitter-tasting substrate of the enzyme called glucosinolate—combine, and some of the glucosinolates are converted into even harsher-tasting isothiocyanates. In other words, the pungency we taste is the plant's defense mechanism when under attack.

The upshot was that the way in which I cut the rabe seemed likely to be at least as important as how I cooked it. I proved this to myself with a quick side-by-side test: I divided a bunch of rabe in half and fully chopped one portion, florets and all. Then, I cut the remaining stalks roughly where the leaves and florets start to branch off from the stems, leaving the leafy parts intact, and cut the stem segments (where less of the enzyme resides) into bite-size pieces. For the sake of ease, I simply sautéed both batches and took a taste. Sure enough, the intact pieces were considerably more mellow. It also turns out that there was another factor at play: The high heat of cooking deactivates the myrosinase enzyme in the vegetable and thus stops the reaction that contributes most of the bitter flavor in the first place.

I could have stopped right there and created a recipe for sautéing chopped stems and whole leaves and florets, but I'd found a few recipes that called for roasting the rabe, which was an interesting alternative. Plus, I hoped that the rabe would brown deeply and take on a rich caramelized flavor that would balance out the remaining bitterness. I prepared another batch, giving the stalks a quick rinse before cutting them using my new technique; tossing them with extra-virgin olive oil, garlic, red pepper flakes, and salt; spreading them on a rimmed baking sheet (which was big enough to arrange them in an even layer); and sliding the sheet into a 400-degree oven.

After 10 minutes, the rabe had caramelized nicely, and the leaves now also offered a delicate crunch—that part was good. But texturally, the stems had suffered, turning soft and stringy by the time they had browned.

Part of the problem, I realized, was that the water droplets left over from washing the rabe were taking a long time to burn off and therefore delaying browning. Going forward, I got serious about drying the greens by rolling them in clean dish towels to blot away as much moisture as possible. I also cranked the heat to 450, but even then the stems were limp by the time they were browned.

It was time to take it up a notch to the broiler. I adjusted the oven rack 4 inches from the heating element, popped in another oiled and salted batch, and kept a close watch. In less than 3 minutes, half the rabe's leaves and florets were lightly charred and crisp at the edges, and the stems were also browned yet still bright green and crisp—so far so good. I gave them a quick toss with tongs and slid the sheet back into the oven. Two minutes later, the results were perfect: lightly charred, crisp leaves and florets and perfectly crisp-tender stalks.

—STEVE DUNN, *Cook's Illustrated*

Broiled Broccoli Rabe

SERVES 4

Because the amount of heat generated by a broiler varies from oven to oven, we recommend keeping an eye on the broccoli rabe as it cooks. If the leaves are getting too dark or not browning in the time specified in the recipe, adjust the distance of the oven rack from the broiler element.

   3   tablespoons extra-virgin olive oil
   1   pound broccoli rabe
   1   garlic clove, minced
   ¾   teaspoon kosher salt
   ¼   teaspoon red pepper flakes
       Lemon wedges

1. Adjust oven rack 4 inches from broiler element and heat broiler. Brush rimmed baking sheet with 1 tablespoon oil.

2. Trim and discard bottom 1 inch of broccoli rabe stems. Wash broccoli rabe with cold water, then dry with clean dish towel. Cut tops (leaves and florets) from stems, then cut stems into 1-inch pieces (keep tops whole). Transfer broccoli rabe to prepared sheet.

3. Combine remaining 2 tablespoons oil, garlic, salt, and pepper flakes in small bowl. Pour oil mixture over broccoli rabe and toss to combine.

4. Broil until half of leaves are well browned, 2 to 2½ minutes. Using tongs, toss to expose unbrowned leaves. Return sheet to oven and continue to broil until most leaves are lightly charred and stems are crisp-tender, 2 to 2½ minutes longer. Transfer to serving platter and serve immediately, passing lemon wedges.

BRUSSELS SPROUTS WITH BACON

WHY THIS RECIPE WORKS: To serve up bitter Brussels sprouts, smoky bacon, and sweet caramelized onions in a single hands-off side dish with each component cooked to perfection, we worked in stages. In order for the bites of bacon to properly crisp and the onions to brown and soften, we gave them a head start. In under 10 minutes, the bacon's hot renderings mingled with the onions, speeding up their caramelization. We arranged halved sprouts cut side down on the hot sheet pan and let everything finish roasting together. Soon enough, these sprouts were browned and tender, infused with the bacon and onions' deep savory flavor.

My go-to method for roasting Brussels sprouts is to toss halved sprouts with olive oil, throw them on a baking sheet, and roast them cut side down at 475 degrees for about 15 minutes. The bottoms caramelize, the insides soften, and even sprout haters admit to enjoying them. But for the holidays, I pictured my roasted sprouts surrounded by crispy bacon and caramelized onions. I just needed to work out the details.

I tossed ¼-inch pieces of thick-cut bacon and a sliced onion with the halved sprouts, transferred the mixture to a baking sheet, and put the sheet in the oven. At the

ROASTED BRUSSELS SPROUTS WITH BACON AND ONION

15-minute mark, the sprouts were tender, but the bacon was still flabby and the onion still crunchy. I let them continue to roast until the bacon and onion were where I wanted them to be, but by that point, my sprouts were way overcooked. Clearly, the bacon and onion had to have a jump start before I added the sprouts.

For my next test, I arranged the bacon pieces on one half of the sheet and then scattered the oil-coated onion over the other half. I slid the sheet into the oven for about 8 minutes, until the bacon was starting to brown, and then added the sprouts to the sheet. I stirred everything together, being careful to nestle the sprouts down onto the sheet to ensure contact. After 15 more minutes in the oven, the bacon was crispy, the onion was tender, and the sprouts were perfectly cooked—pleasantly brown and coated in flavorful bacon fat. A perfect holiday side dish.

—DIANE UNGER, *Cook's Country*

Roasted Brussels Sprouts with Bacon and Onion

SERVES 4 TO 6

Choose Brussels sprouts that are similar in size to ensure even cooking. To keep the sprouts' leaves intact, be sure to trim just a small amount from of the stem before halving the sprouts.

- 1½ pounds Brussels sprouts, trimmed and halved
- 2 tablespoons olive oil
- 1 onion, halved and sliced ¼ inch thick
- 3 slices thick-cut bacon, cut into ¼-inch pieces
- ¼ teaspoon salt
- ¼ teaspoon pepper

1. Adjust oven rack to lowest position and heat oven to 475 degrees. Spray rimmed baking sheet with vegetable oil spray. Toss sprouts and 1 tablespoon oil together in large bowl and set aside. Toss onion and remaining 1 tablespoon oil together in small bowl. Arrange onion in even layer on half of prepared sheet.

Arrange bacon in even layer on other half of sheet. Cook until bacon begins to brown and onion begins to soften, 7 to 9 minutes.

2. Remove sheet from oven and transfer to wire rack. Add sprouts to sheet and stir to combine bacon, onion, and sprouts. Flip sprouts cut side down and nestle into sheet. Return sheet to oven and continue to cook until sprouts are deep golden brown and bacon is crispy, 15 to 17 minutes longer. Sprinkle with salt and pepper. Transfer to platter and serve.

BRAISED CARROTS AND PARSNIPS

WHY THIS RECIPE WORKS: In order to serve a rich side of tender braised root vegetables, we needed to create a braising liquid that infused the vegetables with flavor. We ensured evenly cooked vegetables by cutting sweet carrots and tangy, earthy parsnips into precise ¼-inch-thick slices. For our braising liquid, we cooked minced shallot in butter before pouring in chicken broth and apple cider; sprigs of thyme and bay leaves added fragrant herbal notes. Allowing the liquid to reduce slightly before adding the vegetables concentrated its flavor. We simmered the carrots and parsnips until they turned tender and then we transformed the cooking liquid into a silky sauce by stirring in butter and Dijon mustard. Sweet dried cranberries and fresh parsley offered a bright finish.

My go-to cooking method for root vegetables has always been to roast them in a hot oven until they are caramelized and tender. This year, though, I wanted to come up with something more elegant and interesting that would leave the oven free to cook the holiday roast. Braising—cooking food in a small amount of flavorful liquid that then serves as a sauce—seemed promising. But I wanted to avoid recipes that left the vegetables swimming in bland, soupy liquid or, alternatively, cooked down the sauce to the point that it was a glaze. I wanted my braised vegetables to be swathed in a generous amount of rich, flavorful sauce with appealing body.

BRAISED CARROTS AND PARSNIPS WITH DRIED CRANBERRIES

Carrots possess a sweetness that plays well with a range of flavors—plus, they offer an appealing bright color—so I decided I would pair them with another vegetable in a few different recipes. I started with the classic combination of carrots and parsnips. I began by sautéing a minced shallot in butter. I then added the carrots and parsnips, which I'd cut crosswise into ¼-inch-thick coins to encourage even cooking. I added enough chicken broth to cover the vegetables, brought the mixture to a simmer, covered the pot, and lowered the heat. After 15 minutes, the vegetables were tender, but the sauce was thin in both consistency and flavor.

The quantity of sauce was where I wanted it, so I didn't want to reduce the amount of liquid I started with. As it turned out, the best approach was actually to do the opposite. When I increased the amount of liquid I started with, I was able to reduce it for 5 minutes before adding the vegetables, which gave the sauce better body and a more concentrated flavor. To lend it a bit more silkiness, I also whisked in a couple of tablespoons of butter at the end.

But could I give the sauce even more character? I tried replacing half the broth with white wine, but it made the sauce too tart. I wanted something that would underscore the flavor of the root vegetables yet remain in the background. The answer turned out to be apple cider, which enhanced the earthy sweetness of the vegetables. And its natural sugars, once cooked down, gave the reduced sauce even more body. Bay leaves and thyme sprigs added savoriness, and a tablespoon of mustard gave it a punch. Dried cranberries lent texture, color, and bright, tart flavor while parsley provided a colorful finish.

From here, it was easy to come up with variations on the theme: carrots and celery root with apples and marjoram, carrots and turnips with golden raisins and chives, and carrots and sweet potatoes with candied ginger and cilantro. I'd welcome any one of these side dishes to my holiday table.

—ANDREW JANJIGIAN, *Cook's Illustrated*

Braised Carrots and Parsnips with Dried Cranberries

SERVES 4 TO 6

For a vegetarian version, you can substitute vegetable stock or water for the chicken broth.

- 3 tablespoons unsalted butter, cut into ½-inch pieces
- 1 shallot, minced
- 1 cup chicken broth
- 1 cup apple cider
- 6 sprigs fresh thyme
- 2 bay leaves
  Salt and pepper
- 1 pound carrots, peeled and sliced on bias ¼ inch thick
- 1 pound parsnips, peeled and sliced on bias ¼ inch thick
- ½ cup dried cranberries
- 1 tablespoon Dijon mustard
- 2 tablespoons minced fresh parsley

1. Melt 1 tablespoon butter in large Dutch oven over high heat. Add shallot and cook, stirring frequently, until softened and just beginning to brown, about 3 minutes. Add broth, cider, thyme sprigs, bay leaves, 1½ teaspoons salt, and ½ teaspoon pepper; bring to simmer and cook for 5 minutes. Add carrots and parsnips, stir to combine, and return to simmer. Reduce heat to medium-low, cover, and cook, stirring occasionally, until vegetables are tender, 10 to 14 minutes.

2. Remove pot from heat. Discard thyme sprigs and bay leaves and stir in cranberries. Push vegetable mixture to sides of pot. Add mustard and remaining 2 tablespoons butter to center and whisk into cooking liquid. Stir to coat vegetable mixture with sauce, transfer to serving dish, sprinkle with parsley, and serve.

VARIATIONS

Braised Carrots and Celery Root with Apple
Substitute 1½ pounds celery root, peeled, halved if medium or quartered if large, and sliced ¼ inch thick, for parsnips; 1 Fuji or Honeycrisp apple, cored and cut into ¼-inch dice, for dried cranberries; and 1 teaspoon minced fresh marjoram or thyme for parsley. In step 1, cook celery root in braising liquid by itself for 15 minutes before adding carrots and proceeding with recipe.

Braised Carrots and Turnips with Golden Raisins

Reduce chicken broth and apple cider to ¾ cup each. Substitute turnips, peeled, halved if medium (2- to 3-inch diameter) or quartered if large (3- to 4-inch diameter), and sliced ¼ inch thick, for parsnips; golden raisins for dried cranberries; and 10 chives, cut into 1-inch lengths, for parsley.

Braised Carrots and Sweet Potatoes with Candied Ginger

Substitute 1 pound sweet potatoes, peeled, halved lengthwise, and sliced on bias ¼ inch thick, for parsnips; ¼ cup coarsely chopped candied ginger for dried cranberries; and 3 tablespoons minced fresh cilantro for parsley.

FRENCH-STYLE MASHED POTATOES

WHY THIS RECIPE WORKS: Recipes for these ultrasilky, buttery mashed potatoes can be pretty impossible for the home cook, as most versions require specialty equipment and labor-intensive techniques. To make our *pommes purée* more accessible, we cooked peeled, diced potatoes directly in the milk and butter that we would be incorporating into the mash. This simple change eliminated the need to laboriously beat the butter into the potatoes and it preserved their starches, the key to producing an emulsified texture. Processing the potatoes with a food mill delivered a luxuriously smooth puree with minimal effort.

In the early 1980s, Parisian chef Joël Robuchon turned mashed potatoes into an utterly sublime experience by employing two hallmarks of French cooking: tireless attention to detail and a whole lot of butter.

His method: Boil 2 pounds of whole unpeeled potatoes and then peel them while hot before passing them through a food mill. Next, incorporate a full pound of cold butter, 1 tablespoon at a time, by beating vigorously with a wooden spoon—a 10-minute, arm-numbing process. Finally, thin the puree with warm milk and pass it repeatedly through a *tamis* (a flat, drum-shaped ultrafine sieve). Robuchon's painstaking efforts produced the ultimate example of *pommes purée*, ethereally smooth and laden with butter.

While I love Robuchon's recipe, the scandalous fat content and the drudgery of sieving make it unrealistic for a home cook. But if I could streamline the process and cut back somewhat on the fat, it would be a dish I'd love to make for special occasions.

In France, the puree is made with Ratte potatoes, which are medium-starch fingerlings. I used Yukon Golds, a close substitute. For my first go-round, I cut the amount of butter in half and poured in extra milk to compensate; I used a food mill, but I skipped the tamis.

Was the resulting puree as gloriously smooth as Robuchon's? Perhaps not, but tasters still called it "pillow-soft," so I happily gave up any thoughts of trying to jury-rig a tamis. That said, the potatoes did lack the richness of Robuchon's version. Adding butter back a little at a time, I found that 2½ sticks elevated these spuds to pommes purée status: a rich, silky step above regular mashed potatoes.

Now that I had experienced beating cold butter into potatoes, I was eager to find a way around it. How about melting the butter? Sadly, with so much of it in the mix, the butter and potatoes didn't fully integrate, so the puree was separated and greasy.

Setting that problem temporarily aside, I turned my attention to the literal pain of peeling hot potatoes. I compared a puree made with peeled and diced potatoes (rinsed to remove surface starch) to one made with whole, skin-on spuds. The latter required more than a cup of milk to achieve the proper silken consistency. However, the peeled, diced potatoes absorbed so much cooking water that they could accommodate only ½ cup of milk. The result? A weaker-tasting mash. This got me thinking: Since potatoes are so absorbent, why not peel them and cook them in liquid I'd actually want them to soak up (the milk and butter)? I gave it a try, reserving the buttery cooking milk and whisking it into the milled potatoes. The puree was velvety-smooth and tasted rich and buttery. What's more, it was not at all separated or greasy. This was a double victory: no more beating in cold butter or peeling hot potatoes.

Why did simmering the potatoes directly in milk and butter result in a more cohesive puree than adding melted butter and milk to boiled potatoes? It all comes down to the potato starch, which is critical for helping fat emulsify with potatoes. When peeled potatoes are boiled in water, much of their starch is released and eventually poured down the drain. With too little gluey starch in the mix, the melted butter struggles to form a smooth emulsion with the wet spuds, resulting in a slick, greasy puree. When the potatoes are cooked directly in the milk and butter, none of the released starch gets lost, and it is thus available to help the butter emulsify with the water in the potatoes. (In Robuchon's recipe, the whole, skin-on potatoes retain their starch during cooking; vigorous beating liberates the starch and helps stabilize the emulsion, while the generous amount of butter prevents the released starch from turning the puree gluey.)

In the end, my simplified recipe delivered a rich, silky-smooth mash while allowing me to wave au revoir to an exhausted arm.

—STEVE DUNN, *Cook's Illustrated*

French-Style Mashed Potatoes (Pommes Purée)

SERVES 8

When serving, keep the richness in mind. A small dollop on each plate should suffice.

- 2 **pounds Yukon Gold potatoes, peeled and cut into 1-inch pieces**
- 20 **tablespoons (2½ sticks) unsalted butter**
- 1⅓ **cups whole milk**
-   **Salt and white pepper**

NOTES FROM THE TEST KITCHEN

PUREEING POTATOES
We process the potatoes for Pommes Purée using a food mill, a tool that simultaneously grinds and strains foods. Our favorite model, **RSVP Classic Rotary Food Mill**, purees potatoes quickly and efficiently.

---

1. Place potatoes in fine-mesh strainer and rinse under cold running water until water runs clear. Set aside to drain.

2. Heat butter, milk, and 1 teaspoon salt in large saucepan over low heat until butter has melted. Add potatoes, increase heat to medium-low, and cook until liquid just starts to boil. Reduce heat to low, partially cover, and gently simmer until paring knife can be slipped into and out of centers of potatoes with no resistance, 30 to 40 minutes, stirring every 10 minutes.

3. Drain potatoes in fine-mesh strainer set over large bowl, reserving cooking liquid. Wipe out saucepan. Return cooking liquid to saucepan and place saucepan over low heat.

4. Set food mill fitted with finest disk over saucepan. Working in batches, transfer potatoes to hopper and process. Using whisk, recombine potatoes and cooking liquid until smooth, 10 to 15 seconds (potatoes should almost be pourable). Season with salt and pepper to taste, and serve immediately.

MODERN CAULIFLOWER GRATIN

✓ **WHY THIS RECIPE WORKS:** Our version of this classic vegetable gratin is rich but not overbearing, thanks to cauliflower's ability to become an ultracreamy puree. We separated cauliflower heads into cores, stems, and florets, cutting the latter into slabs for even cooking. We simmered the cores, stems, and some florets in water and butter in the bottom of a Dutch oven while the remaining florets sat aloft in a steamer basket to cook in the steam. The stem mixture blended into a velvety puree and a cornstarch slurry offered some subtle thickening. We poured the creamy mixture over the steamed florets and sprinkled the casserole with toasty panko and Parmesan before finally baking. This new take on gratin was plenty indulgent but still packed with clean cauliflower flavor.

Cauliflower gratin should be a lighter alternative to the rich, starchy classic made with potatoes. Yet most of the recipes I've tried model themselves on that heavy, potato-based template: Cauliflower florets (which have been either boiled or steamed first) are arranged in a baking dish and inevitably buried under a stodgy, flour-thickened, cheesy cream sauce. I had an entirely different dish in mind: a cauliflower gratin with tender florets covered in a velvety sauce that boasted clean cauliflower flavor and was satisfying without the heft.

I started by figuring out the best way to prepare the florets. Cauliflower florets with some of their stem left on look pretty but cook unevenly because the stem is more dense than the floret. Fortunately, I had an easy way to trim the stems and create same-size florets. I first cored the head of cauliflower and then cut it into ½-inch-thick slabs. This made it easy to trim the stems, leaving flat florets about 1½ inches tall. These florets would cook evenly and, because of their flat shape, would also layer neatly in the gratin dish. I found that it took a full two heads' worth of cauliflower to fill a standard 13 by 9-inch baking dish.

Precooking the florets is typical of most recipes and for good reason; cooking them through from start to finish in the sauce would take far too long. In fact, the actual goal of baking the casserole is not to cook the cauliflower but to marry the flavors of sauce and cauliflower. But what was the best way to precook them? Boiling the delicate florets was too aggressive; the jostling made them fall apart. I also gave roasting a try. While this approach imparted a nice toasted, nutty flavor, once I combined the florets with the sauce (a placeholder version for now) and baked the dish for about 15 minutes, I found that the nuttiness detracted from the clean flavor profile I wanted—not to mention that the browned pieces muddied the gratin's appearance. And so I settled on the gentle technique of steaming. I simply loaded my cauliflower florets into a steamer basket and cooked them in a pot over simmering water until a paring knife slipped in and out of them with no resistance.

It was time to move on to the bigger challenge: the sauce. I continued to search for recipes that didn't call for heavy or rich thickeners, such as a béchamel or lots of eggs, and at last found a few unique approaches to try. One featured a sauce made simply of cream thinned with chicken broth in a 2:1 ratio. It sounded lighter than the flour- or egg-thickened sauces, but sadly it was too thin (and too chicken-y). Another skipped liquids altogether and opted to combine the florets with just cheese and spices, plus a bread-crumb topping. The flavor was clean like I wanted, but the dish didn't come together into a cohesive gratin.

NOTES FROM THE TEST KITCHEN

MAKING THE MOST OF CAULIFLOWER
We use two entire heads of cauliflower in our gratin. The florets make up the bulk of the dish while the cores and stems (and a small portion of florets) create the sauce. Here's the most efficient way to prep the vegetable.

1. Pull off tough outer leaves of each head and trim stem.

2. Cut out each core, halve it lengthwise, and slice it thin crosswise. Reserve for sauce.

3. Slice each head into ½-inch-thick slabs.

4. Cut stems from slabs to create flat, 1½-inch-tall florets. Slice stems thin and reserve with sliced cores for sauce.

MODERN CAULIFLOWER GRATIN

Out of ideas, I began browsing cauliflower recipes beyond gratins. A dish from chef Dan Barber of Blue Hill Farm in New York caught my eye. It featured pan-roasted cauliflower nestled in a sauce made of nothing more than cauliflower cooked in milk and water and then pureed with some of the cooking liquid. This recipe takes advantage of the fact that, unlike most vegetables, cauliflower is relatively low in fiber, particularly the insoluble fiber that is resistant to breaking down. This gives cauliflower the unique ability to blend into an ultracreamy puree with no additional liquid

What if cauliflower became my sauce, too? It would be creamy but not too rich, with the benefit of adding another layer of the starring vegetable's flavor. Furthermore, it occurred to me that I wouldn't need to buy another head; I could likely use the stems and cores I had been throwing out. Even if I augmented the scraps with a couple of cups of florets, I would still have plenty of florets for the casserole.

I simmered the stem-core-floret mixture in a few cups of water until the cauliflower was soft, and then I poured the pot's contents into a blender and pureed them until silky-smooth. I poured this sauce over the steamed florets layered in the dish and baked the gratin just until the sauce bubbled around the edges.

I was off to a good start, but the sauce was a bit thin and (not surprisingly, given that the cooking liquid was water) tasted too lean. Adding a little cornstarch improved the consistency. As for amping up the richness without muting flavor or making the sauce too heavy, I found that 6 tablespoons of butter added to the simmering cauliflower and water—this was the simplest approach, and it all would get blended together anyway—improved matters greatly, and the butter's sweet flavor complemented the cauliflower perfectly.

But there was still room for a little more depth and creaminess. I feared that adding cheese might move the sauce into the heavy, gloppy category, but I was happy to discover that ½ cup of grated Parmesan, which I added to the blender, lent a complementary salty richness without weighing the dish down. For more complexity, I added dry mustard, cayenne, and nutmeg. Tossing the florets with the puree so they were fully and evenly coated before they went into the baking dish ensured that there was sauce in every bite.

At this point, all my gratin needed was a classic bread-crumb-and-cheese topping for some added texture, flavor, and color, so I toasted panko bread crumbs in butter until they were golden and then tossed them with additional Parmesan. A sprinkling of minced chives over the finished gratin enlivened its appearance.

Before I was done, I made one more improvement for efficiency's sake. Did I really need two pots, one to steam the florets and one to simmer the sauce? For my next test, I put the stem-core-floret mixture and water in a Dutch oven and arranged my steamer basket, filled with the bulk of the florets, right on top of the mixture before adding the lid. When the florets in the basket were cooked through, I removed the basket and replaced the lid so the sauce mixture could continue to simmer. My double-decker setup was a success.

With that, I had an easy cauliflower gratin that was good enough to require a second helping and light enough to guarantee that there'd be room for it.

—ANNIE PETITO, *Cook's Illustrated*

Modern Cauliflower Gratin
SERVES 8 TO 10

When buying cauliflower, look for heads without many leaves. Alternatively, if your cauliflower does have a lot of leaves, buy slightly larger heads—about 2¼ pounds each. This recipe can be halved to serve four to six; cook the cauliflower in a large saucepan and bake the gratin in an 8-inch square baking dish.

2	heads cauliflower (2 pounds each)
8	tablespoons unsalted butter
½	cup panko bread crumbs
2	ounces Parmesan cheese, grated (1 cup)
	Salt and pepper
½	teaspoon dry mustard
⅛	teaspoon ground nutmeg
	Pinch cayenne pepper
1	teaspoon cornstarch dissolved in 1 teaspoon water
1	tablespoon minced fresh chives

1. Adjust oven rack to middle position and heat oven to 400 degrees.

2. Pull off outer leaves of 1 head of cauliflower and trim stem. Using paring knife, cut around core to remove; halve core lengthwise and slice thin crosswise. Slice head into ½-inch-thick slabs. Cut stems from slices to create florets that are about 1½ inches tall; slice stems thin and reserve along with sliced core. Transfer florets to bowl, including any small pieces that may have been created during trimming, and set aside. Repeat with remaining head of cauliflower. (After trimming you should have about 3 cups of sliced stems and cores and 12 cups of florets.)

3. Combine sliced stems and cores, 2 cups florets, 3 cups water, and 6 tablespoons butter in Dutch oven and bring to boil over high heat. Place remaining florets in steamer basket (do not rinse bowl). Once mixture is boiling, place steamer basket in pot, cover, and reduce heat to medium. Steam florets in basket until translucent and stem ends can be easily pierced with paring knife, 10 to 12 minutes. Remove steamer basket and drain florets. Re-cover pot, reduce heat to low, and continue to cook stem mixture until very soft, about 10 minutes longer. Transfer drained florets to now-empty bowl.

4. While stem mixture is cooking, melt remaining 2 tablespoons butter in 10-inch skillet over medium heat. Add panko and cook, stirring frequently, until golden brown, 3 to 5 minutes. Transfer to second bowl and let cool. Once cool, add ½ cup Parmesan and toss to combine.

5. Transfer stem mixture and cooking liquid to blender and add 2 teaspoons salt, ½ teaspoon pepper, mustard, nutmeg, cayenne, and remaining ½ cup Parmesan. Process until smooth and velvety, about 1 minute (puree should be pourable; adjust consistency with additional water as needed). With blender running, add cornstarch slurry. Season with salt and pepper to taste. Pour puree over cauliflower florets and toss gently to evenly coat. Transfer mixture to 13 by 9-inch baking dish (it will be quite loose) and smooth top with spatula.

6. Scatter bread-crumb mixture evenly over top. Transfer dish to oven and bake until sauce bubbles around edges, 13 to 15 minutes. Let stand for 20 to 25 minutes. Sprinkle with chives and serve.

TO MAKE AHEAD: Follow recipe through step 5, refrigerating gratin and bread-crumb mixture separately for up to 24 hours. When ready to eat, assemble and bake gratin as directed in step 6, increasing baking time by 13 to 15 minutes.

WALKAWAY RATATOUILLE

☑ **WHY THIS RECIPE WORKS:** Ratatouille delivers all the rich flavors of late summer produce in a cozy dish that works as well as a side as it does a vegetable main. To streamline this usually labor-intensive dish, we skipped the time-consuming step of salting and draining the vegetables and instead turned to the oven's even heat to evaporate their excess moisture. Letting the eggplant and tomatoes soften completely allowed us to mash them into a silky sauce. We then added the delicate zucchini and bell peppers and returned the pot to the oven so they could begin to tenderize. To finish, we pulled the pot from the oven, covered it, and let the residual heat turn the vegetables perfectly soft.

Ratatouille is a rustic Provençal specialty that transforms late-summer produce—tomatoes, eggplant, zucchini, and bell peppers—by simmering the vegetables, scented with garlic, onion, and herbs, until they have softened into a rich stew. It's a satisfying dish that can be served as an accompaniment or even turned into a light main course by topping it with an egg, sandwiching it between slices of bread, or spooning it over pasta or rice.

The problem with ratatouille boils down to one thing: water. More specifically, each of the primary ingredients contains more than 90 percent water. If all that liquid isn't dealt with somehow, you end up with a wet, pulpy mess of ingredients that are indistinguishable in taste, color, and texture.

WALKAWAY RATATOUILLE

To remedy this, many cooks complicate what is already a prep-heavy dish (cutting multiple pounds of vegetables into ¼- or ½-inch pieces is the norm). Techniques like salting, microwaving, and pressing are often used to extract excess moisture. The individual vegetables are then typically sautéed in batches to create some flavorful browning before being simmered to cook off more water.

Recipes that skip these steps and call for simply throwing everything into a pot on the stove fared exactly as I anticipated: They were soggy, mushy, and bland. Surely I could come up with a more hands-off approach that would hold ratatouille to its rustic roots but still deliver complex flavor and tender-yet-firm texture.

I definitely wanted to skip any type of pretreatment, and that meant finding a method that could efficiently draw out moisture during cooking. On the stovetop, the heat must be kept low in order to avoid burning the food on the bottom of the pot, but this also means that liquid does not readily evaporate. How about using the oven, where the ambient dry heat would evaporate moisture with less risk of burning?

Roasting the vegetables in batches on baking sheets would be almost as bothersome as sautéing each vegetable individually, so I limited myself to using only a Dutch oven and started with the least amount of chopping that I thought I could get away with. I cut onions, plum tomatoes (meatier than round types, with less watery gel), bell peppers, and zucchini into quarters and an eggplant into eighths, figuring that large pieces would retain their shape and texture better than small ones. I tossed the vegetables with olive oil, salt, and pepper (I'd fiddle with other seasonings later) and slid the Dutch oven, uncovered, into a 400-degree oven. Sure enough, after about 2 hours, the moisture had mostly evaporated and the top layer of vegetables was deeply caramelized. But I wasn't done yet.

It had taken so long for any significant amount of moisture to evaporate from the vegetables that some of them (like the zucchini) were blown out and overcooked. What's more, any intact pieces were unwieldy to eat. I reduced the vegetable size to more manageable 1-inch chunks, which would cook more quickly but still wouldn't require too much time at the cutting board. I also decided to jump-start the cooking of the onions on the stovetop, which would cut down the oven time and give me the opportunity to sauté some smashed garlic cloves before I stirred in the remaining vegetables. These procedural tweaks cut the oven time in half, but even after I stirred partway through, the more delicate vegetables were overdone by the time any browning happened.

The eggplant had even begun to disintegrate, leaving its soft pulp and slivers of peel behind. That was unacceptable. Or was it? If eggplant cooks long enough, its flesh becomes downright silky. Perhaps, I thought, I should embrace eggplant's texture and allow it to break down completely. It just might make for a creamy sauce to unify the stew.

I decided to peel the eggplant to create a smooth sauce with no distractions, and since tomatoes supply so much juice, I added them (also peeled) to the pot with the sautéed onions, garlic, herbs, and seasonings, knowing that their moisture would evaporate for even more concentrated flavor. I would hold the quicker-cooking zucchini and bell peppers back until near the end of the cooking time.

I put my plan into action. After 40 minutes in the oven, the eggplant, onions, and tomatoes were so meltingly soft that they yielded to gentle smashing with a potato masher, turning them into the velvety sauce that I had envisioned. What's more, most of the onions and eggplant had become so deeply browned and full of concentrated flavor that I wouldn't need to worry about getting color on the zucchini and bell peppers. Giving these later additions just a short time in the pot would maintain some pleasing bite to contrast with the smooth sauce.

I stirred in the zucchini and bell peppers and returned the pot to the oven for 20 minutes. When I checked, a few pieces of zucchini were still on the cusp of being done, but rather than return the pot to the oven, I simply covered it and let it rest for 10 minutes. Now a paring knife just slipped in and out of the pieces.

I noticed that the pot had a dark ring of fond around the inside edge. When left to sit with the lid on, the steam moistened the fond, so I could easily scrape the browned bits back into the ratatouille, making for a simple but robust flavor boost. For spice and heady fragrance, I also added red pepper flakes, a bay leaf, and herbes de Provence (a French blend usually consisting of dried basil, fennel, lavender, marjoram, rosemary, savory, and thyme). In fact, the dish now tasted so rich that I felt that some freshening up was in order.

The intensely caramelized ratatouille needed a touch of acid. Although entirely untraditional, a splash of sherry vinegar helped wake up the flavors of the sweet vegetables. Finally, just before serving, I stirred in chopped fresh basil and parsley and gave the stew a glossy drizzle of extra-virgin olive oil. And there it was, a flavorful ratatouille that was truly easy to make.

—ANNIE PETITO, *Cook's Illustrated*

NOTES FROM THE TEST KITCHEN

STREAMLINING RATATOUILLE

Classic ratatouille recipes call for cutting vegetables into small pieces, pretreating them to remove moisture, and then cooking them in batches on the stovetop. Our streamlined oven method eliminates the need for batch cooking and pretreatments; plus, it tastes better.

1. To cut down on oven cooking time, sauté chopped onions and smashed garlic cloves on stovetop.

2. After adding eggplant and tomatoes to base and cooking in oven, mash softened vegetables into thick sauce.

3. Jump-start softening of zucchini and bell peppers in oven; finish, covered, off heat, allowing sauce's residual heat to further soften vegetables.

Walkaway Ratatouille

SERVES 6 TO 8

This dish is best prepared using ripe, in-season tomatoes. If good tomatoes are not available, substitute one 28-ounce can of whole peeled tomatoes that have been drained and chopped coarse. Ratatouille can be served as an accompaniment to meat or fish. It can also be served on its own with crusty bread, topped with an egg, or over pasta or rice. This dish can be served warm, at room temperature, or chilled.

⅓ cup plus 1 tablespoon extra-virgin olive oil
2 large onions, cut into 1-inch pieces
8 large garlic cloves, peeled and smashed
   Salt and pepper
1½ teaspoons herbes de Provence
¼ teaspoon red pepper flakes
1 bay leaf
1½ pounds eggplant, peeled and cut into 1-inch pieces
2 pounds plum tomatoes, peeled, cored, and chopped coarse
2 small zucchini, halved lengthwise and cut into 1-inch pieces
1 red bell pepper, stemmed, seeded, and cut into 1-inch pieces
1 yellow bell pepper, stemmed, seeded, and cut into 1-inch pieces
2 tablespoons chopped fresh basil
1 tablespoon minced fresh parsley
1 tablespoon sherry vinegar

1. Adjust oven rack to middle position and heat oven to 400 degrees. Heat ⅓ cup oil in Dutch oven over medium-high heat until shimmering. Add onions, garlic, 1 teaspoon salt, and ¼ teaspoon pepper and cook, stirring occasionally, until onions are translucent and starting to soften, about 10 minutes. Add herbes de Provence, pepper flakes, and bay leaf and cook, stirring frequently, for 1 minute. Stir in eggplant and tomatoes. Sprinkle with ½ teaspoon salt and ¼ teaspoon pepper and stir to combine. Transfer pot to oven and cook, uncovered, until vegetables are very tender and spotty brown, 40 to 45 minutes.

2. Remove pot from oven and, using potato masher or heavy wooden spoon, smash and stir eggplant mixture until broken down to sauce-like consistency. Stir in zucchini, bell peppers, ¼ teaspoon salt, and ¼ teaspoon pepper and return to oven. Cook, uncovered, until zucchini and bell peppers are just tender, 20 to 25 minutes.

3. Remove pot from oven, cover, and let stand until zucchini is translucent and easily pierced with tip of paring knife, 10 to 15 minutes. Using wooden spoon, scrape any browned bits from sides of pot and stir back into ratatouille. Discard bay leaf. Stir in 1 tablespoon basil, parsley, and vinegar. Season with salt and pepper to taste. Transfer to large platter, drizzle with remaining 1 tablespoon oil, sprinkle with remaining 1 tablespoon basil, and serve.

FREEKEH SALAD

✓ **WHY THIS RECIPE WORKS:** *Freekeh* is a commonly used grain across the eastern Mediterranean and North Africa. We thought its grassy, slightly smoky flavor would work perfectly with sweet roasted winter squash as a hearty lunch or a light dinner. To replace hard-to-find or seasonally restrictive Mediterranean winter squashes, we chose widely available butternut squash. Roasting the squash resulted in lightly charred, beautifully caramelized edges; to give the squash more dimension, we paired it with fenugreek, a slightly sweet and nutty seed with a unique maple-like flavor. To bring all the elements together, we stirred in a rich yet bright tahini-lemon dressing. Chopped walnuts offered complementary crunch.

When I found out I'd be developing salads for *The Complete Mediterranean Cookbook*, I pictured myself pairing various greens and fresh vegetables with zippy dressings and crumbly bites of feta—doable, but hardly exciting. After a bit of research, though, I quickly discovered I'd been underestimating the range of salads hailing from this vast, sunny region of the world. For one thing, it became immensely clear that your everyday Greek salad was just the tiniest tip of the iceberg when it came to the Mediterranean's offerings in that department. From simply dressed servings of leafy greens to punched-up bowls of hearty grains, the options were endless (and delicious). While perusing the grain-centered recipes, one unfamiliar ingredient caught my eye: *freekeh*. Even with my years of experimenting in the test kitchen, this was a grain I had never encountered.

After investigating further, I learned that freekeh, or *farik*, is a grain widely used across the eastern Mediterranean and North Africa. It boasts a nutty yet grassy flavor and is jam-packed with nutrients. Freekeh is made from durum wheat that is harvested while immature and soft (hence its green, vegetal taste); the wheat's chaff or husk is burned off by fire-roasting, creating its toasty flavor. The outer bran is then removed by rubbing, or threshing, which is where the name comes from—freekeh means "to rub" in Arabic—and it is then either left whole or cracked into smaller pieces.

I began brainstorming ways to incorporate freekeh into an authentic Mediterranean salad. Off the bat, I knew I wanted the salad to stay faithful to the flavors of the Mediterranean while keeping the ingredients accessible and easy to source.

The first obstacle was cooking method. Different grains benefit from different cooking techniques: While bulgur can turn tender relatively quickly, readily absorbing its cooking liquid, freekeh bears a greater similarity to wheat berries and farro, tougher grains which do best when prepared like pasta—boiled in water and drained. I followed suit, boiling batches of both whole and cracked freekeh to see which I preferred. Though the cracked grain was plenty flavorful and tender, I fell hard for the chewy yet firm bite of the whole freekeh. With my cooking technique in the bag, I turned my focus to the mix-ins.

Pumpkin and various winter squashes are eaten throughout the Mediterranean, but many of the varieties are hard to source here in the States, so I settled on readily available butternut squash. Naturally sweet

FREEKEH SALAD WITH BUTTERNUT SQUASH, WALNUTS, AND RAISINS

and easy to pair with a punchy vinaigrette, this familiar squash was a shoo-in. I wanted tender bites of squash that complemented the freekeh's smokiness, so some flavor-boosting browning was in order. Peeled, cut into small pieces, tossed with olive oil, and roasted, the squash softened and took on plenty of color in just 30 minutes, but while it tasted great, I still wanted to up its Mediterranean profile. Scanning my spice rack, I decided to bring fenugreek, a common ingredient in Egyptian cuisine, on board. Not only does this seed boast a sweet-nutty flavor that mirrors the contrasts in freekeh, but its subtle maple flavor would be a natural complement to the squash. For my next batch, I stirred some in with the squash and olive oil and slid the pan into the oven. This small change made all the difference, giving the squash the nuance and complexity it needed.

With perfectly cooked freekeh and caramelized, well-seasoned cubes of butternut squash at the ready, this salad was on its way to becoming a satisfying meal, but I needed a vinaigrette to tie it together. My recipe was taking on a distinctly Middle Eastern flavor profile, so I stayed on theme, looking to bring in another regional staple: tahini. This thick paste of toasted sesame seeds has a nutty, buttery flavor that would be the perfect base for a simple but impactful vinaigrette. I whisked a couple of spoonfuls with lemon juice and garlic, thinning out the thick consistency with some water before drizzling in olive oil. This dressing brought out the best in my new favorite grain, highlighting its toasty taste and adding some butteriness to the otherwise lean salad.

Finally, I looked for a quick way to bring some freshness and extra bite to my full-flavored salad. Chopped cilantro introduced some welcome brightness. Sweet golden raisins, plumped in warm water, added juicy bursts that contrasted nicely with the chewy freekeh, and toasted walnuts gave the salad some crunch. Tender, toasty, and hearty, this salad was a real winner.

—ANNE WOLF, *America's Test Kitchen Books*

Freekeh Salad with Butternut Squash, Walnuts, and Raisins

SERVES 4 TO 6

We prefer the texture of whole, uncracked freekeh; cracked freekeh can be substituted, but you will need to decrease the freekeh cooking time in step 2.

- 1½ **pounds butternut squash, peeled, seeded, and cut into ½-inch pieces (4 cups)**
- ¼ **cup plus 1 tablespoon extra-virgin olive oil**
- ½ **teaspoon ground fenugreek**
   Salt and pepper
- 1½ **cups whole freekeh**
- 2½ **tablespoons lemon juice**
- 2 **tablespoons tahini**
- 1 **garlic clove, minced**
- ⅓ **cup golden raisins**
- 1 **cup coarsely chopped cilantro**
- ⅓ **cup walnuts, toasted and chopped**

1. Adjust oven rack to lowest position and heat oven to 450 degrees. Toss squash with 1 tablespoon oil and fenugreek and season with salt and pepper. Arrange squash in single layer in rimmed baking sheet and roast until well browned and tender, 30 to 35 minutes, stirring halfway through roasting; let cool to room temperature.

2. Meanwhile, bring 4 quarts water to boil in Dutch oven. Add freekeh and 1 tablespoon salt, return to boil, and cook until grains are tender, 30 to 45 minutes. Drain freekeh, transfer to large bowl, and let cool completely, about 15 minutes.

3. Whisk lemon juice, tahini, 1 tablespoon water, garlic, ½ teaspoon salt, and ⅛ teaspoon pepper in small bowl. Whisking constantly, slowly drizzle in remaining oil until emulsified.

4. Combine raisins and ¼ cup hot tap water in small bowl and let sit until softened, about 5 minutes; drain raisins. Add squash mixture, raisins, lemon-tahini dressing, cilantro, and walnuts to bowl with freekeh and gently toss to combine. Season with salt and pepper to taste. Serve.

NEW ENGLAND BAKED BEANS

✓ **WHY THIS RECIPE WORKS:** For a pot of classic New England baked beans in less time, we made a few smart tweaks while keeping the traditional flavor intact. Brining the beans jump-started their hydration and softened their skins so they cooked up tender in the oven. Molasses, brown sugar, dry mustard, onion, and salt pork were among the baked bean flavorings we couldn't pass up, but the rich flavor really hit its mark when we added some soy sauce. After bringing everything to a boil on the stovetop, we transferred the beans to the oven, where the cooking liquid slowly thickened into a syrupy sauce. After 2 hours, we uncovered the Dutch oven to allow the beans to turn fully tender while the sauce finished thickening in the last hour of cooking.

In early New England, Puritans baked bread in communal ovens on Saturdays. When the last loaf was pulled from the hearth, the town baker collected bean pots and set them to cook in the residual heat. After bubbling away all afternoon, the beans were served for supper; leftovers were on the table again for breakfast on Sunday. It all worked out to be quite convenient, as cooking was forbidden during the Sabbath (sundown on Saturday through sundown on Sunday).

Today, baked beans are still all about patience: Recipes call for 6, 8, or even 10 hours of cooking to transform modest ingredients—dried beans, smoky pork, bittersweet molasses, mustard, and sometimes onion and brown sugar—into a pot of creamy, tender beans coated in a lightly thickened, sweet, and savory sauce. Delicious, indeed. But must they take so long? I wanted to create the best possible version of this American classic but hopefully without hours and hours of cooking.

White navy beans, which boast a mild flavor and a dense, creamy texture, are typically used for New England baked beans. Step one was to soak them overnight in salty water—an adjustment we make to the usual plain-water soak because we've learned that sodium weakens the pectin in the beans' skins, reducing the number of ruptured beans. That's a good thing,

since when beans burst, they spill their starchy innards, creating a sticky, unappealing texture. Soaked beans also cook faster than unsoaked and seem to absorb water more evenly, so the result is creamier.

To my pot of drained, brined beans, I added some standard flavorings: a cup each of molasses and dark brown sugar, plus dry mustard, black pepper, and a bay leaf. For the pork element, some cooks use bacon, but traditionalists swear by salt pork, and I agreed: It would add meaty depth without the distracting smokiness of bacon. Sticking to the ultrasimple old-fashioned approach, I skipped browning and tossed a few raw chunks of salt pork straight into the pot, where their fat would melt into the beans.

Now, about the long cooking time. The test kitchen has plenty of recipes in which dried beans are fully cooked after simmering in water for only an hour. Baked beans take longer because adding acid to the mix via brown sugar and molasses firms the cell structure of legumes and slows down their cooking—but by how much? To find out, I added enough water to cover the beans by a couple of inches. Then, to jump-start the cooking process, I brought the pot to a boil on the stovetop before placing a lid on it and transferring it to a 300-degree oven. It took 3 hours for the beans to turn perfectly creamy. Longer cooking times, it seemed, were just a holdover from the low-temperature hearth cooking of yesteryear.

Holding back the acidic brown sugar and molasses until the beans had softened could save time, but would there be a flavor sacrifice? I added the molasses and brown sugar to separate batches of beans after 15, 30, and 45 minutes of cooking, tracking how much longer the beans took to soften once the acidic ingredients were added. The results were eye-opening: Adding the molasses and brown sugar at 45 minutes resulted in tender beans in just over an hour, while the 15- and 30-minute batches took twice as long.

The problem was that the longer I waited to add the flavorings, the less they penetrated, leaving the beans pale and bland. Even the batches where the ingredients were added just 15 minutes into simmering didn't

NEW ENGLAND BAKED BEANS

compare to the deeply bronzed beans flavored from the get-go. I would have to live with a 3-hour cooking time—still much shorter than what most recipes call for.

My next tests involved thickening the sauce, which was too soupy. I eventually determined that covering the beans with just ½ inch of water at the start would keep them submerged during cooking and still create a more viscous sauce. But I wanted it even more reduced. Removing the lid for the last hour of cooking helped the sauce cook down just below the beans, creating an attractive browned crust on top and a rich, velvety liquid underneath.

I also needed to adjust the beans' overt sweetness. I cut the molasses in half and reduced the brown sugar to just 2 tablespoons. I also threw a halved yellow onion into the pot. Tasters loved the mild, partly sweet, partly savory note it lent the beans as it softened in the oven (no need to sauté it beforehand).

The beans were now really good, but I felt they needed just a bit more character, so I stirred in a tablespoon of umami-rich soy sauce. My tasters (even the traditionalists) approved of the way it elevated the flavor.

Finally, to capture every last bit of goodness, I made sure to scrape the fond from the pot's inside edge and stirred it into the beans. Tender, creamy, hearty, and glazed in a lightly sweet sauce, these baked beans had it all—in a modest amount of time.

—ANNIE PETITO, *Cook's Illustrated*

New England Baked Beans

SERVES 4 TO 6

You'll get fewer blowouts if you soak the beans overnight, but if you're pressed for time, you can quick-salt-soak your beans. In step 1, combine the salt, water, and beans in a large Dutch oven and bring them to a boil over high heat. Remove the pot from the heat, cover it, and let it stand for 1 hour. Drain and rinse the beans and proceed with the recipe.

Salt
1 pound (2½ cups) dried navy beans, picked over and rinsed
6 ounces salt pork, rinsed, cut into 3 pieces
1 onion, halved
½ cup molasses
2 tablespoons packed dark brown sugar
1 tablespoon soy sauce
2 teaspoons dry mustard
½ teaspoon pepper
1 bay leaf

1. Dissolve 1½ tablespoons salt in 2 quarts cold water in large container. Add beans and let soak at room temperature for at least 8 hours or up to 24 hours. Drain and rinse well.

2. Adjust oven rack to lower-middle position and heat oven to 300 degrees. Combine beans, ¼ teaspoon salt, 4 cups water, salt pork, onion, molasses, sugar, soy sauce, dry mustard, pepper, and bay leaf in large Dutch oven. (Liquid should cover beans by about ½ inch. Add more water if necessary.) Bring to boil over high heat. Cover pot, transfer to oven, and cook until beans are softened and bean skins curl up and split when you blow on them, about 2 hours. (After 1 hour, stir beans and check amount of liquid. Liquid should just cover beans. Add water if necessary.)

3. Remove lid and continue to cook until beans are fully tender, browned, and slightly crusty on top, about 1 hour longer. (Liquid will reduce slightly below top layer of beans.)

4. Remove pot from oven, cover, and let stand for 5 minutes. Using wooden spoon or rubber spatula, scrape any browned bits from sides of pot and stir into beans. Discard onion and bay leaf. (Salt pork can be eaten, if desired.) Let beans stand, uncovered, until liquid has thickened slightly and clings to beans, 10 to 15 minutes, stirring once halfway through. Season with salt and pepper to taste, and serve. (Beans can be refrigerated for up to 4 days.)

FETTUCCINE WITH BUTTER AND CHEESE

✓ **WHY THIS RECIPE WORKS:** We wanted to bring fettuccine Alfredo back to its roots, coating fettuccine in a rich, indulgent sauce using only Parmigiano-Reggiano cheese, butter, and a little salt. The secret? Using some of the pasta's cooking water. After cooking the fettuccine in exactly 3 quarts of water, we reserved 1 cup of the starchy liquid and added it back to the drained pasta along with the remaining ingredients. After a rest and some vigorous stirring, the butter, cheese, and water formed a creamy, emulsified sauce. Serving the pasta in warm bowls kept the pasta hot and the sauce velvety right to the last bite.

Fettuccine with butter and cheese, aka fettuccine Alfredo, consists of Parmigiano-Reggiano cheese, butter, fettuccine, and a pinch of salt. No cream. No eggs. No black pepper. The cheese and butter should combine to create a creamy sauce that coats each strand of pasta. It is one of the world's greatest pasta dishes, but this dish has suffered over the years, mucked up with cream, thickeners, and worse.

Its glory days began in 1914, when Roman restaurateur Alfredo di Lelio needed a high-calorie meal to serve his wife, who was pregnant and having trouble keeping her food down. He created the first version of this cheesy dish, hoping that it would hold her over for a while. Bonus: It was also delicious enough to add to his restaurant's menu.

Cue American silent film stars Mary Pickford and Douglas Fairbanks, who visited Rome and made several meals of di Lelio's dish. They brought the recipe home, and in 1928, it was printed in *The Rector Cook Book*. But because American butter and Parmesan-style cheese weren't as rich and creamy as they are in Italy, the dish began its detour into something di Lelio would not recognize. I was determined to return this dish to its simple origins, using only four ingredients.

OK, five ingredients. I'd also add some of the water I'd cooked the pasta in; using this starchy liquid helps create a silky sauce. The rub proved to be determining exactly how much water to boil the pasta in so that the resulting liquid would have just enough starch. Two quarts was too little, 4 quarts too much. Three quarts of water for a pound of pasta gave me the right consistency.

It's essential to use real Italian Parmigiano-Reggiano cheese; facsimiles won't produce the same creaminess. I tested various amounts and grating styles before settling on 4 ounces of cheese grated on a rasp-style grater for ultrasmall (almost feathery) shreds. These melted more smoothly into the sauce than larger shreds, which clumped.

After cooking dozens of batches using a range of techniques, each fussier than the last, I was thrilled to find that the simplest process also produced the best results: After reserving 1 cup of the cooking water, I drained the pasta; returned it to the pot; added 5 tablespoons of butter, a little salt, the grated cheese, and the reserved cooking water; and vigorously tossed the ingredients with tongs until the sauce covered the pasta. Then—and this step is important—I covered the pot and let the pasta sit for 1 minute to allow any errant drips of water to absorb. I removed the lid and tossed the pasta again to make sure that all the cheese was incorporated.

I transferred the pasta to heated serving bowls and passed them out to the team. The heat of each bowl helped the sauce stay fluid. Would Alfredo di Lelio recognize my dish? I'm certain he would. And he'd love it.

—ASHLEY MOORE, *Cook's Country*

NOTES FROM THE TEST KITCHEN

STIRRING FOR SMOOTH SAUCE

When grated Parmigiano-Reggiano cheese, butter pieces, and pasta cooking water are stirred into still-hot fettuccine, sauce will appear very watery. Cover for 1 minute and then stir vigorously to form creamy emulsion.

Fettuccine with Butter and Cheese

SERVES 4 TO 6

Be sure to use imported Parmigiano-Reggiano cheese here and not the bland domestic cheese labeled "Parmesan." For the best results, grate the cheese on a rasp-style grater. Do not adjust the amount of water for cooking the pasta. Stir the pasta frequently while cooking so that it doesn't stick together. It's important to move quickly after draining the pasta, as the residual heat from the reserved cooking water and pasta will help the cheese and butter melt. For best results, heat ovensafe dinner bowls in a 200-degree oven for 10 minutes prior to serving and serve the pasta hot. If you are using fresh pasta, increase the amount to 1¼ pounds.

    1   pound fettuccine
        Salt
    4   ounces Parmigiano-Reggiano, grated (2 cups), plus
        extra for serving
    5   tablespoons unsalted butter, cut into 5 pieces

1. Bring 3 quarts water to boil in large Dutch oven. Add pasta and 1 tablespoon salt and cook, stirring frequently, until al dente. Reserve 1 cup cooking water, then drain pasta and return it to pot.

2. Add Parmigiano-Reggiano, butter, reserved cooking water, and ½ teaspoon salt to pot. Set pot over low heat and, using tongs, toss and stir vigorously to thoroughly combine, about 1 minute. Remove pot from heat, cover, and let pasta sit for 1 minute.

3. Toss pasta vigorously once more so sauce thoroughly coats pasta and any cheese clumps are emulsified into sauce, about 30 seconds. (Mixture may look wet at this point, but pasta will absorb excess moisture as it cools slightly.) Season with salt to taste.

4. Transfer pasta to individual bowls. (Use rubber spatula as needed to remove any clumps of cheese stuck to tongs and bottom of pot.) Serve immediately, passing extra Parmigiano-Reggiano separately.

PASTA WITH SAUSAGE RAGU

✓ **WHY THIS RECIPE WORKS:** For the long-cooked flavor of classic sausage ragu in under 90 minutes, we needed to maximize flavor and browning with minimal fuss. Whirring a *soffritto* of fennel, onion, and fennel seeds in the food processor combined them evenly, and then pulsing sweet Italian sausage promised tasty bites of meat in every forkful. After browning the sausage, we added the soffritto, building up plenty of deeply flavorful fond. Next we brought in rich tomato paste, minced garlic, and dried oregano to reinforce the recipe's Italian identity. We then turned this concentrated base into a sauce with the addition of red wine for brightness and canned tomatoes speedily chopped in the food processor. From there, a 45-minute simmer was all it took to achieve a supersavory ragu.

Common wisdom says that sausage ragu, a hearty Sunday night staple, requires hours of cooking. But I wanted to capture the long-cooked flavor of this Italian sauce in less than 90 minutes.

The first question to answer was, "What does long-cooked sauce taste like?" After cooking a handful of recipes calling for extended simmering and tasting them against quicker versions, I knew right away: The slow-simmered sauces were deep, savory, and meaty, while the fast ones were less complex and more acidic. Using flavorful sausage gave me a bit of an advantage, but I still had a long way to go.

Every great sauce needs a flavor base of vegetables; in Italian, it's called a *soffritto*. After a test using the usual suspects—chopped onion, carrot, and celery—I realized that the carrot and celery weren't doing much. Just half an onion, plus half a fennel bulb and a tablespoon of fennel seeds, pulsed in the food processor gave me better-defined flavor. But I had other problems to solve.

What kind of sausage should I use? After a few tests, I settled on sweet Italian. I then tested processing it like the vegetables versus breaking it up with a wooden spoon; I preferred using the processor, which evenly dispersed the sausage throughout the finished dish.

I also had to decide on a tomato product. After experimenting with crushed tomatoes and whole peeled tomatoes (pulsed in the food processor), I found that the latter had the silkier texture.

Ingredients settled, I set out to find long-simmered flavor without the long simmering. The answer was simple: careful browning. By browning the sausage and cooking the soffritto thoroughly with the browned meat, I was able to amplify the sauce's flavor and add a subtle sweetness, too, thanks to the caramelized sugars in the onions. I added the remaining ingredients and, after just 45 minutes of simmering, tossed the sauce with pasta and a bit of the cooking water for the perfect consistency. Tasters swore my sauce had been on the stove all day.

—ASHLEY MOORE, *Cook's Country*

Pasta with Sausage Ragu

SERVES 4 TO 6

For a spicier sauce, substitute hot Italian sausage for sweet. You will have 3 cups of extra sauce, which can be used to sauce 1 pound of pasta.

½ fennel bulb, stalks discarded, bulb cored and chopped coarse

½ onion, chopped coarse

1 tablespoon fennel seeds

1 (28-ounce) can whole peeled tomatoes

2 pounds sweet Italian sausage, casings removed

1 tablespoon extra-virgin olive oil, plus extra for drizzling

Salt and pepper

2 tablespoons tomato paste

4 garlic cloves, minced

1½ teaspoons dried oregano

¾ cup red wine

1 pound pappardelle or tagliatelle

Grated Parmesan cheese

1. Pulse fennel, onion, and fennel seeds in food processor until finely chopped, about 10 pulses, scraping down sides of bowl as needed; transfer to separate bowl. Process tomatoes in now-empty processor until smooth, about 10 seconds; transfer to second bowl. Pulse sausage in now-empty processor until finely chopped, about 10 pulses, scraping down sides of bowl as needed.

2. Heat oil in Dutch oven over medium-high heat until shimmering. Add sausage and cook, breaking up meat with spoon, until all liquid has evaporated and meat begins to sizzle, 10 to 15 minutes.

3. Add fennel mixture and ½ teaspoon salt and cook, stirring occasionally, until softened, about 5 minutes.

(Fond on bottom of pot will be deeply browned.) Add tomato paste, garlic, and oregano and cook, stirring constantly, until fragrant, about 30 seconds.

4. Stir in wine, scraping up any browned bits, and cook until nearly evaporated, about 1 minute. Add 1 cup water and pureed tomatoes and bring to simmer. Reduce heat to low and simmer gently, uncovered, until thickened, about 45 minutes. (Wooden spoon should leave trail when dragged through sauce.) Season with salt and pepper to taste; cover and keep warm.

5. Bring 4 quarts water to boil in large pot. Add pasta and 1 tablespoon salt and cook, stirring often, until al dente. Reserve 1 cup cooking water, then drain pasta and return it to pot. Add 3 cups sauce and ½ cup reserved cooking water to pasta and toss to combine. Adjust consistency with remaining reserved cooking water as needed. Transfer to serving dish. Drizzle with extra oil, sprinkle with Parmesan, and serve. (Remaining 3 cups sauce can be refrigerated for up to 3 days or frozen for up to 1 month.)

WEEKNIGHT TAGLIATELLE WITH BOLOGNESE SAUCE

☑ **WHY THIS RECIPE WORKS:** To create a quicker, deep-flavored Bolognese sauce, we looked to ground beef. Treating the beef with a baking soda solution kept it tender. After reducing store-bought beef broth to concentrate its meaty flavor, we pulsed our aromatics with salty pancetta in the food processor and deeply browned the paste to develop a flavorful fond. A healthy dose of tomato paste added depth and pop without much acid or overwhelming tomato flavor. The treated ground beef needed mere minutes to cook through in our sauce's intense base, and we followed it up with more instant flavor builders: dry red wine for brightness and Parmesan cheese for some nuance. When stirred into the sauce, the tagliatelle readily soaked up its rich, meaty, deeply savory flavor.

Six years ago we published a recipe for *ragu alla Bolognese,* the lavish, long-cooked meat sauce named for the northern Italian city from which it hails. It's an "ultimate" version, loaded up with not just ground beef but also ground pork, veal, pancetta, mortadella, and chicken livers. The meats simmer gently with a *soffritto*

WEEKNIGHT TAGLIATELLE WITH BOLOGNESE SAUCE

(softened chopped onion, carrot, and celery), broth, wine, and a goodly amount of tomato paste for about 1½ hours, by which time the sauce is silky, deeply savory, and thick enough that a wooden spoon leaves a trail when dragged along the bottom of the pot. When tossed with eggy ribbons of tagliatelle or pappardelle, it's about as satisfying as a bowl of pasta can get.

Because Bolognese is a long-cooked sauce, it's a perfect project for a winter weekend when I don't mind lingering in the kitchen. But often I don't have the time or patience to make a proper version. That's when I wish I could whip up a streamlined sauce that would closely approximate the meaty depth and richness of the real deal. In fact, I've tried a few recipes called "quick" or "simple" Bolognese that cut the number of meats down to just one (ground beef) and come together in no more than an hour, but none was worth repeating. The most common flaw of these recipes was that they were too tomatoey and acidic—more like meaty marinara than true Bolognese, which actually contains relatively little tomato. Most also lacked the traditional sauce's velvety consistency and ultrasavory flavor; in other words, they tasted like the shortcut sauces they were.

Was it possible to have it both ways—a rich, complex-tasting meat sauce that didn't require half a dozen meats and an afternoon of pot watching? I was about to find out.

I wanted to use ground beef—and only ground beef—as the meat in my sauce. But instead of searing it hard to develop deep color and flavor, which would turn it dry and pebbly, I tossed 1 pound of 85 percent lean ground beef with a little water and baking soda. Odd as it sounds, this has been our routine first move when braising ground beef since we discovered that the alkaline baking soda can raise the meat's pH, helping it retain moisture (without affecting the sauce's flavor).

While the beef soaked, I sautéed finely chopped carrot, onion, and celery in a Dutch oven with a little oil and butter until much of their moisture had evaporated. Then came the tomato component—paste, not canned tomatoes, since I wanted to add savory depth to the sauce and not bright, fruity acidity. I cooked the paste until it developed a rusty hue, an indication that it had caramelized, and then added the meat, which I cooked just until it lost its raw pink color. In went some red wine to deglaze the pot, followed by a cup of beef broth. Some cooks would add dairy at this point;

depending on who you ask, it's either an essential component, lending further richness and supposedly tenderizing the long-cooked meat, or it has no place in the sauce whatsoever. I opted not to, lest the dairy mute the meat's flavor. Instead, I simply simmered the mixture briefly to evaporate some of the liquid before reducing the heat and letting the sauce gurgle gently for about 30 minutes until it thickened up a bit; I then tossed it with the boiled pasta.

This sauce, while not bland, wasn't nearly as meaty-tasting as Bolognese should be. It was also greasy, but that was an easy fix: I switched to 93 percent lean ground beef. Ordinarily, such lean meat can be tough, but the baking soda treatment kept the beef moist and tender.

But what could I do to beef up the flavor? I was still reluctant to brown the ground meat, so I tried another unusual technique we've used in recipes for gravy and shepherd's pie: deeply browning the aromatic vegetables. I sautéed the carrot, onion, and celery for about 10 minutes, which gave me a visibly dark, rich flavor base, and then I finished building the sauce. It was meatier for sure—but still not meaty enough to be called Bolognese.

At this point, I reconsidered my initial ban on other meats. I didn't have to go whole hog, but it would be easy enough to add back something like pancetta, which is widely available and often used in small quantities to flavor Italian braises and sauces. The key would be chopping it very fine so that there would be a lot of surface area for browning and so it could thoroughly integrate into the sauce. I processed 6 ounces in the food processor, and while I was at it, I threw in the aromatic vegetables, too, again to maximize surface area for browning and to save myself the knife work. Once the mixture was paste-like, I spread it into a thin layer in the pot and cooked it.

This was the best-tasting sauce to date, but I had one other ingredient to try: Parmesan cheese. Garnishing each serving with a couple of spoonfuls is the classic way to season Italian pasta dishes with an extra jolt of salty, tangy richness, so why not add some directly to the pot? Sure enough, when I stirred a generous ½ cup into the sauce along with the broth, the final sauce was complex and seriously savory. It wasn't no-holds-barred Bolognese, but it was a convincingly close second.

The sauce tasted great and boasted a thick, velvety consistency that I thought would coat the tagliatelle beautifully. But instead the noodles sucked up all the liquid, leaving the sauce dry and scant.

The problem was that the rough surface of tagliatelle soaks up a lot of liquid. I needed to make the sauce looser so that by the time the tagliatelle absorbed the liquid, the sauce's consistency would tighten up just enough. I would need to scale up the liquid volume without diluting the sauce's now-meaty flavor. I was able to easily accomplish this by reducing 4 cups of beef broth down to 2 cups, which took just 15 minutes and could be done while the beef soaked in the baking soda solution and the vegetables browned.

When I added the concentrated broth to the sauce, I feared I had increased the amount of liquid too much: The sauce looked thin even after cooking for 30 minutes—not a consistency I'd equate with Bolognese. It wasn't until I tossed the sauce with the noodles and they soaked up just enough of the liquid that the sauce looked appropriately thick and clung beautifully to the pasta.

Barely an hour had passed before I was sitting down to a bowl of tagliatelle Bolognese with a savory depth and richness that rivaled long-cooked versions but came together in about half the time.

—ANNIE PETITO, *Cook's Illustrated*

Weeknight Tagliatelle with Bolognese Sauce

SERVES 4 TO 6

If you use our recommended beef broth, Better Than Bouillon Roasted Beef Base, you can skip step 2 and make a concentrated broth by adding 4 teaspoons paste to 2 cups water. To ensure the best flavor, be sure to brown the pancetta-vegetable mixture in step 4 until the fond on the bottom of the pot is quite dark. The cooked sauce will look thin but will thicken once tossed with the pasta. Tagliatelle is a long, flat, dry egg pasta that is about ¼ inch wide; if you can't find it, you can substitute pappardelle. Substituting other pasta may result in a too-wet sauce.

1   pound 93 percent lean ground beef
2   tablespoons water
¼   teaspoon baking soda
    Salt and pepper
4   cups beef broth
6   ounces pancetta, chopped coarse
1   onion, chopped coarse

1   large carrot, peeled and chopped coarse
1   celery rib, chopped coarse
1   tablespoon unsalted butter
1   tablespoon extra-virgin olive oil
3   tablespoons tomato paste
1   cup dry red wine
1   ounce Parmesan cheese, grated (½ cup), plus extra
    for serving
1   pound tagliatelle or pappardelle

1. Toss beef with water, baking soda, and ¼ teaspoon pepper in bowl until thoroughly combined. Set aside.

2. While beef sits, bring broth to boil over high heat in large pot (this pot will be used to cook pasta in step 6) and cook until reduced to 2 cups, about 15 minutes; set aside.

3. Pulse pancetta in food processor until finely chopped, 15 to 20 pulses. Add onion, carrot, and celery and pulse until vegetables are finely chopped, 12 to 15 pulses, scraping down sides of bowl as needed.

4. Heat butter and oil in large Dutch oven over medium-high heat until shimmering. When foaming subsides, add pancetta-vegetable mixture and ¼ teaspoon pepper and cook, stirring occasionally, until liquid has evaporated, about 8 minutes. Spread mixture in even layer in bottom of pot and continue to cook, stirring every couple of minutes, until very dark browned bits form on bottom of pot, 7 to 12 minutes longer. Stir in tomato paste and cook until paste is rust-colored and bottom of pot is dark brown, 1 to 2 minutes.

5. Reduce heat to medium, add beef, and cook, using wooden spoon to break meat into pieces no larger than ¼ inch, until beef has just lost its raw pink color, 4 to 7 minutes. Stir in wine, scraping up any browned bits, and bring to simmer. Cook until wine has evaporated and sauce has thickened, about 5 minutes. Stir in broth and Parmesan. Return sauce to simmer; cover, reduce heat to low, and simmer for 30 minutes (sauce will look thin). Remove from heat and season with salt and pepper to taste.

6. Rinse pot that held broth. While sauce simmers, bring 4 quarts water to boil in now-empty pot. Add pasta and 1 tablespoon salt and cook, stirring occasionally, until al dente. Reserve ¼ cup cooking water, then drain pasta. Add pasta to pot with sauce and toss to combine. Adjust sauce consistency with reserved cooking water as needed. Transfer to platter or individual bowls and serve, passing extra Parmesan separately.

EVERYDAY PAD THAI

EVERYDAY PAD THAI

✔ **WHY THIS RECIPE WORKS:** To create an accessible pad thai with clear sweet, sour, and salty flavors and a mix of textures, we had to replicate the dish's hard-to-find ingredients. Soaking rice noodles in boiling water softened them quickly. We started building the sauce's distinct flavor by sweetening fish sauce with sugar. The sour, fruity taste of tamarind was impossible to mimic, but easy-to-find tamarind juice concentrate rounded out the sauce with authentic taste. We turned to shrimp and egg to bulk up the dish, and we made our own dried shrimp by tossing cut-up shrimp with salt and sugar, microwaving them to shrink them down, and then frying them into crunchy bites. Quick-pickled red radishes were a fitting substitute for preserved daikon. Tossed together with a quick chile vinegar, ours boasted all the complexity of true pad thai.

I once pulled out all the stops to make an entirely authentic version of pad thai, and the result was a real stunner: tender rice noodles entwined in a sweet, sour, salty sauce and stir-fried with garlic, shallot, sweet shrimp, soft curds of scrambled egg, and nuggets of tofu. Chopped dried shrimp and pungent preserved daikon radish contributed intense flavor and chewy, crunchy textures that made me think I'd been transported to Bangkok. Chopped roasted peanuts, crisp bean sprouts, and garlic chives scattered over the top ensured that every bite was as exciting as the next.

My only quibbles? After all that work, the recipe yielded only two servings. Also, although it was incredibly satisfying to eat, my homemade pad thai had required a lot of forethought. Sourcing ingredients like dried shrimp and preserved radish demanded an excursion to an Asian market. Instead, could I create a satisfying version of pad thai using mostly everyday ingredients?

Thankfully, the dried rice noodles that form the base of pad thai are available at most supermarkets. Having dealt with rice noodles before, I knew exactly how to treat them. I put 8 ounces in a bowl with boiling water and let them sit until they were pliant, about 8 minutes. After draining and rinsing the noodles with cold water, I tossed them with oil for antistick insurance.

With the noodles sorted out, I moved on to the sauce. The interplay of salty, sweet, and sour tastes is the primary characteristic of pad thai. These flavors typically come from pungent, saline fish sauce; caramel-like palm sugar; and sour, fruity tamarind. Fish sauce is now available in most supermarkets, so it would need no substitute. Next up: thick palm sugar disks. Rather than hunt them down, I made test batches with brown and white sugar. Finding no discernible flavor difference, I opted to use white.

Tamarind, a fruit that grows as a round, brown pod, is also available as pure tamarind concentrate. I was committed to using everyday ingredients in my recipe, but after some testing I concluded that tamarind is essential to pad thai and is worth seeking out. Happily, tamarind is increasingly available in the Asian or Latin section of supermarkets. I chose the juice concentrate, since it is easier to work with.

On to the protein. Pad thai typically includes three types: firm tofu, shrimp, and eggs. To keep the ingredient list manageable, I omitted the first and added more of the latter two. One pound of large shrimp and four beaten eggs were adequate.

Most recipes call for adding the many ingredients in pad thai to the skillet sequentially. But to avoid overcrowding the pan, the volume of food must be kept low, so only one or two servings can be produced. By cooking in batches rather than gradually adding ingredients to the skillet, I could make enough to serve four. I started with minced garlic and scallion whites (instead of the usual shallot, since I planned on using the scallion greens in place of relatively obscure garlic chives) and then mixed in the shrimp and eggs. Once they were cooked, I transferred them to a bowl and stir-fried the noodles and sauce. I tossed in a handful of bean sprouts and the green parts of the scallions, and the dish was ready to be garnished with lime and chopped peanuts.

My pad thai was now in very good shape, but I pined for those salty bits of chewy dried shrimp and crunchy preserved daikon that help make it unique.

Hoping to replicate the daikon, which has a crunchy texture akin to pickled cabbage, I thought of similar salty, pickled options. Everything from sauerkraut (too vinegary) to pickles (too briny) to dried apricots that I brined (too sweet and sticky) took a turn in the dish. In the end, the most successful option was, not too surprisingly, fresh radishes. Soaking matchsticks of red radish in a warm solution of salt, sugar, and water created a fresh, crunchy, salty mix-in that added its own dimension.

Next, I considered the dried shrimp. In Thailand, the tiny shellfish are peeled, salted, and dried in the sun, giving them a meaty flavor and a firm, chewy texture. In Thai cooking, they are typically fried and used as a garnish or seasoning. My thought was to use a portion of the shrimp I was already calling for—just treated in a different manner. I cut a handful of shrimp into small bits and gently cooked them with the scallions and garlic, hoping to create a kind of shrimp paste. However, the shrimp pieces just plumped as they cooked, making them indistinguishable from the rest.

To produce a better facsimile, I would have to overcook the shrimp. Doing so in a skillet took 20 minutes, so I turned to the microwave. I nuked shrimp pieces until they were shriveled and then fried the nuggets in the skillet until they were golden. I continued with the recipe as before, tossing in makeshift pickled radishes and dried shrimp. Both gave my pad thai authentic character.

Typically pad thai is served with a host of condiments, but to keep things simple, I simply stirred thinly sliced serrano chiles into white vinegar and drizzled it onto the noodles.

My pad thai boasted all the right flavors and textures, and I could have it almost any time I wanted.

—ANNIE PETITO, *Cook's Illustrated*

Everyday Pad Thai

SERVES 4

Since pad thai cooks very quickly, prepare everything before you begin to cook. Use the time during which the radishes and noodles soak to prepare the other ingredients. We recommend using a tamarind juice concentrate made in Thailand in this recipe. If you cannot find tamarind, substitute 1½ tablespoons lime juice and 1½ tablespoons water and omit the lime wedges.

CHILE VINEGAR

⅓ cup distilled white vinegar

1 serrano chile, stemmed and sliced into thin rings

STIR-FRY

Salt

Sugar

2 radishes, trimmed and cut into 1½-inch by ¼-inch matchsticks

8 ounces (¼-inch-wide) rice noodles

3 tablespoons plus 2 teaspoons vegetable oil

¼ cup fish sauce

3 tablespoons tamarind juice concentrate

1 pound large shrimp (26 to 30 per pound), peeled and deveined

4 scallions, white and light green parts minced, dark green parts cut into 1-inch lengths

1 garlic clove, minced

4 large eggs, beaten

4 ounces (2 cups) bean sprouts

¼ cup roasted unsalted peanuts, chopped coarse

Lime wedges

1. FOR THE CHILE VINEGAR: Combine vinegar and chile in bowl and let stand at room temperature for at least 15 minutes.

2. FOR THE STIR-FRY: Combine ¼ cup water, ½ teaspoon salt, and ¼ teaspoon sugar in small bowl. Microwave until steaming, about 30 seconds. Add radishes and let stand for 15 minutes. Drain and pat dry with paper towels.

3. Bring 6 cups water to boil. Place noodles in large bowl. Pour boiling water over noodles. Stir, then let soak until noodles are almost tender, about 8 minutes, stirring once halfway through soaking. Drain noodles and rinse with cold water. Drain noodles well, then toss with 2 teaspoons oil.

4. Combine fish sauce, tamarind concentrate, and 3 tablespoons sugar in bowl and whisk until sugar is dissolved. Set sauce aside.

5. Remove tails from 4 shrimp. Cut shrimp in half lengthwise, then cut each half into ½-inch pieces. Toss shrimp pieces with ⅛ teaspoon salt and ⅛ teaspoon sugar. Arrange pieces in single layer on large plate and microwave at 50 percent power until shrimp are dried and have reduced in size by half, 4 to 5 minutes. (Check halfway through microwaving and separate any pieces that may have stuck together.)

6. Heat 2 teaspoons oil in 12-inch nonstick skillet over medium heat until shimmering. Add dried shrimp and cook, stirring frequently, until golden brown and crispy, 3 to 5 minutes. Transfer to large bowl.

7. Heat 1 teaspoon oil in now-empty skillet over medium heat until shimmering. Add minced scallions and garlic and cook, stirring constantly, until garlic is golden brown, about 1 minute. Transfer to bowl with dried shrimp.

8. Heat 2 teaspoons oil in now-empty skillet over high heat until just smoking. Add remaining whole shrimp and spread into even layer. Cook, without stirring, until shrimp turn opaque and brown around edges, 2 to 3 minutes, flipping halfway through cooking. Push shrimp to sides of skillet. Add 2 teaspoons oil to center, then add eggs to center. Using rubber spatula, stir eggs gently and cook until set but still wet. Stir eggs into shrimp and continue to cook, breaking up large pieces of egg, until eggs are fully cooked, 30 to 60 seconds longer. Transfer shrimp-egg mixture to bowl with scallion-garlic mixture and dried shrimp.

9. Heat remaining 2 teaspoons oil in now-empty skillet over high heat until just smoking. Add noodles and sauce and toss with tongs to coat. Cook, stirring and tossing often, until noodles are tender and have absorbed sauce, 2 to 4 minutes. Transfer noodles to bowl with shrimp mixture. Add 2 teaspoons chile vinegar, drained radishes, scallion greens, and bean sprouts and toss to combine.

10. Transfer to platter and sprinkle with peanuts. Serve immediately, passing lime wedges and remaining chile vinegar separately.

CHEESE AND TOMATO LASAGNA

✓ **WHY THIS RECIPE WORKS:** While meatless lasagna seems like it should be a simple affair, it can result in a dish lacking character and stature. To make a cheese and tomato lasagna that could hold its own, we needed to bring out the best in each component. Tomato paste, minced anchovies, grated Pecorino Romano, and sugar boosted the complexity and body of the sauce, while a small can of diced tomatoes added texture. For the cheeses, we made a few flavorful upgrades, swapping in fontina for mozzarella; Pecorino Romano for Parmesan; and a rich no-cook sauce of cottage cheese, heavy cream, and Pecorino Romano for mild ricotta. Wavy lasagna noodles promised a casserole with a strong structure, and instead of boiling them, we simply soaked them in hot water. As we assembled the layers, we staggered the noodles' placement so the lasagna would bake up level.

When I make lasagna, I usually turn to the Bolognese kind, layered with plenty of ground meats, or perhaps a vegetarian version bulked up with things like eggplant, zucchini, or mushrooms. But I recently decided to try my hand at a simpler classic enjoyed in southern Italy.

Called *lasagne di magro* ("lasagna without meat"), it strips the dish down to its most basic elements: noodles, cheese (usually a trio of ricotta, mozzarella, and Parmesan), and tomato sauce.

I was excited when I found this dish, and trying a few recipes confirmed that it was considerably faster to make than the more familiar kind. But these tests also revealed a shortcoming—namely, that a lasagna with only cheese and tomato can be plain old boring. Without meat and vegetables to add complex flavor, the tomato sauce came across as thin and acidic. The mozzarella and ricotta were bland, and the latter cooked up grainy rather than creamy. These lasagnas also lacked the stature and distinct layering of meat or vegetable versions; the noodles seemed to be swallowed up by the sauce and cheese.

To make this simpler lasagna work, I'd need to amp up the basic elements so that they offered bold, balanced flavor and substance of their own.

There was plenty of room to enhance the flavor and body of the tomato sauce, since the recipes I'd tried called for nothing more than canned tomatoes (usually crushed), garlic, onion, red pepper flakes, and basil. My first additions were tomato paste (a generous ¼ cup) and minced anchovies—both contribute glutamates that would give the sauce a savory boost in the absence of meat (the anchovies leave no trace of fishiness). The tomato paste also added body, but the sauce still came across as thin and one-dimensional. A small can of diced tomatoes in addition to the larger can of crushed ones broke up the uniform texture (they're treated with calcium chloride and thus don't break down much during cooking), while some grated Pecorino Romano tightened up the sauce and further enhanced its savory depth. A touch of sugar tempered the tomatoes' acidity. Those additions, along with a gentle 20-minute simmer, produced a sauce that was altogether different from the starting point: It was complex and balanced, with distinct body and substance.

Ricotta and mozzarella are naturally mild, so my next move was to replace them with stronger, more assertive cheeses. I briefly considered bolstering the ricotta with creamy, tangy additions like mascarpone or cream cheese, but I held off when I remembered that we'd come up with an effective ricotta substitute in other pasta casserole recipes: cottage cheese, which is both creamier and tangier than ricotta. I whisked the cottage cheese together with heavy cream, grated Parmesan, a touch of cornstarch (to prevent the dairy proteins from curdling when cooked), garlic, salt, and pepper to make a quick no-cook sauce. When I swapped in this mixture for the ricotta, it was not only more flavorful but also smoother and more lush. In later versions, I took the flavor boost one step further and traded the Parmesan for saltier, stronger Pecorino Romano.

As for replacing the mozzarella, I needed another good melting cheese that also had enough flavor to stand up to my now-robust tomato sauce. Thankfully, I didn't need to look beyond the Italian border for the perfect candidate: fontina. A great melter prized for its nuttiness, it delivered just as much gooeyness as mozzarella but with a more distinctive flavor.

On to the noodles, which needed to not only separate the lasagna into distinct layers but also provide resiliency and bite. No-boil noodles, which I'd been using for convenience and because they have a delicacy reminiscent of fresh pasta, were the wrong choice here, as demonstrated by the squat, uniformly soft lasagna I'd produced thus far. Switching to thicker, ruffly traditional lasagna noodles would be a convenience trade-off but would, I hoped, yield a taller, more substantial slice.

I boiled the sheets until they were al dente and then layered them in the baking dish with the tomato sauce, cottage cheese sauce, and shredded fontina, topping the layers with a mixture of fontina (tossed with a bit of cornstarch to prevent the shreds from clumping) and Pecorino. I covered the casserole with aluminum foil and baked it for 35 minutes in a moderate oven; I then removed the foil and cranked the heat for the last 15 minutes of cooking so that the top layer of cheese bubbled and browned.

The finished product looked more substantial than past attempts, but by the time the boiled noodles had baked and soaked up moisture from the sauces, they, too, were softer than I wanted, which defeated the purpose of using them in the first place. I could parboil them, but bringing a whole pot of water to a boil just for a quick dip seemed like a lot of fuss. But how about simply soaking them in hot water before baking? I laid the noodles in the dish I would use to bake the lasagna (to keep the dirty dishes to a minimum) and soaked them in boiling water until they were pliable. I drained them and built another lasagna, which turned out to be the best yet, with a good balance of noodles, sauce, and cheese.

I made just two more tweaks: rinsing the soaked noodles before baking to wash off some residual starch that had made the lasagna a tad gummy and reworking the assembly of the noodles. Now that I was simply soaking them before they went into the casserole, they weren't expanding as much, leaving empty spaces at the short sides of the baking dish. I arranged the soaked noodles so only one short side was left uncovered and then laid a half noodle across that open area. To keep the lasagna level, I alternated which short end got the half noodle with every layer.

A lasagna that wasn't a project yet still delivered the satisfying flavor and texture of the meat and vegetable versions? This one should become a classic, too.

—STEVE DUNN, *Cook's Illustrated*

Cheese and Tomato Lasagna

SERVES 8

Do not substitute no-boil noodles for regular noodles, as they are too thin. Alternating the noodle arrangement in step 4 keeps the lasagna level. For a vegetarian version, omit the anchovies.

CHEESE SAUCE

- 4 ounces Pecorino Romano cheese, grated (2 cups)
- 8 ounces (1 cup) cottage cheese
- ½ cup heavy cream
- 2 garlic cloves, minced
- 1 teaspoon cornstarch
- ¼ teaspoon salt
- ¼ teaspoon pepper

TOMATO SAUCE

- ¼ cup extra-virgin olive oil
- 1 onion, chopped fine
- 1½ teaspoons sugar
- ½ teaspoon red pepper flakes
- ½ teaspoon dried oregano
- ½ teaspoon salt
- 4 garlic cloves, minced
- 8 anchovy fillets, rinsed, patted dry, and minced
- 1 (28-ounce) can crushed tomatoes
- 1 (14.5-ounce) can diced tomatoes, drained
- 1 ounce Pecorino Romano cheese, grated (½ cup)
- ¼ cup tomato paste

CHEESE AND TOMATO LASAGNA

LASAGNA

- **14** curly-edged lasagna noodles
- **8** ounces fontina cheese, shredded (2 cups)
- **⅛** teaspoon cornstarch
- **¼** cup grated Pecorino Romano cheese
- **3** tablespoons chopped fresh basil

1. FOR THE CHEESE SAUCE: Whisk all ingredients in bowl until homogeneous. Set aside.

2. FOR THE TOMATO SAUCE: Heat oil in large saucepan over medium heat. Add onion, sugar, pepper flakes, oregano, and salt and cook, stirring frequently, until onions are softened, about 10 minutes. Add garlic and anchovies and cook until fragrant, about 2 minutes. Stir in crushed tomatoes, diced tomatoes, Pecorino, and tomato paste and bring to simmer. Reduce heat to medium-low and simmer until slightly thickened, about 20 minutes.

3. FOR THE LASAGNA: While sauce simmers, lay noodles in 13 by 9-inch baking dish and cover with boiling water. Let noodles soak until pliable, about 15 minutes, separating noodles with tip of paring knife to prevent sticking. Place dish in sink, pour off water, and run cold water over noodles. Pat noodles dry with clean dish towel; dry dish. Cut 2 noodles in half crosswise.

4. Adjust oven rack to middle position and heat oven to 375 degrees. Spread 1½ cups tomato sauce in bottom of dish. Lay 3 noodles lengthwise in dish with ends touching 1 short side, leaving space on opposite short side. Lay 1 half noodle crosswise in empty space to create even layer of noodles. Spread half of cheese sauce over noodles, followed by ½ cup fontina. Repeat layering of noodles, alternating which short side gets half noodle (alternating sides will prevent lasagna from buckling). Spread 1½ cups tomato sauce over second layer of noodles, followed by ½ cup fontina. Create third layer using 3½ noodles (reversing arrangement again), remaining cheese sauce, and ½ cup fontina.

5. Lay remaining 3½ noodles over cheese sauce. Spread remaining tomato sauce over noodles. Toss remaining ½ cup fontina with cornstarch, then sprinkle over tomato sauce, followed by remaining Pecorino.

6. Spray sheet of aluminum foil with vegetable oil spray and cover lasagna. Bake for 35 minutes. Remove lasagna from oven and increase oven temperature to 500 degrees.

7. Remove foil from lasagna, return to oven, and continue to bake until top is lightly browned, 10 to 15 minutes longer. Let lasagna cool for 20 minutes. Sprinkle with basil, cut into pieces, and serve.

GRILLED PIZZA

✓ **WHY THIS RECIPE WORKS:** To re-create the crisp, perfectly charred pizzas we tasted in Providence, Rhode Island, we started with the dough. Kneading together bread flour, sugar, yeast, water, oil, and salt in the food processor and allowing the dough to ferment in the refrigerator promised a crust with complex flavor and a tight crumb. Using a somewhat high percentage of water and stretching the dough on an oiled baking sheet made for a relatively slack dough that easily stretched without turning sticky. The oil also helped the exterior fry and crisp. After imparting great char on both sides of the crust, we protected the crisp crust from turning soggy under the toppings by sprinkling it with Parmesan. Warming the pizza sauce, dolloping it over the surface, and using a combination of quick-melting fresh mozzarella and finely grated Parmesan meant all of the pizza's elements finished cooking at once.

I like to host pizza parties year-round, but come summertime the last thing I want to do is crank up the oven and cook in a hot kitchen. That's when I opt to grill pizza. Not only does this approach allow me to move both the kitchen and the party outdoors, but when made well, the pie is a lighter and fresher style of pizza, perfect for summer appetites: a thin, audibly crisp, lightly charred crust that's tender within and topped judiciously (so as not to saturate the crust) with a simple tomato sauce, pockets of cheese, and fresh herbs.

My standards for grilled pizza are admittedly high, since I was introduced to this style at Al Forno in Providence, Rhode Island, the restaurant where the dish is said to have been invented more than three decades ago. There, the pies are cooked on a custom-made wood-fired grill, which produces a gorgeously charred, crisp-tender oblong crust that the kitchen tops with alternating islands of bright, well-rounded tomato sauce and gooey melted cheese, a few shallow pools of rich olive oil, and zippy raw scallion curls.

But as proficient as I am at baking pizzas, I've found it much trickier to grill one. That's because unlike an oven, which browns pizza from both the bottom and the top, a grill cooks pizza entirely from the bottom, which leaves the top soft and blond and the toppings undercooked, even when the grill is covered. To brown the second side, many recipes call for flipping the dough before applying any toppings, but I've found that this also causes the dough to puff up from edge to edge—more like a flatbread than pizza.

The grill at Al Forno avoids this problem because it features a brick enclosure that absorbs heat and then reflects it back onto the top of the pie, much like an oven would. Without that setup, I'd need to test other ways to achieve the results I was after.

Grilling the dough on both sides was a must if I wanted flavorful browning on the top and bottom, so I focused my first tests on keeping the dough flat. I used our Thin-Crust Pizza dough as a jumping-off point; it's a mixture of bread flour, instant yeast, water, vegetable oil, salt, and sugar that comes together in minutes in the food processor and stretches beautifully without tearing or springing back. It also boasts a tight crumb with complex flavor thanks to a prolonged fermentation in the fridge, where the dough's yeast produces sugars, alcohol, and acids. As for the grill setup, for now I'd cook the pies on a gas grill with all the burners set to high and revisit the method later if necessary.

Back to the puffiness issue: I wondered if the solution might be as simple as pressing the dough as thin as possible, which I tried with both my hands and a rolling pin. But neither of the mechanical methods worked: No matter how thin I stretched it, the dough inevitably puffed back up once it hit the grill. My only recourse was to try tweaking the dough formula itself. First I halved the amount of yeast, which did minimize the air bubbles but didn't make the dough easier to stretch. What I really needed was a looser dough that would naturally spread more, so I gradually upped the amount of water until the dough was soft enough to stretch into a thin sheet but not so wet that it was soupy.

The difference—an extra ½ ounce of water—made for a dough that not only stretched thinner and puffed less but also boasted a moister, more tender crumb.

But adding more water presented a catch-22: The wetter dough was stickier and required a liberal dusting of flour to keep it from clinging to my fingers and the grill grate (which I'd already oiled generously), but more flour made the exterior of the crust leathery and tough.

Stumped, I arranged a visit with Al Forno's executive chef, David Reynoso, hoping there was more to the restaurant's great results than the custom grill. And as it turned out, there was a subtle but significant difference to his method. Rather than stretching the dough in flour, he did so in a generous amount of olive oil. It made sense, as the fat not only kept the dough from sticking but essentially fried the exterior a bit and helped it crisp: As water in the dough's exterior is driven away by the high temperatures, the starch molecules lock into place, forming a rigid, brittle network with a porous, open structure.

Back at work, I whipped up another batch of dough. This time I poured ¼ cup of olive oil onto a rimmed baking sheet, dipped both sides of the dough ball into it, and then used my palms to stretch and spread the dough into a thin oval sheet that measured roughly 16 by 12 inches, just about filling the pan. It was a little messy, but the dough stretched easily beneath my hands and peeled cleanly from my fingers and the grate: So far so good. The finished product was proof that using lots of oil was worth it: This pie was thin, tender, and flavorful, with a crisp shell—and it wasn't the least bit greasy.

NOTES FROM THE TEST KITCHEN

AVOIDING HOT SPOTS ON THE GRILL

Arrange coals around perimeter of kettle (rather than evenly across it) to create even layer of heat.

GRILLED PIZZA

I should clarify that these pies had cooked nicely on a gas grill with the lid closed, but when I tried mimicking the results over a single-level charcoal fire, things got trickier. Simply put, it was much harder to maintain even heat over the entire surface, and the bottom of the crust tended to burn in the center before the outer edges had browned and the cheese had melted.

It wasn't that the fire was too strong; I proved that to myself when I reduced the amount of charcoal and the same bull's-eye effect happened, only more slowly. The problem was the shape of the kettle grill; even though the coals were spread in an even layer, the curved walls reflected heat and created a hot spot at the very center. The solution was to make the shape of the grill work in my favor by arranging the coals in a ring around the exterior of the grill with a void at the center; that way, the concentrated heat on the outside edge would reflect in. With that setup, I was able to achieve a more-even spread of heat from edge to edge.

However, this setup meant that I could cook just one pie at a time. But this was just as well: I'd also realized during testing that grilled pizza is more ephemeral than other styles and goes from perfectly crisp to limp in minutes, so serving one at a time was better. Going forward, I made sure to have everything I needed—all three sheets of stretched dough, sauce, cheese, and tools—at the ready so that I could cook and serve the pies as quickly as possible. In fact, it was best to pargrill all three pies before topping, grilling, and serving them one by one.

With my dough and my cooking method locked down, it was time to turn my attention to finessing the toppings, which, up to this point, had been just a coarse puree of whole tomatoes and seasonings along with some shredded mozzarella. The sauce needed nothing more than a little olive oil and sugar to balance the tomatoes' bright acidity, but the cheese, which was a tad bland and had never fully melted in previous tests, needed rethinking. After a few tests, I switched from the block mozzarella we typically use on pizza to the softer, faster-melting fresh kind and supplemented it with salty-sharp finely grated Parmesan.

I was also strategic about how and when I added the toppings: First, I applied a thin but even layer of Parmesan (plus a little more olive oil), which created a flavorful barrier against the other toppings' moisture, ensuring that the crust would stay crisp. Since slathering the thin dough with sauce and cheese would surely thwart crispness, I instead dolloped spoonfuls of sauce (warmed on the stove first to ensure it would be piping hot by the time the pizza was done) over the pargrilled dough surface, along with bite-size pieces of the mozzarella. I slid the pie back over the heat for 3 to 5 minutes to crisp up the crust and cook the toppings, checking the underside and rotating the pizza as necessary to make sure that it browned evenly. When it came off the grill, I finished it with chopped fresh basil, one more drizzle of oil, and a bit of coarse salt for crunch.

This was the closest replica of the Al Forno pie that I'd ever had: a crisp-tender crust that boasted richness from that oil bath and just a touch of smoke and char, simply and judiciously covered with pockets of bright, balanced sauce and just enough gooey cheese. It didn't need any other toppings (though applying certain fresh items that don't weigh down the pie after cooking is fine) and was as addictive to eat as it was fun to make.

—ANDREW JANJIGIAN, *Cook's Illustrated*

Grilled Pizza

SERVES 4 TO 6

The dough must sit for at least 24 hours before shaping. We prefer the high protein content of King Arthur bread flour for this recipe, though other bread flours are acceptable. For best results, weigh your ingredients. It's important to use ice water in the dough to prevent it from overheating in the food processor. Grilled pizza cooks quickly, so it's critical to have all of your ingredients and tools ready ahead of time. We recommend pargrilling, topping, and grilling in quick succession and serving the pizzas one at a time, rather than all at once.

DOUGH

- 3 cups (16½ ounces) King Arthur bread flour
- 1 tablespoon sugar
- ¼ teaspoon instant or rapid-rise yeast
- 1¼ cups plus 2 tablespoons ice water (11 ounces)
- 1 tablespoon vegetable oil, plus extra for counter
- 1½ teaspoons salt

SAUCE

- 1 (14-ounce) can whole peeled tomatoes, drained with juice reserved
- 2 tablespoons extra-virgin olive oil
- 2 teaspoons minced fresh oregano
- ½ teaspoon sugar, plus extra for seasoning
  Salt
- ¼ teaspoon red pepper flakes

PIZZA

- ½ cup plus 1 tablespoon extra-virgin olive oil, plus extra for drizzling
- 3 ounces Parmesan cheese, grated (1½ cups)
- 8 ounces fresh whole-milk mozzarella cheese, torn into bite-size pieces (2 cups)
- 3 tablespoons shredded fresh basil
  Coarse sea salt

1. FOR THE DOUGH: Process flour, sugar, and yeast in food processor until combined, about 2 seconds. With processor running, slowly add ice water; process until dough is just combined and no dry flour remains, about 10 seconds. Let dough stand for 10 minutes.

2. Add oil and salt to dough and process until dough forms satiny, sticky ball that clears sides of bowl, 30 to 60 seconds. Transfer dough to lightly oiled counter and knead until smooth, about 1 minute. Divide dough into 3 equal pieces (about 9⅓ ounces each). Shape each piece into tight ball, transfer to well-oiled baking sheet (alternatively, place dough balls in individual well-oiled bowls), and coat top of each ball lightly with oil. Cover tightly with plastic wrap (taking care not to compress dough) and refrigerate for at least 24 hours or up to 3 days.

3. FOR THE SAUCE: Pulse tomatoes in food processor until finely chopped, 12 to 15 pulses. Transfer to medium bowl and stir in reserved juice, oil, oregano, sugar,

½ teaspoon salt, and pepper flakes. Season with extra sugar and salt to taste, cover, and refrigerate until ready to use.

4. One hour before cooking pizza, remove dough from refrigerator and let stand at room temperature.

5A. FOR A CHARCOAL GRILL: Open bottom vent halfway. Light large chimney starter three-quarters filled with charcoal briquettes (4½ quarts). When top coals are partially covered with ash, pour into ring around perimeter of grill, leaving 8-inch clearing in center. Set cooking grate in place, cover, and open lid vent halfway. Heat grill until hot, about 5 minutes.

5B. FOR A GAS GRILL: Turn all burners to high, cover, and heat grill until hot, about 15 minutes. Leave all burners on high.

6. While grill is heating, transfer sauce to small saucepan and bring to simmer over medium heat. Cover and keep warm.

7. FOR THE PIZZA: Clean and oil cooking grate. Pour ¼ cup oil onto center of rimmed baking sheet. Transfer 1 dough round to sheet and coat both sides of dough with oil. Using your fingertips and palms, gently press and stretch dough toward edges of sheet to form rough 16 by 12-inch oval of even thickness. Using both your hands, lift dough and carefully transfer to grill. (When transferring dough from sheet to grill, it will droop slightly to form half-moon or snowshoe shape.) Cook (over clearing if using charcoal; covered if using gas) until grill marks form, 2 to 3 minutes. Using tongs and spatula, carefully peel dough from grate, then rotate dough 90 degrees and continue to cook (covered if using gas) until second set of grill marks appears, 2 to 3 minutes longer. Flip dough and cook (covered if using gas) until second side of dough is lightly charred in spots, 2 to 3 minutes. Using tongs or pizza peel, transfer crust to cutting board, inverting so side that was grilled first is facing down. Repeat with remaining

---

NOTES FROM THE TEST KITCHEN

CHOOSING CANNED TOMATOES
Using canned whole peeled tomatoes gives our Grilled Pizza's sauce fresh flavor year round. Our favorite brand is **Muir Glen Organic Whole Peeled Tomatoes**.

2 dough rounds, adding 1 tablespoon oil to sheet for each round and keeping grill cover closed when not in use to retain heat.

8. Drizzle top of 1 crust with 1 tablespoon oil. Sprinkle one-third of Parmesan evenly over surface. Arrange one-third of mozzarella pieces, evenly spaced, on surface of pizza. Dollop one-third of sauce in evenly spaced 1-tablespoon mounds over surface of pizza. Using pizza peel or overturned rimmed baking sheet, transfer pizza to grill; cover and cook until bottom is well browned and mozzarella is melted, 3 to 5 minutes, checking bottom and turning frequently to prevent burning. Transfer pizza to cutting board, sprinkle with 1 tablespoon basil, drizzle lightly with extra oil, and season with salt to taste. Cut into wedges and serve. Repeat with remaining 2 crusts.

TURKISH PIDE

✔ **WHY THIS RECIPE WORKS:** *Pide* is a Turkish flatbread that can be easily identified by its signature canoe shape. Like Italian pizza, pide varies from region to region and even from family to family, so the first task in developing our recipe was to identify what we liked. First, we focused on the dough. We tested a few traditional recipes and found that tasters preferred a cold-fermented dough with a crisp outer crust and chewy, irregular interior. Next, we turned to toppings. Tasters loved the classic Turkish combination of eggplant, red bell pepper, and tomatoes. We found that salting the eggplant was unnecessary since sautéing the veggies eliminated any excess moisture. Pulsing canned whole tomatoes in the food processor gave our topping the best texture. We accented the vegetables with smoky paprika and spicy red pepper flakes, a healthy amount of mint, and some briny, creamy feta. Shaping the flatbreads on individual parchment sheets made transferring the little boats to our preheated baking stone easy and efficient.

Pide is Turkey's answer to pizza, marked by its thin, canoe-like shape and distinctly Mediterranean toppings, from fragrant spiced lamb to tender spinach to any number of local cheeses. I knew this traditional flatbread needed to be included in our new collection of Mediterranean recipes, so in order to develop my own, my first step was to give a few different doughs a try.

Working with just a basic pizza sauce as my placeholder filling, I formed my first *pideler* using the handful of different doughs I found during my research, along with the test kitchen's favorite recipe for pizza dough. Though I noticed some slight differences among the traditional doughs—varying amounts of olive oil, sugar, and in one case, Greek yogurt—all sought to infuse the crust with nuance and tang. Luckily, tasters favored the taste of our pizza dough, which develops great complexity during an extended rest in the fridge. It requires some advance planning, but the recipe is largely hands-off—and totally foolproof. Plus, it's sturdy enough to hold up under any number of fillings.

With the dough decided, it was time to figure out my shaping technique. Looking back at the traditional recipes, I saw that some called for rolling the edges up over the filling, creating a lip around the border; others vaguely described pressing indentations around the perimeter before spreading on the filling; and others stopped at forming the oval. An edgeless pide was all well and good for a simple tomato sauce, but I knew I wanted my pide loaded with a saucy, chunky filling, so the technique of rolling the edges in for a crust seemed like the most logical approach.

Next, I began to consider my filling. Much as I liked the idea of a meaty lamb or spicy sausage pide, in keeping with the vegetables-first mindset of the Mediterranean diet, I decided to reshift my focus toward a Turkish standard: eggplant. Spiced up and paired with a bright tomato-based sauce and cheese, an eggplant pide seemed like a great introduction to this dish. To keep the sauce easy and accessible year-round, I worked with ingredients I could get my hands on in any season. I cut a 1-pound eggplant into hearty ½-inch chunks and sautéed them in olive oil, concentrating the earthy flavors and expelling any excess liquid while bringing in some browning. For a bit of contrasting sweetness, I softened chopped red bell pepper with the eggplant, allowing both to cook down and intensify. Fresh tomatoes are iffy in the colder months, so I grabbed a few cans of whole peeled tomatoes and pulsed them in the

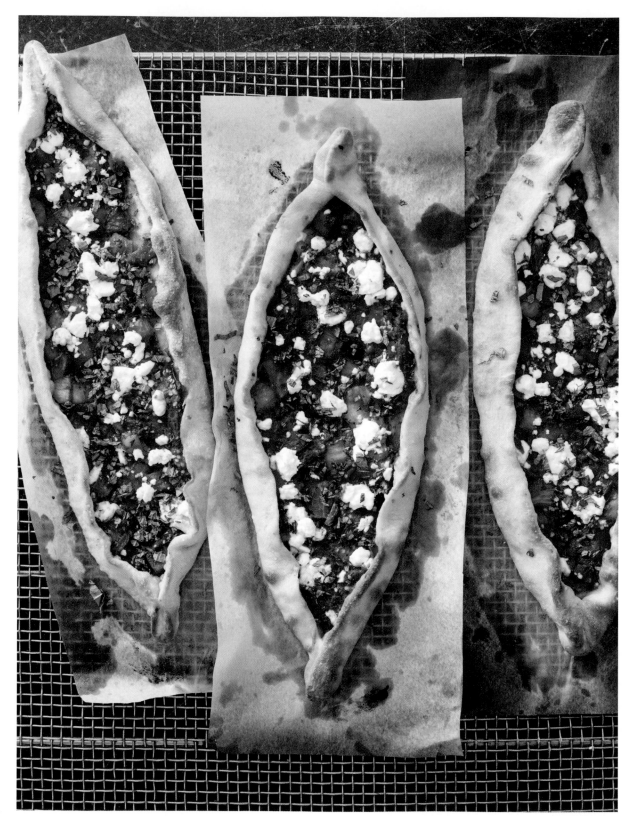

TURKISH PIDE

food processor, creating a chunky puree. I poured the tomatoes into the eggplant mixture to simmer and thicken. I wanted to add some more authenticity to the filling, so I started tinkering with spices. A few tests revealed that my tasters enjoyed the additions of garlic, spicy red pepper flakes, and smoked paprika.

The deep red filling was plenty striking, but I wanted to make my pide's flavors really pop, so I decided to introduce some cheese. Briny, crumbly feta was a natural choice, pairing well with the Turkish flavor profile. I also brought in some fresh, herbal flavor by adding chopped mint. This filling boasted deep, multilayered flavors that I knew would put your everyday pizza toppings to shame.

My pizza dough recipe made enough to crank out two large pies, but baking on a smaller scale seemed far more manageable, since the long, narrow shape was hard to maneuver. I divided the dough into six portions, rolled them into balls, and gave them another hour's rest before I pressed and stretched the first ball of dough into a long oval and brushed it with olive oil. It is customary to shape and fill the flatbreads before lifting and moving them to the oven—the weight of the filling supposedly gives the dough a final stretch before it bakes—but in practice this was tricky. Instead, I prepared each pide on its own sheet of parchment paper, which I could use to transfer them to and from the oven. I then spread on the eggplant mixture and folded up the sides to create a lip around the edges. Pinching the ends together sealed everything in and gave them the traditional shape.

I transferred my assembled flatbreads to a pizza peel one by one, using the parchment paper to safely lift and place each one. Pideler are traditionally baked in the blazing heat of a wood-fired oven, but I made do by preheating a baking stone at 500 degrees for an hour. Baked in that intense heat just inches from the broiler element, the flatbreads needed just 10 minutes or so for the crusts to turn golden and crisp and the filling to brown.

I sprinkled the finished flatbreads with mint, sliced them up, and called in my tasters. We were all in agreement: From the richly spiced vegetables to the briny bites of feta to the flavorful, crisp crust, my Turkish pide gave even the best slice of pizza a run for its money.

—KATHERINE PERRY, *America's Test Kitchen Books*

Turkish Pide

MAKES 6 PIDELER, SERVING 6 TO 8

It is important to use ice water in the dough to prevent it from overheating in the food processor. We recommend King Arthur brand bread flour. Press and roll the remaining three dough balls into ovals while the first set of flatbreads bake, but don't top and shape them until right before baking.

DOUGH

3 cups (16½ ounces) bread flour

2 teaspoons sugar

½ teaspoon instant or rapid-rise yeast

1⅓ cups ice water

1 tablespoon extra-virgin olive oil

1½ teaspoons salt

TOPPINGS

1 (28-ounce) can whole peeled tomatoes

5 tablespoons extra-virgin olive oil

1 pound eggplant, cut into ½-inch pieces

½ red bell pepper, chopped

Salt and pepper

3 garlic cloves, minced

¼ teaspoon red pepper flakes

½ teaspoon smoked paprika

6 tablespoons minced fresh mint

6 ounces feta cheese, crumbled (1½ cups)

1. FOR THE DOUGH: Pulse flour, sugar, and yeast in food processor until combined, about 5 pulses. With processor running, slowly add ice water and process until dough is just combined and no dry flour remains, about 10 seconds. Let dough rest for 10 minutes.

2. Add oil and salt to dough and process until dough forms satiny, sticky ball that clears sides of bowl, 30 to 60 seconds. Transfer dough to lightly oiled counter and knead by hand to form smooth, round ball, about 30 seconds. Place dough seam side down in lightly greased large bowl or container, cover tightly with plastic wrap, and refrigerate for at least 24 hours or up to 3 days.

3. FOR THE TOPPINGS: Pulse tomatoes and their juice in food processor until coarsely ground, about 12 pulses. Heat 2 tablespoons oil in 12-inch nonstick skillet over medium-high heat until shimmering. Add eggplant, bell pepper, and ½ teaspoon salt and cook, stirring occasionally, until softened and beginning to brown, 5 to 7 minutes. Stir in garlic, pepper flakes, and paprika and cook until fragrant, about 30 seconds.

4. Add tomatoes, bring to simmer, and cook, stirring occasionally, until mixture is very thick and measures 3½ cups, about 10 minutes. Off heat, stir in ¼ cup mint and season with salt and pepper to taste; let cool completely before using.

5. One hour before baking, adjust oven rack 4 inches from broiler element, set baking stone on rack, and heat oven to 500 degrees. Press down on dough to deflate. Transfer dough to clean counter and divide in half, then cut each half into thirds (about 4¾ ounces each); cover loosely with greased plastic. Working with 1 piece of dough at a time (keep remaining pieces covered), form into rough ball by stretching dough around your thumbs and pinching edges together so that top is smooth. Space balls 3 inches apart, cover loosely with greased plastic, and let rest for 1 hour.

6. Cut six 16 by 6-inch pieces of parchment paper. Generously coat 1 dough ball with flour and place on well-floured counter. Press and roll into 14 by 5½-inch oval. Arrange oval on parchment rectangle and reshape

as needed. (If dough resists stretching, let it relax for 10 to 20 minutes before trying to stretch it again.) Repeat with 2 more dough balls and parchment rectangles.

7. Brush dough ovals with oil, then top each with ½ cup eggplant mixture and ¼ cup feta, leaving ¾-inch border around edges. Fold long edges of dough over filling to form canoe shape and pinch ends together to seal. Brush outer edges of dough with oil and transfer flatbreads (still on parchment rectangles) to pizza peel.

8. Slide flatbreads (each on its parchment rectangle) onto baking stone, spacing them at least 1 inch apart. Bake until crust is golden brown and edges are crisp, 10 to 15 minutes. Transfer flatbreads to wire rack, discard parchment, and let cool for 5 minutes. Sprinkle with 1 tablespoon mint, slice, and serve. Repeat with remaining 3 dough balls, 3 parchment rectangles, oil, and toppings.

NOTES FROM THE TEST KITCHEN

SHAPING TURKISH PIDE

1. Press and roll 1 dough ball into 14 by 5½-inch oval on well-floured counter. Arrange oval on parchment rectangle and reshape as needed.

2. Brush oval with oil, then top with ½ cup eggplant mixture and ¼ cup feta, leaving ¾-inch border around edges.

3. Fold long edges of dough over filling to form canoe shape and pinch ends together to seal.

CRISPY SKILLET TURKEY BURGERS

✔ **WHY THIS RECIPE WORKS:** For juicy, full-flavored turkey burgers we could prepare in a skillet, we needed to keep the moisture in the patties. Taking inspiration from our favorite meatloaf recipes, we created a panade, working panko bread crumbs, Monterey Jack cheese, and mayonnaise into juicy ground turkey. The panade created rich pockets of fat and kept the patties from turning too dense. Even better, the cheese encouraged some appealing crisping around the edges of the burger. Our supersimple turkey burgers cooked through quickly, needing just 5 minutes per side, and while they tasted great topped with all the usual burger fixings, their rich flavors paired particularly well with tangy pickled onions.

So much can go wrong with a turkey burger. Even when made with care, it can be dry, dense, or totally lacking in flavor. We've cracked the code before in the test kitchen, but our process involved grinding our own turkey meat. I wanted a moist, flavorful turkey burger using store-bought ground turkey. And what's more, I wanted it to have slightly crispy edges.

First I had to rectify the pitfalls of most turkey burgers—dryness and denseness—without changing the culprits: the relative lack of fat and the need to cook turkey to 160 degrees.

To fight dryness, you can add moisture, which usually means adding fat. Using fattier ground turkey (usually a blend of white and dark meat and about 93 percent lean) instead of ground turkey breast (white meat only and up to 99 percent lean) made a difference. So did adding a bit of mayonnaise to the mix, which was easy to incorporate.

But in the end it was the density of bad turkey burgers that clued me in to the most transformative fix: a panade. We often add a panade of bread crumbs and dairy to our meatloaf mixture to create juicy pockets within the ground meat and keep it from coagulating too tightly when cooked. Much like meatloaf, my turkey burgers needed a bit of internal physical disruption to keep them from being so dense.

After several experiments, I settled on a combination of panko bread crumbs and shredded cheese; with the mayonnaise, this served as a panade. The cheese—just

2 ounces for four burgers—also added a delicate savory flavor. And the exposed cheese on the tops and bottoms of the burgers crisped up into a browned, *frico*-like crust—a crispy, savory foil to the tender juiciness inside.

Talk about easy: All four burgers could be cooked together in a nonstick skillet over medium heat until deeply browned and crunchy. Flipping the burgers just once made the process a snap. My final recipe required no more than 10 minutes and one skillet.

Since the flavors of the mayonnaise and cheese are subtle, these burgers are a great canvas for any additional flavors. Standards like ketchup, mustard, lettuce, and tomato dress up the turkey burgers in a classic style. If you like southwestern flavors, try layering some pickled jalapeños on the patties and a smear of mashed avocado on the buns. Or give the burgers a smoky slant with some barbecue sauce and a couple of slices of bacon.

—KATIE LEAIRD, *Cook's Country*

Crispy Skillet Turkey Burgers

SERVES 4

Be sure to use 93 percent lean ground turkey, not 99 percent fat-free ground turkey breast, in this recipe or the burgers will be tough. Serve with your favorite burger toppings, including Pickled Onions (recipe follows).

- 1 **pound ground turkey**
- 1 **cup panko bread crumbs**
- 2 **ounces Monterey Jack cheese, shredded (½ cup)**
- ¼ **cup mayonnaise**
  Salt and pepper
- 1 **tablespoon vegetable oil**
- 4 **hamburger buns, toasted and buttered**

1. Combine turkey, panko, Monterey Jack, mayonnaise, ½ teaspoon salt, and ½ teaspoon pepper in bowl. Using your hands, pat turkey mixture into four ¾-inch-thick patties, about 4 inches in diameter. Season patties with salt and pepper.

2. Heat oil in 12-inch nonstick skillet over medium heat until shimmering. Add patties and cook until well browned and meat registers 160 degrees, about 5 minutes per side.

3. Place burgers on buns and serve.

MAKES ABOUT 2 CUPS

1 **small red onion, halved and sliced thin**

2 **jalapeño chiles, stemmed and sliced into thin rings**

1 **cup white wine vinegar**

2 **tablespoons lime juice**

1 **tablespoon sugar**

1 **teaspoon salt**

Combine onion and jalapeños in medium bowl. Bring vinegar, lime juice, sugar, and salt to boil in small saucepan. Pour vinegar mixture over onion mixture and let sit for at least 30 minutes. (Pickled onions can be made in advance and refrigerated for up to 1 week.)

SHREDDED CHICKEN TACOS

✓ **WHY THIS RECIPE WORKS:** For deeply flavorful *tinga de pollo*, we cooked the chicken directly in its tomato-and-chipotle-based sauce. After browning meaty chicken thighs, we built a complex, smoky sauce on top of the residual fond using fire-roasted diced tomatoes, chipotle chiles, a touch of brown sugar, and lime juice and zest. Meaty-tasting chicken broth thinned the sauce out just enough so the thighs could cook through as it simmered. As soon as the chicken was cooked, we plucked it from the pot and shredded it. We pureed the sauce and returned it to the stove, stirring in the chicken and allowing it to thicken. Spooned into tortillas and topped with a host of creamy, cool, and crunchy fixings, these chicken tacos were saucy, rich, and simple enough to prepare any day of the week.

I've long been a fan of pork *tinga,* a taco filling hailing from the Puebla region of Mexico that features super-tender shredded pork in a boldly flavored sauce anchored by tomatoes and smoky-spicy chipotle chiles. Toppings like cilantro, salty Cotija cheese, and a squeeze of lime provide a perfect contrast to the rich, meaty filling. But since it's usually made with cuts that take several hours to turn tender, pork tinga isn't practical for a weeknight. I'd thought about adapting a recipe to work with chicken, but after a little research I realized there was no need:

Lots of authentic recipes for *tinga de pollo* already exist.

I gave the most common—and speedy—approach I found a test run. Similar to the recipe for pork tinga, it called for poaching the chicken (I chose boneless breasts) in water in one pot as you prepare the sauce in another. This was as simple as softening some chopped onions with oil before simmering them with canned diced tomatoes, chicken broth, and—of course—a few tablespoons of minced chipotle chiles in adobo sauce. As soon as the chicken was poached, I shredded it and stirred it into the pot with the sauce. After cooking the mixture briefly to give the flavors a chance to meld, I gave it a taste. Fast? Yes. But as I had suspected, the time savings just weren't worth it. The chicken was bland, and the sauce was thin in both flavor and texture. Could I deliver the full-flavored smoky, spicy, hearty filling that I craved while keeping the recipe weeknight-friendly?

I began by making three immediate changes. First, I swapped out the breasts for more flavorful boneless thighs. This was such an obvious improvement that I couldn't believe more recipes didn't call for it, particularly since the thighs took only about 15 minutes to cook through, barely longer than the breasts I'd used in my first attempt. Second, I ditched one of my pots. By cooking the chicken and sauce in separate pots, I had missed an opportunity to infuse both components with more flavor. Instead, I simmered them together from the start. And third, to address the sauce's watery consistency, I dialed back on the tomatoes and chicken broth, going from a 28-ounce can of tomatoes to a 14.5-ounce can and from 1 cup to ½ cup of chicken broth.

These changes helped, but they weren't enough. Most tinga de pollo recipes didn't call for browning the meat, but this would certainly give the chicken more flavor as well as leave behind flavorful bits of fond in the pot that could be stirred into the sauce (and wouldn't add much more time). I also wondered if browning the onions instead of just softening them would make a difference. After browning the chicken on both sides and setting it aside, I added the onions to the pot and let them go several minutes longer before introducing the other ingredients and proceeding with the recipe. I also decided to cook the chicken a little longer, until it reached 195 degrees. Though we typically cook thigh meat to 175 degrees, longer braising allows even more of its collagen to break down, delivering meat that's

SHREDDED CHICKEN TACOS (TINGA DE POLLO)

more tender. For my purposes, this meant the meat was easier to shred. Tasters approved of all these changes: The chicken was more tender, and the thick sauce now boasted savory flavor and depth. But I had higher ambitions: I wanted the dish to have even more complexity.

The diced tomatoes in the sauce were fine, but what if I swapped them for a can of the fire-roasted kind? One test confirmed that their lightly charred flavor enhanced the smokiness of the chipotles. I also opted to add some of the adobo sauce from the can of chipotles; just 2 teaspoons added a layer of vinegary, smoky complexity. I continued to experiment with other ingredients I'd seen in tinga recipes. Tasters thought that oregano made my recipe taste like Italian pasta sauce, so it was out. Tomatillos, thyme, and bay leaf didn't offer enough flavor to justify their inclusion. However, garlic and cumin, plus a little warmth from cinnamon, earned a thumbs-up. Authentic recipes seemed to end here, but I found that stirring in just ½ teaspoon of brown sugar had a surprisingly big impact, lending

a necessary balancing sweetness. A little acidity and floral flavor from fresh lime juice and zest brightened the dish just enough. With just these simple pantry ingredients, I had the richly smoky, spicy, tomatoey sauce that I'd wanted.

There was just one thing I still wasn't happy with: The shreds of chicken and the sauce seemed like separate entities, with much of the sauce dripping from the chicken as I dished it out of the pot. But I had an idea. Thanks to the fact that I was cooking the chicken to 195 degrees, its muscle fibers were looser than they would have been at 175 degrees. So instead of briefly warming the shredded chicken in the pureed sauce before serving, as I'd been doing, I let it simmer for a full 10 minutes. As I'd hoped, the simmering action loosened the muscle fibers even further and gave the sauce a chance to really take hold of the meat. It also allowed the sauce to thicken further. The upshot: a more cohesive taco filling with sauce that clung to the meat.

All I had left to do was iron out the toppings. Minced fresh cilantro and scallions, some avocado pieces, crumbled Cotija cheese, and fresh lime juice added the right amount of contrasting fresh, cool flavors. For some textural interest, I also whipped up a quick *escabèche,* a traditional quick-pickled Mexican condiment, as the chicken cooked. All it took was giving some sliced red onion, jalapeño, and carrots a 30-minute soak in a spiced pickling brine. With that, I had tacos that satisfied all my cravings—plus a simple recipe that also had deep, complex flavor.

—STEVE DUNN, *Cook's Illustrated*

NOTES FROM THE TEST KITCHEN

WARMING TORTILLAS, THREE WAYS

GAS FLAME: Using tongs, place tortilla directly over medium flame of gas burner until lightly charred, about 30 seconds per side.

SKILLET: Toast tortilla in dry nonstick skillet over medium-high heat until softened and spotty brown, 20 to 30 seconds per side.

MICROWAVE: Wrap up to 6 tortillas in damp, clean dish towel and microwave until warm, 30 to 45 seconds.

Shredded Chicken Tacos (Tinga de Pollo)
SERVES 6

In addition to the Mexican-Style Pickled Vegetables (Escabèche) (recipe follows) and the toppings included here, Mexican *crema* (or sour cream) and minced onion are also good choices. If you can't find Cotija cheese, you can substitute crumbled feta.

CHICKEN

- 2 **pounds boneless, skinless chicken thighs, trimmed**
  Salt and pepper
- 2 **tablespoons vegetable oil**
- 1 **onion, halved and sliced thin**

3 garlic cloves, minced

1 teaspoon ground cumin

¼ teaspoon ground cinnamon

1 (14.5-ounce) can fire-roasted diced tomatoes

½ cup chicken broth

2 tablespoons minced canned chipotle chile in adobo sauce plus 2 teaspoons adobo sauce

½ teaspoon brown sugar

1 teaspoon grated lime zest plus 2 tablespoons juice

TACOS

12 (6-inch) corn tortillas, warmed

1 avocado, halved, pitted, and cut into ½-inch pieces

2 ounces Cotija cheese, crumbled (½ cup)

6 scallions, minced

Minced fresh cilantro

Lime wedges

1. FOR THE CHICKEN: Pat chicken dry with paper towels and season with salt and pepper. Heat 1 tablespoon oil in large Dutch oven over medium-high heat until shimmering. Add half of chicken and brown on both sides, 3 to 4 minutes per side. Transfer to large plate. Repeat with remaining chicken.

2. Reduce heat to medium, add remaining 1 tablespoon oil to now-empty pot, and heat until shimmering. Add onion and cook, stirring frequently, until browned, about 5 minutes. Add garlic, cumin, and cinnamon and cook until fragrant, about 1 minute. Add tomatoes, broth, chipotle and adobo sauce, and sugar and bring to boil, scraping up any browned bits.

3. Return chicken to pot, reduce heat to medium-low, cover, and simmer until meat registers 195 degrees, 15 to 20 minutes, flipping chicken after 5 minutes. Transfer chicken to cutting board.

4. Transfer cooking liquid to blender and process until smooth, 15 to 30 seconds. Return sauce to pot. When cool enough to handle, use two forks to shred chicken into bite-size pieces. Return chicken to pot with sauce. Cook over medium heat, stirring frequently, until sauce is thickened and clings to chicken, about 10 minutes. Stir in lime zest and juice. Season with salt and pepper to taste.

5. FOR THE TACOS: Spoon chicken into center of each warm tortilla and serve, passing avocado, Cotija, scallions, cilantro, and lime wedges separately.

Mexican-Style Pickled Vegetables (Escabèche)
MAKES ABOUT 2 CUPS

For less spicy pickled vegetables, remove the seeds from the jalapeño.

½ teaspoon coriander seeds

¼ teaspoon cumin seeds

1 cup cider vinegar

½ cup water

1½ teaspoons sugar

¼ teaspoon salt

1 red onion, halved and sliced thin

2 carrots, peeled and sliced thin

1 jalapeño chile, stemmed and sliced thin into rings

Toast coriander seeds and cumin seeds in medium saucepan over medium heat, stirring frequently, until fragrant, about 2 minutes. Add vinegar, water, sugar, and salt and bring to boil, stirring to dissolve sugar and salt. Remove saucepan from heat and add onion, carrots, and jalapeño, pressing to submerge vegetables. Cover and let cool completely, 30 minutes. (Cooled vegetables can be refrigerated for up to 1 week.)

FARRO BOWLS WITH TOFU, MUSHROOMS, AND SPINACH

WHY THIS RECIPE WORKS: Vegetable-and-grain bowls give you the freedom to mix things up at dinnertime. To bring that flexibility to our own table, we made a vegan bowl with a hearty base of nutty farro, a satisfying grain often used in western Mediterranean cooking. We wanted to prove that full-flavored and nutritious farro could work well outside of Italian dishes, so we ventured to pair it with bold Asian-inspired ingredients. For toppings, we chose crispy seared tofu planks, which we attractively fanned on top of the grains, along with a simple sauté of mushrooms, shallot, and spinach. We partnered these easy-to-prepare toppings with our potent, perfectly drizzlable Miso-Ginger Sauce.

With tastings to attend at every hour of the workday, I rarely leave the test kitchen at lunchtime. When I do make it out, though, it's because I'm craving something hearty and satisfying. In my more recent quests for a healthful lunch, I've noticed a clear trend toward grain bowls. From burrito joints to the neighborhood sandwich shop, these bowls are cropping up everywhere, offering an ever widening array of flavors and ingredients to choose from. I, for one, am a big fan, but regularly ducking out to pick up a bowl of my favorite greens and grains isn't exactly a frugal habit. Hoping to make these bowls an at-home possibility, I set out to make my own.

Since a healthy, satisfying bowl was my end goal, I decided to make my recipe one that vegans and non-vegans alike could enjoy. To make my version stand out in a category overrun with quinoa, I deferred to a different grain as my base: sweet, nutty, chewy farro.

I knew from past experience that farro is best prepared using the pasta cooking method—boiled until tender and drained—so the main focus of this recipe's development would be its flavors. Although farro has close ties to Tuscan cuisine, I wanted my bowl to break away from its Italian roots. Neutral-tasting tofu seemed like an easy way to incorporate a plant-based protein into my bowl, and that decision inspired me to work towards an Asian flavor profile, bringing the flavors to life across the board.

Starting with the tofu, I grabbed a brick of the firm variety, sliced it into cubes, and drained it on paper towels to absorb its excess liquid. Dredging the cubes in cornstarch (rather than in flour or cornmeal) promised a delicate crisp crust without turning bready or gritty when fried. I cooked the coated tofu cubes in a hot skillet, but by the time their surfaces were evenly browned, the bites had begun to shrivel and overcook. Perhaps cubes were not the answer. I tried again, this time slicing the tofu crosswise into planks. Following the same prep steps as before, I fried up a new batch and was pleased to see the broad planks turn uniformly golden brown before the insides overcooked. Check that off the list.

It was time to bring in some vegetables. I was already using my skillet to fry the tofu, so I decided to streamline by keeping all of the cooking on the stovetop. Mushrooms were a must—their earthy flavor would give my bowls a strong savory backbone, and they cook quickly while still staying firm. White mushrooms would be too mild for this dish but the more mature, deep flavor of cremini mushrooms seemed fitting. I chopped some cremini and tossed them into my skillet, browning them along with a minced shallot for more complex flavor. They tasted meaty and rich, and a hit of sherry vinegar brought in some nutty flavor, echoing that of my key ingredient, the farro.

I wanted to incorporate some greenery, if only to bring some color to my bowl, so I added a few handfuls of baby spinach to the skillet when the mushrooms were nearly done cooking. These tender leaves cooked down in no time, but when I portioned my spinach-mushroom mixture over a small serving of farro, one thing became abundantly clear: the spinach was too sparse. There was no way I could fit more spinach in the already full skillet, so I decided to separate the two components. After preparing the mushrooms, I cleared out the skillet, heated up some oil, and began wilting the quick-cooking leaves in batches. With this simple swap, I was able to bring in a more generous helping.

I began assembling the bowls, piling farro high with crisp tofu, earthy cremini, and tender spinach. A sprinkling of scallions made for a fresh finish, but the winning touch came when I drizzled on a quick vegan mayo–based sauce flavored with red miso, maple syrup, sesame oil, more sherry vinegar, and some fresh ginger. With that, I had the soul-satisfying bowl I'd been craving.

—KATHERINE PERRY, *America's Test Kitchen Books*

Farro Bowls with Tofu, Mushrooms, and Spinach
SERVES 4 TO 6

We prefer the flavor and texture of whole-grain farro; pearled farro can be used, but the texture may be softer. We found a wide range of cooking times among various brands of farro, so start checking for doneness after 10 minutes. Do not use quick-cooking farro in this recipe.

1½	cups whole farro
	Salt and pepper
2	teaspoons toasted sesame oil
1	teaspoon sherry vinegar
14	ounces firm tofu, sliced crosswise into 8 equal slabs
⅓	cup cornstarch
¼	cup vegetable oil, plus extra as needed
10	ounces cremini mushrooms, trimmed and chopped coarse
1	shallot, minced
2	tablespoons dry sherry
10	ounces (10 cups) baby spinach
1	recipe Miso-Ginger Sauce (recipe follows)
2	scallions, sliced thin

1. Bring 4 quarts water to boil in Dutch oven. Stir in farro and 1 tablespoon salt, return to boil, and cook until grains are tender with slight chew, 15 to 30 minutes. Drain farro and return to now-empty pot. Drizzle with sesame oil and vinegar, toss to coat, and cover to keep warm.

2. While farro cooks, spread tofu on paper towel–lined baking sheet and let drain for 20 minutes. Gently press dry with paper towels and season with salt and pepper.

3. Spread cornstarch in shallow dish. Coat tofu thoroughly in cornstarch, pressing gently to adhere; transfer to plate. Heat 1 tablespoon vegetable oil in 12-inch nonstick skillet over medium-high heat until just smoking. Add tofu and cook until both sides are crisp and browned, about 4 minutes per side, adding more oil as necessary to prevent charring. Transfer to paper towel–lined plate to drain and tent with aluminum foil.

4. In now-empty skillet, heat 2 tablespoons vegetable oil over medium-high heat until shimmering. Stir in mushrooms, shallot, and ⅛ teaspoon salt and cook until vegetables begin to brown, 5 to 8 minutes. Stir in sherry and cook, scraping up any browned bits, until skillet is nearly dry, about 1 minute; transfer to bowl.

5. Heat remaining 1 tablespoon vegetable oil over medium-high heat in now-empty skillet until shimmering. Add spinach, 1 handful at a time, and cook until just wilted, about 1 minute.

6. Divide farro among individual bowls, then top each bowl with tofu, mushroom mixture, and spinach. Drizzle with miso-ginger sauce, sprinkle with scallions, and serve.

Miso-Ginger Sauce
MAKES ABOUT ¾ CUP

Our favorite vegan mayonnaise is Just Mayo.

¼ cup vegan mayonnaise

3 tablespoons red miso

2 tablespoons water

1 tablespoon maple syrup

1 tablespoon sesame oil

1½ teaspoons sherry vinegar

1½ teaspoons grated fresh ginger

Whisk all ingredients in bowl until well combined.

SKILLET SPANAKOPITA

WHY THIS RECIPE WORKS: Spanakopita is a Greek spinach-and-cheese pie with a crisp phyllo shell. To turn this appealing meal into a streamlined one-pan supper, our first challenge was to simplify the crust. The traditional method of buttering or oiling and stacking sheets of phyllo dough creates flaky layers, but this seemed too labor-intensive. Instead, we sprayed sheets of phyllo with olive oil spray, crumpled each into a ball, and placed them on top of the filling. This created plenty of surface area without tedious layering; plus, it didn't matter if a sheet tore. As for the filling, we used our skillet to drive off any remaining moisture from the thawed spinach so our crust wouldn't steam in the oven. A mix of feta and ricotta cheeses added briny flavor and rich, creamy texture, while scallions, mint, and dill delivered an herbal backbone.

If there's one thing I hate about cooking at home, it's the aftermath: Most of my favorite meals leave me with a staggering pile of pots, pans, and dishes to tackle. When I'm cooking at work, I'm pretty spoiled—we have a staff of dishwashers who power through the mountains of kitchen equipment we use all day—but when I'm home and responsible for my own cleanup, my patience runs thin. My anti-dishwashing prayers were soon answered when our new book of streamlined, single-vessel recipes, *One-Pan Wonders*, became my next assignment.

One-pan cooking is nothing new. Here in the test kitchen, we have been touting the virtues of slow-cooker dinners and sheet pan suppers for years, but when I looked closer at our recipes and those in other cookbooks, it became clear that many "one pan" claims were only half true. Whether they called for browning in a skillet before moving food to a sheet pan, or preparing rice or pasta in a separate pot from the sauce and accompaniments, existing recipes didn't deliver the truly streamlined, one-pan meals they promised. I was determined to deliver the real deal, so I started my recipe development with the most familiar vessel of all: the skillet.

When it comes to skillet suppers, there are the usual suspects—like stir-fries and chicken and rice—but I was on a mission to make one-pan cooking fresh and exciting so I started with something a little more exotic: spanakopita. I set out to convert this traditional Greek spinach pie into a satisfying skillet dinner, using the

SKILLET SPANAKOPITA

vessel to both cook and serve the dish. The crisp phyllo crust was sure to be my greatest challenge, so I decided to settle on the filling first.

Tender spinach and briny feta are the stars of spanakopita, so I made them my first priority. Although fresh spinach is a breeze to work with, thawed frozen spinach tasted just as fresh and eliminated precooking (and any extra pans)—all I had to do was squeeze the already tender leaves to remove excess liquid. I started warming up the spinach by cooking it in butter and then, to infuse this base with complex, authentic flavor, I bloomed minced garlic, nutmeg, and cayenne right among the leaves. I transferred the spinach to a bowl and stirred in some crumbly, briny feta (my tasters preferred freshly crumbled cheese to precrumbled, which had a gritty texture). Eggs bound the filling, but to really boost my spanakopita's creamy, rich quality, I turned to a nontraditional ingredient: whole-milk ricotta cheese. With that final addition, my filling was fragrant, rich, and easy to pull together, but I also wanted to give my weeknight spanakopita some panache. The classic Greek combination of mint and dill offered fresh brightness, and sliced scallions added a touch of oniony bite without overpowering the other flavors. I spread this thick, verdant filling back into my empty skillet, and prepared to tackle the crust.

Using convenient store-bought phyllo was an easy decision, but determining how to incorporate it was another matter. Traditional spanakopita has layers of phyllo on the top and bottom, each sheet being laid down one at a time and brushed with olive oil to help it crisp and brown. This technique seemed entirely too tedious for my simple meal; I instead set out to find an innovative way to speed up the oil coating process without sacrificing any of the appealing browning along the way.

For my first attempt, I tore phyllo into shreds, tossed them in oil, and attempted to place the oiled strips over the surface of the filling. This was a major letdown: The oil dunk made for an uneven coating and caused the phyllo to clump together, producing a floury, starchy topping. Easier? Yes. Better? Not by a long shot. For my next batch, I tried using a lighter touch by spraying each sheet with olive oil spray. Unlike my first attempt, this ensured each sheet was evenly coated with fat, banning those unpleasant starchy bites for good. Working with one coated sheet at a time, I crumpled the phyllo and placed it atop the waiting filling, covering its surface with craggy rosettes.

A mere 25 minutes in the oven produced a perfectly browned crust. I scooped out a portion of the rich spinach pie and was astounded. Not only did it have all the classic flavors of a traditional recipe, but the crumpled phyllo, with its many crags and crannies, was also crispier than any of the layered pies I'd ever tried. The best part? I was left with only a bowl and a skillet to scrub down later.

—STEPHANIE PIXLEY, *America's Test Kitchen Books*

Skillet Spanakopita

SERVES 4

Phyllo dough is also available in larger 18 by 14-inch sheets; if using, cut them in half to make 14 by 9-inch sheets. Don't thaw the phyllo in the microwave; let it sit in the refrigerator overnight or on the counter for 4 to 5 hours. You will need a 10-inch ovensafe nonstick skillet for this recipe.

1	tablespoon unsalted butter
20	ounces frozen chopped spinach, thawed and squeezed dry
¼	teaspoon salt
¼	teaspoon pepper
3	garlic cloves, minced
⅛	teaspoon ground nutmeg
⅛	teaspoon cayenne pepper
8	ounces feta cheese, crumbled (2 cups)
6	ounces (¾ cup) whole-milk ricotta cheese
4	scallions, sliced thin
2	large eggs, lightly beaten
¼	cup minced fresh mint
2	tablespoons minced fresh dill
20	(14 by 9-inch) phyllo sheets, thawed
	Olive oil spray

1. Adjust oven rack to lower-middle position and heat oven to 375 degrees. Melt butter in 10-inch nonstick skillet over medium heat. Add spinach, salt, and pepper and cook until mixture is dry, about 4 minutes. Stir in garlic, nutmeg, and cayenne and cook until fragrant, about 30 seconds. Transfer mixture to large bowl and let cool slightly, about 5 minutes.

2. Stir feta, ricotta, scallions, eggs, mint, and dill into cooled spinach mixture until well combined. Spread mixture evenly into now-empty skillet.

3. Working with 1 sheet phyllo at a time, lay flat on clean counter and spray liberally with oil spray. Crumple oiled phyllo into 2-inch ball and place on top of spinach mixture in skillet.

4. Transfer skillet to oven and bake until phyllo is golden brown and crisp, about 25 minutes, rotating skillet halfway through baking. Remove skillet from oven (skillet handle will be hot). Let cool for 10 minutes before serving.

NOTES FROM THE TEST KITCHEN

TOPPING SPANAKOPITA WITH PHYLLO DOUGH

1. Working with 1 sheet at a time, spray surface of phyllo with oil spray.

2. Using your hands, gently crumple oiled sheet of phyllo into 2-inch ball.

3. Place crumpled phyllo ball on top of spinach mixture.

DOUBLE-CRUST CHICKEN POT PIE

WHY THIS RECIPE WORKS: Chicken pot pie is the perfect all-in-one meal and we had our hearts set on an ambitious double-crust version that towered above the rest. Using a food processor, we created a pie dough enriched with egg and sour cream for a touch of tang. The gravy came together quickly when we softened onion, carrots, and celery in butter before adding flour, broth, and half-and-half to finish it off. Using a shredded rotisserie chicken kept the pie streamlined, and frozen peas offered bursts of sweetness to our supersavory filling. After pouring the filling into a dough-lined pie plate, topping it off with the second crust, and brushing with egg for some appealing luster, we started the pie in a hot oven to rapidly bake the crust. Reducing the temperature to 375 degrees to finish allowed the crust to brown deeply, and letting the pie sit before serving set the filling for tidy slices.

It's hard to imagine anything more comforting than a pot pie: savory chicken and vegetables suspended in a velvety cream gravy and topped with a flaky pie crust. That is, unless you imagine a slice of this rich, savory pie standing tall on a plate, with a second buttery crust underneath.

I started with a favorite test kitchen pie dough, which I bolstered with a beaten egg for richness (and to make it easier to work with), as well as a healthy dose of sour cream to lend it a slightly tangy flavor. The dough came together easily in the food processor and, after a quick knead to bring it all together and an hour-long chill in the fridge, it rolled out easily and neatly on my very lightly floured counter. I was ready to tackle the filling.

I wanted the pie's filling to be satisfying but also simple to make. I sautéed vegetables (onion, carrots, and celery) with butter in a large saucepan, thickened the mixture with a generous sprinkling of flour, and whisked in chicken broth and half-and-half. I cut a potato into tiny cubes and added them to the sauce, where they cooked through in just 8 minutes. After stirring in fresh thyme and some salt and pepper for thorough seasoning, I had a flavorful base ready for cooked chicken.

In the past, we've used many methods for cooking chicken before adding it to pie filling, including poaching, sautéing, and baking. But all of these required additional pots and pans and quite a bit of time—and since this pie was already a project, I wanted an easier route. So I grabbed a grocery store rotisserie chicken, shredded the already-cooked meat—both light and dark—and stirred it into my filling. Not only was this a timesaver, but my filling turned out flavorful and moist.

I spooned the filling into the bottom crust and topped it with the rolled-out top crust before crimping the edges, cutting slits in the top for ventilation, and baking the pie for about 20 minutes at 450 degrees and 15 minutes longer at 375, until the crust was a gorgeous golden brown.

By now, the only trouble I was having was with serving. Whenever I sliced into the pie and lifted out a piece, the piping-hot filling just flowed out. It needed to thicken up.

I was hesitant to increase the amount of flour for fear of turning the silky sauce into glue. I was equally wary of cornstarch. While I considered my options for a spell, the answer revealed itself: Simply letting the fully baked pie rest for 45 minutes gave it time to tighten up and become satisfyingly sliceable. And my crust didn't sog out at all. (Don't worry, it was still warm enough to eat.)

The hardest part of this recipe is waiting for the filling to firm up before slicing and serving the pie. I have no advice to offer other than, "Good luck with that."

—KATIE LEAIRD, *Cook's Country*

Double-Crust Chicken Pot Pie

SERVES 6 TO 8

The pie may seem loose when it comes out of the oven; it will set up as it cools. You can substitute 3 cups of turkey meat for the chicken, if desired.

CRUST

- ½ cup sour cream, chilled
- 1 large egg, lightly beaten
- 2½ cups (12½ ounces) all-purpose flour
- 1½ teaspoons salt
- 12 tablespoons unsalted butter, cut into ½-inch pieces and chilled

FILLING

- 4 tablespoons unsalted butter
- 1 onion, chopped fine
- 2 carrots, peeled and cut into ¼-inch pieces (⅔ cup)
- 2 celery ribs, cut into ¼-inch pieces (½ cup)
- ½ teaspoon salt
- ½ teaspoon pepper
- 6 tablespoons all-purpose flour
- 2¼ cups chicken broth
- ½ cup half-and-half
- 1 small russet potato (6 ounces), peeled and cut into ¼-inch pieces (1 cup)
- 1 teaspoon minced fresh thyme
- 1 (2½-pound) rotisserie chicken, skin and bones discarded, meat shredded into bite-size pieces (3 cups)
- ¾ cup frozen peas
- 1 large egg, lightly beaten

1. FOR THE CRUST: Combine sour cream and egg in bowl. Process flour and salt in food processor until combined, about 3 seconds. Add butter and pulse until only pea-size pieces remain, about 10 pulses. Add half of sour cream mixture and pulse until combined, 5 pulses. Add remaining sour cream mixture and pulse until dough begins to form, about 10 pulses.

2. Transfer mixture to lightly floured counter and knead briefly until dough comes together. Divide dough in half and form each half into 4-inch disk. Wrap disks tightly in plastic wrap and refrigerate for 1 hour. (Wrapped dough can be refrigerated for up to 2 days or frozen for up to 2 months. If frozen, let dough thaw completely on counter before rolling.)

3. Let chilled dough sit on counter to soften slightly, about 10 minutes, before rolling. Roll 1 disk of dough into 12-inch circle on lightly floured counter. Loosely roll dough around rolling pin and gently unroll it onto 9-inch pie plate, letting excess dough hang over edge. Ease dough into plate by gently lifting edge of dough with your hand while pressing into plate bottom with your other hand.

4. Roll other disk of dough into 12-inch circle on lightly floured counter, then transfer to parchment paper–lined baking sheet; cover with plastic. Refrigerate both doughs for 30 minutes.

5. FOR THE FILLING: Meanwhile, adjust oven rack to lowest position and heat oven to 450 degrees. Melt butter in large saucepan over medium heat. Add onion, carrots, celery, salt, and pepper and cook until vegetables begin to soften, about 6 minutes. Add flour and cook, stirring constantly, until golden, 1 to 2 minutes. Slowly stir in broth and half-and-half and bring to boil over medium-high heat.

6. Stir in potato and thyme. Reduce heat to medium and simmer until sauce is thickened and potato is tender, about 8 minutes. Off heat, stir in chicken and peas.

7. Transfer filling to dough-lined pie plate. Loosely roll remaining dough round around rolling pin and gently unroll it onto filling. Trim overhang to ½ inch beyond lip of plate. Pinch edges of top and bottom crusts firmly together. Tuck overhang under itself; folded edge should be flush with edge of plate. Crimp dough evenly around edge of plate using your fingers. Cut four 2-inch slits in top of dough.

8. Brush top of pie with egg. Place pie on rimmed baking sheet. Bake until top is light golden brown, 18 to 20 minutes. Reduce oven temperature to 375 degrees, rotate sheet, and continue to bake until crust is deep golden brown, 12 to 15 minutes longer. Let pie cool on wire rack for at least 45 minutes. Serve.

TO MAKE AHEAD: At end of step 6, transfer filling to bowl and refrigerate until fully chilled, about 1½ hours. Continue with step 7, then wrap pie tightly in plastic wrap and then aluminum foil. Freeze for up to 1 month. When ready to bake, unwrap frozen pie, cover with foil, and place on rimmed baking sheet (do not thaw). Place sheet on middle rack of cold oven and set oven to 375 degrees. Bake for 1¼ hours. Uncover pie and brush with egg. Rotate sheet and continue to bake until crust is golden brown and filling is beginning to bubble up through slits and registers at least 150 degrees, 55 minutes to 1¼ hours longer. Let cool for 45 minutes before serving.

NOTES FROM THE TEST KITCHEN

COOLING BEFORE SLICING

Letting our Double-Crust Chicken Pot Pie cool for at least 45 minutes gives the filling time to firm up just enough to hold together during slicing. (Don't worry, it will still be plenty hot.)

PUB-STYLE STEAK AND ALE PIE

✓ **WHY THIS RECIPE WORKS:** Steak pie is classic British comfort food, and to make ours authentic yet approachable, we kept things simple. First, we skipped the traditional browning of the meat (which had to be done in several time-consuming batches) and browned the mushrooms and onion instead, building a flavorful fond. Adding flour early in the process and limiting the amount of stock we added to the pot meant that the gravy formed as the meat cooked so we could bypass the usual sauce-building steps. To make sure the limited moisture didn't mean limited flavor, we added bacon, garlic, and thyme. We substituted beer for some of the stock and boosted browning with the addition of a small amount of baking soda. Adding egg and sour cream to the dough made it sturdy enough to go over the filling while it was hot, and it baked up flaky yet substantial.

Steak pie in Britain isn't made with what Americans would call "steak" (British cooks use the word "steak" broadly, so it encompasses cuts like chuck and shank), and it often lacks a bottom crust. Some might argue that it's not a pie. But if you get hung up on what steak pie isn't, you'll miss out on what it is: a powerful, delicious antidote to spring's last chilly days.

Here's how most versions come together: Brown the meat, usually with onion and maybe bacon or mushrooms. Braise it in stock and perhaps beer for several hours, and then thicken the liquid to a gravy consistency. Transfer the filling to a pie plate and let it cool before topping it with pastry and baking it until the crust is crisp.

About that optional bottom crust: There's no denying the heft of a meat-only pie, so I endorse skipping it. That also means a bit of time saved, though even without it most of the steak pie recipes I saw seemed too involved. Surely I could do something about that.

My first timesaving move was to opt for boneless short ribs. They offer good beefy flavor, cook relatively quickly, and require little trimming. After cutting 3 pounds of short ribs into ¾-inch chunks, I realized that searing them would be problematic. Even after dividing the meat into three batches, there wasn't enough room in the pot for proper browning; the meat

PUB-STYLE STEAK AND ALE PIE

steamed. I pressed on. I sautéed an onion and 4 ounces of mushrooms until they were tender before returning the beef to the pot and adding 4 cups of broth. This was less than I'd seen in other recipes, but adding less liquid to begin with would mean less time spent reducing it on the back end; eventually I hoped to eliminate that tiresome step altogether. When it all came to a simmer, I covered the pot and transferred it to a 350-degree oven. While the filling cooked, I mixed up a half batch of the pie dough I use for fruit pies and put it in the fridge.

In less than 1½ hours, the beef was tender. I fished it out with a slotted spoon and transferred it to a pie plate; I then reduced the cooking liquid to 2 cups. It was still too thin, so I whisked in a *beurre manié*, a paste of raw flour and butter, to thicken it. I poured the hot gravy over the meat and rolled out the dough.

Most recipes recommend letting the filling cool before topping it with the dough, but since I was trying to streamline, I went for it. Not a good idea. The buttery, moist dough melted as I fluted the edges of the pie, and it turned to mush in the oven.

It was a modest first attempt. The beef was meltingly tender, but the gravy was pale and tasted flat. I identified the lack of fond and the smaller portion of beef stock as the culprits, and that second problem was especially worrisome: I'd have to decrease the liquid even further if I wanted to skip the reducing and thickening steps, but how could I do that without losing even more flavor? And clearly the crust needed work.

I decided to skip the fussy searing step and boost meaty flavor with a couple of slices of bacon and a full pound of glutamate-rich mushrooms. When the mushrooms had released most of their juices, I added the onion along with garlic and thyme. The heady aroma was encouraging, considering I hadn't added the beef,

but even more encouraging was the fond that began to form. I let it get really brown, and then I added flour, which I hoped would sufficiently thicken the gravy as the meat cooked, allowing me to skip both the beurre manié and the reducing step at the end.

Next I deglazed the pan with ¼ cup of beef stock, and when the fond lifted, I added ¾ cup of beer for more complexity. I opted for a straightforward ale (I grabbed a Newcastle), which would boost flavor without being obtrusive. Then I added the rest of the beef stock, a mere 1½ cups this time.

Before adding the beef, I decided to use the test kitchen's trick of tossing it with a little baking soda (diluted with water). We typically do this because baking soda changes the meat's pH and makes it more tender. The meat in my previous pie was plenty tender, but the higher pH would also boost browning, deepening the color and flavor of my gravy.

Worried that some of the limited moisture would evaporate before the meat cooked, I covered the Dutch oven with foil before putting on the lid and moving the pot to the oven. After 1 hour, I stirred the meat. It was almost tender, but the cooking liquid was still a little thin, so I replaced the lid but not the foil and returned the pot to the oven for 30 minutes more. After a total of 1½ hours of oven time, the meat was beautifully tender and the gravy was a deep, glossy brown, thick enough to coat the meat generously—no reducing or thickening required. And the fond, extra mushrooms, beer, thyme, and garlic had done wonders for the flavor. It was time for the crust.

The test kitchen's Foolproof Pie Dough is my go-to for fruit pie, but its high moisture and fat content made it too soft to place on a warm filling. For a dough that was sturdy yet flaky, I chose a dough we've used for chicken pot pie that includes an egg for strength; it also substitutes sour cream for some of the fat. Less butter meant less fat that would melt with heat, so I was able to place this dough on the warm filling with no problems. And how did it bake? Beautifully. The edge held its attractive crispness, and the crust was flaky but substantial. Now that I've got this recipe in my back pocket, I'm looking forward to the next chilly day.

—ANDREA GEARY, *Cook's Illustrated*

NOTES FROM THE TEST KITCHEN

PICKING THE BEST ALE FOR PIE
For the broadest appeal, English pale and brown ales worked best in our Pub-Style Steak and Ale Pie. Bitter, hoppy, or floral beers were too pronounced, while American lagers were barely noticeable.

Pub-Style Steak and Ale Pie

SERVES 6

Don't substitute bone-in short ribs; their yield is too variable. Instead, use a 4-pound chuck-eye roast, well trimmed of fat. Use a good-quality beef broth for this recipe; the test kitchen's favorite is Better Than Bouillon Roasted Beef Base. If you don't have a deep-dish pie plate, use an 8 by 8-inch baking dish and roll the pie dough into a 10-inch square. We prefer pale and brown ales for this recipe.

FILLING

- **3** tablespoons water
- **½** teaspoon baking soda
- **3** pounds boneless beef short ribs, trimmed and cut into ¾-inch chunks
- **½** teaspoon salt
- **½** teaspoon pepper
- **2** slices bacon, chopped
- **1** pound cremini mushrooms, trimmed and halved if medium or quartered if large
- **1½** cups beef broth
- **1** large onion, chopped
- **1** garlic clove, minced
- **½** teaspoon dried thyme
- **¼** cup all-purpose flour
- **¾** cup beer

CRUST

- **1** large egg, lightly beaten
- **¼** cup sour cream, chilled
- **1¼** cups (6¼ ounces) all-purpose flour
- **½** teaspoon salt
- **6** tablespoons unsalted butter, cut into ½-inch pieces and chilled

1. FOR THE FILLING: Combine water and baking soda in large bowl. Add beef, salt, and pepper and toss to combine. Adjust oven rack to lower-middle position and heat oven to 350 degrees.

2. Cook bacon in large Dutch oven over high heat, stirring occasionally, until partially rendered but not browned, about 3 minutes. Add mushrooms and ¼ cup broth and stir to coat. Cover and cook, stirring occasionally, until mushrooms are reduced to about half their original volume, about 5 minutes. Add onion, garlic, and thyme and cook, uncovered, stirring occasionally, until onion is softened and fond begins to form on bottom of pot, 3 to 5 minutes. Sprinkle flour over mushroom mixture and stir until all flour is moistened. Cook, stirring occasionally, until fond is deep brown, 2 to 4 minutes. Stir in beer and remaining 1¼ cups broth, scraping up any browned bits. Stir in beef and bring to simmer, pressing as much beef as possible below surface of liquid. Cover pot tightly with aluminum foil, then lid; transfer to oven. Cook for 1 hour.

3. Remove lid and discard foil. Stir filling, cover, return to oven, and continue to cook until beef is tender and liquid is thick enough to coat beef, 15 to 30 minutes longer. Transfer filling to deep-dish pie plate. (Once cool, filling can be covered with plastic wrap and refrigerated for up to 2 days.) Increase oven temperature to 400 degrees.

4. FOR THE CRUST: While filling is cooking, measure out 2 tablespoons beaten egg and set aside. Whisk remaining egg and sour cream together in bowl. Process flour and salt in food processor until combined, about 3 seconds. Add butter and pulse until only pea-size pieces remain, about 10 pulses. Add half of sour cream mixture and pulse until combined, about 5 pulses. Add remaining sour cream mixture and pulse until dough begins to form, about 10 pulses. Transfer mixture to lightly floured counter and knead briefly until dough comes together. Form into 4-inch disk, wrap in plastic, and refrigerate for at least 1 hour or up to 2 days.

5. Roll dough into 11-inch round on lightly floured counter. Using knife or 1-inch round biscuit cutter, cut round from center of dough. Drape dough over filling (it's OK if filling is hot). Trim overhang to ½ inch beyond lip of plate. Tuck overhang under itself; folded edge should be flush with edge of plate. Crimp dough evenly around edge of plate using your fingers or press with tines of fork to seal. Brush crust with reserved egg. Place pie on rimmed baking sheet. Bake until filling is bubbling and crust is deep golden brown and crisp, 25 to 30 minutes. (If filling has been refrigerated, increase baking time by 15 minutes and cover with foil for last 15 minutes to prevent overbrowning.) Let cool for 10 minutes before serving.

MEATBALLS AND MARINARA

✓ **WHY THIS RECIPE WORKS:** We wanted to use our food processor to make the ultimate meatball, with all the rich flavor and tender texture you can get only from the perfect cut of meat. A 2:1 ratio of steak tips to short ribs produced meatballs with beefy, unctuous flavor. We chilled the meat in the freezer before processing to prevent it from turning pasty, and treating it with a small amount of baking soda allowed us to cut back on the milk–bread crumb panade. The end result? Even meatier meatballs. Roasting our big batch of meatballs all at once in a hot oven kept the cooking hands-off while still producing a nice browned crust. A simmer in a quick homemade tomato sauce offered the perfect finish.

Spaghetti and meatballs are my kind of comfort food. The tender, seasoned bites of meat bathed in bright marinara sauce instantly transport me back to lazy Sunday suppers with family—the kinds of happy memories that prompt me to pull out my pasta pot whenever company is coming. I thought nothing could top the ease and richness of the test kitchen's standby recipe, which calls for kneading a milk–bread crumb panade into ground beef and sweet Italian sausage; the classic combination of Parmesan, parsley, and garlic rounds out the flavors. However, I then tasted a burger made with sirloin steak tips ground at home using a food processor. Unlike patties made with store-bought ground beef, this burger was incredibly meaty and juicy, and it made me wonder if my favorite meatballs would see similar improvements with freshly ground meat. I couldn't wait to find out.

No matter the protein or flavor profile, there are a few meatball rules that the test kitchen nearly always follows. First: Use a panade. This mixture of bread and liquid (usually milk) keeps the meatballs juicy; without this key component, the meatballs inevitably turn out disappointingly dry and crumbly. Second: Don't be afraid of seasoning. Even the most flavorful cut of beef can benefit from a handful of spices, some grated Parmesan, or fresh herbs. And third: Incorporate more than one cut of meat. Whether it's using store-bought meatloaf mix (a mixture of beef, pork, and veal) or starting with two different meats and kneading them together, combining different cuts is beneficial

for both flavor and structure. With these tenets in mind, I made it my goal to use my food processor to turn out the best meatballs I'd ever tasted.

That ground-sirloin burger had really knocked my socks off, so I started out with sirloin tips. For my first attempt, I pulsed some hefty chunks in the food processor and instantly saw the error in my ways: The meat had quickly turned pasty, no better than store-bought ground meat. In order to get a really superior texture, I'd need the steak to hold up a little better against the blade, so for my next batch, I cut the steak into ½-inch pieces just as before, but this time I put them in the freezer long enough to firm them up. When I pulsed the chilled meat, the blade chopped rather than pulverized it, leaving me with supremely tender beef.

Before I traveled too far down the ground sirloin path, I decided to introduce a second cut of meat to really heighten the meatballs' flavor. I ran a few tests, working in everything from chuck steak to country-style ribs. When my tasters and I tested out these plain-and-simple batches, our preference was obvious: Even without seasoning, the meaty, indulgent flavor of beef short ribs was the hands-down winner. This juicy cut promised just the right amount of moisture needed to keep the meatballs tender, while the lean steak tips maintained some structure. With that, I readied my next batch, cutting up and chilling my two cuts of beef.

I wanted to keep this recipe efficient, so I used the chilling time to pull together an easy marinara sauce. The food processor was already shaping up to be the hero of this recipe, so I used it to pulse onions, garlic, oregano, and pepper flakes, creating an evenly mixed marinara sauce base. After softening the onion mixture in a skillet, I reserved some of the base as a flavorful mix-in for the meatballs and worked the rest into a simple stovetop sauce. I deepened the sauce's base with tomato paste and dry red wine before adding in water and canned crushed tomatoes. I let this bright, fragrant sauce simmer away while I turned my attention back to the meatballs.

Even with juicy short ribs in the mix, a panade was a must, so I mashed torn bread slices with milk and kneaded the mixture into the freshly ground beef. I planned on making a couple dozen meatballs at once, so I baked this batch on a wire rack–lined baking sheet (our go-to method for browning meatballs en masse).

MEATBALLS AND MARINARA

These meatballs emerged deeply browned but disappointingly soggy. The moisture-boosting panade had apparently worked against me. Distressed, I consulted some of my fellow test cooks and learned that I'd been underestimating my home-ground beef. While supermarket ground beef tends to be overprocessed and therefore demands lots of moisture-boosting panade to compensate, my food processor–ground meat had retained more of its natural moisture, meaning I could scale back my panade. Another colleague suggested incorporating baking soda for extra tenderizing insurance, as it prevents the proteins from bonding. I heeded her advice as well and began again.

Since I was already using my food processor, I decided to use it to whir together the panade's fixings. This made quick work of my panade: I simply tore apart some slices of bread and quickly pulsed them together with the milk. I kept the flavors decidedly Italian-inspired, adding Parmesan, fresh parsley, and my reserved onion mixture, plus two eggs for just the right amount of binding. I kneaded the speedy panade and a teaspoon of baking soda into the waiting ground beef, rolled the mixture into balls, and baked them. After just 20 minutes in the oven, these meatballs emerged beautifully browned and, at last, perfectly tender. Finished off in the simmering sauce, the meatballs boosted my simple pantry marinara's taste tenfold, giving it meaty depth in no time.

Spooned over a heaping plate of spaghetti, my upgraded meatballs and marinara were a real step up from my old favorites.

—SARA MAYER, *America's Test Kitchen Books*

Meatballs and Marinara

**MAKES 24 MEATBALLS AND ABOUT 14 CUPS SAUCE,
ENOUGH FOR 2 POUNDS PASTA**

Sirloin steak tips are often sold as flap meat. We prefer using a mix of steak tips and short ribs in this recipe; however, you can use all steak tips, if desired. To save time, prepare the other ingredients while the beef is in the freezer.

MEATBALLS

2 pounds sirloin steak tips, trimmed and cut into ½-inch pieces
1 pound boneless beef short ribs, trimmed and cut into ½-inch pieces
1 teaspoon baking soda
2 slices hearty white sandwich bread, torn into 1-inch pieces
2 large eggs
2 ounces Parmesan cheese, grated (1 cup)
½ cup fresh parsley leaves
¼ cup milk
2 teaspoons salt

SAUCE

3 onions, cut into 1-inch pieces
8 garlic cloves, peeled and smashed
1 tablespoon dried oregano
¾ teaspoon red pepper flakes
¼ cup extra-virgin olive oil
1 (6-ounce) can tomato paste
1 cup dry red wine
1 cup water
4 (28-ounce) cans crushed tomatoes
   Salt and pepper
¼ cup minced fresh basil

1. FOR THE MEATBALLS: Toss steak tips and short ribs together in rimmed baking sheet and spread into single layer. Freeze until very firm and starting to harden around edges but still pliable, about 45 minutes.

2. FOR THE SAUCE: Meanwhile, pulse onions, garlic, oregano, and pepper flakes in food processor until finely chopped, about 10 pulses. Heat oil in Dutch oven over medium heat until shimmering. Add onion mixture and cook until softened and lightly browned, 10 to 15 minutes. Set aside half of onion mixture for meatballs.

3. Stir tomato paste into remaining onion mixture and cook over medium heat until fragrant, about 1 minute. Stir in wine, scraping up any browned bits, and cook until slightly thickened, about 2 minutes. Stir in water, tomatoes, and 1 teaspoon salt. Bring to simmer and cook until sauce is no longer watery, 45 minutes to 1 hour.

4. Meanwhile, adjust oven rack to upper-middle position and heat oven to 475 degrees. Set wire rack in aluminum foil–lined rimmed baking sheet and spray with vegetable oil spray. Sprinkle baking soda evenly over beef. Working in 6 batches, pulse beef in now-empty food processor until finely ground into 1/16-inch pieces, about 20 pulses, stopping to redistribute meat as needed; transfer to large bowl.

5. Process bread, eggs, Parmesan, parsley, milk, salt, and remaining onion mixture in again-empty processor until smooth, about 20 seconds, scraping down sides of bowl as needed. Transfer bread mixture to bowl with beef and knead with your hands until well combined.

6. Pinch off and roll beef mixture into 2-inch meatballs (you should have 24 meatballs), place on prepared rack, and bake until well browned, about 20 minutes. Transfer meatballs to pot with sauce and simmer for 15 minutes. Stir in basil and season with salt and pepper to taste. Serve. (Meatballs and marinara can be refrigerated for up to 3 days or frozen for up to 1 month.)

GRILLED FROZEN STEAKS

✔ **WHY THIS RECIPE WORKS:** Rather than follow the convention of thawing frozen steaks before grilling them, we discovered that we could get perfectly cooked steaks by cooking them straight from the freezer, no planning ahead required. A big challenge was choosing the right type of steak: It had to be flavorful since a marinade or spice rub wasn't an option, and it had to be thick so the interior wouldn't overcook while the exterior browned. We found that 1½-inch-thick rib eyes or New York strips were perfect. We started them over a hot fire to develop a distinct crust on both sides, seasoning with salt and pepper after each flip, and then we slid them to the cooler side of the grill to reach the desired internal temperature.

I recently watched in disbelief as a fellow test cook took a rock-hard steak from the freezer and clunked it into a screaming-hot skillet. I'm all for questioning conventional wisdom, but really—could this possibly end well?

He seared the steak until it was well browned, about 90 seconds on each side, and then transferred it to the oven for 20 minutes to finish cooking. After letting it rest briefly, he sliced it. It was perfect. The exterior had developed an impressive sear while the super-chilled interior was resistant to overcooking, so the meat within was juicy and rosy from edge to edge.

The approach is clever, and skipping the thawing step is certainly appealing for those of us who like to keep steaks on hand in the freezer. But the prospect of a perfectly cooked steak, even one that is really convenient to make, isn't quite enough to induce me to fire up both an oven and a stovetop skillet on a hot summer evening. So what about adapting the technique for the grill?

I knew from the outset that I'd use a two-level fire. The hotter side of the grill would stand in for the skillet; I'd cook my steak there until it was deeply browned all over. The cooler side of the grill would play the part of the oven, where the interior of the steak would come up to temperature more slowly. If I could make it work, I'd happily stock my freezer with steaks so I could grill them on the spur of the moment—with no forethought about thawing them—all summer long.

But before I focused on perfecting my grilling method, I'd have to decide what kind of steak to use. My colleague had done his indoor testing with thick-cut steaks (think rib eye and strip), so I'd certainly test those. But thin, quick-cooking flank and skirt steaks are favorites on the grill, so I wanted to give them a try, too. I froze my assortment of steaks overnight until they were solid.

I started by grilling the flank and skirt steaks, and I quickly learned an important lesson: Searing in a hot skillet is very different from cooking on a grill. The browning step took three times longer on the grill than it had in my colleague's skillet. That's because the radiant energy of the average grill isn't nearly as focused or efficient as the conductive energy of a heated skillet.

The longer period over high heat on the grill meant that these thinner steaks thawed quickly, and the interiors overcooked by the time the exteriors were properly charred. The flavor was also a bit lackluster. I usually apply a spice rub to flank steak before grilling, but applying a rub or even just salt and pepper to a frozen steak is like seasoning a brick: Everything bounces right off.

Though somewhat discouraging, these initial results actually made me hopeful about my chances with the thicker steaks. Rib-eye and strip steaks taste great with very little embellishment—there's no need for a spice-heavy rub—so a bit of salt and pepper sprinkled on as the steaks thawed on the grill would probably be sufficient. And at about 1½ inches thick, these steaks would be less vulnerable to overcooking.

I put my frozen rib-eye and strip steaks on the grill, first cooking them over the hotter side until they were nicely charred, about 7 minutes per side, and then sliding them over to the cooler side. At that point the internal temperature was a reassuring 70 degrees—no overcooking here.

After about 12 minutes over indirect heat, the temperature had risen to 115 degrees, so I took the steaks off the grill and let them rest before slicing them. These steaks were perfect: crusty and charred on the outside yet still pink and juicy inside, with a big beefy flavor that needed nothing else. Best of all, they had taken less than 30 minutes to go from freezer to serving platter.

To make the most of my summery grilled steak, I also paired it with an Italian-style dinner salad. I sliced the steaks, shingled the slices on a platter, and topped them with arugula dressed with lemony vinaigrette and studded with shards of salty Parmesan. I sprinkled more Parmesan on top, and I was done in less than 40 minutes. From now on, I'll definitely be stocking my freezer so I can grill a steak whenever the urge strikes.

—ANDREA GEARY, *Cook's Illustrated*

Grilled Frozen Steaks

SERVES 4

Do not substitute thinner steaks for the thick-cut steaks called for in this recipe. Thinner steaks cannot be grilled successfully when taken directly from the freezer.

- **2 (1-pound) frozen boneless strip or rib-eye steaks, 1½ inches thick, trimmed**
- **Kosher salt and pepper**

1A. FOR A CHARCOAL GRILL: Open bottom vent completely. Light large chimney starter mounded with charcoal briquettes (7 quarts). When top coals are partially covered with ash, pour evenly over half of grill. Set cooking grate in place, cover, and open lid vent completely. Heat grill until hot, about 5 minutes.

1B. FOR A GAS GRILL: Turn all burners to high, cover, and heat grill until hot, about 15 minutes. Leave primary burner on high and turn off other burner(s).

2. Clean and oil cooking grate. Place steaks on hotter side of grill and cook (covered if using gas) until browned and charred on first side, 5 to 7 minutes. Flip steaks, season with salt and pepper, and cook until browned and charred on second side, 5 to 7 minutes. Flip steaks, season with salt and pepper, and move to cooler side of grill, arranging so steaks are about 6 inches from heat source. Continue to cook until meat registers 115 to 120 degrees (for rare) or 120 to 125 degrees (for medium-rare), 10 to 15 minutes longer. Transfer steaks to wire rack set in rimmed baking sheet and let rest for 5 minutes before serving.

VARIATION

Grilled Frozen Steaks with Arugula and Parmesan
SERVES 4 TO 6

Use the large holes of a box grater to shred the Parmesan.

- **1 recipe Grilled Frozen Steaks**
- **6 tablespoons extra-virgin olive oil**
- **2 tablespoons lemon juice, plus lemon wedges for serving**
- **¾ teaspoon salt**
- **¼ teaspoon pepper**
- **8 ounces (8 cups) baby arugula**
- **2 ounces Parmesan cheese, shredded (⅔ cup)**

Slice steaks thin against grain. Fan slices on either side of large platter. Whisk oil, lemon juice, salt, and pepper together in large bowl. Add arugula and three-quarters of Parmesan and toss to combine. Arrange arugula down center of platter, allowing it to overlap steak. Sprinkle remaining Parmesan over steak and arugula. Serve with lemon wedges.

GRILLED BONELESS SHORT RIBS

✔ **WHY THIS RECIPE WORKS:** To get tender, smoky boneless short ribs with great charred flavor and juicy interiors, we set up the grill with two heat zones: one hotter, one cooler. To render the short ribs' excess fat while building deep smoky flavor, we started them on the cooler side of the grill, positioned over a smoking wood chip packet and covered to trap the smoke. We then moved the ribs over to the hotter side to deeply sear them. To cut the ribs' richness, we served them with a bold sauce based on Argentinian *criolla*: We cooked sweet red bell pepper with red onion, garlic, paprika, cumin, and cayenne and then added cilantro and lemon juice for a fresh finish.

Layered with fat and ribboned with bands of chewy cartilage, boneless English-style short ribs are not a common choice for grilling in America. We typically use low-and-slow cooking methods, like braising, to unlock this cut's rich flavor.

But in Argentina, where beef is king and grilling is an art form, boneless hunks of short rib are cooked over hardwood coals to a rosy medium-rare. Sliced thin and served with a tangy herb sauce or piquant pepper relish, the ribs take top billing at the *churrascaria*. I wanted to help us get into the action up here in North America.

I prepared a handful of existing recipes to help set my course and was knocked sideways by the results. The best of the bunch produced juicy ribs with a deep, meaty savor rivaling that of the best—and most expensive—steaks I have tasted. Unfortunately, producing ribs that were an even medium-rare—and weren't scorched by flare-ups—required frequent flipping and steady supervision. There had to be an easier way.

Technically speaking, "short rib" is a vague name applied to ribs taken from three locations along the cow's rib cage, each exhibiting slightly different thickness and attributes. The thickest, leanest, beefiest of the bunch are referred to as "chuck" short ribs, and when I grilled all three styles the chuck ribs won handily. Consult your butcher if necessary; otherwise, look for the thickest ribs available and trim away the exterior membrane and fat before cooking.

I thought it best to treat the ribs like a thick steak, for which there are two prevailing—and opposing—cooking methods: sear quickly on the hotter side of the grill to develop a crust and then finish on the cooler side, or flip the script and cook them through slowly on the cooler side before finishing on the hotter side to develop a crust. In this case, the first method yielded beautifully browned ribs that, once sliced, revealed a band of well-done meat encircling rare meat—and way too much thick, unrendered fat. The latter method came closer but still featured too much fat.

I needed to cook the ribs as slowly as I could, rendering as much fat as possible, before browning them quickly over a very hot fire. To that end, I piled all the coals on one side of the grill and cooked the ribs on the opposite side with the grill covered (essentially, grill roasting) before sliding them over the hot coals to finish. The method produced passable results, but covering the grill quashed much of the coals' heat, making it nearly impossible to create a crust without overcooking the meat.

I turned to a favorite test kitchen trick, capping the ribs with a disposable aluminum roasting pan and waiting patiently for any sign that the meat was cooking. Apparently, there simply wasn't enough heat for this method to work. But after tinkering, it did work when I spread a single thin layer of coals beneath the ribs (piling the majority of coals on the opposite side); the ribs cooked through and rendered their fat, ready for the hot sear.

These ribs were the best to date—evenly cooked, richly browned, and free of gnarly fat chunks—though I wanted a smokier flavor in the meat. This proved easy to do: I slid a foil packet filled with soaked wood chips beneath the ribs during the first step. The disposable pan captured the upwelling smoke, bathing the meat in its flavors. (As an added benefit, the foil packet shielded the coals from the dripping fat, reducing flare-ups).

The ribs tasted terrific on their own, though I still wanted a quick-and-easy accompaniment to cut the richness. An Argentine-style *criolla* sauce of minced raw onion, sweet bell pepper, garlic, olive oil, and vinegar tasted good, albeit a bit raw. I much preferred the blend once I sautéed the ingredients and rounded it out with pungent cumin, fresh cilantro, and spicy

GRILLED BONELESS SHORT RIBS WITH ARGENTINE-STYLE PEPPER SAUCE

cayenne pepper and substituted lemon juice for the vinegar. Welcome to America, grilled short ribs. There's plenty of room at the table.

—MATTHEW CARD, *Cook's Country*

Grilled Boneless Short Ribs with Argentine-Style Pepper Sauce

SERVES 4 TO 6

The thickness and marbling of boneless short ribs can vary a good deal. Look for lean ribs cut from the chuck. If in doubt, ask your butcher for the cut by its technical designation: NAMP 130A. If you need to buy bone-in English-style ribs, slice off the ribs, cartilage, and excess fat. If your short ribs are a single slab, cut them into 2- to 3-inch-wide strips. Plan ahead: The salted short ribs need to sit for at least an hour before grilling.

2½–3	pounds boneless beef short ribs, 1½ to 2 inches thick, 2 inches wide, and 4 to 5 inches long, trimmed
	Kosher salt and pepper
1½	cups wood chips
½	cup finely chopped red bell pepper
⅓	cup finely chopped red onion
¼	cup extra-virgin olive oil
3	garlic cloves, minced
1	teaspoon paprika
½	teaspoon ground cumin
¼	teaspoon cayenne pepper
⅓	cup minced fresh cilantro
2	tablespoons lemon juice
1	(13 by 9-inch) disposable aluminum roasting pan (if using charcoal)

1. Pat beef dry with paper towels and sprinkle all over with 1 tablespoon salt. Let sit at room temperature for at least 1 hour before grilling. Just before grilling, soak wood chips in water for 15 minutes, then drain.

2. Meanwhile, combine bell pepper, onion, oil, garlic, paprika, cumin, cayenne, and ½ teaspoon salt in small saucepan. Cook over medium-high heat until vegetables are softened, about 5 minutes. Remove from heat and stir in cilantro and lemon juice. Transfer to bowl and set aside.

3A. FOR A CHARCOAL GRILL: Using large piece of heavy-duty aluminum foil, wrap soaked chips in 12 by 10-inch foil packet. (Make sure chips do not poke holes in sides or bottom of packet.) Cut 3 evenly spaced 2-inch slits in top of packet. Open bottom vent completely. Light large chimney starter mounded with charcoal briquettes (7 quarts). When top coals are partially covered with ash, pour two-thirds evenly over half of grill, then pour remaining coals over other half of grill. Place wood chip packet on smaller pile of coals, set cooking grate in place, cover, and open lid vent completely. Heat grill until hot and wood chips are smoking, about 5 minutes.

3B. FOR A GAS GRILL: Using large piece of heavy-duty aluminum foil, wrap soaked chips in 8 by 4½-inch foil packet. (Make sure chips do not poke holes in sides or bottom of packet.) Cut 2 evenly spaced 2-inch slits in top of packet. Remove cooking grate and place wood chip packet directly on primary burner. Set grate in place, turn all burners to high, cover, and heat grill until hot and wood chips are smoking, about 15 minutes. Turn primary burner to medium and secondary burner(s) to medium-high.

4. Clean and oil cooking grate. Season beef with pepper. Place beef on grill directly over foil packet. Cover beef with disposable pan if using charcoal (if using gas, close lid) and cook for 5 minutes. Flip beef and cook 5 minutes longer, covering in same manner.

5. Slide beef to hotter side of grill and cook, covered if using gas, until well browned on all sides and beef registers 125 degrees, 4 to 8 minutes, turning often. Transfer beef to carving board, tent with foil, and let rest for 10 minutes. Slice beef against grain as thin as possible. Serve with pepper sauce.

NOTES FROM THE TEST KITCHEN

SLICING SHORT RIBS

Cutting meat perpendicular to the grain creates a tender texture, but when the direction of the grain isn't obvious, make a test slice. If you've cut parallel to the grain, turn the meat 90 degrees before cutting again.

POMEGRANATE-BRAISED BEEF SHORT RIBS

✔ **WHY THIS RECIPE WORKS:** This braise takes its cue from a popular pairing in Moroccan tagines: tender beef and sweet, tangy prunes. Short ribs offered intense, beefy flavor, and we started by roasting them in the oven; this step enabled us to render and discard a significant amount of fat before braising. Using pomegranate juice as the braising liquid gave our sauce the perfect touch of tartness to balance the meatiness of the beef and the sweetness of the prunes. *Ras el hanout*, a complex blend of warm Moroccan spices, added a pleasing, piquant aroma. After braising, we defatted the cooking liquid and then blended it with the vegetables and some of the prunes to create a velvety sauce. We added the remaining prunes to the sauce for pops of sweetness and garnished with sesame seeds and cilantro.

I love rich, meaty braised short ribs, and while Western approaches often derive their depth from red wine and fragrant herbs like thyme and bay leaf, home cooks across the Mediterranean defer to dried fruits and spice blends for complexity in their braises. I wanted to apply this approach to my next short rib feast, and considering that meat is rarely the center of the meal in that region's cuisine, I knew I needed this dish to be exceptional enough for a special occasion.

Braises are tailor-made for turning tough cuts of meat tender through extended low-and-slow cooking, and bone-in beef short ribs are far and away my favorite cut for this technique. To infuse this indulgent cut with a new range of flavors, I looked to Moroccan tagines (stews slow-cooked in covered earthenware pots) for inspiration. Unlike the wallop of richness in many of my favorite braises, tagines are a study in contrasts, boasting layers of sweetness, tang, and warmth. One traditional pairing really sparked my interest: beef and prunes. Slow-cooked along with the beef, the juicy prunes promised bright, fruity sweetness to complement the indulgent meat. I loved this idea, and to make sure the prunes' impact wasn't so subtle as to be drowned out, I decided I'd back them up with another sweet-tart ingredient common in North Africa: pomegranate juice. Puckery and bright, a few cups of this deep red juice would be just the reinforcement I needed. Last, to incorporate that critical layer of warm spice, I would add *ras el hanout*. This spice blend is a staple in Moroccan cooking, and while products in the supermarket were passable, I was pleased to learn that I could just as easily prepare my own by combining a handful of spices I already had in my pantry, like coriander, cumin, nutmeg, and cinnamon. Between the mellow, rich sweetness of the prunes, the brightness of the pomegranate juice, and the complexity of my homemade ras el hanout, I knew I was on track to have the nuanced sauce I wanted, so I moved on to determine my cooking technique.

Hoping to extract as much beefy flavor as possible, I began by browning the short ribs in a Dutch oven, working in batches to prevent overcrowding. After a few rounds of browning and discarding the rendered fat, I decided that this approach was too fussy. I traded my Dutch oven for a roomier option—a roasting pan—and this time was able to brown and render fat from all of the ribs at once in the oven. As an added bonus, this method was hands-off and far less messy. When I finally poured off the fat, I discovered that the ribs had left behind a generous amount of fond, the perfect starting place for my sauce. I deglazed the pan with pomegranate juice, scraped the browned bits into the sweet-tart liquid, and thinned it out with water to tame its intensity. Tempted as I was to finish building the sauce in the roasting pan, I enlisted my Dutch oven here so I could fully submerge the ribs using less braising liquid.

After softening some aromatics in oil and blooming my superfragrant homemade ras el hanout, I poured in the pomegranate-fond mixture, dropped in some halved prunes, nestled in the ribs, and brought everything to a simmer before covering the Dutch oven and transferring it to a 300-degree oven. From there, the beefy ribs gradually turned meltingly tender and what emerged was a rich, rustic braise, but the braising liquid hadn't quite turned into the lush sauce I'd wanted. Rather than dilute my dish's signature flavors with an outside thickener, I defatted the thin liquid and gave it a spin in a blender along with the strained solids before returning it to a simmer, adding in a few more sweet, succulent prunes and returning the ribs to the pot. This subtly thickened sauce napped the ribs perfectly, and a hit of vinegar gave it some welcome brightness.

These tagine-inspired short ribs had it all—richness and brightness, sweetness and tartness—and, after a sprinkling of sesame seeds and fresh cilantro, they proved an elegant, occasion-worthy dish.

—NICOLE KONSTANTINAKOS,
America's Test Kitchen Books

Pomegranate-Braised Beef Short Ribs with Prunes and Sesame

SERVES 6 TO 8

Short ribs come in two styles: English-style ribs contain a single rib bone and a thick piece of meat. Flanken-style ribs are cut thinner and have several smaller bones. While either will work here, we prefer the less expensive and more readily available English-style ribs. If using flanken-style ribs, flip the ribs halfway through roasting in step 1. We prefer to use our Ras el Hanout (recipe follows), but you can substitute store-bought ras el hanout if you wish, though flavor and spiciness can vary greatly by brand.

- 4 **pounds bone-in English-style short ribs, trimmed**
  Salt and pepper
- 4 **cups unsweetened pomegranate juice**
- 1 **cup water**
- 2 **tablespoons extra-virgin olive oil**
- 1 **onion, chopped fine**
- 1 **carrot, peeled and chopped fine**
- 2 **tablespoons ras el hanout**
- 4 **garlic cloves, minced**
- ¾ **cup prunes, halved**
- 1 **tablespoon red wine vinegar**
- 2 **tablespoons toasted sesame seeds**
- 2 **tablespoons chopped fresh cilantro**

1. Adjust oven rack to lower-middle position and heat oven to 450 degrees. Pat short ribs dry with paper towels and season with salt and pepper. Arrange ribs bone side down in single layer in large roasting pan and roast until meat begins to brown, about 45 minutes.

2. Discard any accumulated fat and juices in pan and continue to roast until meat is well browned, 15 to 20 minutes. Transfer ribs to bowl and tent loosely with aluminum foil; set aside. Stir pomegranate juice and water into pan, scraping up any browned bits; set aside.

3. Reduce oven temperature to 300 degrees. Heat oil in Dutch oven over medium heat until shimmering. Add onion, carrot, and ¼ teaspoon salt and cook until softened, about 5 minutes. Stir in ras el hanout and garlic and cook until fragrant, about 30 seconds.

4. Stir in pomegranate mixture from roasting pan and half of prunes and bring to simmer. Nestle short ribs bone side up into pot and bring to simmer. Cover,

transfer pot to oven, and cook until ribs are tender and fork slips easily in and out of meat, about 2½ hours.

5. Transfer short ribs to bowl, discard any loose bones, and tent loosely with aluminum foil. Strain braising liquid through fine-mesh strainer into fat separator; transfer solids to blender. Let braising liquid settle for 5 minutes, then pour defatted liquid into blender with solids and process until smooth, about 1 minute.

6. Transfer sauce to now-empty pot and stir in vinegar and remaining prunes. Return short ribs and any accumulated juices to pot, bring to gentle simmer over medium heat, and cook, spooning sauce over ribs occasionally, until heated through, about 5 minutes. Season with salt and pepper to taste. Transfer short ribs to serving platter, spoon 1 cup sauce over top, and sprinkle with sesame seeds and cilantro. Serve, passing remaining sauce separately.

Ras el Hanout

MAKES ABOUT ½ CUP

Ras el hanout is a complex Moroccan spice blend that traditionally features a host of warm spices. If you can't find Aleppo pepper, you can substitute ½ teaspoon paprika and ½ teaspoon red pepper flakes.

- 16 **cardamom pods**
- 4 **teaspoons coriander seeds**
- 4 **teaspoons cumin seeds**
- 2 **teaspoons anise seeds**
- ½ **teaspoon allspice berries**
- ¼ **teaspoon black peppercorns**
- 4 **teaspoons ground ginger**
- 2 **teaspoons ground nutmeg**
- 2 **teaspoons ground dried Aleppo pepper**
- 2 **teaspoons ground cinnamon**

1. Toast cardamom, coriander, cumin, anise, allspice, and peppercorns in small skillet over medium heat until fragrant, shaking skillet occasionally to prevent scorching, about 2 minutes. Let cool to room temperature.

2. Transfer toasted spices, ginger, nutmeg, Aleppo, and cinnamon to spice grinder and process to fine powder. (Ras el hanout can be stored at room temperature in airtight container for up to 1 year.)

BEEF TENDERLOIN WITH SMOKY POTATOES

✔ **WHY THIS RECIPE WORKS:** To turn out rich, elegant beef tenderloin and a generous side of potatoes using just one cooking vessel, we looked to our roomy roasting pan. After seasoning and tying the roast, we let the beef rest while we bloomed minced scallions, minced garlic, and smoky paprika on the stovetop. After stirring small red potatoes into the smoky, seasoned base, we moved the pan to the oven, giving the potatoes a 15-minute head start before adding the beef. Placing the tenderloin atop the potatoes allowed the dry heat to circulate around the meat, encouraging plenty of browning without overcooking it. The potatoes finished roasting just as the beef reached a juicy medium-rare, and a quick persillade relish of parsley, capers, and cornichons finished off the dish.

In the pantheon of high-end cuts of beef, tenderloin stands on its own. Extremely tender with a pleasantly mild flavor, this cut is usually reserved for the holidays, if only because it comes with such a hefty price tag. I'm a big fan of this special roast, but when I'm entertaining, the last thing I want is the stress of preparing a showstopping roast as well as a side in time for dinner. With the harried holiday host in mind, I decided to turn this stately roast into a streamlined one-pan meal, making it just fancy enough to work for a special occasion while keeping it accessible and foolproof.

The test kitchen's go-to technique for preparing beef tenderloin is to prop it up on a wire rack to encourage even browning all over its surface, but that approach wouldn't necessarily lend itself well to simultaneously preparing a side. What if I kept the roasting pan but instead incorporated a side that held the beef aloft (or at least protected it from direct contact with the bottom of the pan)? Now my wheels were really beginning to turn.

Beef tenderloin needs little embellishment, so I simply seasoned it with salt and pepper before tying it into a tight cylinder with kitchen twine. Though they wouldn't raise the roast high, slender green beans, mushrooms, and delicate pearl onions seemed like suitably elegant sides that would offer some level of insulation for my tenderloin. I tossed the trio in oil and spread them across the bottom of the roasting pan before placing the beef on top. Roasted together,

this first attempt was promising, but it was clear where I needed to make some adjustments. The beef had roasted beautifully, taking on some subtle color while maintaining a juicy, rich interior. The vegetables were another story. The moisture-rich mushrooms had all but drowned the beans and onions, steaming them until they were unappealingly limp, and the green beans themselves had taken on an unattractive army green hue during the extended cooking time. It was clear I needed a sturdier accompaniment.

At face value, the humble potato struck me as a gauche partner for my upscale centerpiece—I wasn't about to serve up beef tenderloin as your everyday meal of meat and potatoes—but then I considered red potatoes. Small, tender, and certainly sophisticated, these spuds would serve me well.

The beauty of using a roasting pan for a one-pan meal is that it can transition seamlessly from stovetop to oven; I took full advantage of this, heating oil in the pan (set over two burners) to bloom some spices and briefly jump-start the potatoes' cooking. I kept the tender, thin red skins intact and embellished them with the impactful combination of minced scallions, minced garlic, and smoky paprika. Knowing the potatoes would need more time than the beef to cook through, I gave them a head start in the oven, roasting the spiced-up spuds for 15 minutes before placing the tied tenderloin on top. From there, the beef roasted to a rosy medium-rare and the potatoes turned tender and deeply flavorful in around 35 minutes.

In under an hour, I'd managed to pull together a tenderloin feast that was at once classic and foolproof, but I wasn't quite satisfied: My smoky, crimson-tinged potatoes and rich meat needed some contrasting brightness. A verdant persillade relish was just the thing, delivering the fresh, zippy pop needed to tie this effortlessly elegant meal together.

—RUSSELL SELANDER, *America's Test Kitchen Books*

Beef Tenderloin with Smoky Potatoes and Persillade Relish
SERVES 6 TO 8

Use extra-small red potatoes measuring less than 1 inch in diameter. Center-cut beef tenderloin roasts are sometimes sold as Châteaubriand.

BEEF AND POTATOES

1 (3-pound) center-cut beef tenderloin roast, trimmed
¼ cup extra-virgin olive oil
   Salt and pepper
3 pounds extra-small red potatoes, unpeeled
5 scallions, minced
4 garlic cloves, minced
1 tablespoon smoked paprika
⅓ cup water

PERSILLADE RELISH

¾ cup minced fresh parsley
½ cup extra-virgin olive oil
6 tablespoons minced cornichons plus 1 teaspoon brine
¼ cup capers, rinsed and chopped coarse
3 garlic cloves, minced
1 scallion, minced
1 teaspoon sugar
¼ teaspoon salt
¼ teaspoon pepper

1. FOR THE BEEF AND POTATOES: Adjust oven rack to middle position and heat oven to 425 degrees. Pat roast dry with paper towels, coat with 2 tablespoons oil, and season with salt and pepper. Tie roast with kitchen twine at 1½-inch intervals; set aside at room temperature.

2. Heat remaining 2 tablespoons oil in 16 by 12-inch roasting pan over medium-high heat (over 2 burners, if possible) until shimmering. Add potatoes, scallions, garlic, paprika, ½ teaspoon salt, and ¼ teaspoon pepper and cook until scallions are softened, about 1 minute. Off heat, stir in water, scraping up any browned bits. Transfer roasting pan to oven and roast potatoes for 15 minutes.

3. Remove roasting pan from oven, stir potato mixture, and lay beef on top. Return pan to oven and roast until beef registers 120 to 125 degrees (for medium-rare), 35 to 50 minutes.

4. FOR THE PERSILLADE RELISH: While beef roasts, combine all ingredients in bowl.

5. Remove pan from oven. Transfer roast to carving board, tent with aluminum foil, and let rest 15 minutes. Cover potatoes left in pan with foil to keep warm. Remove twine from roast, slice into ½-inch-thick slices, and serve with potatoes and persillade relish.

BONELESS RIB ROAST WITH YORKSHIRE PUDDING AND JUS

✓ **WHY THIS RECIPE WORKS:** To turn out an impressive roast with plenty of custardy Yorkshire pudding to soak up the jus, we started with the beef. Richly marbled, full of meaty flavor, and easy to slice, a hefty boneless rib roast was our cut of choice. We trimmed and salted the beef for thorough seasoning, gently roasted it to a juicy medium-rare, and let it rest before searing it in a hot skillet to boost its flavorful browning. Yorkshire pudding is a traditional British accompaniment, and we made enough to satisfy a crowd by baking it the same roasting pan. Preheating the pan and melting down the roast's drippings and some of the fat cap trimmings to use as the pudding's cooking fat guaranteed a flavorful, custardy result, and giving the batter a rest before baking maximized its rise. To finish things off, we pulled together a savory jus by softening onions and whisking in beef broth, cornstarch, and thyme. A bracing horseradish sauce tied the dish together.

As our friends in the United Kingdom have known for generations, a crusty, custardy Yorkshire pudding is without peer as an accompaniment to a resplendent roast beef. It swabs up and soaks up all those drippings and gravy in the most rewarding way. This year I set out to create a foolproof recipe for both items—roast and pudding—that would have them ready for the table at the same time.

I started, naturally, with the beef. While I love the impressive stature of a bone-in standing rib roast, it can be tricky to carve at the table. So this year I opted for a boneless rib roast. Its rich marbling would guarantee plenty of beefy flavor, and searing and slicing the roast would be much easier.

To prepare it, I called upon the tried-and-true test kitchen method for bone-in rib roast. I salted the roast a day in advance to ensure complete seasoning. I then roasted it in a 250-degree oven until it hit 120 degrees (for medium-rare) and set it aside for an hour before searing the exterior in a piping-hot skillet. Next I made a quick sauce—a jus—with chopped onion, reduced beef broth, cornstarch for thickening, and a sprig of thyme. Even without the bones, this technique yielded a seasoned, crusty exterior enveloping a rosy, juicy interior.

While the roast was resting for an hour before its final sear, I set my sights on the slightly more complicated portion of my feast. Making a Yorkshire pudding—a savory pancake of milk (or water), flour, and eggs, similar to a Dutch baby or popover—can be a fraught process. It's all about texture: You want a custardy, moist interior with a contrasting crunchy exterior. The existing recipes I researched had a lot of folklore to wade through, often with "unbreakable" rules for success. I was skeptical.

Almost all British chefs agree that you need to use a preheated pan and a hot oven in order to get a better rise in your pudding. And despite my skepticism, this claim held true. After experimenting, I found that pouring the batter into a hot pan (and I mean really hot—preheated at 425 degrees until the fat was beginning to smoke) not only caused the pudding to achieve a towering height but also kept it from sticking to the pan. This was excellent news, as it meant I could use the same pan I roasted my beef in and thus take full advantage of those flavorful drippings.

Only one problem: There weren't enough drippings for my Yorkshire pudding. For a full, roasting-pan-size Yorkshire pudding, I'd need 6 tablespoons of fat, and my boneless roast was yielding less than half that. So for my next test, I chopped up the trimmings I'd removed from the roast's fat cap and placed about ¾ cup of them in the roasting pan when the beef went in. This ensured that I'd have plenty of rendered fat for my pudding.

I was more doubtful about the existing recipes' call to stir together the batter and let it sit at room temperature before baking. Yet after a few tests, this rule, too, proved essential: I found that letting the batter sit at room temperature for 1 hour yielded a taller pudding. Why? Our science editor confirmed that the hour-long rest allowed time for the gluten formed when mixing the batter to relax, so the pudding was able to rise more quickly in the oven.

With a succulent roast, a deeply savory jus, and my golden, gloriously tall Yorkshire pudding, all I needed was one final traditional condiment. I chose a sharp, bracing, supersimple stir-together horseradish sauce. I was now ready for the holiday feast—and even my friends in the United Kingdom would be happy.

—MORGAN BOLLING, *Cook's Country*

Boneless Rib Roast with Yorkshire Pudding and Jus

SERVES 8 TO 10

At the butcher counter, ask for a roast with an untrimmed fat cap, ideally ½ inch thick, in order to get enough trimmings to cook the pudding. The roast must be salted and refrigerated for at least 24 hours before cooking. The roast and Yorkshire pudding can also be made separately from one another. To make only the roast, do not add the trimmed fat to the roasting pan. To make only the Yorkshire pudding, proceed with step 6, substituting 6 tablespoons of vegetable oil for the beef fat. Our winning roasting pan is the Calphalon Contemporary Stainless Roasting Pan with Rack. If you're using a dark, nonstick roasting pan, reduce the cooking time for the Yorkshire pudding by 5 minutes. Serve with Horseradish Sauce (recipe follows), if desired.

ROAST AND PUDDING

- 1 (5- to 5½-pound) first-cut boneless beef rib roast with ½-inch fat cap
  Kosher salt and pepper
- 2½ cups (12½ ounces) all-purpose flour
- 4 cups milk
- 4 large eggs
- 1 tablespoon vegetable oil, plus extra as needed

JUS

- 1 onion, chopped fine
- 1 teaspoon cornstarch
- 2½ cups beef broth
- 1 sprig fresh thyme

1. FOR THE ROAST AND PUDDING: Using sharp knife, trim roast's fat cap to even ¼-inch thickness and refrigerate trimmings for later use. Cut 1-inch crosshatch pattern in fat cap, being careful not to cut into meat. Rub 2 tablespoons salt over entire roast and into crosshatch. Transfer to large plate and refrigerate, uncovered, for at least 24 hours.

2. Adjust oven rack to lower-middle position and heat oven to 250 degrees. Spray roasting pan with vegetable oil spray. Cut reserved trimmings into ½-inch pieces. Place 3 ounces (about ¾ cup) trimmings in bottom of prepared pan. Set V-rack over trimmings in pan.

BONELESS RIB ROAST WITH YORKSHIRE PUDDING AND JUS

3. Season roast with pepper and place fat side up on V-rack. Roast until meat registers 115 degrees for rare, 120 degrees for medium-rare, or 125 degrees for medium, 2½ to 3 hours.

4. Meanwhile, combine flour and 1 tablespoon salt in large bowl. Whisk milk and eggs in second bowl until fully combined. Slowly whisk milk mixture into flour mixture until smooth. Cover with plastic wrap and let rest at room temperature for 1 hour.

5. Transfer V-rack with roast to carving board, tent with aluminum foil, and let rest for 1 hour. Using fork, remove solids in pan, leaving liquid fat behind (there should be about 6 tablespoons; if not, supplement with extra vegetable oil). Increase oven temperature to 425 degrees.

NOTES FROM THE TEST KITCHEN

TRIMMING AND PREPPING THE FAT CAP

Ask the butcher directly for a first-cut boneless beef rib roast with an untrimmed fat cap, ideally ½ inch thick; you may have to call ahead and special-order this roast. Here's how to prep this hefty roast.

1. Using sharp knife, trim fat cap to even ¼-inch thickness. Refrigerate trimmings.

2. Cut 1-inch crosshatch pattern into fat cap, being careful not to cut into meat.

3. Place 3 ounces of reserved trimmings in roasting pan (rendered fat will be used for Yorkshire pudding).

6. When oven reaches 425 degrees, return pan to oven and heat until fat is just smoking, 3 to 5 minutes. Rewhisk batter and pour into center of pan. Bake until pudding is dark golden brown and edges are crisp, 40 to 45 minutes.

7. Meanwhile, pat roast dry with paper towels. Heat 1 tablespoon oil in 12-inch skillet over medium-high heat until just smoking. Sear roast on all sides until evenly browned, 5 to 7 minutes. Transfer roast to carving board.

8. FOR THE JUS: Return skillet to medium-high heat and add onion. Cook until onion is just softened, about 3 minutes, scraping up any browned bits. Whisk cornstarch into broth. Add broth mixture and thyme sprig to skillet and bring to boil. Reduce heat to medium-low and simmer until reduced by half and slightly thickened, about 7 minutes. Strain jus through fine-mesh strainer set over small saucepan; discard solids. Cover and keep warm.

9. Slice roast ¾ inch thick. Cut pudding into squares in roasting pan. Serve beef with Yorkshire pudding and jus.

TO MAKE AHEAD: Roast can be refrigerated for up to 4 days in step 1. Batter can be covered and refrigerated for up to 24 hours in step 4. Let come to room temperature before proceeding with recipe.

Horseradish Sauce

MAKES ABOUT 1 CUP

Buy refrigerated prepared horseradish, not the shelf-stable kind, which contains preservatives and additives. This sauce can be refrigerated for up to two days.

- ½ **cup sour cream**
- ½ **cup prepared horseradish**
- 1½ **teaspoons kosher salt**
- ⅛ **teaspoon pepper**

Combine all ingredients in bowl. Cover and refrigerate for at least 30 minutes to allow flavors to meld.

SMOTHERED PORK CHOPS

✓ **WHY THIS RECIPE WORKS:** To serve up the ultimate braised pork chops, we started with ¾- to 1-inch-thick bone-in blade chops. We prepared a traditional Southern seasoning mixture using Lawry's Seasoned Salt, onion powder, granulated garlic, paprika, and pepper, and we called on that mixture three times over: on the chops, in the flour dredge that the chops were coated in, and in the gravy. We first browned the coated chops well and then built a gravy in the same skillet using vegetable oil and flour. We cooked the roux until it was the color of peanut butter, stirred in onions and water, and poured the mixture over the chops. After cooking in the gravy for about 1½ hours, the pork chops were supertender and flavorful.

To "smother" meat is to cook it low-and-slow in rich gravy until the meat is ridiculously tender. Unfortunately, that gravy is often just a cloak to mask subpar meat or, worse, a barrier obscuring perfectly good meat. What I wanted was thick, meaty, ultratender chops nestled in a rich gravy made lightly nutty by a golden-brown roux.

To find the best chop for smothering, I started by testing rib, loin, and blade chops. Both the rib and loin chops cooked up tough and dry, no matter how gentle the heat. But blade chops have more fat and connective tissue and stand up well to aggressive browning (for good flavor) and long braising (for tenderizing).

Margaret Boyd of Mrs. B's Home Cooking in Montgomery, Alabama, is famous for her chops, and she generously explained her cooking process to me over the phone. Following her lead, I started by making a spice blend to season the chops. Her secret ingredient? Not so secret: It's Lawry's Seasoned Salt. I mixed some with onion powder, granulated garlic, paprika, and pepper and made enough of it to season the chops, the flour I'd use to coat them before frying, and the gravy.

Although Boyd dredges her chops in flour and deep-fries them before braising, I opted to shallow-fry them in just ½ cup of oil, two at a time, until the exteriors were a deep golden brown. I then transferred them to a wire rack to await the gravy.

All great gravies start with a roux, a cooked mixture of flour and fat; Boyd cooks hers until it is the color of peanut butter. I poured off all but ¼ cup of fat from the skillet before stirring in flour and cooking the mixture, stirring, until the kitchen started to smell like popcorn and the roux achieved the correct color. This took about 3 minutes. I then added the rest of the spice mixture and sliced onions and cooked it all for 2 minutes before stirring in 3 cups of water (my tasters preferred water to broth, which was deemed too savory). I poured the gravy over the chops in a baking dish and covered it with aluminum foil before transferring it to the oven.

I tested oven temperatures ranging from 250 to 400 degrees before settling on 350 degrees. In 1½ hours of hands-off time, the chops were supertender.

I transferred the chops to a big platter while I finished my gravy by skimming some of the accumulated fat with a spoon and adding a splash of vinegar to brighten the flavor. I set a pot of cooked rice next to my steaming platter of chops and called my tasters. The pork chops were so tender you could cut them with a thought. The gravy was thick, rich, silky, and packed with flavor. "I just want to curl up with these chops," said one taster.

—DIANE UNGER, *Cook's Country*

Southern-Style Smothered Pork Chops
SERVES 4

Try to find chops of the same thickness for even cooking. For proper sauce consistency, it's important to measure the amount of fat left in the skillet before making the roux. Serve with steamed white rice.

- 2 tablespoons Lawry's Seasoned Salt
- 1 tablespoon onion powder
- 1 teaspoon granulated garlic
- 1 teaspoon paprika
  Pepper
- 4 (8- to 10-ounce) bone-in blade-cut pork chops, ¾ to 1 inch thick, trimmed
- 1 cup all-purpose flour
- ½ cup vegetable oil
- 2 onions, quartered through root end and sliced thin crosswise
- 3 cups water
- 1 tablespoon cider vinegar

1. Adjust oven rack to middle position and heat oven to 350 degrees. Set wire rack in rimmed baking sheet. Combine seasoned salt, onion powder, granulated garlic, paprika, and 1 teaspoon pepper in bowl. Pat chops dry with paper towels and sprinkle each chop with 1 teaspoon spice mixture (½ teaspoon per side).

2. Combine ½ cup flour and 4 teaspoons spice mixture in shallow dish. Dredge chops lightly in seasoned flour, shake off excess, and transfer to prepared rack.

3. Heat oil in 12-inch skillet over medium-high heat until just smoking. Add 2 chops to skillet and fry until deep golden brown, 3 to 5 minutes per side. Let excess oil drip from chops, then return chops to rack. Repeat with remaining 2 chops.

4. Transfer fat left in skillet to liquid measuring cup. Return ¼ cup fat to skillet and stir in remaining ½ cup flour. Cook over medium heat, stirring constantly, until roux is color of peanut butter, 3 to 5 minutes. Add onions and remaining 4 teaspoons spice mixture and cook, stirring constantly, until onions begin to soften slightly, about 2 minutes.

5. Slowly stir water into roux mixture until gravy is smooth and free of lumps. Bring to simmer and cook until gravy begins to thicken, about 2 minutes. Pour half of gravy into 13 by 9-inch baking dish. Nestle browned chops in dish, overlapping slightly as needed. Pour remaining gravy over chops and cover dish tightly with aluminum foil. Bake until chops are fully tender, about 1½ hours.

6. Carefully transfer chops to serving dish. (Chops will be delicate and may fall apart.) Use wide spoon to skim fat from surface of gravy. Add vinegar to gravy and season with pepper to taste. Pour gravy over chops. Serve.

PAN-SEARED THICK-CUT BONELESS PORK CHOPS

✔ **WHY THIS RECIPE WORKS:** We wanted to serve juicy boneless pork chops with a distinct, flavorful crust straight from our skillet, so we started with the meat. Thick-cut pork chops can be hard to find, so we cut them ourselves from a boneless center-cut pork loin roast. To maximize the crisp crust, we skipped brining or salting and instead thoroughly dried the exteriors by patting the chops with paper towels. Searing the chops in a preheated cast-iron skillet and flipping them every 2 minutes imparted a distinct crust while also keeping the meat perfectly moist.

Pork chops seem like a good candidate for a weeknight meal: They're quick to cook and, when given a nice crusty sear, are flavorful. But since most pork is pretty lean, chops are easy to overcook, resulting in leathery, dried-out meat. Thicker chops—which require more time to cook through—give you a wider window of time to build up a solid sear before the interiors are overdone. But after looking for thick-cut (1½ inches or thicker) chops at a number of supermarkets and coming up short, I realized that if I wanted a juicy interior and a substantial crust, I was going to have to butcher a pork roast into chops myself.

Although rib bones insulate meat from heat, helping prevent overcooking, I decided right off the bat that I'd cut boneless chops for two reasons. First, the rib bones can be a challenge to slice through. Second, you don't get to decide how thick to make the chops, since that is dictated by the spacing between the ribs (usually about an inch). Starting with a boneless roast would make it possible to fashion chops of any thickness.

As for the type of roast, I considered both blade-end and center-cut loin roasts. Blade-end roasts come from near the shoulder of the animal and contain more fat, which made for slightly juicier chops. But that wasn't enough to overcome the cut's drawbacks: For one thing, the fattier parts are found only at the very end of the roast, meaning that you can't cut four identical chops. This roast also tends to widen toward the blade end, making it impossible to cut chops of equal thickness and weight. On the other hand, a center-cut roast, which comes from the pig's back, is compact, cylindrical, and lean from end to end, making it ideal for home-cut chops. What's more, it's readily available in most supermarkets.

I cut my center-cut pork loin roast crosswise into four even pieces. The thickness of the chops varied slightly depending on the diameter of the loin, but I found that starting with a 2½-pound roast guaranteed chops at least 1½ inches thick.

We typically brine or salt pork to season it and enhance or maintain the meat's juiciness. But since the moisture added by brining would impede browning, I dismissed it—I didn't want to wait 45 minutes for the surface to dry out. As it turned out, salting the meat also interfered with developing a rich crust since it brought some of the meat's moisture to the surface. I decided to simply season the meat just prior to cooking. But here was the crux of the problem: To get the rich mahogany crust and juicy interior I was after, I needed to cook the meat both at high heat and more gently at the same time, a seeming contradiction.

PAN-SEARED THICK-CUT BONELESS PORK CHOPS

Until now, I'd been using a basic approach to searing, cooking the chops in a stainless-steel skillet with a couple of teaspoons of oil over high heat and flipping them once. But the skillet never got hot enough to produce a great crust. I switched to a cast-iron skillet, which gets—and stays—exceptionally hot, even when four thick chops (which absorb a lot of heat from the metal) are added. The trick with cast iron is to preheat it thoroughly, so I put it in a cold oven set to 500 degrees and waited for the oven to come to temperature, by which time the pan would be well saturated with heat. I also added more oil (2 tablespoons total) to the pan, which ensured that the chops, which tended to pull away from the pan here and there as they cooked, made full contact with the heat and seared evenly.

Now that the exterior was gorgeously brown, I focused on the interior. The chops needed to hit 140 degrees for serving, but that didn't mean I had to keep them in the pan to get them there, since they'd continue to cook off the heat—the phenomenon referred to as carryover cooking. Usually, we remove meat from direct heat about 5 to 10 degrees shy of the serving temperature to avoid overcooking, but I wondered if the extreme heat I was getting on the chops' exteriors would allow me to take the meat off the heat sooner. In other words, could I use the high heat to my advantage?

It sounded counterintuitive, but it actually worked brilliantly. By the time the chops were seared on both sides, the meat registered 125 degrees, and there was more than enough residual heat on their surfaces to push them to 140 as they rested under foil. The only flaw was the gray band of overcooked meat that developed just below the surface as each side spent several minutes sitting over the heat to sear. The fix was to flip the chops every couple of minutes as they cooked, which slowed down cooking and just about eliminated the overcooked layer of meat.

The chops ultimately spend the same amount of time in contact with the pan as they would with uninterrupted searing on each side, but with every flip, some of the heat that accumulates in the chop dissipates, preventing overcooking on the interior.

No brining. No salting. No fancy techniques. These were by far the easiest pork chops I'd ever made, and they looked and tasted great. But to give the recipe plenty of utility—even for company, since thick-cut chops are nice for entertaining—I decided to develop a few sauces to dress up the chops. I made them intensely flavored and relatively rich to give the meat plenty of character, but they're still quick enough to whip up any night of the week. In a nod to the vinegar-pepper topping commonly found in Italian pork chop recipes, I created a roasted red pepper–vinegar sauce. I also pulled together a couple of pesto-like concoctions: a French mint persillade (a parsley-based sauce with garlic and oil) and a Sicilian-inspired walnut and raisin pesto.

—ANDREW JANJIGIAN, *Cook's Illustrated*

Pan-Seared Thick-Cut Boneless Pork Chops

SERVES 4

Look for a pork loin that is 7 to 8 inches long and 3 to 3½ inches in diameter. We strongly prefer using natural pork here. Using pork that is enhanced (injected with a salt solution) will inhibit browning. This recipe works best in a cast-iron skillet, but a 12-inch stainless-steel skillet will work. Serve the chops with one of our sauces (recipes follow), if desired.

1 (2½- to 3-pound) boneless center-cut pork loin roast, trimmed

    Kosher salt and pepper

2 tablespoons vegetable oil

1. Adjust oven rack to middle position, place 12-inch cast-iron skillet on rack, and heat oven to 500 degrees. Meanwhile, cut roast crosswise into 4 chops of equal thickness.

2. When oven reaches 500 degrees, pat chops dry with paper towels and season with salt and pepper. Using potholders, remove skillet from oven and place over high heat. Being careful of hot skillet handle, add oil and heat until just smoking. Add chops and cook, without moving them, until lightly browned on first side, about 2 minutes. Flip chops and cook until lightly browned on second side, about 2 minutes.

3. Flip chops and continue to cook, flipping every 2 minutes and adjusting heat as necessary if chops brown too quickly or slowly, until exteriors are well browned and meat registers 125 to 130 degrees, 10 to

12 minutes longer. Transfer chops to platter, tent with aluminum foil, and let rest for 15 minutes (temperature will climb to 140 degrees). Serve.

Roasted Red Pepper–Vinegar Sauce

MAKES ABOUT 1 CUP

Red wine vinegar or sherry vinegar can be substituted for the white wine vinegar, if desired.

- ¾ cup jarred roasted red peppers, rinsed and patted dry
- 2 jarred hot cherry peppers, stems removed
- 2 garlic cloves, peeled
- 2 teaspoons dried rosemary, lightly crushed
- 2 anchovy fillets, rinsed and patted dry
- ½ teaspoon salt
- ⅛ teaspoon pepper
- ¼ cup water
- 2 tablespoons white wine vinegar
- ⅓ cup extra-virgin olive oil
- 2 tablespoons minced fresh parsley

Pulse red peppers, cherry peppers, garlic, rosemary, anchovies, salt, and pepper in food processor until finely chopped, 15 to 20 pulses. Add water and vinegar and pulse briefly to combine. Transfer mixture to medium bowl and slowly whisk in oil until fully incorporated. Stir in parsley.

Mint Persillade

MAKES ABOUT 1 CUP

You can substitute 1½ teaspoons of anchovy paste for the fillets, if desired.

- 1 cup fresh mint leaves
- 1 cup fresh parsley leaves
- 3 garlic cloves, peeled
- 3 anchovy fillets, rinsed and patted dry
- 1 teaspoon grated lemon zest plus 1 tablespoon juice
- ½ teaspoon salt
- ⅛ teaspoon pepper
- ⅓ cup extra-virgin olive oil

Pulse mint, parsley, garlic, anchovies, lemon zest, salt, and pepper in food processor until finely chopped, 15 to 20 pulses. Add lemon juice and pulse briefly to combine. Transfer mixture to medium bowl and slowly whisk in oil until fully incorporated.

Walnut-Raisin Pesto

MAKES ABOUT 1 CUP

You can substitute pine nuts or pecans for the walnuts, if desired.

- 1 cup walnuts
- ½ cup golden raisins
- 4 garlic cloves, peeled
- 1 teaspoon dried oregano
- ½ teaspoon salt
- ⅛ teaspoon pepper
- ⅓ cup extra-virgin olive oil
- 3 tablespoons water
- 2 tablespoons white wine vinegar
- 2 tablespoons minced fresh parsley

Pulse walnuts, raisins, garlic, oregano, salt, and pepper in food processor until finely chopped, 15 to 20 pulses. Transfer walnut mixture to 12-inch skillet and stir in oil. Heat, stirring frequently, over medium-low heat until garlic and oregano are fragrant, about 5 minutes. Remove skillet from heat and stir in water and vinegar. Transfer to medium bowl and stir in parsley.

NOTES FROM THE TEST KITCHEN

MAKING THICK-CUT CHOPS

If necessary, trim roast to square off ends. Divide roast in half crosswise. Divide each half again crosswise to form 4 equal-size chops.

CRUMB-CRUSTED PORK TENDERLOIN

CRUMB-CRUSTED PORK TENDERLOIN

✅ **WHY THIS RECIPE WORKS:** For a kicked-up, weeknight-friendly pork tenderloin with an appealingly crisp crust, we needed a coating that really clung. We boosted the flavor of crunchy panko bread crumbs by stirring them into a rich mixture of butter, mustard, garlic, rosemary, and cayenne and baking them, allowing the panko to crisp and absorb plenty of flavor. We got this crunchy crust to adhere to the pork by dredging each tenderloin in flour and egg before pressing on the seasoned panko. Baking the pork on a wire rack–lined baking sheet protected the coating's texture and ensured evenly cooked meat.

Inexpensive, quick-cooking, and lean, pork tenderloin is a fine choice for a weeknight supper, but it doesn't have a lot of pizzazz. I wanted to add a flavorful crust to make something a little more filling and a lot more exciting.

It's easy to create a crumb crust that's flavorful but more difficult to create one that sticks. I started with an assortment of crumbs, each with a different texture: fresh bread, panko, and saltines. After trying all of them and using a variety of cooking methods, my least favorite option was saltine crumbs, which turned gray and greasy. Fresh bread crumbs tended to turn soggy. But crunchy-crisp panko bread crumbs were excellent, proving why they're a longtime test kitchen favorite.

Panko has a strong structure but lacks flavor, so I searched for ways to add some. Melted butter was a must and would act as my primary glue. Knowing that pork loves mustard, I stirred some together with the crumbs, choosing whole-grain mustard for its rustic texture. Minced garlic was another must. But something was still missing—possibly a strong herb that could withstand the roasting process? Fresh rosemary fit the bill, and I sloshed in a bit of white wine vinegar for vibrancy.

Because I was adding liquid—vinegar—to the crumbs, I knew I'd have to bake them before coating the tenderloin; otherwise they would turn soggy and slide off the meat as it cooked. Baking the panko mixture briefly on a baking sheet dried it out so that it could more easily adhere. I chose to stick to the typical flour and egg wash to coat the tenderloin and create a sticky surface for the bread crumbs.

In early tests, I experimented with pan searing, shallow frying, and even deep frying, but simply roasting the crumb-crusted pork proved to be the most successful method. By placing the pork on a wire rack and nestling this rack into a rimmed baking sheet, I was able to keep the crumbs on the bottom from turning soggy and allow airflow around the pork to ensure that it cooked evenly.

Crunchy, savory, mustardy, and meaty, my pork tenderloin delivered much more satisfaction than its simple technique would suggest.

—ALLI BERKEY, *Cook's Country*

Crumb-Crusted Pork Tenderloin

SERVES 4 TO 6

Transferring the baked panko bread-crumb mixture to a 13 by 9-inch baking dish in step 2 provides a little extra wiggle room for coating the tenderloins in step 4.

- 5 tablespoons unsalted butter, melted
- ¼ cup whole-grain mustard
- 1½ tablespoons white wine vinegar
- 2 garlic cloves, minced
- 2 teaspoons minced fresh rosemary
  Kosher salt and pepper
  Pinch cayenne pepper
- 1½ cups panko bread crumbs
- ¼ cup all-purpose flour
- 3 large egg whites
- ⅓ cup grated Parmesan cheese
- 2 (1- to 1¼-pound) pork tenderloins, trimmed

1. Adjust oven rack to middle position and heat oven to 350 degrees. Whisk melted butter, mustard, vinegar, garlic, rosemary, ¾ teaspoon salt, ½ teaspoon pepper, and cayenne in bowl until combined. Stir in panko until fully combined.

2. Spread panko mixture in even layer on rimmed baking sheet, breaking up any clumps. Bake, stirring every 5 minutes, until golden brown, 15 to 18 minutes. Transfer crumbs to 13 by 9-inch baking dish and let cool completely, about 10 minutes. Break up any large clumps with your fingers. Increase oven temperature to 400 degrees.

3. Set wire rack in now-empty sheet. Place flour in shallow dish. Whisk egg whites together in second shallow dish. Stir Parmesan into cooled crumb mixture. Pat tenderloins dry with paper towels and season with salt and pepper.

4. Working with 1 tenderloin at a time, dredge in flour, shaking off excess; dip in egg whites to thoroughly coat, letting excess drip back into dish; then coat with crumbs, pressing gently to adhere. Transfer tenderloins to prepared rack. Bake until pork registers 140 degrees, 25 to 30 minutes. Let tenderloins rest on rack for 10 minutes. Slice and serve.

SMOKED PORK LOIN WITH DRIED-FRUIT CHUTNEY

✔ **WHY THIS RECIPE WORKS:** We wanted a pork roast that delivered barbecue's meaty, smoky flavor in a fraction of the time, so we looked to quicker-cooking pork loin. A salt–brown sugar rub and an overnight rest thoroughly seasoned the mild blade-end roast and promised a perfectly caramelized exterior. We set up our grill for low-and-slow cooking, protecting the roast from direct heat by placing it right above a water-filled aluminum roasting pan. A single wood chip packet infused the pork with just enough smoke. While the roast cooked, we prepared a sweet-tart chutney to contrast its deep, smoky flavor.

I haven't met many people who can resist a plateful of smoky, tender barbecue like pork butt or ribs, but I also haven't met many who can regularly commit to the half-day required to make them. So what can you do to create a meaty, smoky pork roast fit for a crowd in less time? After some thinking, I settled on using a pork loin. Because it isn't loaded with collagen, a pork loin doesn't require nearly as much cooking time as ribs or a pork butt—maybe a couple of hours, tops. It has a drawback, though—namely, a very mild flavor. But smoking seemed like a great way to give this mild cut a big flavor boost. The challenge? I'd need to be careful with the smoke. I'd want enough to amplify the roast's meaty taste but not overwhelm it. And because pork loin doesn't have much fat and has a tendency to dry out, I'd also need to take steps to ensure that my roast came off the grill tender and juicy.

My first step was to pick the best cut from the loin. Here's the thing: All pork loin roasts are not created equal. You've actually got two options: blade-end or center-cut. The blade roast comes from the end of the loin closest to the shoulder, so it has relatively more fat (and flavor) than roasts cut from the center of the loin. That made the blade-end roast my clear choice.

I also knew I'd either salt or brine my roast since both of these pretreatments season the meat and help it retain juices during cooking. In both cases, the salt works its way into the meat and alters the meat's muscle proteins, making them better at holding on to water. Though brining tends to be quicker, it also impedes browning and would require making room for a large container in the fridge, so I settled on salting. Covering a roast with ¼ cup kosher salt, which is easier to distribute than table salt, and refrigerating it for 6 hours before grilling (I used a stripped-down grilling method for now) worked well enough. But letting it sit overnight worked much better, giving the salt time to penetrate deeper into the meat.

Following the lead of a few of the roast pork recipes the test kitchen has done in the past, I decided to add a good amount of brown sugar to the salt rub. This would have several benefits. First, like salt, sugar would help the meat retain moisture and stay juicy (it's less effective at the job but still makes a difference). Second, sugar dissolved on the surface of the meat would encourage caramelization, delivering both more flavor and improved color. Finally, opting for brown sugar over granulated would add a hint of molasses flavor that would nicely complement the pork.

With my pork roast ready to go, I headed outside. First up: the grill setup. A lean roast like pork loin benefits from low-and-slow indirect cooking since this allows the interior to cook through evenly and gently, helping it retain as much moisture as possible. We've had a lot of experience with indirect cooking on the grill, so I arranged our standard setup: I banked the coals on one side of the grill and placed the roast opposite them, on the cooler side, with a pan filled with water beneath it to help keep the meat moist. The water pan also kept the temperature in the grill stable by absorbing heat.

So how low, exactly, did I need to go? I began with a grill temperature of 375 degrees (7 quarts of charcoal), but the roast came out dry. So I worked my way down in temperature. While lower temperatures led to better results, too low was too hard to maintain and took too long to cook the pork through. I found that 300 degrees was my best bet for a juicy roast in a reasonable time frame. Cooked at this temperature, the roast needed 1½ to 2 hours to hit the ideal internal temperature of 140 degrees.

The problem was, I had to refuel my fire partway through. Luckily, we had already devised a solution for this when developing our recipe for Memphis-Style Barbecued Spareribs: We arranged a layer of unlit coals in the grill and then topped those with a layer of lit coals. This stretched out the life of the flame, so there was no need to refuel. To achieve the steady 300 degrees that I wanted, I just needed to bump up the coal count from the rib recipe since that recipe calls for a grill temperature of 275 degrees. Some simple math and a few roasts later, I found that a combination of 25 unlit and 40 lit coals (or 4 quarts) was just the ticket for a 300-degree fire that would burn for 2 hours.

And what about a browning step? We often brown the exterior of a roast for deeper flavor and improved color. Happily, the salt–brown sugar rub contributed enough on both fronts that I could skip it.

The final detail was the smoke. As wood smolders, it breaks down into numerous flavorful compounds that vaporize, waft up, and settle on the food, infusing it with smoky, spicy pungency but also a complex sweetness. Combined with the flavor that grilling adds—which would mainly be Maillard browning along with some flavor from the coals since pork loin has little to offer in the way of fatty drippings—smoking meat delivers a lot of bang for the buck. But how much smoke did my recipe need?

I started with 4 cups of wood chips, but that much smoke was overkill for mild pork loin. Two cups produced just the right amount of smoke to add flavor but not overwhelm, and setting the lid vents over the meat ensured that the smoke drifted by the meat before exiting the grill. The smoking process also gave my roast a beautifully lacquered appearance.

Translating my charcoal-grilled recipe to gas was easy enough: I placed the wood chip packet on the primary burner and placed the roast beside it so that the smoke would drift over the meat on its way out of the vents at the back.

As a finishing touch, I put together a quick dried-fruit chutney to serve alongside the roast. Brightened with vinegar, ginger, and mustard, it was the perfect complement to the deeply smoky meat. This recipe certainly satisfied my barbecue cravings, and I didn't have to put in half a day's work to enjoy it.

—STEVE DUNN, *Cook's Illustrated*

Smoked Pork Loin with Dried-Fruit Chutney
SERVES 6

Note that the roast needs to be refrigerated for at least 6 hours or up to 24 hours after the salt rub is applied. A blade-end roast is our preferred cut, but a center-cut boneless loin roast can also be used. Any variety of wood chip except mesquite will work; we prefer hickory. If you'd like to use wood chunks instead of wood chips when using a charcoal grill, substitute two medium wood chunks, soaked in water for 1 hour, for the wood chip packet.

PORK
- ½ cup packed light brown sugar
- ¼ cup kosher salt
- 1 (3½- to 4-pound) blade-end boneless pork loin roast, trimmed
- 2 cups wood chips
- 1 (13 by 9-inch) disposable aluminum roasting pan (if using charcoal) or 1 (9-inch) disposable aluminum pie plate (if using gas)

CHUTNEY
- ¾ cup dry white wine
- ½ cup dried apricots, diced
- ½ cup dried cherries
- ¼ cup white wine vinegar
- 3 tablespoons water
- 3 tablespoons packed light brown sugar
- 1 shallot, minced
- 2 tablespoons grated fresh ginger
- 1 tablespoon unsalted butter
- 1 tablespoon Dijon mustard
- 1½ teaspoons dry mustard
  Kosher salt

1. FOR THE PORK: Combine sugar and salt in small bowl. Tie roast with twine at 1-inch intervals. Rub sugar-salt mixture over entire surface of roast, making sure roast is evenly coated. Wrap roast tightly in plastic wrap, set roast in rimmed baking sheet, and refrigerate for at least 6 hours or up to 24 hours.

2. Just before grilling, soak wood chips in water for 15 minutes, then drain. Using large piece of heavy-duty aluminum foil, wrap soaked chips in 8 by 4½-inch foil packet. (Make sure chips do not poke holes in sides or bottom of packet.) Cut 2 evenly spaced 2-inch slits in top of packet.

3A. FOR A CHARCOAL GRILL: Open bottom vent halfway. Arrange 25 unlit charcoal briquettes over half of grill and place disposable pan filled with 3 cups water on other side of grill. Light large chimney starter two-thirds filled with charcoal briquettes (4 quarts). When top coals are partially covered with ash, pour evenly over unlit briquettes. Place wood chip packet on coals. Set cooking grate in place, cover, and open lid vent halfway. Heat grill until hot and wood chips are smoking, about 5 minutes.

3B. FOR A GAS GRILL: Remove cooking grate and place wood chip packet directly on primary burner. Place disposable pie plate filled with 1 inch water directly on other burner(s). Set grate in place, turn all burners to high, cover, and heat grill until hot and wood chips are smoking, about 15 minutes. Turn primary burner to medium and turn off other burner(s). (Adjust primary burner as needed to maintain grill temperature of 300 degrees.)

NOTES FROM THE TEST KITCHEN

SETTING UP A GRILL FOR SMOKED PORK LOIN

Placing roast on opposite side of grill from burners or hot coals and above water-filled aluminum pan allows meat to cook through gently and retain juices.

4. Clean and oil cooking grate. Unwrap roast and pat dry with paper towels. Place roast on grill directly over water pan about 7 inches from heat source. Cover (position lid vent over roast if using charcoal) and cook until meat registers 140 degrees, 1½ to 2 hours, rotating roast 180 degrees after 45 minutes.

5. FOR THE CHUTNEY: Combine wine, apricots, cherries, vinegar, water, sugar, shallot, and ginger in medium saucepan. Bring to simmer over medium heat. Cover and cook until fruit is softened, 10 minutes. Remove lid and reduce heat to medium-low. Add butter, Dijon, and dry mustard and continue to cook until slightly thickened, 4 to 6 minutes. Remove from heat and season with salt. Transfer to bowl and let stand at room temperature.

6. Transfer roast to cutting board, tent with foil, and let stand for 30 minutes. Remove and discard twine. Slice roast into ¼-inch-thick slices and serve with chutney.

RACK OF PORK WITH POTATOES AND ASPARAGUS

✓ **WHY THIS RECIPE WORKS:** In order to bring a juicy rack of pork to the table along with perfectly cooked sides, we had to tinker with timing and oven temperatures. We discovered that the pork's heat-retaining bones were contributing to the carryover cooking of the roast, so we roasted the meat in a hot oven for just 1½ hours, bringing its internal temperature to 130 degrees. The meat's temperature gradually rose to a safe 145 degrees as it rested. Roasting herb-tossed Yukon Gold potatoes below the pork gave the spuds a head start; as soon as we removed the roast, we arranged asparagus over the partially cooked potatoes and returned the pan to the oven long just enough for the spears to turn crisp-tender and the potatoes to finish roasting. A speedy salsa verde offered a bright finishing touch.

Resplendent rack of pork—a rich, meaty roasted loin with the rib bones still attached—is just as worthy a holiday centerpiece as the celebrated prime rib roast of beef. But what makes it especially welcome at our table is its price: It costs about one-quarter as much as the beef.

The bones aren't just for show. Over the years we've learned that in the oven, heat travels more slowly through bone than through meat. In essence, the bones insulate much of the roast and keep it from cooking too quickly—a big deal considering that pork loin is so lean. Even a touch too much heat or a few too many minutes in the oven can render it unpalatably dry. So when I wanted juicy, deeply seasoned, rosy pork, along with some lovely roasted vegetables (potatoes and asparagus), I hoped the bones would help me achieve it.

To start, I rubbed a bone-in roast with brown sugar and salt and let it sit for a few hours to ensure good browning and juicy meat. I placed the pork on a rack set in a roasting pan, tossed some Yukon Gold potatoes under it, and put the pan in a 250-degree oven. Considering that the temperature of the meat rises a few extra degrees once it's pulled from the oven, I removed my first roast about 5 degrees shy of my target temperature of 145 degrees.

The undercooked potatoes were the least of my worries: The temperature of the pork rose more than 15 degrees in just 10 minutes of resting and showed no signs of stopping. When I sliced into it, I was faced with dry, gray meat. Tapping the bones with the tip of my finger revealed the reason: heat.

At such a low oven temperature, the meat really didn't need the bones for insulation while it roasted, and once it was out of the oven, the heat held in the bones was accelerating the carryover cooking. I had to figure out how to use the bones to my advantage.

A higher oven temperature would help the potatoes cook through. Perhaps I could exploit the increased carryover cooking rate and roast the pork in a hotter oven. The bones would insulate the meat and help keep it juicy. And I'd remove the pork earlier, when it registered 130 degrees, relying on the heat in the bones to help it reach a perfect 145.

I tested oven temperatures of 375, 400, and 425 degrees. About 1½ hours at 400 degrees, followed by a 30-minute rest, was the best option. But my potatoes were still slightly undercooked.

These underdone potatoes proved to be less a problem than a solution for how to cook the final component, asparagus. The spears would need just a few minutes

in the oven, so I cooked the pork and seasoned potatoes together, transferred the pork to a carving board to rest, laid the asparagus over the potatoes, and returned the pan to the oven. By the time the roast was ready to carve, the potatoes were browned on the outside and creamy on the inside and the asparagus was crisp yet tender.

Running my knife between the ribs and meat, I separated the meat from the bones and carved it into thin slices. The ribs had served their purpose. There was just one thing left to do with them: Pick them clean.

—CECELIA JENKINS, *Cook's Country*

Rack of Pork with Potatoes and Asparagus
SERVES 8

Use small Yukon Gold potatoes measuring 1 to 2 inches in diameter. The roast's bones trap heat, so the meat continues to cook during the resting period, which is why we pull it from the oven at 130 degrees; the temperature will climb to 145 degrees. Monitoring the roast with a probe thermometer is best. If you use an instant-read thermometer, open the oven door as infrequently as possible and remove the roast from the oven before taking its temperature. Serve with Quick Salsa Verde (recipe follows).

1 tablespoon packed dark brown sugar
  Kosher salt and pepper
1 (4- to 5-pound) center-cut bone-in pork rib roast, chine bone removed
2 pounds small Yukon Gold potatoes, unpeeled, halved
5 teaspoons vegetable oil
1 tablespoon minced fresh rosemary
2 pounds asparagus, trimmed

1. Combine sugar and 1 tablespoon salt in bowl. Trim fat on roast to ¼-inch thickness. Pat roast dry with paper towels and sprinkle with sugar mixture. Wrap roast in plastic wrap and refrigerate for at least 6 hours or up to 24 hours.

2. Adjust oven rack to lower-middle position and heat oven to 400 degrees. Toss potatoes with 1 tablespoon oil, rosemary, ½ teaspoon salt, and ½ teaspoon pepper in bowl, then arrange cut side down in large roasting pan.

3. Nestle V-rack among potatoes in pan. Unwrap roast and brush off any excess sugar mixture. Sprinkle roast with 1 teaspoon pepper and place fat side up on V-rack.

4. Roast until center of pork registers 130 degrees, about 1½ hours. Transfer pork and V-rack to carving board, tent with aluminum foil, and let rest for 30 minutes.

5. Meanwhile, toss asparagus with remaining 2 teaspoons oil, ⅛ teaspoon salt, and ⅛ teaspoon pepper in bowl and place on top of potatoes. Return pan to oven and cook until asparagus is bright green and potatoes are browned on bottom, 18 to 20 minutes.

6. Remove bones from roast by running sharp knife down length of bones, following contours as closely as possible. Carve meat into ¼-inch-thick slices and cut ribs between bones. Serve.

Quick Salsa Verde

MAKES 1 CUP

- 1 **cup minced fresh parsley**
- ½ **cup extra-virgin olive oil**
- 2 **tablespoons capers, rinsed and minced**
- 4 **teaspoons lemon juice**
- 2 **anchovy fillets, rinsed and minced**
- 1 **garlic clove, minced**
- ¼ **teaspoon salt**

Whisk all ingredients together in bowl.

NOTES FROM THE TEST KITCHEN

REMOVING THE BONES FROM RACK OF PORK

Secure roast with your hand (using clean dish towel to grip it). With your other hand, use sweeping motion to run sharp boning knife down length of bones, following contours as closely as possible.

PORCHETTA

⊘ WHY THIS RECIPE WORKS: The complex herbal flavors of Italian *porchetta* seemed perfectly suited to a more elegant treatment, so we turned it into a roast. Using a whole pig is traditional, but we opted for readily available, well-marbled pork butt for our recipe. We infused the roast with flavor by carving slits into the meat and applying a paste of fennel seeds, rosemary, thyme, and garlic. We replicated the texture of the crisp skin in whole-hog porchetta by carving a crosshatch pattern into the pork butt's fat cap and treating it with salt and baking soda to dry it out and encourage browning. We shortened the porchetta's cooking time by halving the pork butt to make two smaller roasts and covering the roasting pan with foil, allowing the pork to steam and cook through while still remaining moist. A direct blast of heat at the end delivered a flavorful burnished crust.

Italy's porchetta—fall-apart tender, rich pieces of slow-cooked pork, aromatic with garlic, fennel seeds, rosemary, and thyme and served with pieces of crisp skin on a crusty roll—is one of the world's greatest street foods. Traditionally a whole pig is boned and the meat is rubbed with an herb-spice paste. The pig is then tied around a spit and allowed to sit overnight. The next day, it's slow-roasted over a wood fire until the meat is ultra-tender and the skin is burnished and crackling-crisp.

Recently, porchetta came to mind as I pondered my holiday roast options. It may sound strange, given that a sandwich doesn't offer much in the way of presentation, but it's such a knockout for flavor that I had to wonder: Could I make a few tweaks to transform porchetta from street-fare sandwich to holiday centerpiece?

Going whole hog wasn't an option, so my first task was picking the right substitute. Some recipes call for wrapping a pork belly around a pork loin. I ruled out that scenario from the get-go for being too fussy; plus, pork loin takes more work to keep juicy. Pork belly alone is also a popular choice since it comes with skin attached and it's very fatty (it's what you make bacon from, after all). I found that it was easy to tie into a compact roll that sliced neatly, its skin cooked up crisp and crackly, and the meat was tender and moist.

PORCHETTA

But I ultimately decided against it, too, since it's often composed of more fat than meat—fine for bacon but a bit much for porchetta.

Pork butt, cut from the upper portion of the shoulder, was my best bet. It generally cooks up flavorful and moist, and it's fatty without being over the top. Its lack of skin was a drawback, but I decided I could live with it since I suspected I could brown and crisp the fat cap as a stand-in.

That said, the recipes I tried featuring pork butt left something to be desired. Even though the meat was tender and juicy at the center, it got progressively drier and tougher toward the exterior. The herb paste was poorly distributed, and the irregular, loose shape of the roast meant it was hard to slice into neat pieces elegant enough for a holiday dinner.

When cooking a pork butt, low-and-slow is best since it allows the ample collagen time to melt, creating an ultratender roast; it also helps mitigate the difference in cooking between the interior and exterior. I found that 6 hours produced the best results, but that was just too long. Cutting the roast in half lengthwise decreased the cooking time by almost half, and it gave me two cylindrical roasts that sliced nicely, especially when I tied them with twine.

Now the meat was cooking through more evenly and more quickly, but the exterior was still a bit dry. I had noticed when testing the pork belly version that all of the meat was juicy and tender despite having been cooked at a much higher temperature than my pork butts were. Was it the greater amount of fat? Or was it the fact that when tied into a roll, the meat in the pork belly was entirely encased within a layer of skin?

Increasing the amount of fat in my pork butt wasn't on the table, but I had a notion for how to fake a layer of skin around it: aluminum foil. For my next test, I covered the roasting pan tightly with foil, roasted the pork until its interior registered 180 degrees, and then removed the foil. A billow of steam wafted up, and I noticed that the meat had shed about a cup of brothy liquid into the pan—good signs. While the roasts were pale and wan on the exterior, the meat was tender and juicy throughout, with little discernible difference between the exterior and the core. Here's why: The steam kept the surface temperature of the roast from exceeding the boiling point of water (212 degrees), preventing the exterior from overcooking as the interior

came up to temperature. Cooking with steam also sped up the cooking, since steam is a better conductor of heat than air is. The cooking time was down to about 2 hours.

I drained the juices from the pan, untied the roasts, and returned them to a 500-degree oven for a short stint to brown.

Next, I shifted my focus to the paste. Some recipes called for rubbing the paste onto the roast, with the hope that the flavor would penetrate. Others called for poking holes in the roast with a knife and stuffing the paste into them. The latter approach worked better than the former, but it was slow work and impossible to tell whether I'd done a good job until serving time. There had to be a better way.

I tried pulling each roast apart along the seams while still keeping the pieces attached to each other—basically unfolding each roast—and then rubbing the paste all over before tying each piece back together. That worked in terms of distribution, but the roasts fell apart at the seams during slicing. A similar thing happened when I butterflied the roasts along their length. The problem in both cases was that I had created seams that ran perpendicular to the direction in which the roast would be sliced. So what if the cuts ran in the same direction as the slices?

For my next test, I cut a series of parallel slits through each roast along its length, stopping 1 inch from each end. Getting the paste into the roast was easy since the slits were big enough to let me use my hands to push the paste in from both sides. I rubbed each roast with salt, applied the paste, and let the roasts sit overnight in the fridge, which gave the salt time to penetrate the meat. This worked perfectly and guaranteed that every serving was deeply flavored and that the meat would slice neatly.

All that remained was to improve the appearance and texture of the fat cap "skin." I had avoided putting the herb paste on the fat cap to give it a better chance of crisping up, but it was still a bit pale, and the fat just below the surface wasn't particularly well rendered. To improve things, I used a sharp knife to create 1-inch-wide crosshatches through the cap, which would let heat penetrate and the fat render out. To help it dry out and thus crisp up, I rubbed the fat cap with salt and left the roasts uncovered for their overnight rest. Finally, to boost browning, I added a bit of baking soda to the salt rub. Baking soda creates a more alkaline environment, which makes browning reactions more likely to occur. Crisp, rich, and deeply browned, the fat cap was the perfect complement to the tender, moist, boldly flavored meat beneath. This porchetta might have simple street-food roots, but it's worthy of taking center stage on any holiday table.

—ANDREW JANJIGIAN, *Cook's Illustrated*

Porchetta

SERVES 8 TO 10

Pork butt roast is often labeled Boston butt in the supermarket. Look for a roast with a substantial fat cap. If fennel seeds are unavailable, substitute ¼ cup of ground fennel. The porchetta needs to be refrigerated for 6 to 24 hours once it is rubbed with the paste, but it is best when it sits for a full 24 hours.

- **3** tablespoons fennel seeds
- **½** cup fresh rosemary leaves (2 bunches)
- **¼** cup fresh thyme leaves (2 bunches)
- **12** garlic cloves, peeled
  Kosher salt and pepper
- **½** cup extra-virgin olive oil
- **1** (5- to 6-pound) boneless pork butt roast, trimmed
- **¼** teaspoon baking soda

1. Grind fennel seeds in spice grinder or mortar and pestle until finely ground. Transfer ground fennel to food processor and add rosemary, thyme, garlic, 1 tablespoon pepper, and 2 teaspoons salt. Pulse mixture until finely chopped, 10 to 15 pulses. Add oil and process until smooth paste forms, 20 to 30 seconds.

2. Using sharp knife, cut slits in surface fat of roast, spaced 1 inch apart, in crosshatch pattern, being careful not to cut into meat. Cut roast in half with grain into 2 equal pieces.

3. Turn each roast on its side so fat cap is facing away from you, bottom of roast is facing toward you, and newly cut side is facing up. Starting 1 inch from short end of each roast, use boning or paring knife to make slit that starts 1 inch from top of roast and ends 1 inch from bottom, pushing knife completely through roast. Repeat making slits, spaced 1 to 1½ inches apart, along length of each roast, stopping 1 inch from opposite end (you should have 6 to 8 slits, depending on size of roast).

4. Turn roast so fat cap is facing down. Rub sides and bottom of each roast with 2 teaspoons salt, taking care to work salt into slits from both sides. Rub herb paste onto sides and bottom of each roast, taking care to work paste into slits from both sides. Flip roast so that fat cap is facing up. Using 3 pieces of kitchen twine per roast, tie each roast into compact cylinder.

5. Combine 1 tablespoon salt, 1 teaspoon pepper, and baking soda in small bowl. Rub fat cap of each roast with salt–baking soda mixture, taking care to work mixture into crosshatches. Transfer roasts to wire rack set in rimmed baking sheet and refrigerate, uncovered, for at least 6 hours or up to 24 hours.

6. Adjust oven rack to middle position and heat oven to 325 degrees. Transfer roasts, fat side up, to large roasting pan, leaving at least 2 inches between roasts. Cover tightly with aluminum foil. Cook until pork registers 180 degrees, 2 to 2½ hours.

7. Remove pan from oven and increase oven temperature to 500 degrees. Carefully remove and discard foil and transfer roasts to large plate. Discard liquid in pan. Line pan with foil. Remove twine from roasts; return roasts to pan, directly on foil; and return pan to oven. Cook until exteriors of roasts are well browned and interiors register 190 degrees, 20 to 30 minutes.

8. Transfer roasts to carving board and let rest for 20 minutes. Slice roasts ½ inch thick, transfer to serving platter, and serve.

NOTES FROM THE TEST KITCHEN

PREPPING PORK BUTT

1. After crosshatching surface, halve pork butt, creating 2 smaller roasts.

2. Cut deep slits into sides of roasts, then rub salt and herb paste over roasts and into slits.

GRILLED CITRUS CHICKEN

✔ **WHY THIS RECIPE WORKS:** We wanted to infuse perfectly grilled chicken with bright, distinct citrus taste, so we began by immersing boneless, skinless breasts in an intense "brinerade," a salt brine solution boosted with garlic, sugar, and orange, lemon, and lime zests. Soaking the chicken in this mixture promised well-seasoned, supermoist meat with clear citrus notes, and the sugar encouraged plenty of browning on the grill. Starting the breasts out on the cooler side of the grill cooked the meat without drying it out; finishing on the hotter side gave the chicken plenty of flavorful char. We finished the chicken with more citrus flavor by adding a quick sauce made with the juices of grill-charred orange, lemon, and lime halves.

Boneless, skinless chicken breasts are often tagged as a boring, easily overcooked substitute for more-flavorful thighs. I disagree. Call me Pollyanna (it wouldn't be the first time), but I think of this lean, mild meat as a blank canvas just waiting for a creative boost.

I love citrus juices—lemon, lime, and orange—but when they're used in a marinade, their acidity can toughen meat. I needed another way to bring these flavors to grilled chicken.

Years of testing have taught us that marinades do most of their work on the surface of the meat, while a solution of salt and water deeply seasons meat and helps keep it moist. By combining the two into a salty marinade, or "brinerade," we season the meat throughout while also adding flavor to the exterior.

I assembled a brinerade of salt, pepper, garlic, sugar (to aid in browning), vegetable oil, and a few tablespoons of water and added equal parts lemon, lime, and orange zest (less acidic than juice) for a balance of sour and sweet. I poured this mixture into a zipper-lock bag, added the chicken breasts, and let them soak for an hour.

Our favorite method for grilling chicken is to build a half-grill fire (piling all the coals on one side of the grill). We cook the chicken on the cooler side, covered with a disposable pan to help trap heat and smoke, until it reaches an internal temperature of 140 degrees. We then transfer it to the hotter side to sear.

Right off the grill, my chicken was juicy and well seasoned, with pronounced citrus flavors—but the orange zest overwhelmed, so I tweaked the ratio (2 parts each lemon and lime zest to 1 part orange).

For one last pop of flavor, I halved the fruit I'd zested and grilled the pieces over direct heat. I used the warm, slightly smoky juices to make a quick citrus-mint sauce, bringing the best bits of summer to this simple dish.

—CHRISTIE MORRISON, *Cook's Country*

Grilled Citrus Chicken

SERVES 4

Plan ahead: The chicken needs to marinate for at least an hour. Do not marinate it longer than 12 hours or it will be too salty. Use a rasp-style grater to zest the citrus. The chicken takes longer to cook on a gas grill, so begin checking it at the end of the range in step 3.

- 1 orange
- 1 lemon
- 1 lime
- 7 tablespoons vegetable oil
- 3 tablespoons water
- 3 garlic cloves, minced
- 2½ teaspoons sugar
- Salt and pepper
- 4 (6- to 8-ounce) boneless, skinless chicken breasts, trimmed
- 1 (13 by 9-inch) disposable aluminum roasting pan (if using charcoal)
- 1 teaspoon mayonnaise
- 1 teaspoon Dijon mustard
- 1 tablespoon minced fresh mint

1. Grate 1 teaspoon zest from orange, 2 teaspoons zest from lemon, and 2 teaspoons zest from lime. Place all citrus zest in bowl. Halve orange, lemon, and lime and set aside. Add 3 tablespoons oil, water, two-thirds of garlic, 2 teaspoons sugar, 1½ teaspoons salt, and ½ teaspoon pepper to citrus zest and whisk to combine. Transfer brinerade to 1-gallon zipper-lock bag. Add chicken, press out air, seal bag, and turn to distribute brinerade. Refrigerate for at least 1 hour or up to 12 hours.

2A. FOR A CHARCOAL GRILL: Open bottom vent completely. Light large chimney starter filled with charcoal briquettes (6 quarts). When top coals are partially covered with ash, pour evenly over half of grill. Set cooking grate in place, cover, and open lid vent completely. Heat grill until hot, about 5 minutes.

GRILLED CITRUS CHICKEN

2B. FOR A GAS GRILL: Turn all burners to high, cover, and heat grill until hot, about 15 minutes. Leave primary burner on high and turn off other burner(s).

3. Clean and oil cooking grate. Place chicken skinned side down on cooler side of grill, with thicker ends facing coals. (Edges of chicken should be no more than 4 inches from center of primary burner if using gas.) Cover with disposable pan (if using gas, close lid) and cook until bottom of chicken just begins to develop light grill marks and is no longer pink, 6 to 9 minutes.

4. Flip chicken and rotate so that thinner ends face coals. Cover as before and continue to cook until chicken registers 140 degrees, 6 to 9 minutes longer.

5. Remove disposable pan and transfer chicken and citrus halves, cut side down, to hotter side of grill. Cook chicken, uncovered (covered if using gas), until dark grill marks appear, 2 to 4 minutes. Flip chicken and cook, uncovered (covered if using gas), until marked on second side and chicken registers 160 degrees, 2 to 4 minutes longer. Cook citrus halves until lightly charred, about 4 minutes.

6. Transfer chicken to cutting board, tent with aluminum foil, and let rest for 5 minutes. Squeeze 3 tablespoons orange juice, 1 tablespoon lemon juice, and 1 tablespoon lime juice into bowl. Whisk in mayonnaise, Dijon, remaining one-third of garlic, remaining ½ teaspoon sugar, ¼ teaspoon salt, and ⅛ teaspoon pepper. Whisking constantly, slowly drizzle in remaining ¼ cup oil until emulsified. Stir in mint and season with salt and pepper to taste. Slice each breast on bias ¼ inch thick. Serve, drizzled with citrus sauce.

NOTES FROM THE TEST KITCHEN

HARNESSING THE GRILL'S HEAT

When using a charcoal grill, covering our Grilled Citrus Chicken with an overturned disposable aluminum roasting pan traps intense heat around the food while still allowing oxygen to reach the coals.

STOVETOP-ROASTED CHICKEN WITH LEMON-HERB SAUCE

✔ **WHY THIS RECIPE WORKS:** To serve up juicy chicken that boasted a crisp, golden-brown skin without ever heating the oven, we turned to bone-in skin-on chicken parts and a nonstick skillet. We patted the chicken dry to eliminate any skin-sogging moisture and seasoned the pieces with minced fresh rosemary before placing them skin side down in a cold skillet. As the skillet heated up on the stovetop, the chicken gradually cooked and rendered much of its fat. We ramped up the heat to finish it off, deeply browning the skin. This simple chicken dish warranted an easy but impactful accompaniment, so we used some of the rendered fat to build a bright lemon-herb pan sauce.

Bone-in chicken parts, from kid-friendly drumsticks to parent-pleasing breasts and thighs, are one of my favorite weeknight suppers. Bone-in pieces are juicier and more economical than boneless. But they are usually relegated to the oven, and they take time to cook. I wanted roast-chicken flavor with crispy skin in one skillet on the stovetop, with delicious browned bits left in the skillet to make a pan sauce.

The variables: which pan to use and at what temperature, if and when to flip the pieces, and if and when to cover them. I tested a variety of techniques, but none was easy or foolproof enough. Then I came across a method that intrigued me: chicken arranged skin side down in a cold nonstick skillet.

Why not? I nestled the pieces in the skillet and then turned the heat to high. Once the skin had browned, I covered the skillet to help the chicken cook through. I was sure the chicken was going to stick to the skillet, or worse, turn out steamy and greasy. But to my surprise, the skin was golden and crispy and the meat supertender. The stove, however, was a mess, splattered with chicken grease from corner to corner.

So for my next test, I again placed the chicken in a cold nonstick skillet, but this time I covered the pan before browning the chicken over a more moderate medium heat, hoping that covering the skillet the whole time would trap the mess and keep the chicken moist. After about 15 minutes, I cranked the heat to medium-high and cooked the chicken 10 to 15 minutes longer. Bingo: The skin was deep golden brown and every piece was cooked through and juicy.

The gorgeous browned bits in the pan were perfect for a quick sauce. I cooked rosemary and garlic until they were fragrant and added lemon juice and water. Off the heat, I whisked in butter and chives. Adding capers, sun-dried tomatoes, or cornichons with other herbs made easy, flavorful variations.

—DIANE UNGER, *Cook's Country*

Stovetop-Roasted Chicken with Lemon-Herb Sauce

SERVES 4

For even cooking, it's important to buy chicken pieces within the specifications given. If you prefer all dark meat, this recipe will work with a total of eight bone-in thighs or drumsticks; if you prefer all white meat, you can use four bone-in breasts. Note that the chicken is started in a cold skillet to give the fat time to render.

CHICKEN

- 2 (10- to 12-ounce) bone-in split chicken breasts, trimmed
- 4 (5- to 7-ounce) bone-in chicken thighs or drumsticks, trimmed

  Salt and pepper
- ½ teaspoon minced fresh rosemary

LEMON-HERB SAUCE

- 2 garlic cloves, minced
- ½ teaspoon minced fresh rosemary
- 2 tablespoons water
- ½ teaspoon grated lemon zest plus 1 tablespoon juice
- 6 tablespoons unsalted butter, cut into 6 pieces
- 1 tablespoon minced fresh chives

  Salt and pepper

1. FOR THE CHICKEN: Pat chicken dry with paper towels. Place breasts on cutting board, bone side down, and cover with plastic wrap. Using meat pounder, pound thick ends of breasts to ¾- to 1-inch thickness.

Season all chicken pieces with salt and pepper. Place chicken, skin side down, in cold 12-inch nonstick skillet and sprinkle with rosemary.

2. Cover skillet and place over medium heat. (If using electric stove, preheat burner for 3 minutes over medium heat.) Cook chicken, without moving it, until skin is light golden brown, about 15 minutes.

3. Increase heat to medium-high and continue to cook, covered, until skin is deep golden brown and crispy and breasts register 160 degrees and thighs/drumsticks register at least 175 degrees, 10 to 15 minutes longer, rotating skillet halfway through cooking. (If using drumsticks, flip them during last 5 minutes of cooking.) Transfer chicken, skin side up, to platter and tent with aluminum foil.

4. FOR THE LEMON-HERB SAUCE: While chicken rests, pour off all but 2 teaspoons fat from skillet. Add garlic and rosemary and cook over medium heat until fragrant, about 30 seconds, scraping up any browned bits. Off heat, stir in water and lemon zest and juice. Whisk in butter, 1 piece at a time, until smooth and emulsified.

5. Stir in chives and any accumulated chicken juices; season with salt and pepper to taste. Spoon sauce over chicken and serve.

VARIATIONS

Stovetop-Roasted Chicken with Lemon-Caper Sauce

Add 2 tablespoons minced capers to skillet with garlic in step 4. Substitute ½ teaspoon minced fresh thyme for chives.

Stovetop-Roasted Chicken with Lemon-Cornichon Sauce

Add 2 tablespoons minced cornichons to skillet with garlic in step 4. Substitute 2 teaspoons minced fresh tarragon for chives.

Stovetop-Roasted Chicken with Lemon–Sun-Dried Tomato Sauce

Add ¼ cup oil-packed sun-dried tomatoes, chopped, to skillet with garlic in step 4. Increase rosemary in sauce to 1 teaspoon and omit chives.

HAWAIIAN FRIED CHICKEN

✔ **WHY THIS RECIPE WORKS:** Hoping to re-create Hawaii's crisp, boldly flavored *karaage* chicken at home, we started by marinating meaty boneless chicken thighs in a mixture of soy sauce, ginger, garlic, brown sugar, and sesame oil. We ensured a crisp, even coating by pressing on a mixture of potato starch and baking powder and refrigerating the coated chicken, allowing the coating to fully hydrate and cling. Frying the chicken in batches in peanut oil ensured it was evenly cooked and flavorful, and serving it with a dipping sauce of rice vinegar, soy sauce, and lemon juice made for an authentic finish.

In Hawaii, fried chicken is often served as part of a "plate lunch" with macaroni salad and steamed rice. But not all fried chicken in Hawaii is the same. *Mochiko* chicken features boneless, skinless thighs marinated in soy sauce and battered with sweet rice flour. *Katsu*-style chicken is coated in crisp panko crumbs and fried. *Karaage* chicken is marinated in soy sauce or tamari, brown sugar, sake, and lots of ginger and garlic; coated in potato starch; and then fried and served with a sharp dipping sauce. The common denominator is utter deliciousness.

I made versions of each style and gathered tasters. Each style had its fans, but the flavorful karaage was the most popular; we used it as a primary inspiration. I found a few more recipes to test out the nuances. Some recipes called for marinating the chicken overnight, making for supersalty chicken. Others had so much potato starch that the elements were out of proportion. I wanted the chicken to be seasoned throughout but not too salty. And I wanted the coating to be thin and crispy, with a dipping sauce that united the flavors and balanced the chicken's richness.

My first decision was to use boneless, skinless chicken thighs, for both ease and maximum flavor. For the marinade, soy sauce (you can substitute tamari if you'd like your chicken gluten-free), brown sugar, and a heavy dose of ginger and garlic were a given, but how to get the biggest bang for the buck was a balancing act. My first tests were too salty, so I decided to dilute the concentration of the soy sauce with another liquid. The easiest and best-tasting option was water, at a ratio of 2 parts water to 1 part soy sauce.

I used the food processor to make a garlic and ginger paste; doing so let me skip the tedious step of peeling the ginger, as the final result was so finely ground that it didn't matter. Sweetened with 3 tablespoons of brown sugar, the paste adhered nicely to the chicken.

The traditional coating for this chicken is straight-up potato starch, but no matter how many times and techniques I tried (and there were plenty, believe me), I couldn't get an evenly fried, crispy exterior that didn't turn an unsightly blotchy white. I tried combinations of potato starch mixed with rice flour, cornstarch, all-purpose flour, and even tapioca starch, but all left me with blotchy, too-thick, unevenly cooked coatings. I nearly threw in the towel.

But I'm no quitter when it comes to fried chicken, so for my next test I removed the chicken from the marinade, let the excess drip off, and transferred each piece to a mixture of potato starch and baking powder that I'd seasoned with salt, pepper, and sesame seeds. I coated each piece lightly and transferred it to a parchment-lined baking sheet. Once the pieces were coated, I firmly pressed the coating into the meat and then refrigerated it, tightly covered, for at least 30 minutes. This process allowed the potato starch to become fully saturated with absorbed marinade, allowing it to cook evenly when fried at a temperature of 375 degrees. Finally—perfect, lightly golden chicken pieces.

For a dipping sauce, I combined ½ cup of seasoned rice vinegar and ¼ cup each of fresh lemon juice and soy sauce. I fried up a final batch of chicken, gathered my tasters, and stood back to watch them greedily devour the crispy, crunchy, sweet, sour, salty chicken and then come back for more.

—DIANE UNGER, *Cook's Country*

Hawaiian-Style Fried Chicken

SERVES 4 TO 6

You will need at least a 6-quart Dutch oven for this recipe. The chicken marinates for at least an hour before breading. Pressing the chicken after dredging it in the starch ensures a more uniform coating.

CHICKEN

- 1 **(3-ounce) piece ginger, unpeeled, cut into ½-inch pieces**
- 4 **garlic cloves, peeled**
- 1 **cup water**
- ½ **cup soy sauce**

3 tablespoons packed light brown sugar

1 tablespoon toasted sesame oil

2 pounds boneless, skinless chicken thighs, trimmed and halved crosswise

2¼ cups potato starch

2 tablespoons sesame seeds

1½ teaspoons baking powder

Salt and pepper

3 quarts peanut or vegetable oil

DIPPING SAUCE

½ cup seasoned rice vinegar

¼ cup soy sauce

¼ cup lemon juice (2 lemons)

Pepper

1. FOR THE CHICKEN: Process ginger and garlic in food processor until finely chopped, about 15 seconds; transfer to large bowl. Add water, soy sauce, sugar, and sesame oil and whisk to combine. Add chicken and press to submerge. Cover bowl with plastic wrap and refrigerate for at least 1 hour or up to 3 hours.

2. FOR THE DIPPING SAUCE: Whisk vinegar, soy sauce, and lemon juice together in bowl. Season with pepper to taste.

3. Line rimmed baking sheet with parchment paper. Set wire rack in second rimmed baking sheet. Whisk potato starch, sesame seeds, baking powder, 1 teaspoon salt, and 1 teaspoon pepper together in large bowl.

4. Working with 1 piece of chicken at a time, remove from marinade, allowing excess to drip back into bowl. Dredge chicken in potato starch mixture, pressing to adhere. Gently shake off excess and transfer chicken to parchment-lined sheet. Coating will look mottled; using your hand, press on chicken to smooth out coating. Cover sheet tightly with plastic and refrigerate for at least 30 minutes or up to 1 hour.

5. Add peanut oil to large Dutch oven until it measures about 2 inches deep; heat oil over medium-high heat to 375 degrees. Carefully add one-third of chicken to pot and fry until deep golden brown and cooked through, about 5 minutes, stirring gently as needed to prevent pieces from sticking together. Adjust burner, if necessary, to maintain oil temperature between 350 and 375 degrees.

6. Transfer chicken to prepared rack. Return oil to 375 degrees and repeat in 2 more batches with remaining chicken. Serve chicken with sauce.

ARROZ CON POLLO

✔ **WHY THIS RECIPE WORKS:** For streamlined *arroz con pollo* at home, we began with this dish's flavor backbone: a *sofrito* of onions, peppers, garlic, and spices. This zesty blend infused the cooking liquid (chicken broth) and the dish's quick herbal sauce with bright, bold flavors. Browning skin-on chicken thighs and discarding the skin left us with flavorful rendered fat, which we used to soften chopped onion, toast the rice, and bloom the classic Latin spice blend, *sazón*. Baking the rice and chicken in the broth promised rich, deep flavor and stirring in halved green olives, capers, bay leaves, and lemon juice added layer upon layer of flavor to this one-pot meal.

Many cuisines around the world have a version of chicken and rice, from Spanish paella to Singaporean chicken rice. But among the most famous, and popular, is Latin American–style *arroz con pollo* ("rice with chicken"), with fall-off-the-bone chicken nestled in creamy, flavorful rice—a dish you might encounter in Miami, perhaps, or New York City.

Before starting, I spent hours on the phone talking to professional chefs, home cooks, and others who'd grown up with arroz con pollo and make it regularly. They waxed enthusiastically about Puerto Rican versions, Cuban versions, Central American versions, and more. I made six recipes and ordered the dish from a few local restaurants. What I found was that there are as many

---

NOTES FROM THE TEST KITCHEN

PICKING POTATO STARCH

In our Hawaiian-Style Fried Chicken, potato starch produced the crunchiest results because it fried up into a crispy, porous coating faster than either cornstarch or wheat starch (flour). This meant we had a crunchy coating in the time required to fry the chicken, whereas a cornstarch or flour coating would need to fry longer, resulting in overcooked chicken.

ARROZ CON POLLO (RICE WITH CHICKEN)

recipes for arroz con pollo as there are people who cook it. If you grew up with this dish, the version served in your house when you were young remains the only "authentic" version. I set out to make an all-purpose version that nodded to Puerto Rican tradition.

While the common denominators are the chicken and rice, the flavor backbone comes from a *sofrito,* a stable but invigorating base found in many similar dishes. Sofritos vary by the cook but often contain a mixture of onions, peppers, garlic, and herbs. For my sofrito I mixed finely chopped onion, garlic, cumin, cilantro, and a Cubanelle pepper (similar to green bell pepper but slightly sweeter and milder). I set the sofrito aside while I browned mixed chicken parts in a Dutch oven. I then removed them and sautéed onion and rice in the chicken fat left behind. Once the rice was nice and toasty, I stirred in chicken broth and the sofrito, added the browned chicken back to the pot, and covered it.

It took about 20 minutes of covered simmering for the rice to become tender and the chicken to cook through, releasing savory aromas into the kitchen. But the rice was unevenly cooked—mushy in certain spots and crunchy in others. And while the chicken's dark meat stayed juicy, the white meat was dry.

One fix was easy: I switched from mixed chicken parts to more-forgiving (and more-flavorful) thighs. I also removed the skin after browning the pieces; the skin added flavor early on but became gummy if I left it on as the chicken finished cooking.

The second fix was also easy: I moved the covered Dutch oven from the stovetop to the more-diffuse heat of the oven. I also left the lid on for 15 minutes after removing the pot from the oven to allow the rice to gently finish cooking to a consistent texture.

But it still wasn't perfect; my rice was too sticky. I was using a standard ratio of 3 cups chicken broth to 2 cups rice, but because the chicken was letting off liquid as it cooked, I had rice that was flavorful but mushy. After a couple of tests, I decided to scale back to 2½ cups of broth, just enough to cook the rice through without it feeling stodgy.

Most of the cooks I interviewed told me that medium-grain rice was preferred for this dish. Extensive cross-testing confirmed that medium-grain rice gave me the most creamy, cohesive, evenly cooked result. But I found that long-grain rice worked, too.

I was already adding capers and olives, sometimes sold together as *alcaparrado,* for a briny flavor and including a couple of bay leaves for earthiness. But something was missing. Some recipes I found called for marinating the chicken in bitter orange juice, but this resulted in mealy meat. Instead, inspired by recipes from home cooks, I chose a different option: *sazón* spice blend.

In the same way Creole seasoning in New Orleans and Old Bay in Maryland are go-to blends, sazón is common in many Latin home kitchens. It's easy to find, available in most international or Latin American food aisles. Just 1 tablespoon added complexity and brilliant color.

One version of arroz con pollo I found called for a tangy herb sauce on the side. Inspired by this, I stirred together a quick sauce using a couple of tablespoons of my already-made sofrito, which I'd set aside before cooking, along with a little mayonnaise and some lemon juice. Drizzling this over the dish gave it a final punch of freshness.

—MORGAN BOLLING, *Cook's Country*

Arroz con Pollo (Rice with Chicken)

SERVES 6

Sazón is a spice blend common in Latin American cooking. We developed this recipe with Goya Sazón with Coriander and Annatto (or *con Culantro y Achiote*). It can be found in the international aisle of most supermarkets; however, other brands will work. (One tablespoon of Goya Sazón equals about two packets.) If you can't find sazón, use our homemade version (recipe follows). You can substitute ¾ cup of chopped green bell pepper for the Cubanelle pepper. Allow the rice to rest for the full 15 minutes before lifting the lid to check it. Long-grain rice may be substituted for medium-grain, but the rice will be slightly less creamy.

1 cup fresh cilantro leaves and stems, chopped

1 onion, chopped (1 cup)

1 Cubanelle pepper, stemmed, seeded, and chopped (¾ cup)

5 garlic cloves, chopped coarse

1 teaspoon ground cumin

½ cup mayonnaise

3½ tablespoons lemon juice (2 lemons), plus lemon wedges for serving

Salt and pepper

6 (5- to 7-ounce) bone-in chicken thighs, trimmed

1 tablespoon vegetable oil

2 cups medium-grain rice, rinsed

1 tablespoon Goya Sazón with Coriander and Annatto

2½ cups chicken broth

¼ cup pimento-stuffed green olives, halved

2 tablespoons capers, rinsed

2 bay leaves

½ cup frozen peas, thawed (optional)

1. Adjust oven rack to middle position and heat oven to 350 degrees. Process cilantro, ½ cup onion, Cubanelle, garlic, and cumin in food processor until finely chopped, about 20 seconds, scraping down bowl as needed. Transfer sofrito to bowl.

2. Process mayonnaise, 1½ tablespoons lemon juice, ⅛ teaspoon salt, and 2 tablespoons sofrito in now-empty processor until almost smooth, about 30 seconds. Transfer mayonnaise-herb sauce to small bowl, cover, and refrigerate until ready to serve.

3. Pat chicken dry with paper towels and sprinkle with 1 teaspoon salt and ¼ teaspoon pepper. Heat oil in Dutch oven over medium heat until shimmering. Add chicken to pot skin side down and cook without moving it until skin is crispy and golden, 7 to 9 minutes. Flip chicken and continue to cook until golden on second side, 7 to 9 minutes longer. Transfer chicken to plate; discard skin.

4. Pour off all but 2 tablespoons fat from pot and heat over medium heat until shimmering. Add remaining ½ cup onion and cook until softened, 3 to 5 minutes. Stir in rice and Sazón and cook until edges of rice begin to turn translucent, about 2 minutes.

5. Stir in broth, olives, capers, bay leaves, remaining sofrito, remaining 2 tablespoons lemon juice, 1 teaspoon salt, and ½ teaspoon pepper, scraping up any browned bits. Nestle chicken into pot along with any accumulated juices and bring to vigorous simmer. Cover, transfer to oven, and bake for 20 minutes.

6. Transfer pot to wire rack and let stand, covered, for 15 minutes. Fluff rice with fork and stir in peas, if using. Discard bay leaves. Serve with mayonnaise-herb sauce and lemon wedges.

Homemade Sazón

MAKES 1 TABLESPOON

We add paprika in place of annatto for color. In addition to flavoring our Arroz con Pollo, this blend makes a great seasoning for eggs, beans, and fish. Store it in an airtight container for several months.

1 teaspoon garlic powder

¾ teaspoon salt

½ teaspoon paprika

½ teaspoon ground coriander

¼ teaspoon ground cumin

Combine all ingredients in bowl.

STICKY CHICKEN

✓ **WHY THIS RECIPE WORKS:** For rich, supertender sticky chicken easy enough to prepare on a weeknight, we looked for a quick way to infuse chicken thighs with flavor. Braising bone-in thighs in a zippy mixture of pantry staples like cider vinegar, honey, soy sauce, and ketchup imparted plenty of complexity in no time, and starting the thighs skin side down encouraged the fat to render and contribute lots of flavor to the liquid. After baking it for 20 minutes, we flipped the chicken, allowing the now-exposed skin to brown in the oven's dry heat. While the chicken rested, we turned its braising liquid into a lush, sticky sauce, thickening it on the stovetop with the help of some cornstarch. To serve, we returned the thighs to the skillet and coated them in the sauce. Sprinkling on some toasted sesame seeds offered a final flourish.

Sticky chicken isn't just a great recipe name, it's a great dish, too—deeply flavored roasted chicken with a sticky, slightly sweet, lacquered exterior. It wasn't hard finding existing recipes for this dish—but good recipes? That was a steeper hill to climb.

Most of the recipes I found called for marinating chicken pieces in a mixture of soy sauce, ketchup, and some sort of sweetener (such as brown sugar or honey) for at least 30 minutes; searing them on the stovetop to begin crisping the skin; and then covering the pan or transferring the pan to the oven to finish cooking the chicken. In some cases the chicken was dry and unevenly cooked, and in others it was inedibly salty. I wanted a happy medium: well-seasoned meat, nicely rendered skin, and a sweet and sticky sauce. And it had to be easy and fast enough for a weeknight meal.

My first big decision was to switch from chicken parts to just bone-in chicken thighs, which rarely dry out. Eight would be enough to serve four people. I also took marinating off the table (no time for that). But I did want the chicken to be packed with flavor. So I whisked together a braising liquid of cider vinegar, honey, soy sauce, and ketchup—all pantry staples— tasting the sauce as I went along to ensure the right balance of sweet and salty. I added granulated garlic and red pepper flakes for a punch of flavor.

I assumed that searing the chicken skin side down on the stovetop before adding the braising liquid would give me wonderfully crispy skin (initially), but I could fit only six thighs in my skillet in order to get even browning. What's more, I'd be dousing them with braising liquid anyway, so why bother chasing crispiness? I decided to ditch this step.

Instead, I laid eight chicken thighs skin side down in my cold skillet. My idea was to cook the chicken slowly in my flavorful sauce to begin rendering the fat from the skin. Then I'd turn the chicken skin side up to finish cooking with the skin above the level of the cooking liquid, presumably drying it out a bit and browning it in the process.

I set the skillet in a 425-degree oven. After about 20 minutes skin side down and 20 minutes skin side up, my chicken had reached an internal temperature of 175 degrees. But it looked awful. I kept cooking the chicken for a few more minutes until the skin turned an appetizing brown (chicken thighs can withstand longer cooking, and they actually get more tender when cooked to a higher temperature). Satisfied with the appearance of the skin, I transferred the chicken to a platter and turned my attention to finishing the sauce.

What had started as 1¾ cups of sauce had swelled to 3 cups of liquid from the addition of the chicken's juices. I ran the liquid through a fat separator, returned the defatted liquid to the skillet along with a small amount of cornstarch, and reduced it to ¾ cup, at which point it was just thick enough to coat the chicken and give it the shiny glaze I was looking for.

I gathered my tasters for servings of chicken with some extra sauce for dipping and a sprinkling of toasted sesame seeds. Thumbs up all around. The chicken was tender, and the sauce was balanced and just sweet enough. Mission accomplished: Sweet, savory sticky chicken in less than an hour.

—DIANE UNGER, *Cook's Country*

Sticky Chicken

SERVES 4

Trim any fatty pockets from the edges of the chicken thighs to ensure well-rendered skin. Cooking the thighs to 195 degrees melts the tough connective tissues while keeping the meat moist. This dish is best served with white rice.

8   (5- to 7-ounce) bone-in chicken thighs, trimmed
     Pepper
¾   cup cider vinegar
½   cup honey
¼   cup soy sauce
¼   cup ketchup
1   teaspoon granulated garlic
¼   teaspoon red pepper flakes
1   teaspoon cornstarch
1   teaspoon water
2   teaspoons toasted sesame seeds

1. Adjust oven rack to upper-middle position and heat oven to 425 degrees. Season chicken with pepper and arrange skin side down in 12-inch ovensafe skillet. Whisk vinegar, honey, soy sauce, ketchup, granulated garlic, and pepper flakes together in bowl and pour over chicken. (Skillet will be full.)

2. Bake chicken for 20 minutes. Flip chicken skin side up and continue to bake until skin is spotty brown and meat registers 195 to 200 degrees, 20 to 25 minutes longer. Transfer chicken to serving platter. Carefully pour pan juices into fat separator (skillet handle will be hot) and let settle for 5 minutes.

3. Dissolve cornstarch in water in small bowl. Return defatted juices to skillet and whisk in cornstarch mixture. Bring sauce to boil over high heat and cook until syrupy and spatula leaves trail when dragged through sauce, 7 to 9 minutes. (You should have about ¾ cup sauce.) Season with pepper to taste.

4. Off heat, return chicken to skillet and turn to coat with sauce. Flip chicken skin side up and sprinkle with sesame seeds. Serve.

CHICKEN MOLE POBLANO

✔ **WHY THIS RECIPE WORKS:** By stripping down mole poblano to only the most essential elements and steps, we turned this Mexican classic into an easy-to-make, yet still highly flavorful, dish. We built a pared-down chile paste in the food processor using ancho and chipotle chiles for a smoky, sweet, and subtly spicy base. Sesame seeds and almonds added richness and body while a slice of sandwich bread further bound the paste; a handful of herbs and dried spices rounded out its complex flavor. A couple ounces of unsweetened chocolate lent warmth and just enough bitterness. Instead of frying or toasting the various paste ingredients, we "oven-fried" the paste itself by adding more oil to the pot and letting it cook gently for 30 minutes in the oven. We then gently stewed chicken parts directly in the sauce so they could pick up its flavor.

Even if you've never tasted mole poblano, you might know of its prominent place in Mexican cuisine. The legends associated with its origin all seem to agree on one thing: This rich, velvety, deeply complex sauce, the hallmark of the Puebla region and widely considered the country's national dish, was conceived centuries ago to serve to dignitaries. To make it, cooks spent days gathering, frying or roasting, and then grinding nuts and seeds, dried chiles, herbs and warm spices, dried fruit, aromatics such as garlic and onion, and tomatoes into a paste thickened with stale bread or tortillas. The earthy, faintly bitter, fruity-sweet, smoky, and subtly spicy mixture (the term *mole* stems from the Nahuatl word *molli*, which means "sauce" or "concoction") was then fried to deepen its flavor; enriched with a little dark chocolate; thinned with liquid left over from poaching a chicken or turkey to yield a smooth, dark sauce; and poured over the poached poultry. Sopping it up with corn tortillas or rice meant not a drop was wasted.

To this day, preparing mole is a ritual in Mexican households, one that's often tackled over multiple days and reserved for special occasions. But stateside, it's also become a familiar dish in traditional Mexican restaurants and one that home cooks are often tempted to try. There are plenty of published recipes to choose from, many of which, I've found, are quite good—and, not surprisingly, incredibly labor-intensive. Then there are approaches that reduce the ingredients and the work to convenience products like commercial chili powder and no more than an hour or so of prepping and cooking, but they result in a rather lackluster sauce.

What I wanted was a mole recipe that struck a compromise between the depth and complexity of authentic versions and the more reasonable workload of modern approaches. My strategy: Start with a classic formula, and then, testing carefully, evaluate which components and steps could be simplified or cut altogether without undermining the end result.

I would begin with the chiles. Some recipes call for as many as six varieties, the most common being rich, raisiny sweet anchos; fruity and slightly spicy pasillas; and smoky chipotles (or mulatos). I tried a blend of all three, toasting them in the oven before letting them cool; removing their stems, seeds, and ribs; tearing them into pieces; and then soaking them so that they softened. To prepare the rest of the paste, I fried sesame seeds, peanuts, almonds, walnuts, and pecans in oil (rather than the traditional lard), followed by coriander and cumin and a couple of corn tortillas; pureed the nut-seed mixture with raisins (plumped beforehand in warm water), onion, garlic, tomato, dried oregano and thyme, ground cinnamon, and the drained chiles; and finally fried the paste to deepen and meld the flavors. In went a few ounces of bittersweet Mexican chocolate, which had been hard to track down but made the paste richer, darker, and a touch more bitter. I thinned it with chicken broth and then ladled it over a whole poached chicken—my placeholder poultry for the moment.

The sauce certainly was complex, but with so many components in the mix, the flavors of the individual chiles were subtle, and I guessed that only a very attuned palate would notice if I further downsized the list. Anchos made a good base chile, especially since I could enhance their earthy-sweet profile with the nuts, spices, raisins, and dark chocolate I was already using. Chipotles

CHICKEN MOLE POBLANO

were a must for their smokiness and heat, but instead of fussing with another dried chile, I minced a tablespoon of the easier-to-find canned kind, which also came with the benefit of punchy adobo sauce. The others could go.

I spent my next few tests weeding out some of the nuts. Ultimately, almonds were the only essential variety; they provided a baseline of richness and body, and the sesame seeds offered their distinctively earthy flavor, making walnuts, pecans, and peanuts superfluous. I also switched from corn tortillas to a slice of white sandwich bread—an ingredient I am more likely to have on hand—and no one was the wiser.

Those changes took care of the earthy, smoky, and spicy flavors I'd wanted to hit, but I also needed to tweak the tomato component. Tomato paste was better than the fresh tomatoes I'd been using: A couple of tablespoons rounded out the sauce with acidity as well as depth, and it was more convenient to use.

Finally, I circled back to the Mexican chocolate: The two biggest differences between this kind and European and American chocolate are that the former boasts a relatively coarse, rustic texture and is scented with cinnamon and sometimes other warm spices. You can really taste the difference between the two types if you try them in bar form, but once melted into the mole, the Mexican chocolate's distinctiveness was almost imperceptible. Unsweetened chocolate made a fine stand-in.

I'd cut the ingredient list down considerably, and I was anxious to do the same with the method—particularly the frying part, since frying each component once before grinding and then for a second time as a paste was a laborious process.

Instead, I tried toasting the chiles, nuts, seeds, spices, and bread together on a rimmed baking sheet in the oven and happily found that this delivered comparably rich-tasting results. And as long as I added the same amount of oil to the food processor as I had been using to fry, the consistency and richness of the paste weren't any different. But as it turned out, I didn't even need to go that far. Just to see how streamlined I could make the recipe, I skipped the toasting and simply fried the paste, and my tasters still didn't pick up on the change. I did need to toast the anchos to make them pliable enough to stem and seed, but otherwise I'd eliminated about an hour of work with no loss in flavor.

I also made a few tweaks to the soaking and frying steps. I sped up the soaking process by zapping the anchos and raisins together in the microwave. After processing all the ingredients for the paste, instead of frying it on the stove, where it required constant stirring to prevent scorching, I moved the pot to a low oven, where it required just a few stirs.

Back to my placeholder poached chicken: The broth it produced worked nicely for thinning the paste, but simply pouring the sauce over the cooked bird didn't yield a very cohesive dish. Switching to chicken parts allowed me to stew the meat directly in the sauce, where it soaked up much more flavor; plus, it enabled me to increase the amount of meat to serve at least six guests (mole is a for-company dish, after all). For the sauce base, I simply switched to using store-bought chicken broth, and that was fine.

When I tallied up all my changes, I'd cut the ingredient list by 30 percent (and limited it to supermarket staples only) and the marathon-like process by several hours—taking this from a dish I'd like to make to one that I actually would. But the most convincing part was the flavors, which were deeply complex and balanced.

—ANDREW JANJIGIAN, *Cook's Illustrated*

Chicken Mole Poblano

SERVES 6 TO 8

Our preference is to cook the chicken with the skin on, but it can be removed before cooking, if desired. Serve with white rice and/or corn tortillas. Vary the amount of cayenne (or omit it altogether) depending on how spicy you like your food.

- 3 ounces (6 to 8) dried ancho chiles
- 3½ cups chicken broth
- ½ cup raisins
- 1 onion, cut into 1-inch pieces
- ¼ cup vegetable oil
- 2 tablespoons tomato paste
- 4 garlic cloves, peeled
- 1 tablespoon minced canned chipotle in adobo sauce
- ¾ cup sliced almonds
- 1 slice hearty white sandwich bread, torn into 1-inch pieces
- 3 tablespoons sesame seeds

2 teaspoons salt

1–2 teaspoons cayenne pepper (optional)

1 teaspoon dried oregano

½ teaspoon dried thyme

½ teaspoon ground cinnamon

½ teaspoon ground cumin

½ teaspoon ground coriander

½ teaspoon pepper

2 ounces unsweetened chocolate, chopped coarse

4 pounds bone-in chicken pieces (split breasts cut in half, drumsticks, and/or thighs), trimmed

1. Adjust oven rack to middle position and heat oven to 325 degrees. Place anchos on rimmed baking sheet and toast until fragrant and pliable, about 5 minutes. Transfer to medium bowl and let cool for 5 minutes. Remove seeds, stems, and ribs from anchos and discard; tear flesh into ½-inch pieces and return pieces to bowl.

2. Add 2 cups broth and raisins to bowl with anchos, cover, and microwave until steaming, about 2 minutes. Let stand until softened, about 5 minutes. Drain mixture in fine-mesh strainer set over bowl, reserving liquid.

3. Process onion, 2 tablespoons oil, tomato paste, garlic, chipotle, and ancho-raisin mixture in food processor until smooth, about 5 minutes, scraping down sides of bowl as needed. Add almonds; bread; 2 tablespoons sesame seeds; salt; cayenne, if using; oregano; thyme; cinnamon; cumin; coriander; pepper; and ¼ cup reserved ancho soaking liquid and continue to process until smooth paste forms, about 3 minutes, scraping down sides of bowl as needed and adding additional soaking liquid if necessary.

4. Heat remaining 2 tablespoons oil in Dutch oven over medium-high heat until shimmering. Add mole paste and cook, stirring frequently, until steaming, about 3 minutes. Stir in chocolate until incorporated. Transfer pot to oven and cook, uncovered, for 30 minutes, stirring twice. (Paste will darken during cooking.) (Paste can be refrigerated for up to 1 week or frozen for up to 1 month.)

5. Place pot over medium-high heat and whisk remaining reserved soaking liquid and remaining 1½ cups broth into mole paste until smooth. Place chicken in even layer in pot, reduce heat to low, cover, and cook until breasts register 160 degrees and drumsticks/thighs register 175 degrees, 25 to 30 minutes, stirring halfway through cooking. Transfer chicken pieces to serving dish as they come up to temperature. Pour sauce over chicken, garnish with remaining 1 tablespoon sesame seeds, and serve.

GRILLED SPICE-RUBBED CHICKEN DRUMSTICKS

✓ **WHY THIS RECIPE WORKS:** Meaty chicken drumsticks are sorely underutilized, but they are a great choice for grilling. After brining to season them and help them retain their juices, we coated the drumsticks with a lively spice rub. Cooking the chicken over indirect heat until it reached an internal temperature of 190 degrees gave the connective tissue plenty of time to soften while the skin gradually rendered and crisped; the result was juicy, ultratender meat and skin that released from the grill grate with ease. We finished by cooking the drumsticks briefly over the coals to capture some tasty char before serving.

Chicken breasts have been the most popular part of the chicken for decades, thighs are currently trendy, and wings are a sports-bar standby. Drumsticks, on the other hand, have been neglected. Maybe that's because when you eat them as part of a whole chicken, they don't seem that special. In fact, they can be chewy and tough. Nevertheless, with their built-in handles and conveniently small size, they are tailor-made for a cookout. They also happen to be the most economical part of the bird.

I decided to devise a foolproof way to grill drumsticks to perfection. In my book, that means fully rendered, nicely browned skin and moist, flavorful meat. And if I really wanted to start a drumstick fad, I'd have to make sure my method was easy, even for grill novices.

There aren't a lot of drumstick-specific recipes out there; most just lump them under the heading "parts." And most of the recipes I managed to find followed a similar pattern: Soak chicken in a marinade for a few hours or simply dust it with a spice rub and then grill it over a medium fire until it's done. If a final internal temperature was specified, it was usually 165 degrees.

I decided to put off marinades and spice rubs until I had figured out the best grilling strategy. My first stop was the popular grill-over-medium-fire-until-done approach, which took only about 25 minutes, but speed turned out to be its only virtue. Fat from the drumsticks

GRILLED SPICE-RUBBED CHICKEN DRUMSTICKS

dripped onto the coals, causing flames to shoot up, so I was frantically moving the pieces around to avoid scorching, which was difficult because the chicken skin was still stuck to the grate. Because the drumsticks cooked pretty quickly, the skin, though inevitably scorched and torn in spots, was still blubbery and soft underneath. Meanwhile, the meat was tough and even a bit dry.

I had a pretty good idea of how to fix that last problem. All parts of the chicken are safe to eat at 160 degrees. Taking white meat any higher dries it out, but dark meat is different. We've found that it benefits from being cooked to as high as 190 degrees, especially if it's brought to that temperature slowly. That's because the legs and thighs have a lot of connective tissue, which is made up of a sturdy protein called collagen. This can work to the smart cook's advantage because, given time, that collagen transforms into rich gelatin, which lubricates the muscle fibers so the meat is juicy and tender. Collagen begins to break down at 140 degrees. The more time the meat spends between 140 degrees and its final temperature, the more collagen will be converted into gelatin and the more tender and juicy the meat will be.

Slowing down the cooking was imperative. On a grill, that means cooking over indirect heat. I lit a full chimney of charcoal, and when it was partially covered with ash, I poured it over half the grill. I placed the chicken, skin side down, on the cooler side; covered the grill; and settled in to enjoy one of my favorite features of indirect grilling: doing nothing.

Except for one moment when I rearranged the pieces so that they all had equal time close to the coals, I carried on doing nothing for a full 50 minutes. But in that time, good things were happening inside the grill. The drumsticks were shedding their excess fat, but without any coals beneath them, there were no flare-ups to contend with. This meant I didn't need to frantically move them around to avoid scorching—they clung lightly to the grill grate but were easily dislodged. Once the drumsticks reached 185 degrees, they easily released from the grate, so I moved them over to the hotter side to char and crisp up a bit, which took only about 5 minutes.

This batch was a big improvement over the previous one. The skin was rendered, not rubbery, and the meat was tender and reasonably juicy. I wondered if adding one step to my ultrasimple process might be worthwhile.

I almost always brine or salt white meat (and whole birds) before cooking. It seasons the meat, but more important, it changes the meat's proteins in such a way that they hold on to more of their moisture when cooked. This extra step usually isn't necessary when cooking fattier dark meat because it is not as easily overcooked. But I was cooking the drumsticks for an unusually long time in the grill's dry heat, so I figured some kind of salt treatment might be advantageous.

Salting takes at least 6 hours, but brining takes only 30 minutes, so I opted for brining. Sure enough, the saltwater soak plus my mostly hands-off cooking method produced the juiciest drumsticks I had ever eaten. If only the flavor were a bit more interesting.

In the test kitchen, we often avoid marinating. The oil tends to drip and cause flare-ups on the grill (admittedly, this would be less of a problem with my indirect cooking strategy), and the acid turns the exterior of the meat mealy and mushy. Glazes can add interest, but they make eating chicken out of hand a messy proposition. I opted for a spice rub instead.

I started with sugar, which would melt and turn tacky to help the spices stick. I then added paprika, chili powder, garlic powder, cayenne, salt, and pepper. After brining the chicken, I patted it dry and coated it with the rub. One hour later I had chicken that would be the star of any cookout. I also developed two more spice rubs. After all, a single flavor profile might not be enough to sustain a new drumstick-eating trend, and I wanted this craze to have legs.

—ANDREA GEARY, *Cook's Illustrated*

Grilled Spice-Rubbed Chicken Drumsticks
SERVES 6

Before applying the spice rub, smooth the skin over the drumsticks so it is covering as much surface area as possible. This will help the skin render evenly and prevent the meat from drying out.

½ **cup salt**

5 **pounds chicken drumsticks**

1 **recipe spice rub (recipes follow)**

1. Dissolve salt in 2 quarts cold water in large container. Submerge drumsticks in brine, cover, and refrigerate for 30 minutes to 1 hour.

2. Place spice rub on plate. Remove chicken from brine and pat dry with paper towels. Holding drumstick by bone end, press lightly into rub on all sides. Pat gently to remove excess rub. Repeat with remaining drumsticks.

3A. **FOR A CHARCOAL GRILL:** Open bottom grill vent halfway and light large chimney starter filled with charcoal briquettes (6 quarts). When top coals are partially covered with ash, pour evenly over half of grill. Set cooking grate in place, cover, and open lid vent halfway. Heat grill until hot, about 5 minutes.

3B. **FOR A GAS GRILL:** Turn all burners to high, cover, and heat grill until hot, about 15 minutes. Leave primary burner on high and turn off other burner(s). (If your grill has three burners, you may need to turn on burner next to primary burner to maintain grill temperature between 325 and 350 degrees.)

4. Clean and oil cooking grate. Place chicken, skin side down, on grate over cooler side of grill. Cover grill and cook for 25 minutes. Rearrange pieces so that drumsticks that were closest to edge are now closer to heat source and vice versa. Cover grill and cook until chicken registers 185 to 190 degrees, 20 to 30 minutes.

5. Move all chicken to hotter side of grill and cook, turning occasionally, until skin is nicely charred, about 5 minutes. Transfer to platter, tent with foil, and let rest for 10 minutes. Serve.

Barbecue Spice Rub

MAKES ABOUT ⅓ CUP

Granulated garlic can be substituted for the garlic powder, if desired.

- 3 tablespoons packed brown sugar
- 1 tablespoon paprika
- 1 tablespoon chili powder
- 2 teaspoons garlic powder
- ¾ teaspoon salt
- ¾ teaspoon pepper
- ¼ teaspoon cayenne pepper

Combine all ingredients in small bowl.

Jerk-Style Spice Rub

MAKES ABOUT ¼ CUP

If whole allspice berries are unavailable, you can substitute 2 teaspoons of ground allspice.

- 1 tablespoon allspice berries
- 1 tablespoon black peppercorns
- 1½ teaspoons dried thyme
- 2 tablespoons packed brown sugar
- 2 teaspoons garlic powder
- 1½ teaspoons dry mustard
- ¾ teaspoon salt
- ¾ teaspoon cayenne pepper

Grind allspice, peppercorns, and thyme in spice grinder or mortar with pestle until coarsely ground. Transfer to bowl and stir in remaining ingredients.

Ras el Hanout Spice Rub

MAKES ABOUT ½ CUP

This North African spice blend delivers a complex flavor from a mix of warm spices. Though not strictly authentic, smoked paprika may be substituted for half the sweet paprika to produce an even more complex flavor.

- 2 tablespoons paprika
- 4 teaspoons ground coriander
- 4 teaspoons ground cumin
- 1 tablespoon packed brown sugar
- 1 teaspoon ground cardamom
- 1 teaspoon ground cinnamon
- ¾ teaspoon salt
- ½ teaspoon ground cloves
- ½ teaspoon ground nutmeg
- ½ teaspoon cayenne pepper

Combine all ingredients in bowl.

ITALIAN-STYLE TURKEY MEATBALLS

✓ **WHY THIS RECIPE WORKS:** Our turkey meatballs rival those made from beef or pork, thanks to a few test kitchen tricks. A traditional milk-and-bread panade made the meatballs too wet, so instead we worked egg and fresh bread crumbs into ground turkey. A small amount of unflavored gelatin boosted the lean turkey's juiciness, and Parmesan cheese, anchovies, tomato paste, and shiitake mushrooms reinforced the dish's savory flavor. We chilled the rolled meatballs in the refrigerator to help them set before browning them in a skillet. Once the meatballs had taken on some good color, we pulled together a simple pantry tomato sauce. Letting the meatballs finish cooking in the simmering sauce made for a flavorful finish.

I can see the appeal of using ground turkey in place of beef or pork in a meatball, since many folks these days want to eat less red meat. But when I swapped ground turkey into my usual meatball recipe (an Italian red-sauce version), I got something that was altogether disappointing. The meat mixture was so wet that it was difficult to shape, and the meatballs slumped during the frying step, leaving them more pyramid-shaped than spherical. Once cooked, they were mushy overall yet grainy inside. And their flavor was entirely uninspiring. I wanted an easy-to-form turkey meatball with the same traits as a knockout beef or pork version: a moist, tender, slightly springy texture and rich, savory flavor.

My standard meatball recipe (like most) goes like this: Combine ground meat and seasonings with egg and a panade—a moistened bread-crumb mixture that helps the meat hold on to liquid as it cooks and keeps its texture open and tender. With beef or pork, you want to handle the mixture as gently as possible, since overworking can cause the meat proteins to tighten up, creating a too-springy, sausage-like consistency. But as I had already discovered, turkey is another beast altogether: Although it contains the same sticky proteins as beef and pork, it also has a higher moisture content (ground turkey contains about 71 percent moisture versus 66 and 61 percent for pork and beef, respectively). This means that even after a good amount of mixing, ground turkey remains wet and hard to work

with. Commercially ground turkey also has a finer texture than beef or pork, which is why it cooks up mushy. The fine consistency also means the meat has a harder time holding on to moisture.

There are three options when buying commercially ground turkey: 85 percent lean, 93 percent lean, and 99 percent lean. I tried all three, and I wasn't surprised when the 99 percent lean type produced ultradry, nearly inedible results. I would go with the fattier options, both of which produced moister meatballs.

My recipe called for panko (Japanese dried bread crumbs, which we like for their consistently dry texture) soaked in milk. Since the turkey was so wet to begin with, I figured that the milk was unnecessary and probably partly why the meatballs were so difficult to roll. Indeed, when I left out the milk and just stirred the meat, egg, and panko together, the mixture was stiffer and easier to work with—but the cooked meatballs were somewhat dense.

A better solution was switching to sandwich bread, which I ground to fine crumbs in a food processor. In terms of moisture content, the crumbs were midway between milk-soaked panko and dry panko—dry enough to soak up some of the water in the turkey yet still moist enough to keep the meatballs from becoming dense.

But the meatballs were still too mushy, and they continued to be grainy. In an attempt to repair the mushiness, I added another egg, hoping it would firm up the meatballs once cooked, but the extra liquid once again made the mixture too hard to work with. Ultimately, I found that a 15-minute postshaping refrigeration period was the key to creating a springy, not mushy, texture in the cooked meatballs. That's because it gave the myosin, a sticky, soluble protein in meat, time to bind the meat together. (It also firmed up the mixture, making it the easiest yet to shape.)

Finally, it occurred to me that adding some powdered gelatin might help mitigate the graininess of the meat by trapping some of its moisture, and indeed it did. The slick gelatin also created a juicy mouthfeel.

I'd solved the textural problems; now I needed to work on flavor. Italy isn't the only country known for its meatballs, so I knew I'd want to come up with some variations once I'd perfected my Italian version. I considered Parmesan cheese, which is rich in glutamates, compounds that enhance the meaty umami flavor of foods; it added a savory boost but was subtle enough to work with any flavor profile. Glutamate-rich anchovies worked similarly, amplifying meatiness without announcing their presence.

The last umami-enhancing ingredient I used was a seemingly unusual one: dried shiitake mushrooms. Shiitakes are naturally high in glutamates, and though they are most commonly used in Asian cooking, their flavor is relatively neutral, so I knew they'd work no matter how I flavored the meatballs. I reconstituted them in hot water (making sure to add the soaking liquid to the sauce to retain all of the mushrooms' flavor) and then chopped them fine in the food processor.

Lastly, I tackled the cooking method. For ease, I'd been browning the meatballs in oil in a skillet before removing them, making a quick tomato sauce, and returning them to the skillet to cook through. As they simmered in the sauce, the meatballs picked up that rich flavor.

Move over, pork and beef. I'll still use you to make meatballs—but maybe not quite as often.

—ANDREW JANJIGIAN, *Cook's Illustrated*

Italian-Style Turkey Meatballs

SERVES 4 TO 6

Serve with spaghetti.

1	cup chicken broth
½	ounce dried shiitake mushrooms
2	slices hearty white sandwich bread, torn into 1-inch pieces
1	ounce Parmesan cheese, grated (½ cup), plus extra for serving
1	tablespoon chopped fresh parsley
1½	teaspoons unflavored gelatin
	Salt and pepper
4	anchovy fillets, rinsed, patted dry, and minced
1½	pounds 85 or 93 percent lean ground turkey
1	large egg, lightly beaten
4	garlic cloves, minced
1	(14.5-ounce) can whole peeled tomatoes
½	teaspoon dried oregano
⅛	teaspoon red pepper flakes
3	tablespoons extra-virgin olive oil
2	tablespoons tomato paste
¼	cup chopped fresh basil
	Sugar

1. Microwave broth and mushrooms in covered bowl until steaming, about 1 minute. Let sit until softened, about 5 minutes. Drain mushrooms in fine-mesh strainer and reserve liquid.

2. Pulse bread in food processor until finely ground, 10 to 15 pulses; transfer bread crumbs to large bowl (do not wash processor bowl). Add Parmesan, parsley, gelatin, 1 teaspoon salt, and ¼ teaspoon pepper to bowl with bread crumbs and mix until thoroughly combined. Pulse mushrooms and half of anchovies in food processor until chopped fine, 10 to 15 pulses. Add mushroom mixture, turkey, egg, and half of garlic to bowl with bread-crumb mixture and mix with your hands until thoroughly combined. Divide mixture into 16 portions (about ¼ cup each). Using your hands, roll each portion into ball; transfer meatballs to plate and refrigerate for 15 minutes.

3. Pulse tomatoes and their juice in food processor to coarse puree, 10 to 15 pulses. Combine oregano, pepper flakes, remaining anchovies, remaining garlic, and ¼ teaspoon pepper in small bowl; set aside.

4. Heat oil in 12-inch nonstick skillet over medium-high heat until shimmering. Add meatballs and cook until well browned all over, 5 to 7 minutes. Transfer meatballs to paper towel–lined plate, leaving fat in skillet.

5. Add reserved anchovy mixture to skillet and cook, stirring constantly, until fragrant, about 30 seconds. Increase heat to high; stir in tomato paste, reserved mushroom liquid, and pureed tomatoes; and bring to simmer. Return meatballs to skillet, reduce heat to medium-low, cover, and cook until meatballs register 160 degrees, 12 to 15 minutes, turning meatballs once. Transfer meatballs to platter, increase heat to high, and simmer sauce until slightly thickened, 3 to 5 minutes. Stir in basil and season with sugar, salt, and pepper to taste. Pour sauce over meatballs and serve, passing extra Parmesan separately.

ITALIAN-STYLE TURKEY MEATBALLS

Asian-Style Turkey Meatballs
SERVES 4 TO 6

Serve with white rice.

1½	cups chicken broth
½	ounce dried shiitake mushrooms
2	slices hearty white sandwich bread, torn into 1-inch pieces
1	ounce Parmesan cheese, grated (½ cup)
6	scallions, white parts minced, green parts sliced thin on bias
1	tablespoon sugar
2½	teaspoons unflavored gelatin
	Salt
1½	teaspoons white pepper
2	anchovy fillets, rinsed and patted dry
1½	pounds 85 or 93 percent lean ground turkey
1	large egg, lightly beaten
2	tablespoons water
3	tablespoons vegetable oil
2	garlic cloves, minced
1	tablespoon soy sauce
2	teaspoons sesame oil

1. Microwave broth and mushrooms in covered bowl until steaming, about 1 minute. Let sit until softened, about 5 minutes. Drain mushrooms in fine-mesh strainer and reserve liquid.

2. Pulse bread in food processor until finely ground, 10 to 15 pulses; transfer bread crumbs to large bowl (do not wash processor bowl). Add Parmesan, scallion whites, half of scallion greens, sugar, 1½ teaspoons gelatin, 1 teaspoon salt, and 1 teaspoon white pepper to bowl with bread crumbs and mix until thoroughly combined. Pulse mushrooms and anchovies in food processor until chopped fine, 10 to 15 pulses. Add mushroom mixture, turkey, and egg to bowl with bread-crumb mixture and mix with your hands until thoroughly combined. Divide mixture into 16 portions (about ¼ cup each). Using your hands, roll each portion into ball; transfer meatballs to plate and refrigerate for 15 minutes.

3. Sprinkle remaining 1 teaspoon gelatin over water in bowl and let stand until gelatin softens, about 5 minutes. Heat vegetable oil in 12-inch nonstick skillet over medium-high heat until shimmering. Add meatballs and cook until well browned all over, 5 to 7 minutes. Transfer meatballs to paper towel–lined plate, leaving fat in skillet.

4. Add garlic to skillet and cook, stirring constantly, until fragrant, about 30 seconds. Increase heat to high, stir in soy sauce, sesame oil, reserved mushroom liquid, gelatin mixture, and remaining ½ teaspoon white pepper and bring to simmer. Return meatballs to skillet, reduce heat to medium-low, cover, and cook until meatballs register 160 degrees, 12 to 15 minutes, turning meatballs once. Transfer meatballs to platter. Season sauce with salt to taste, pour over meatballs, garnish with remaining scallion greens, and serve.

Moroccan-Style Turkey Meatballs
SERVES 4 TO 6

Serve with white rice or couscous.

2	slices hearty white sandwich bread, torn into 1-inch pieces
1½	teaspoons unflavored gelatin
1	ounce Parmesan cheese, grated (½ cup)
½	cup chopped fresh cilantro
2	tablespoons chopped fresh parsley
1	tablespoon paprika
1½	teaspoons ground cumin
1	teaspoon ground coriander
	Salt and pepper
½	teaspoon ground cinnamon
¼	teaspoon ground nutmeg
¼	teaspoon cayenne pepper
2	carrots, peeled and cut into 1-inch pieces
2	anchovy fillets, rinsed and patted dry
1½	pounds 85 or 93 percent lean ground turkey
1	large egg, lightly beaten
1	onion, cut into 1-inch pieces
3	tablespoons extra-virgin olive oil
2	tablespoons tomato paste
¼	teaspoon ground ginger
1	cup chicken broth
¼	teaspoon saffron threads, crumbled

1. Pulse bread in food processor until finely ground, 10 to 15 pulses; transfer bread crumbs to large bowl (do not wash processor bowl). Add gelatin, Parmesan, 2 tablespoons cilantro, parsley, 2 teaspoons paprika, cumin, coriander, 1 teaspoon salt, ½ teaspoon pepper, cinnamon, nutmeg, and ⅛ teaspoon cayenne and mix until thoroughly combined. Pulse carrots and anchovies in food processor until carrots are chopped fine, 10 to 15 pulses. Add carrot mixture, turkey, and egg to bowl with bread-crumb mixture and mix with your hands until thoroughly combined. Divide mixture into 16 portions (about ¼ cup each). Using your hands, roll each portion into ball; transfer meatballs to plate and refrigerate for 15 minutes.

2. Pulse onion in food processor until finely chopped, 10 to 15 pulses. Heat oil in 12-inch nonstick skillet over medium-high heat until shimmering. Add meatballs and cook until well browned all over, 5 to 7 minutes. Transfer meatballs to paper towel–lined plate, leaving fat in skillet.

3. Add tomato paste, ginger, and onion to skillet and cook, stirring constantly, until onion is softened, about 4 minutes. Increase heat to high; add broth, saffron, ¼ cup cilantro, remaining 1 teaspoon paprika, and remaining ⅛ teaspoon cayenne; and bring to simmer. Return meatballs to skillet, reduce heat to medium-low, cover, and cook until meatballs register 160 degrees, 12 to 15 minutes, turning meatballs once. Transfer meatballs to platter, increase heat to medium-high, and simmer sauce until slightly thickened, 3 to 5 minutes. Season sauce with salt and pepper to taste. Pour sauce over meatballs, garnish with remaining 2 tablespoons cilantro, and serve.

NOTES FROM THE TEST KITCHEN

GRINDING TURKEY AT HOME

If you have the time, grinding your own turkey thighs yields excellent meatballs.

Start with one 2-pound turkey thigh, skinned, boned, trimmed, and cut into ½-inch pieces. Place pieces on large plate in single layer. Freeze until pieces are very firm and hardened around edges, 35 to 45 minutes. Pulse one-third of turkey in food processor until chopped into ⅛-inch pieces, 18 to 22 pulses, stopping and redistributing turkey around bowl as needed to ensure even grinding. Transfer turkey to large bowl and repeat 2 times with remaining turkey. Yields 1½ pounds.

EASIER ROAST TURKEY WITH GRAVY

✓ **WHY THIS RECIPE WORKS:** For a crisp, juicy, and, above all, hassle-free holiday turkey, we looked to maximize flavor and browning while minimizing work. To infuse the mild bird with seasoning and boost its moisture retention, we salted it at least 24 hours ahead of time; applying a baking powder rub before roasting ensured browned, crisp skin. By preheating a heat-retaining baking stone as well as our roasting pan, we were able to jump-start the meaty leg quarters' cooking so the light and dark meat would finish cooking at the same time. We protected the quicker-cooking breast meat from the intense heat using a foil shield. For a burnished finish, we dropped the oven temperature, removed the foil shield, and allowed the breast to brown while the bird finished cooking. The extreme heat helped the turkey's juices brown and reduce into concentrated drippings, which we turned into a flavorful gravy while the turkey rested.

An idyllic roast turkey isn't hard to envision: Picture crispy, well-browned skin and moist, juicy, well-seasoned meat. And don't forget a lightly thickened, full-flavored gravy. But alas, the perfect bird is not easy to come by. Crispy skin is elusive, and an ever-present hurdle when roasting whole poultry is that while the dark meat needs to reach 175 degrees, the delicate breast meat will dry out if it's cooked beyond 160 degrees. The gravy is easier to get right, but it takes about an hour of simmering to produce rich, well-rounded flavor.

Over the years, we've jumped through all kinds of hoops to try to get both the dark and white meat properly cooked: roasting the breast and leg quarters separately, butterflying the turkey so it lies flat, flipping the hot turkey over partway through roasting, and even icing down the breasts before putting the turkey in the oven. But this year, I wanted to find a simpler way: In other words, I wanted all the advantages of a great roasted turkey with none of the disadvantages.

First on my agenda: salt, which alters the proteins in meat and helps it retain moisture as it cooks. There are two ways to introduce salt into a turkey: brining and salting. A brine penetrates the flesh rather quickly, in

6 to 12 hours, but there are drawbacks. For one, brining adds water to the skin, which hinders browning. Another is that the process requires a container large enough to hold 2 gallons of brine along with a 14-pound turkey—that takes up a lot of refrigerator space.

Salting a turkey (underneath the skin, for proper penetration) works a little differently. Salt draws out moisture from the meat, and this moisture mixes with the salt to form a concentrated brine. Over time, the salt migrates back into the meat, seasoning it and helping keep it juicy. Salt also dries out the skin, so it browns more readily. And although salting requires more time—24 to 48 hours—it eventually results in fully seasoned meat. Another bonus of salting is that it occupies less fridge space since no large container is required.

Salting, it seemed, was the way to go, and while I was at it, I also wanted to incorporate sugar, which helps accentuate turkey's mild flavor. I found that 4 teaspoons of sugar and 4 tablespoons of salt were the right amounts for a 12- to 14-pound bird. Using my fingers, I loosened the skin of the turkey and then rubbed my salt-sugar blend on the flesh and in the cavity of the bird. I then arranged the bird on a wire rack set in a rimmed baking sheet, transferred it to the fridge, and waited 24 hours for the salt to do its work.

Because the dark meat needs to cook to a higher temperature than the white meat, some of our turkey recipes call for starting the bird breast side down on a V-rack set inside a roasting pan, an arrangement that shields the breast from some of the heat. The bird is then flipped breast side up partway through cooking. But handling a heavy, steaming-hot bird in the middle of the roasting period is never an easy task. In the spirit of producing a supersimple recipe, I looked at our recipe for Weeknight Roast Chicken. There, we skip the awkward flip by placing the bird breast side up directly in a preheated skillet. The pan transfers heat into the portion of the bird that needs it most—the thighs and legs. At the same time, the convection currents act more slowly on the breasts. The result? A perfectly cooked chicken.

A skillet was too small for a turkey, but a roasting pan would work. I placed one on the bottom rack of the oven and turned the dial to 500 degrees. When the oven was up to temperature, I swirled 2 tablespoons of oil into the hot pan before setting my salted turkey in place. To avoid overheating the oil and smoking out the kitchen, I dropped the oven temperature to 425 degrees immediately after putting in the turkey. Then, after about 45 minutes, I reduced the temperature to 325 degrees for a gentle finish. An hour and a half later, the breast hit 160 degrees. However, the dark meat was well short of the 175 degrees I was shooting for. I needed a better way to slow down the breast and speed up the leg quarters.

Turning the oven above 500 degrees wasn't possible. If I couldn't get the oven any hotter, I needed to find a way to store some of the heat it produced and then direct that heat at the turkey. How about using a baking stone? Baking stones are designed to absorb heat and then deliver that heat to whatever is placed on top of them. For my next go-round, I slipped a baking stone under my roasting pan in the oven. While they preheated, I covered the turkey's breast with a double layer of aluminum foil, which would shield it from some heat. I would remove the foil when I turned the oven down to 325 so that the breast could brown. Sure enough, this approach produced exactly the results I wanted. This was no small victory: With no extra effort—just a strategically placed piece of kitchenware—the turkey legs and thighs registered 175 degrees just as the breasts reached 160.

My only critique was that the skin wasn't quite brown or crispy enough, so I employed a test kitchen trick that makes all the difference: rubbing baking powder onto the skin. Baking powder has alkaline properties that speed up browning. It also causes proteins in the skin to break down more readily and produce crispier results.

I prepared one last bird, salting it overnight and then rubbing 1 teaspoon of baking powder (combined with 1½ teaspoons of oil for easy distribution) on top before following my new roasting protocol. When I pulled this bird out of the oven, I knew instantly that the baking powder had done its job. The skin was deeply bronzed and beautifully crispy. I transferred the turkey to a carving board to rest while I contemplated the drippings.

When I tasted the drippings, one thing jumped out at me: They were salty and intensely flavorful. The supplementary heat from the baking stone had caused the juices to reduce far more than usual, making them superconcentrated. I transferred the drippings to a fat separator, making sure to scrape the flavorful fond from the bottom of the pan. I proceeded with a classic gravy-making routine, starting with browning the neck and giblets from the turkey along with onion, carrot, and herbs in some of the reserved fat and then stirring in flour to make a roux. Finally, I whisked in chicken broth and white wine and let the gravy simmer to thicken.

After about 10 minutes (the drippings were so intense that no real reduction was necessary), I dipped a spoon in for a taste and found that the superconcentrated jus had produced a gravy that was far too salty, even though I hadn't added any additional seasonings. The solution was simple: Instead of using chicken broth, I swapped in water (unsalted broth was an option, but it seemed unnecessary since I already had flavor in spades). Now I had a deeply flavorful gravy—in record time.

Roasting a turkey was now less of a hassle, and I could produce the gravy while the bird rested. From now on, the first thing I'll be reaching for when roasting a turkey is a baking stone.

—LAN LAM, *Cook's Illustrated*

Easier Roast Turkey with Gravy

SERVES 10 TO 12

Note that this recipe requires refrigerating the seasoned bird for 24 to 48 hours. This recipe was developed and tested using Diamond Crystal Kosher Salt. If you have Morton Kosher Salt, which is denser than Diamond Crystal, reduce the salt in step 1 to 3 tablespoons and rub 1 tablespoon of the salt mixture into each breast, 1½ teaspoons into each leg, and the remainder into the cavity. If using a self-basting turkey (such as a frozen Butterball) or a kosher turkey, do not apply the salt mixture to the bird. The success of this recipe is dependent on saturating the baking stone and roasting pan with heat.

Kosher salt and pepper
4 teaspoons sugar
1 (12- to 14-pound) turkey, neck and giblets removed and reserved for gravy
2½ tablespoons vegetable oil
1 teaspoon baking powder
1 small onion, chopped fine
1 carrot, sliced thin

5 sprigs fresh parsley
2 bay leaves
5 tablespoons all-purpose flour
3¼ cups water
¼ cup dry white wine

1. Combine 4 tablespoons salt and sugar in bowl. Place turkey, breast side up, on counter. Using your fingers, carefully loosen skin covering breast and legs. Rub 4 teaspoons salt-sugar mixture under skin of each breast, 2 teaspoons under skin of each leg, and remaining salt-sugar mixture inside cavity. Tuck wings behind back and tie legs together with kitchen twine. Place turkey on wire rack set in rimmed baking sheet and refrigerate, uncovered, for 24 to 48 hours.

2. At least 30 minutes before roasting turkey, adjust oven rack to lowest position, set baking stone on rack, set roasting pan on baking stone, and heat oven to 500 degrees. Combine 1½ teaspoons oil and baking powder in small bowl. Pat turkey dry with paper towels. Rub oil mixture evenly over turkey. Cover turkey breast with double layer of aluminum foil.

3. Remove roasting pan from oven. Drizzle remaining 2 tablespoons oil into roasting pan. Place turkey, breast side up, in pan and return pan to oven. Reduce oven temperature to 425 degrees and roast for 45 minutes.

4. Remove foil, reduce oven temperature to 325 degrees, and continue to roast until breast registers 160 degrees and drumsticks/thighs register 175 degrees, 1 to 1½ hours longer.

NOTES FROM THE TEST KITCHEN

WINGING THE TURKEY NECK
Not all turkeys come with a neck—a standard gravy flavor booster. Luckily, a portion of the wings makes a great substitute.

Use kitchen shears to cut between midsection and drumette of each wing, leaving drumette in place both for appearance and to keep bird stable during roasting and carving. Use chef's knife to separate wingtip and midsection.

5. Using spatula, loosen turkey from roasting pan; transfer to carving board and let rest, uncovered, for 45 minutes. While turkey rests, using wooden spoon, scrape up any browned bits from bottom of roasting pan. Strain mixture through fine-mesh strainer set over bowl. Transfer drippings to fat separator and let rest for 10 minutes. Reserve 3 tablespoons fat and defatted liquid (you should have 1 cup; add water if necessary). Discard remaining fat.

6. Heat reserved fat in large saucepan over medium-high heat until shimmering. Add reserved neck and giblets and cook until well browned, 10 to 12 minutes. Transfer neck and giblets to large plate. Reduce heat to medium; add onion, carrot, parsley sprigs, and bay leaves; and cook, stirring frequently, until vegetables are softened, 5 to 7 minutes. Add flour and cook, stirring constantly, until flour is well coated with fat, about 1 minute. Slowly whisk in reserved defatted liquid and cook until thickened, about 1 minute. Whisk in water and wine, return neck and giblets to pan, and bring to simmer. Simmer for 10 minutes, then season with salt and pepper to taste. Discard neck. Strain gravy through fine-mesh strainer, discarding solids, and transfer to serving bowl. Carve turkey and arrange on serving platter. Serve with gravy.

COD IN SAFFRON BROTH WITH CHORIZO AND POTATOES

✔ **WHY THIS RECIPE WORKS:** For tender, perfectly cooked cod served in an elegant, fragrant broth, we needed to take a gentle approach. Braising is a great way to gradually cook delicate fish, so we prepared a flavorful broth by enhancing white wine and clam juice with garlic, chopped onion, spicy Spanish-style chorizo, and saffron. Waxy red potatoes, sliced into coins to mirror the slices of chorizo, added some heft and brought just the right creaminess to the flavorful broth. After adding a hit of lemon for brightness, we ladled the broth over the cooked fillets for serving. A sprinkling of parsley and a drizzle of olive oil over the flaky fish brought it all together.

Home cooks in countries bordering the Mediterranean Sea know their way around fresh seafood, and when I began work on *The Complete Mediterranean Cookbook*, my research introduced me to the dizzying number of ways they put the daily catch to good use. One approach really sparked my interest: firm whitefish bathed in a golden, saffron-infused broth. A popular preparation in Spain, it was not quite a soup but not quite a braise, either. I didn't want to get hung up on labels, though—I wanted to develop a recipe of my own.

My first roadblock came when I went to the fish counter. Hake is a commonly used fish in Spanish cooking. Firm and mild tasting, it takes well to a whole host of flavors and preparations, but I soon discovered it's not widely available stateside. I wanted my dish to be authentic, but I needed to come up with some alternatives if I was going to pull it off in New England. Though cod isn't native to Mediterranean waters, its medium-firm texture and clean, mild flavor comes close to hake's; equally mild haddock would also pass muster.

With my star ingredient at the ready, I worked on the flavor profile. Saffron was a must—not only would it give the broth a gorgeous golden hue, but it would also infuse the dish with its distinct balance of honey and grass notes plus some subtle bitterness. I wanted to use a judicious amount of this premium spice, so for my first attempt, I added it last so its flavor wouldn't be drowned out during cooking. After browning chopped onion to create my broth's base, I poured in both water and clam juice for a clean, seafood-forward taste. Using a single bottle of clam juice and a cup or so of water gave me enough liquid to gently cook the fish without turning the dish into a soup. Next, I added the cod fillets and let them gently cook through, covered, in the simmering broth. When the fillets were halfway done, I added the crumbled saffron threads, allowing their rich color to suffuse the broth.

I plated this first version, spooning some of the broth over the cod before tasting it. The broth was subtle—almost too much so. Adding the saffron late had had the opposite effect I wanted: Its flavor was muted, leaving the broth bland and doing the mild cod no favors. Furthermore, this brothy dish would hardly serve as a meal. For my next try, I needed to bump up the flavor and add some more heft.

This time, I enhanced the browned onion base with some garlic and bloomed the saffron right in among those aromatics, instantly bringing the sparse red threads to life. To bulk up the dish while also infusing it with more impactful flavors, I stirred sliced Spanish-style chorizo into this fragrant base. I knew this bold addition threatened to overpower the mild-mannered cod, so I

COD IN SAFFRON BROTH WITH CHORIZO AND POTATOES

used a mere 3 ounces, just enough to introduce savory heat and occasional meaty bites of chorizo to contrast the flaky fish.

For the liquid components, I cut back on water slightly, brightened the savory broth with white wine, and added a bay leaf for some herbal nuance. Small red potatoes seemed like an easy way to turn this dish into a satisfying meal, so I sliced them into thin rounds and added them along with the cod. Just 10 minutes later the broth was deeply fragrant and the cod was fully cooked, but the potatoes were still too firm. I knew that continuing to cook the potatoes would result in overcooked fish, so I began once again, this time giving the potatoes a 10-minute head start before adding in the cod.

Before serving, I took a quick taste of my broth, and decided it could do with another touch of bright acid. A squeeze of lemon did the trick, and sprinkling on some fresh parsley gave my elegant, fragrant bowl some welcome freshness. With such a refined recipe now in my repertoire, I felt fortunate to have stumbled upon this satisfying segment of Mediterranean cooking.

—AFTON CYRUS, *America's Test Kitchen Books*

Cod in Saffron Broth with Chorizo and Potatoes

SERVES 4

Haddock and hake are good substitutes for the cod. Use small red potatoes measuring 1 to 2 inches in diameter. Serve with crusty bread to dip into the broth.

- 1 tablespoon extra-virgin olive oil, plus extra for serving
- 1 onion, chopped fine
- 3 ounces Spanish-style chorizo sausage, sliced ¼ inch thick
- 4 garlic cloves, minced
- ¼ teaspoon saffron threads, crumbled
- 1 (8-ounce) bottle clam juice
- ¾ cup water
- ½ cup dry white wine
- 4 ounces small red potatoes, unpeeled, sliced ¼ inch thick
- 1 bay leaf
- 4 (4- to 6-ounce) skinless cod fillets, 1 to 1½ inches thick
  Salt and pepper
- 1 teaspoon lemon juice
- 2 tablespoons minced fresh parsley

1. Heat oil in 12-inch skillet over medium heat until shimmering. Add onion and chorizo and cook until onion is softened and lightly browned, 5 to 7 minutes. Stir in garlic and saffron and cook until fragrant, about 30 seconds. Stir in clam juice, water, wine, potatoes, and bay leaf and bring to simmer. Reduce heat to medium-low, cover, and cook until potatoes are almost tender, about 10 minutes.

2. Pat cod dry with paper towels and season with salt and pepper. Nestle cod skinned side down into skillet and spoon some broth over top. Bring to simmer, cover, and cook until potatoes are fully tender and cod flakes apart when gently prodded with paring knife and registers 140 degrees, 10 to 12 minutes.

3. Carefully transfer cod to individual shallow bowls. Using slotted spoon, divide potatoes and chorizo evenly among bowls. Discard bay leaf. Stir lemon juice into broth and season with salt and pepper to taste. Spoon broth over cod, sprinkle with parsley, and drizzle with extra oil. Serve.

NOTES FROM THE TEST KITCHEN

TASTING SAFFRON

Sometimes known as "red gold," saffron is the world's most expensive spice. It's made from the delicate, hand-harvested dried stigmas of *Crocus sativus* flowers. Luckily, a little saffron goes a long way, adding a distinct reddish-gold color, notes of honey and grass, and a slight hint of bitterness to dishes like bouillabaisse, paella, and risotto. You can find it as powder or threads, but we've found threads are more common. The major producers are Iran and Spain; the saffron you find in the supermarket is usually Spanish. When buying saffron, look for dark red threads without any interspersion of yellow or orange threads; our favorite brand is **Morton & Bassett Saffron Threads**.

ONE-PAN MEDITERRANEAN SHRIMP

☑ **WHY THIS RECIPE WORKS:** To incorporate quick-cooking shrimp into a flavor-packed one-pan meal, we created an easy Mediterranean profile with potatoes, fennel, feta, and olives. We gave the vegetables a head start, roasting them while we readied the shrimp. Oregano and lemon zest boosted the shrimp's flavor, and baking them atop the partially cooked potatoes and fennel protected them from the pan's direct heat. Briny, crumbly feta, sprinkled on before roasting, added a soft, subtly creamy dimension and reinforced the Mediterranean flavors. The shrimp cooked through in minutes, and serving them with olives and a drizzle of buttery olive oil offered a refined finish.

It's common to see shrimp skewered on the grill, sizzling in butter in a hot skillet, or frying in a pool of hot oil in a Dutch oven. But an alternate option, a one-baking-sheet meal with shrimp as the centerpiece, calls for the oven.

The beauty of using shrimp for a speedy supper is that they cook through quickly when exposed to any sort of heat. And unlike other proteins that need direct contact with a hot surface or flame to achieve an appetizing sear, shrimp taste great without it.

But this is also the danger of shrimp—it's far too easy to overcook them. If they spend too long in the oven, their delicate flesh turns tough and rubbery. After a few initial tests, I discovered that 6 to 8 minutes in a 450-degree oven was perfect.

Finding vegetables that shared this short cooking time was a futile exercise—almost nothing I tried would cook through in that time frame. I knew I'd have to give the vegetables a good head start in the oven and then add the shrimp for just the final few minutes. Potatoes were easy enough to incorporate using this method.

But what about something green? I tried broccolini, an underused vegetable that I love, but it turned into an unappealing swampy mess on the baking sheet. Spinach just turned slimy. My breakthrough came when a coworker suggested I try fennel.

Though its pale color made it appear less vibrant than other green vegetables, the slightly sweet, licorice-like flavor of roasted fennel paired beautifully with the briny shrimp. By slicing the fennel bulb into wedges through the stem end, I was able to keep the layers intact as they cooked; plus, this thick cut provided more surface area for flavorful browning.

To liven things up and give the dish a Mediterranean flavor profile, I tossed the shrimp with oregano and lemon zest before adding them to the pan with crumbled feta and sliding it back into the oven. When the shrimp were cooked through, I scattered a handful of chopped kalamata olives over the top. A sprinkling of parsley and a squeeze of lemon put the final fresh touches on this satisfying Mediterranean-style shrimp supper.

—KATIE LEAIRD, *Cook's Country*

One-Pan Mediterranean Shrimp
SERVES 4 TO 6

We prefer all-natural shrimp that aren't treated with sodium or preservatives. If buying frozen shrimp, make sure the ingredient label lists only "shrimp."

- 1½ pounds Yukon Gold potatoes, peeled and sliced ½ inch thick
- 2 fennel bulbs, stalks discarded, bulbs halved lengthwise and cut into 1-inch-thick wedges through stem end
- 3 tablespoons extra-virgin olive oil, plus extra for drizzling
  Salt and pepper
- 2 pounds jumbo shrimp (16 to 20 per pound), peeled, deveined, and tails removed
- 2 teaspoons dried oregano
- 1 teaspoon grated lemon zest, plus lemon wedges for serving
- 4 ounces feta cheese, crumbled (1 cup)
- ½ cup pitted kalamata olives, halved
- 2 tablespoons chopped fresh parsley

1. Adjust oven rack to lower-middle position and heat oven to 450 degrees. Toss potatoes, fennel, 2 tablespoons oil, 1 teaspoon salt, and ¼ teaspoon pepper together in bowl. Spread vegetables in single layer on rimmed baking sheet and roast until just tender, about 25 minutes.

2. Pat shrimp dry with paper towels. Toss shrimp, oregano, lemon zest, remaining 1 tablespoon oil, ½ teaspoon salt, and ¼ teaspoon pepper together in bowl.

3. Using spatula, flip potatoes and fennel so browned sides are facing up. Scatter shrimp and feta over top. Return to oven and roast until shrimp are cooked through, 6 to 8 minutes. Sprinkle olives and parsley over top and drizzle with extra oil. Serve with lemon wedges.

PAELLA ON THE GRILL

PAELLA ON THE GRILL

✓ **WHY THIS RECIPE WORKS:** For a large-scale grilled paella with plenty of the crisp rice known as *socarrat*, we turned to our roomy, sturdy roasting pan. Building a large fire and fueling it with unlit coals ensured that the heat output would last throughout cooking; we shortened the cooking time by streamlining the traditional *sofrito* and grilling (rather than searing) the chicken thighs. To ensure that the various elements finished cooking at the same time, we staggered their addition to the pan. After lightly toasting the Arborio rice in oil, we arranged the charred thighs around the cooler perimeter of the pan and poured in our cooking liquid: a flavorful mixture of broth, clam juice, and sherry. The shrimp, sausage, and clams came next, gently cooking through in the simmering liquid. Sweet frozen peas added pops of color and brightness to finish off this crowd-pleasing paella.

If you've ever made paella, you probably know that no two versions of this famous Spanish rice dish are prepared the same way. The basic template consists of medium-grain rice cooked in a wide, shallow vessel (traditionally, a *paellera*) with a flavor base called *sofrito*, broth and maybe wine, and a jumble of meat and/or seafood. Within this framework, the proteins can be anything from poultry to pork to any species of shellfish; the seasonings may include garlic, saffron, smoked paprika, or all of the above; and the embellishments might be peas, bell peppers, or lemon. As the rice absorbs the liquid, the grains in contact with the pan form a caramelized crust known as *socarrat*—the most prized part of the dish. The final product is colorful and flavor-packed: a one-pot showpiece that's perfect for entertaining.

What you might not know is that while most modern recipes are cooked on the stove or in the oven, paella was originally made on the grill, and many Spanish cooks still make it that way today. The live fire gives the dish a subtle smokiness and provides an extra-large cooking surface that encourages even socarrat development—a distinct advantage over a stove's burners or the indirect heat of an oven, which often yield a spotty or pale crust.

But in my experience, grilling comes with challenges of its own. Besides the usual problem—the quicker-cooking proteins overcook while they wait for heartier items to cook through—keeping a charcoal fire alive can be tricky. Plus, most recipes call for a paella pan, which only enthusiasts keep on hand.

The grilled paella I had in mind would feature tender-chewy rice strewn with moist chicken, sausage, and shellfish; a uniformly golden, crisp crust; and an efficient, reliable cooking method.

A paella pan alternative had to be grill-safe, deep enough to accommodate the food (I wanted a recipe that serves eight), and broad to maximize the amount of socarrat. A disposable aluminum pan was large enough, but its flimsy walls made it a nonstarter given the hefty amount of food I was cooking. But a sturdy stainless-steel roasting pan was easy to maneuver, and its surface area was generous—three times as spacious as a large Dutch oven. I worried that the pan's underside would darken on the grill, but during testing I quickly discovered that the exterior stayed remarkably clean on both charcoal and gas grills.

As for the fire setup, I needed a single layer of coals to expose the pan's base to even heat, but I also needed long-lasting heat output that wouldn't require refueling. So I lit 7 (rather than our usual 6) quarts of charcoal and poured them evenly across the kettle's surface, hoping that would be enough. (On a gas grill, I'd simply crank the burners to high.)

Knowing I'd have to stagger the additions of the proteins to get them to finish cooking at the same time, I first set the roasting pan over the fire and browned boneless, skinless chicken thighs (richer in flavor than breasts) that I'd halved for easier portioning. From there, I pushed the meat to the side, sautéed the sofrito (finely chopped onion, bell pepper, and tomato) until it softened, and followed with minced garlic, smoked paprika, and saffron. Then came the rice. Traditional Bomba and Valencia have more bite than other medium-grain rices, but Arborio is easier to find and made a good substitute. I stirred it in with a mixture of chicken broth, clam juice, and dry sherry that I hoped would highlight the proteins. Once the rice had absorbed most of the liquid, I scattered chunks of slightly spicy, smoky, cured Spanish chorizo; shrimp (seasoned first with oil, garlic, smoked paprika, and salt); and littleneck clams over the top and let the paella cook until the grains were plump and the underside sizzled—the audible cue that a flavorful crust was forming.

My staggering strategy wasn't quite right. The chicken was a tad dry, while the sausage wasn't warmed through and the shellfish were just shy of done. Maybe part of the problem was not only when I was adding the proteins but also where I was placing them in the pan. Thinking that the thighs would stay moist if they cooked more gently, I arranged them around the cooler perimeter of the pan. As for the chorizo, shrimp, and clams, they merely sat on top of the rice and received relatively little heat when I added them after most of the liquid had been absorbed. Instead, I partially submerged the shrimp and clams (hinge side down so that their juices could be absorbed by the rice) in the center of the rice after the liquid came to a simmer and then scattered the chorizo over top. As the liquid reduced, all three components would stay warm without overcooking.

Back to the heat output: The larger fire almost held out until the rice was cooked. But to completely close the gap between the cooking time and the fuel output, I made adjustments to both.

First, I covered the lit coals with 20 fresh briquettes that would gradually ignite during cooking. Next, I seared the chicken thighs directly on the grates rather than in the roasting pan (they'd still finish cooking at the edges of the pan). They browned in half the time and picked up valuable grill flavor.

Then, I retooled the sofrito to make it quicker. Instead of waterlogged fresh peppers and tomato, I used roasted red peppers and tomato paste—shortcuts to the caramelized sweetness achieved in a long-cooked sofrito. I also divided the sofrito into two parts, sautéing the peppers with the onions in the roasting pan but adding the tomato paste and aromatics (toasted first to deepen their flavor) to the cooking liquids. Finally,

I brought the seasoned broth to a boil in a saucepan so that it would quickly simmer when I poured it into the roasting pan.

Finally, the proteins were spot-on, but I took a couple of extra steps to ensure that the rice cooked evenly from top to bottom, periodically shuffling the pan around over the fire to avoid any hot spots and scraping a corner of the rice with a spoon to track the socarrat development. When the grains were almost cooked through, I scattered thawed frozen peas over the surface (they would add sweet pop and color) and covered the grill so that the trapped steam would heat them through and finish cooking any underdone grains at the surface.

The finished paella was a stunner—as impressive to eat as it was to behold. And now that I have the blueprint for making it successfully on the grill, I'm not sure I'll ever go back to the indoor version.

—LAN LAM, *Cook's Illustrated*

Paella on the Grill

SERVES 8

This recipe was developed using a light-colored 16 by 13.5-inch tri-ply roasting pan; however, it can be made in any heavy roasting pan that measures at least 14 by 11 inches. If your roasting pan is dark in color, the cooking times will be on the lower end of the ranges given. The recipe can also be made in a 15- to 17-inch paella pan. If littlenecks are unavailable, use 1½ pounds shrimp in step 1 and season them with ½ teaspoon salt.

1½ **pounds boneless, skinless chicken thighs, trimmed and halved crosswise**
  Salt and pepper
12 **ounces jumbo shrimp (16 to 20 per pound), peeled and deveined**
 6 **tablespoons extra-virgin olive oil**
 6 **garlic cloves, minced**
1¾ **teaspoons hot smoked paprika**
 3 **tablespoons tomato paste**

4 cups chicken broth

1 (8-ounce) bottle clam juice

⅔ cup dry sherry

Pinch saffron threads (optional)

1 onion, chopped fine

½ cup jarred roasted red peppers, chopped fine

3 cups Arborio rice

1 pound littleneck clams, scrubbed

1 pound Spanish-style chorizo, cut into ½-inch pieces

1 cup frozen peas, thawed

Lemon wedges

1. Place chicken on large plate and sprinkle both sides with 1 teaspoon salt and 1 teaspoon pepper. Toss shrimp with 1 tablespoon oil, ½ teaspoon garlic, ¼ teaspoon paprika, and ¼ teaspoon salt in bowl until evenly coated. Set aside.

2. Heat 1 tablespoon oil in medium saucepan over medium heat until shimmering. Add remaining garlic and cook, stirring constantly, until garlic sticks to bottom of saucepan and begins to brown, about 1 minute. Add tomato paste and remaining 1½ teaspoons paprika and continue to cook, stirring constantly, until dark brown bits form on bottom of saucepan, about 1 minute. Add broth, clam juice, sherry, and saffron, if using. Increase heat to high and bring to boil. Remove saucepan from heat and set aside.

3A. FOR A CHARCOAL GRILL: Open bottom vent completely. Light large chimney starter mounded with charcoal briquettes (7 quarts). When top coals are partially covered with ash, pour evenly over grill. Using tongs, arrange 20 unlit briquettes evenly over coals. Set cooking grate in place, cover, and open lid vent completely. Heat grill until hot, about 5 minutes.

3B. FOR A GAS GRILL: Turn all burners to high, cover, and heat grill until hot, about 15 minutes. Leave all burners on high.

4. Clean and oil cooking grate. Place chicken on grill and cook until both sides are lightly browned, 5 to 7 minutes total. Return chicken to plate. Clean cooking grate.

5. Place roasting pan on grill (turning burners to medium-high if using gas) and add remaining ¼ cup oil. When oil begins to shimmer, add onion, red peppers, and ½ teaspoon salt. Cook, stirring frequently, until onion begins to brown, 4 to 7 minutes. Add rice (turning burners to medium if using gas) and stir until grains are well coated with oil.

6. Arrange chicken around perimeter of pan. Pour broth mixture and any accumulated juices from chicken over rice. Smooth rice into even layer, making sure nothing sticks to sides of pan and no rice rests atop chicken. When liquid reaches gentle simmer, place shrimp in center of pan in single layer. Arrange clams in center of pan, evenly distributing with shrimp and pushing hinge sides of clams into rice slightly so they stand up. Distribute chorizo evenly over surface of rice. Cook (covered if using gas), moving and rotating pan to maintain gentle simmer across entire surface of pan, until rice is almost cooked through, 12 to 18 minutes. (If using gas, heat can also be adjusted to maintain simmer.)

7. Sprinkle peas evenly over paella, cover grill, and cook until liquid is fully absorbed and rice on bottom of pan sizzles, 5 to 8 minutes. Continue to cook, uncovered, checking bottom of pan frequently with metal spoon, until uniform golden-brown crust forms, 8 to 15 minutes longer. (Rotate and slide pan around grill as necessary to ensure even crust formation.) Remove pan from grill, cover with aluminum foil, and let stand for 10 minutes. Serve with lemon wedges.

NOTES FROM THE TEST KITCHEN

PICKING THE BEST ROASTING PAN

Handsome, heavy-duty, and with plenty of room to produce a feast, the roasting pan is an ultraversatile tool, perfect for everything from classic roast turkey to Paella on the Grill. Our favorite pan, **Calphalon Contemporary Stainless Roasting Pan with Rack,** is lightweight, with roomy handles for safe, easy maneuvering.

PERFECT POACHED EGGS

WHY THIS RECIPE WORKS: Producing a tender, tidy white is the hardest part of poaching eggs. To guarantee success every time, we began by cracking the eggs into a colander. This simple step eliminated a ragged, wispy finish by allowing the loose whites to slip away before cooking. Using a measuring cup to deposit the drained eggs in the water prevented any jostling, and boiling 6 cups of water in a roomy Dutch oven created plenty of steam to fully cook the gooey portion of the white nearest the yolk. To ensure that the whites would set up quickly while the yolks remained runny, we treated the water with salt and vinegar and allowed the eggs to finishing poaching off the heat in the still-warm water and hot steam. After just 3 minutes, we had the perfect poached eggs we wanted.

You could argue that poaching eggs is an ambitious goal from the start. Drop a delicate raw egg, without its protective shell, into a pot of simmering water in the hope that it will emerge perfectly cooked. That means a tender, fully set white—no ring of gelatinous, translucent goo surrounding the yolk—and a yolk that's fluid but thickened, almost saucy. Equally important: The white must not be raggedy or wispy at the edges and must boast a plump, ovoid flying-saucer shape that's ideal for nestling atop an English muffin or a bed of salad greens.

Since a raw egg cooked in simmering water wants to spread out in all directions before it sets, it's this latter issue that's the trickiest to overcome. I was determined to figure out a solution, and I would have plenty of help: There are dozens of recipes, essays, and videos claiming to produce perfect results. I would try them all and see where I landed.

First I experimented with the more novel suggestions I found. These ranged from poaching eggs in a muffin tin in the oven to microwaving each egg individually in a small bowl of shallow water to parcooking them in the shell before releasing them directly into the simmering water. I wasn't too surprised when most of these ideas proved to be dead ends. Conventional methods worked better, but they also had their limitations. The most common trick was to swirl the water around the eggs to create a vortex that kept the white from spreading, all the while folding any loose stragglers back on the yolk.

The whirlpool worked, but it meant I could only poach one or two eggs a time. Another approach involved lowering an egg into the water in a large metal spoon and keeping it there while using a second spoon to block the loose white from straying too far. The results were perfect—but who wants to juggle spoons like that to cook a single egg?

The most useful trick I found didn't try to corral the white during cooking but instead started by draining the raw eggs in a colander. At first I found this step counterintuitive—wouldn't all the white just drain off through the holes? It turns out that every egg contains two kinds of white, thick and thin. The thicker portion clings more tightly to the yolk, while the thinner portion is looser and can break away and slip through the colander holes. It is this thinner white that is most prone to spreading out into wispy tendrils in the water, so eliminating it went a long way toward fixing this issue. I also found that starting with the freshest eggs possible increased the chance that more of the white was thick, so less of it would drain away, leaving me with a plumper poached egg.

I next tried a common method targeted at a different issue: ensuring that the yolks stay runny while the whites, which solidify at a much higher temperature, reach the right degree of tender firmness. This approach calls for adding a few splashes of vinegar to the simmering water before slipping in the eggs. Acid lowers the water's pH, which makes the proteins in the white set faster. The only issue? For the vinegar to be effective, you have to add so much that it gives the eggs a sour taste. I found that the upper limit was ½ teaspoon per cup of water, which wasn't enough to be much help. But there was something else I could add that also makes egg proteins bond faster: salt. Using vinegar and salt together meant I didn't need much of either one. After a few tests, I worked out my formula: 1 tablespoon vinegar and 1 teaspoon salt to 6 cups water.

But there was still more I could do to keep the whites tidy—I could get the eggs into the water as gently as possible. Gingerly sliding them into the water from bowls held close to the water's surface, as many recipes suggest, kept the white contained, but pouring multiple bowls at once—I was poaching four eggs to serve two people—was awkward. Cracking all the eggs into a

2-cup liquid measuring cup and pouring them in one by one at different spots in the water was easier. Plus, I could retrieve them in the order they were added, so they cooked to the same degree. It made sense at this point to switch from a large saucepan to a broader Dutch oven, which made bringing the measuring cup close to the water easier.

After bringing the water to a boil, I added the vinegar and salt, deposited the drained eggs around the water's surface, and then considered whether to lower the heat to a bare simmer or shut it off completely and cover the pot, allowing residual heat to do the cooking. I'd seen recipes calling for both methods, and after a quick test, I settled on the latter for two reasons: First, even though it was very gentle, the residual heat was still enough to allow the egg whites to set, and it was extra insurance that the yolk would stay beautifully runny. Second, in the covered environment, steam could cook the white at the very top of the eggs, which can be the most stubborn to set, without constantly turning the egg over in the water. Though timing varied slightly depending on the size of the eggs, I found that it took about 3 minutes for the white, including the top, to become nicely opaque. Plus, one advantage of poaching eggs as opposed to cooking them in their shells is that you can actually see the results and return the eggs to the pot if necessary.

And with that, I really had it: a foolproof recipe for perfect poached eggs. As ambitious as it had seemed at first, poaching eggs now felt like a quick, simple way to add protein to any meal, from eggs Benedict and corned beef hash to a salad or pasta to fried rice to polenta.

—ANDREW JANJIGIAN, *Cook's Illustrated*

Perfect Poached Eggs

SERVES 2

For the best results, be sure to use the freshest eggs possible. Cracking the eggs into a colander will rid them of any watery, loose whites and result in perfectly shaped poached eggs. This recipe can be used to cook from one to four eggs. To make two batches of eggs to serve all at once, transfer four cooked eggs directly to a large pot of 150-degree water and cover them. This will keep them warm for 15 minutes or so while you return the poaching water to a boil and cook the next batch. We like to serve these eggs on buttered toast or toasted and buttered English muffins or on salads made with assertively flavored greens.

4 **large eggs**
1 **tablespoon distilled white vinegar**
 Salt and pepper

1. Bring 6 cups water to boil in Dutch oven over high heat. Meanwhile, crack eggs, one at a time, into colander. Let stand until loose, watery whites drain away from eggs, 20 to 30 seconds. Gently transfer eggs to 2-cup liquid measuring cup.

2. Add vinegar and 1 teaspoon salt to boiling water. With lip of measuring cup just above surface of water, gently tip eggs into water, one at a time, leaving space between them. Cover pot, remove from heat, and let stand until whites closest to yolks are just set and opaque, about 3 minutes. If after 3 minutes whites are not set, let stand in water, checking every 30 seconds, until eggs reach desired doneness. (For medium-cooked yolks, let eggs sit in pot, covered, for 4 minutes, then begin checking for doneness.)

3. Using slotted spoon, carefully lift and drain each egg over Dutch oven. Season with salt and pepper to taste, and serve.

NOTES FROM THE TEST KITCHEN

PERFECTING POACHED EGGS

1. Drain eggs before cooking to remove loose whites, preventing messy, wispy tendrils.

2. Transfer eggs to measuring cup before adding to water to minimize jostling.

EGGS PIPÉRADE

✔ **WHY THIS RECIPE WORKS:** Eggs *pipérade* is a humble Basque breakfast that pairs tender scrambled eggs with a vibrant mix of peppers, onions, and tomatoes, but this dish is only successful when all the elements are cooked properly. For a flavorful sauté of vegetables that wouldn't water down the eggs, we had to eliminate any excess moisture. Cooking Cubanelle and red bell peppers in a covered skillet softened them up, and adding chopped canned peeled tomatoes offered plenty of fresh, bright flavor void of papery cooked skins. Cooked down with the canned tomatoes' juices, a hit of sherry vinegar, and some minced fresh parsley, the simple pairing of tomatoes and peppers emerged with bold, concentrated flavor. Next, rather than scramble the eggs in among the perfectly cooked vegetables, we prepared them separately, cooking the eggs into tender, moist curds. We preserved the perfect textures and flavors of our pipérade by serving the eggs and vegetables side by side with a sprinkling of parsley.

You can bulk up scrambled eggs with any mix of vegetables, but one of my favorites is the pepper and tomato sauté called *pipérade*, a preparation that originated in the Basque region of northern Spain and southern France. Pipérade delivers richness, acidity, and tempered heat from a combination of sweet or mildly spicy fresh peppers, tomatoes, olive oil, garlic, and onion; fragrant spices, such as paprika; and a subtly spicy, fruity dried pepper called *piment d'Espelette* that is widely grown in the area. If you've scrambled eggs with vegetables, you know the challenges: how to incorporate watery produce without leaving the eggs in a puddle of liquid, and how to prevent the eggs from cooking up as stringy bits rather than pillowy curds.

To help maximize my chances of tender curds, I'd use the test kitchen's recipe for Perfect Scrambled Eggs. Its combination of high and low heat (the initial blast causes the eggs to puff up, while a slow finish keeps them soft and moist), a generous amount of fat (we use half-and-half), and a gentle folding technique produce rich, tender results.

Most pipérade recipes call for precooking the vegetables to evaporate excess liquid. I started by sautéing the aromatics—chopped onion, a bay leaf, a few cloves of minced garlic, paprika, and red pepper flakes, which contributed at least some of the fruitiness of hard-to-find piment d'Espelette—in olive oil and then added red and green bell pepper strips and some salt. I covered the pan and let the mixture cook for about 10 minutes to soften the peppers. I stirred in a few coarsely chopped fresh tomatoes and cooked the mixture uncovered for another 10 minutes or so to concentrate the flavors and evaporate the tomato liquid. Out came the bay leaf, and in went a couple of tablespoons of minced fresh parsley. The mixture was nicely thickened, and it tasted rich, if a bit flat, so I added a last-minute splash of sherry vinegar. What didn't go over well were the bits of chewy tomato skin, so I made subsequent batches with a can of whole peeled tomatoes (drained of most of their excess liquid). I also tried swapping the green bell peppers for mild Cubanelle peppers, which tasters preferred for their less vegetal taste.

Where many recipes go wrong is scrambling the eggs directly in the pipérade. The liquid in the produce causes the eggs to cook up stringy and wet rather than creamy and smooth; it also muddies their soft yellow color. I figured I could just push the cooked pipérade to the side of the pan, scramble the eggs, and fold the two components together, but even then some liquid bled into the eggs. So I further separated the two components by removing the pipérade from the skillet and wiping the pan clean before scrambling the eggs. I also swapped the half-and-half for fruity olive oil, which better complemented the dish. To keep up the tidy appearance, I plated the two components side by side rather than folding the cooked eggs into the peppers (though the latter is traditional and a fine option), and I garnished the platter with minced parsley. The finished product was attractive enough for company, quick and easy enough for everyday, and incredibly satisfying.

—ADAM RIED, *Cook's Illustrated*

Eggs Pipérade

SERVES 4

We like Cubanelle peppers here, but you can substitute green bell peppers, if desired. To serve the dish the traditional way, fold the eggs gently into the pepper mixture.

EGGS PIPÉRADE

6 tablespoons extra-virgin olive oil

1 large onion, cut into ½-inch pieces

1 large bay leaf

Salt and pepper

4 garlic cloves, minced

2 teaspoons paprika

1 teaspoon minced fresh thyme

¾ teaspoon red pepper flakes

3 red bell peppers, stemmed, seeded, and cut into ⅜-inch strips

3 Cubanelle peppers, stemmed, seeded, and cut into ⅜-inch strips

1 (14-ounce) can whole peeled tomatoes, drained with ¼ cup juice reserved, chopped coarse

3 tablespoons minced fresh parsley

2 teaspoons sherry vinegar

8 large eggs

1. Heat 3 tablespoons oil in 12-inch nonstick skillet over medium heat until shimmering. Add onion, bay leaf, and ½ teaspoon salt and cook, stirring occasionally, until onion is softened and just starting to brown, about 6 minutes. Add garlic, paprika, thyme, and pepper flakes and cook, stirring occasionally, until fragrant, about 1 minute. Add bell peppers, Cubanelle peppers, and 1 teaspoon salt; cover and cook, stirring occasionally, until peppers begin to soften, about 10 minutes.

2. Uncover and stir in tomatoes and reserved juice. Reduce heat to medium-low and cook, uncovered, stirring occasionally, until mixture appears dry and peppers are tender but not mushy, 10 to 12 minutes. Discard bay leaf; stir in 2 tablespoons parsley and vinegar. Season with salt and pepper to taste. Transfer pepper mixture to serving dish and wipe skillet clean with paper towels.

3. While pepper mixture cooks, beat eggs, 2 tablespoons oil, ½ teaspoon salt, and ¼ teaspoon pepper with fork until eggs are thoroughly combined and color is pure yellow.

4. Return now-empty skillet to medium-high heat, add remaining 1 tablespoon oil, and heat until shimmering. Add egg mixture and, using rubber spatula, constantly and firmly scrape along bottom and sides of skillet until eggs begin to clump and spatula just leaves trail on bottom of pan, 30 to 60 seconds. Reduce heat to low and gently but constantly fold eggs until clumped

and just slightly wet, 30 to 60 seconds. Immediately transfer eggs to serving dish with pepper mixture, sprinkle with remaining 1 tablespoon parsley, and serve.

BROCCOLI AND FETA FRITTATA

✔ **WHY THIS RECIPE WORKS:** For a hearty, satisfying frittata, we paired the eggs with a bold, well-seasoned filling. We made sure the eggs stayed tender throughout cooking by following a two-step cooking technique: After stirring the eggs on the stovetop, allowing large curds to form, we moved the skillet to the oven where the more even heat cooked the eggs through gently. Stirring feta into the beaten eggs and pouring the egg mixture over small pieces of lightly browned, red pepper–flecked broccoli made for a rich, evenly distributed filling that turned our frittata into a real meal.

The frittata is sometimes called a lazy cook's omelet. After all, it contains the same ingredients but doesn't require folding the eggs around the filling, a skill that takes practice to master. But it's not just the fold that distinguishes the two. Frittatas sport a golden-brown exterior, whereas any browning on a French-style omelet is a sign of poor technique. Also, an omelet should be custardy and just set, whereas a frittata must be firm enough to hold a filling in place.

But even the practical frittata requires a little know-how, lest the bottom turn rubbery or the center end up loose and wet. I wanted to uncover the keys to a tender, evenly cooked, cohesive frittata. I also wanted it to be big and hearty enough to serve at least four for dinner.

With plenty of filling ingredients and a 12-inch non-stick skillet at the ready, I evaluated common cooking methods. I immediately dismissed what I call "the inversion method," since it can be even harder to pull off than folding an omelet. It calls for cooking the frittata in an oiled skillet on the stove until the bottom sets, sliding it onto a plate, placing the overturned skillet on top of the frittata, inverting it back into the skillet, and returning the skillet to the stove to finish cooking. Yes, it's as tricky as it sounds. No thanks.

Instead, I tried a method that skips the difficult flipping step and calls for covering the skillet to trap the steam and cook the eggs through. I poured a dozen beaten eggs (enough to serve four to six people) on top of 3 cups of a hot placeholder filling (the right amount for a substantial frittata) and gave it a try. Unfortunately, this was a miss: While I waited for the eggs to set, the bottom of the frittata overcooked.

Another popular approach, cooking the frittata entirely in the oven, didn't fare much better. Recipes were either too time-consuming, requiring a low temperature and at least 40 minutes to cook the eggs, or they called for the use of a broiler, which produced a spotty brown top that hid runny pockets.

In the end, I got the best results using a hybrid stove-oven approach. But it wasn't as straightforward as pouring the eggs over a filling on the stovetop, letting it cook for a couple of minutes, and then popping the pan into the oven. When made this way, the frittata overcooked on the bottom.

Stirring the eggs as they began to set on the stovetop was crucial. After pouring the eggs over the filling, I scraped the bottom of the pan as curds formed. This action prevented overcooking by pushing the partially cooked egg away from the pan bottom and allowing raw egg to flow in. After just 30 seconds, my spatula left a wide trail through the curds, at which point I smoothed the eggs into an even layer and transferred the skillet to a 350-degree oven, where the frittata finished cooking in less than 10 minutes. Progress, indeed: This frittata was evenly cooked from top to bottom and edge to edge. However, the eggs were rather rubbery. Here was my next challenge.

Many frittata recipes call for the addition of dairy, claiming that it tenderizes eggs. So I whipped up frittatas using milk, heavy cream, sour cream, and crème fraîche, happily finding that they all produced roughly the same tender texture—any variation in richness wasn't noticeable because of the substantial filling. And because any subtle flavor differences in the dairy were also obscured by the filling, I settled on milk. One-third cup of milk per dozen eggs was just the right amount. Any more made the eggs too delicate.

It was at this point that a colleague made an interesting observation. The frittata was emerging piping hot from the oven; when I took its temperature, it registered between 185 and 195 degrees. Scrambled eggs cooked to that temperature would be tough and bouncy—and yet the frittata was still tender. Exactly what was the milk doing to keep the eggs tender?

Here's what I learned: First, when it comes to tenderizing eggs, there's nothing special about dairy; any liquid will do the job. That said, after experimenting with water (too bland), chicken broth (too chicken-y), and even wine (too acidic), I decided to stick with understated milk.

To understand how liquid makes eggs tender, you first need to understand the composition of an egg: It is mainly water, fat, and proteins. At room temperature, the proteins are isolated and coiled up. But when heat is added, the proteins begin to unwind and move more. As they move, they bump into each other, and because they are unwound, they tangle and form a mesh that holds the water and fat in place. This reaction starts when the eggs hit 160 degrees, the temperature at which curds first take shape. As the temperature increases, the number of bonds increases and the mesh gets stronger. As this happens, the eggs move from just set to firm to rubbery.

That's where the extra liquid comes in: Liquid dilutes the proteins, making it harder for them to coagulate and turn rubbery even as the temperature rises. What's more, even when they do bond, there is a lot of extra water in the mesh, which further contributes to tenderness. The result is eggs that remain tender even when heated to nearly 200 degrees.

As I read about egg cookery, I was reminded that the salt I was using for seasoning also played a role in protein coagulation. Salt weakens the protein network, a disruption that further tenderizes the eggs.

To finish, I drew up some guidelines for the fillings. First, I chose bold ingredients to complement the mild eggs, cooking them in the skillet before building the frittata. Second, I chopped the ingredients into ½-inch pieces (or smaller) because large chunks broke up the frittata's structure, making it prone to falling apart. Third, I seasoned not just with salt but also with a touch of acid, which provided a flavor boost without affecting the texture of the eggs.

My first creation was a broccoli and feta frittata seasoned with lemon and red pepper flakes. As I worked my way through other combinations, three favorites

BROCCOLI AND FETA FRITTATA

emerged: asparagus with tangy goat cheese, Yukon Gold potatoes paired with garlicky chorizo, and earthy shiitake mushrooms with nutty Pecorino Romano cheese. Move over, omelets—when eggs are for dinner, a simple frittata will be my new go-to dish.

—LAN LAM, *Cook's Illustrated*

Broccoli and Feta Frittata

SERVES 4 TO 6

This frittata can be served warm or at room temperature. When paired with a salad, it can serve as a meal.

- **12 large eggs**
- **⅓ cup whole milk**
- **Salt**
- **1 tablespoon extra-virgin olive oil**
- **12 ounces broccoli florets, cut into ½-inch pieces (4 cups)**
- **Pinch red pepper flakes**
- **3 tablespoons water**
- **½ teaspoon grated lemon zest plus ½ teaspoon juice**
- **4 ounces feta cheese, crumbled into ½-inch pieces (1 cup)**

1. Adjust oven rack to middle position and heat oven to 350 degrees. Whisk eggs, milk, and ½ teaspoon salt in bowl until well combined.

2. Heat oil in 12-inch ovensafe nonstick skillet over medium-high heat until shimmering. Add broccoli, pepper flakes, and ¼ teaspoon salt; cook, stirring frequently, until broccoli is crisp-tender and spotty brown, 7 to 9 minutes. Add water and lemon zest and juice; continue to cook, stirring constantly, until broccoli is just tender and no water remains in skillet, about 1 minute longer.

3. Add feta and egg mixture and cook, using rubber spatula to stir and scrape bottom of skillet until large curds form and spatula leaves trail through eggs but eggs are still very wet, about 30 seconds. Smooth curds into even layer and cook, without stirring, for 30 seconds. Transfer skillet to oven and bake until frittata is slightly puffy and surface bounces back when lightly pressed, 6 to 9 minutes. Using rubber spatula, loosen frittata from skillet and transfer to cutting board. Let stand for 5 minutes before slicing and serving.

VARIATIONS

Asparagus and Goat Cheese Frittata

This recipe works best with thin and medium-size asparagus.

Substitute 1 pound asparagus, trimmed and cut into ¼-inch lengths, for broccoli and ¼ teaspoon pepper for pepper flakes. Reduce cooking time in step 2 to 3 to 4 minutes. Omit water. Substitute goat cheese for feta and add 2 tablespoons chopped fresh mint to eggs with cheese.

Chorizo and Potato Frittata

Be sure to use Spanish-style chorizo, which is dry-cured and needs only to be heated through.

Substitute 1 pound Yukon Gold potatoes, peeled and cut into ½-inch pieces, for broccoli and ¼ teaspoon ground cumin for pepper flakes. In step 2, cook potatoes until half are lightly browned, 8 to 10 minutes. Substitute 1 teaspoon sherry vinegar for lemon zest and juice and add 6 ounces Spanish-style chorizo sausage, cut into ¼-inch pieces, along with water. Omit feta and add ½ cup chopped fresh cilantro to skillet with egg mixture in step 3.

Shiitake Mushroom Frittata with Pecorino Romano

While the shiitake mushrooms needn't be cut into exact ½-inch pieces, for a cohesive frittata, make sure that no pieces are much larger than ¾ inch.

Substitute 1 pound shiitake mushrooms, stemmed and cut into ½-inch pieces, for broccoli and ¼ teaspoon pepper for pepper flakes. Reduce water to 2 tablespoons and substitute 2 minced scallion whites, 1 tablespoon sherry vinegar, and 1½ teaspoons minced fresh thyme for lemon zest and juice. Substitute ¾ cup shredded Pecorino Romano for feta and add 2 thinly sliced scallion greens to eggs with cheese.

TEXAS BREAKFAST TACOS

✓ **WHY THIS RECIPE WORKS:** For an authentic take on Texas's egg-filled breakfast tacos, we started by making our tortillas from scratch. After kneading together the simple dough and chilling it, we rolled out 6-inch rounds and cooked them one at a time in a lightly oiled skillet. For a hearty filling that came together quickly, we crisped smoky chopped bacon, leaving some of its fat in the skillet to help soften and flavor chopped onion and minced jalapeño. We added the eggs last, scrambling them among the vegetables and bacon. Topped with Monterey Jack cheese, our warm Salsa Roja, and a squeeze of lime, this Texan breakfast was ready in no time.

Texans, especially south Texans, love their breakfast tacos. In the Austin area alone, more than 370 spots sell these plump, egg-filled treats. And they're cheap—you can buy one for $1 or $2 at your local gas station (just one of the reasons why college students love them). Essential to all tacos is the tortilla—specifically a flour tortilla, the traditional choice for breakfast tacos. It should be tender and chewy yet sturdy enough to hold the substantial fillings, with a clean, slightly wheaty flavor. Unfortunately, most packaged versions fall short of this ideal.

Homemade flour tortillas are simpler to make than you might think, and they require no special equipment. They're just a basic blend of flour, water, salt, and lard or shortening that is kneaded together, allowed to rest, shaped into flat rounds, and cooked quickly in a skillet. In testing, tasters preferred shortening, as grocery-store lard imparted a sour flavor. Letting the dough rest in the fridge after mixing made it easier to roll out and yielded more-tender tortillas. Given that I'm not a morning person, I was happy to discover that these tortillas could be made a couple of days ahead and stayed just as pliable as fresh.

I wanted to keep the fillings for my version ultrasimple. Most breakfast tacos feature scrambled eggs with a few add-ins. Conversations with breakfast taco experts informed me that potato, bacon, and chorizo (all mixed with scrambled eggs) were the most popular fillings, though some menus offer mix-ins like stewed cow's cheek, cactus, or mini beef franks. (I passed on these more challenging options.) Whipping up the egg-based fillings was a breeze, even first thing in the morning.

Salsas or hot sauce often live on the table at breakfast taco spots, and my recipe wouldn't be complete without one. So I made a cooked tomato salsa, similar to one found in south Texas, that came together quickly in the microwave.

Once I'd assembled all the components, my spicy, egg-stuffed tacos made an excellent breakfast. Or lunch, for that matter. Or even dinner.

—MORGAN BOLLING, *Cook's Country*

Texas Breakfast Tacos

SERVES 4 TO 6

It's important to follow visual cues when making the eggs, as your pan's thickness will affect the cooking time. If you're using an electric stovetop for the eggs, heat a second burner on low and move the skillet to it when it's time to adjust the heat. You can substitute store-bought tortillas for the homemade. This recipe makes enough filling for twelve 6-inch tacos.

    12 large eggs
        Salt and pepper
     6 slices thick-cut bacon, cut into ½-inch pieces
     1 small onion, chopped fine
     1 jalapeño chile, stemmed, seeded, and minced
     1 recipe Homemade Taco-Size Flour Tortillas
        (recipe follows)
     1 recipe Salsa Roja (recipe follows)
        Shredded Monterey Jack cheese
        Thinly sliced scallions
        Lime wedges

1. Whisk eggs, ½ teaspoon salt, and ¼ teaspoon pepper in bowl until thoroughly combined and mixture is pure yellow, about 1 minute. Set aside.

2. Cook bacon in 12-inch nonstick skillet over medium heat until crispy, 8 to 10 minutes. Pour off all but 2 tablespoons fat from skillet (leaving bacon in skillet). Add onion and jalapeño and cook until vegetables are softened and lightly browned, 4 to 6 minutes.

3. Add egg mixture and, using heat-resistant rubber spatula, constantly and firmly scrape along bottom and sides of skillet until eggs begin to clump and spatula leaves trail on bottom of skillet, 1½ to 2½ minutes.

4. Reduce heat to low. Gently but constantly fold egg mixture until clumped and slightly wet, 30 to

60 seconds. Season with salt and pepper to taste. Fill tortillas with egg mixture and serve immediately, passing salsa, Monterey Jack, scallions, and lime wedges separately.

Homemade Taco-Size Flour Tortillas

MAKES 12 (6-INCH) TORTILLAS

Lard can be substituted for the shortening, if desired.

- 2 cups (10 ounces) all-purpose flour
- 1¼ teaspoons salt
- 5 tablespoons vegetable shortening, cut into ½-inch chunks
- ⅔ cup warm tap water
- 1 teaspoon vegetable oil

1. Combine flour and salt in large bowl. Using your fingers, rub shortening into flour mixture until mixture resembles coarse meal. Stir in water until combined.

2. Turn dough out onto counter and knead briefly to form smooth, cohesive ball. Divide dough into 12 equal portions, about 2 tablespoons each; roll each into smooth 1-inch ball between your hands. Transfer to plate, cover with plastic wrap, and refrigerate until dough is firm, at least 30 minutes or up to 2 days.

3. Cut twelve 6-inch squares of parchment paper. Roll 1 dough ball into 6-inch circle on lightly floured counter. Transfer to parchment square and set aside. Repeat with remaining dough balls, stacking rolled tortillas on top of each other with parchment squares between.

4. Heat oil in 12-inch nonstick skillet over medium heat until shimmering. Wipe out skillet with paper towels, leaving thin film of oil on bottom. Place 1 tortilla in skillet and cook until surface begins to bubble and bottom is spotty brown, about 1 minute. (If not browned after 1 minute, turn heat up slightly. If browning too quickly, reduce heat.) Flip and cook until spotty brown on second side, 30 to 45 seconds. Transfer to plate and cover with clean dish towel. Repeat with remaining tortillas.

TO MAKE AHEAD: Cooled tortillas can be layered between parchment paper, covered with plastic wrap, and refrigerated for up to 3 days. To serve, discard plastic, cover tortillas with clean dish towel, and microwave at 50 percent power until heated through, about 20 seconds.

Salsa Roja

MAKES ABOUT 1½ CUPS

This salsa is a welcome addition to our Texas Breakfast Tacos, but you can also serve it with tortilla chips or as an accompaniment to pork, chicken, or fish. To make this salsa spicier, reserve and add the chile seeds to the blender before processing.

- 1 pound plum tomatoes, cored and chopped
- 2 garlic cloves, chopped
- 1 jalapeño chile, stemmed, seeded, and chopped
- 2 tablespoons chopped fresh cilantro
- 1 tablespoon lime juice
  Salt
- ¼ teaspoon red pepper flakes

1. Combine tomatoes and garlic in bowl and microwave, uncovered, until steaming and liquid begins to pool in bottom of bowl, about 4 minutes. Transfer tomato mixture to fine-mesh strainer set over bowl and let drain for 5 minutes.

2. Combine jalapeño, cilantro, lime juice, 1 teaspoon salt, pepper flakes, and drained tomato mixture in blender. Process until smooth, about 45 seconds. Season with salt to taste. Serve warm. (Salsa can be refrigerated for up to 3 days. Cover and microwave briefly to rewarm before serving.)

VARIATIONS

Texas Breakfast Tacos with Chorizo

Substitute 8 ounces Mexican-style chorizo sausage, casings removed, for bacon. Cook chorizo in skillet over medium heat, breaking up meat with wooden spoon, until well browned, 6 to 8 minutes, before adding onion and jalapeño.

Texas Breakfast Tacos with Potato

Omit bacon. Melt 2 tablespoons unsalted butter in skillet over medium heat. Add 1 (8-ounce) russet potato, peeled and cut into ½-inch cubes, and ¼ teaspoon salt and cook until tender, 6 to 8 minutes, before adding onion and jalapeño.

ONE-PAN BREAKFAST

✓ **WHY THIS RECIPE WORKS:** We wanted to cook up breakfast favorites—eggs, toast, potatoes, and sausage—without using every pan in our kitchen, so we did some streamlining and decided to cook everything together on a single sheet pan. The potatoes and sausages would need the longest cooking time, so we gave them a head start, seasoning and parbaking potato chunks first before then adding the links. We corralled the eggs by cutting rounds out of the middle of each slice of buttered bread, making room on the sheet pan for the slices, and, after briefly toasting the bread in the oven, cracking an egg into each hole. From there, the eggs needed mere minutes in the oven before our all-in-one breakfast was ready to serve.

Breakfast is great any time of day. But even greater is tucking into the works—crispy potatoes, juicy sausage links, runny egg yolks, and buttery toast—with only one pan to clean.

To make it all work, I knew I'd need a baking sheet. But even with the extra surface area, would all that food fit? I could cook components in groups and remove them to make space for the eggs at the end, but those first-cooked items would get cold and the eggs would run all over the sheet and cook unevenly. I needed a plan.

A test kitchen recipe for eggs-in-a-hole gave me a clue as to how to pull this off: I'd preheat a baking sheet, toast bread and cut holes in it, and then crack eggs into the holes and bake.

Starting the potatoes and sausages first and then moving them to one side ensured that the sheet would be hot enough to cook the eggs. But together the sausages and ½-inch potato chunks crowded the pan, steaming rather than browning. Bigger potato chunks (about 1 inch) browned much better but needed to cook for longer, which made the sausages turn dry and black.

Staggering the cooking process, I gave the potatoes a head start before adding the sausages. The sausages didn't brown much, but I didn't want them to dry out so I pressed on, moving them into a pile with the potatoes and resigning myself to lightly browned sausages. But to my surprise, the sausages in the pile browned nicely since they were slightly elevated in the circulating hot oven air, while those buried at the bottom continued to brown from contact with the sheet.

Next up: the toast. Buttering the bread and the sheet helped the toast brown and prevented sticking. To ensure that the toast and eggs finished together, I toasted one side of the bread and flipped it before adding the eggs.

With the oven at a very intense 500 degrees, I had been turning out an uneven mix of runny and chalky yolks. Lowering the temperature to 475 degrees still provided the initial blast of heat needed to cook the eggs through without sacrificing those luxurious runny yolks. Serving up a full breakfast (or dinner!) for four on a single pan? Mission accomplished.

—CECELIA JENKINS, *Cook's Country*

One-Pan Breakfast

SERVES 4

We prefer to use raw breakfast sausage links for this recipe, but fully cooked frozen links can also be used; Jimmy Dean Fully Cooked Original Pork Sausage Links are our favorite. Both types of sausage links cook in the same amount of time. The potatoes can be cut, submerged in water, and refrigerated for up to 24 hours. Dry them thoroughly with a dish towel before using.

- 2 **pounds Yukon Gold potatoes, unpeeled, cut into 1-inch chunks**
- 1 **tablespoon vegetable oil**
  Salt and pepper
- 4 **slices hearty white sandwich bread**
- 3 **tablespoons unsalted butter, softened**
- 12 **ounces breakfast sausage links**
- 4 **large eggs**

1. Adjust oven rack to middle position and heat oven to 475 degrees. Spray rimmed baking sheet with vegetable oil spray. Toss potatoes with oil, 1 teaspoon salt, and ¼ teaspoon pepper on prepared sheet and spread into even layer. Bake until potatoes are spotty brown on tops and sides, about 20 minutes.

2. Meanwhile, spread 1 side of bread slices evenly with 2 tablespoons butter. Using 2½-inch biscuit cutter or sturdy drinking glass of similar diameter, cut circle from center of each bread slice; reserve cut-out bread rounds.

3. Remove sheet from oven. Distribute sausages over potatoes (it's OK if some fall onto sheet), return sheet to oven, and bake until sausages are lightly browned on top, about 12 minutes.

4. Remove sheet from oven. Using metal spatula, push potatoes and sausages into pile occupying about one-third of sheet, creating enough room for bread. Place remaining 1 tablespoon butter on now-empty part of sheet and use spatula to distribute evenly. Place all bread, buttered side up, on empty part of sheet (do not place cut-out bread rounds in holes). Bake until bread is lightly toasted on bottom, about 4 minutes.

5. Remove sheet from oven. Flip bread. Crack 1 egg into each bread hole and season eggs with salt and pepper. Bake until yolks have clouded over but still give slightly when touched, 3 to 4 minutes. Transfer sheet to wire rack and let sit until whites are completely set, about 2 minutes. Serve immediately.

NATURALLY SWEET ANISE–POPPY SEED MUFFINS

✔ **WHY THIS RECIPE WORKS:** We wanted to make poppy seed muffins with less sugar while maintaining the rich flavor, fluffy, tender interiors, and golden crusts expected from this breakfast treat. The molasses-y flavor of Sucanat in place of sugar worked well here, and grinding it in a spice grinder ensured it was evenly distributed. To boost the muffins' flavor, we upped their perceived sweetness by increasing the vanilla; the sweet, subtle licorice flavor of ground anise seeds rounded out the muffins perfectly. Cake flour (rather than all-purpose) produced muffins with a fine crumb, and a combination of baking powder and baking soda ensured good rise and good browning. A hot oven and a raised oven rack gave the muffins a perfect golden crust.

Muffins are notoriously high in sugar, so when we started working on a new collection of low-sugar, naturally sweetened recipes, I knew this breakfast treat was the perfect candidate for a makeover. Hoping to keep things simple, I set my sights on a flavor I assumed fell on the lower end of the sugar spectrum: lemon–poppy seed. Unlike some of its obviously sugar-packed cousins (I'm looking at you, triple-chocolate), this muffin's appeal resides in the nuanced flavors of bright citrus and toasty poppy seeds rather than in white sugar's sweetness.

Or so I thought. When I learned that each muffin contained a whopping 22 grams of sugar, I made it my goal to slash that amount down to 11 grams while also introducing a less refined sweetening agent to the mix. I had plenty of natural sweeteners to choose from, but I was immediately drawn to Sucanat. Unlike granulated sugar, this minimally processed sweetener is made by beating sugar cane juice with paddles to form granules. It has a deep molasses flavor and works well in a wide range of applications. With this natural cane sugar in hand, I baked off my first test batch, cutting the sugar amount from 8 ounces to 4 ounces.

While tasters enjoyed the satisfying sweetness and subtle molasses flavor the Sucanat contributed to the muffins, the bright citrus taste I loved in the original recipe was now lost. Incorporating more lemon juice was a nonstarter—adding more pucker would just necessitate more Sucanat—so instead I doubled the lemon zest in my next batch. Much to my dismay, this batch was even worse, with muffins that tasted soapy, not citrusy. Through each round, the poppy seeds maintained their toasty taste, so I decided to take the focus off of the lemon flavor and seek out something new to pair with the poppy seeds.

Half the pleasure of a fresh baked muffin is its enticing aroma, so in an attempt make my next batch temptingly fragrant, I added a tablespoon of vanilla. The muffins smelled heavenly and even tasted sweeter. I also tested out a few additional aromatic ingredients. After tasting my way through muffins flavored with the likes of lavender, sage, almond extract, and ground anise, I settled on the latter. Like the vanilla, the anise's sophisticated licorice taste made the muffin taste instantly sweeter.

I had been using melted butter in my test batches, so I decided to try doubling down on flavor by browning the butter for extra toasty, nutty nuance to echo the Sucanat and poppy seeds. With that small adjustment, my muffins were finally superfragrant, sophisticated, and just sweet enough. Their structure, however, was another story.

Sugar helps baked goods hold on to moisture, so reducing the sugar amount left me with drier muffins. Sugar also inhibits gluten formation, so less sugar meant more gluten—and therefore, a tougher crumb. I was sure that cutting the all-purpose flour with some

NATURALLY SWEET ANISE–POPPY SEED MUFFINS

lower-protein cake flour would lighten the crumb, but after a few test runs, I discovered that the softest, most appealing texture came from a full-on swap for all cake flour. I addressed the dryness by replacing the low-fat yogurt with whole-milk yogurt, which gave the muffins added richness.

I now had tender muffins with an even, moist crumb, but they were still baking up pale and speckled. It dawned on me that the flecked appearance was caused by the Sucanat. While traditional sugar is manufactured to have uniform crystals, Sucanat's minimal processing yields granules of irregular sizes and shapes, so no matter how much I stirred, the granules never fully dissolved into the batter. This was an easy fix, though: Grinding the Sucanat into a powder made it disappear right into the batter of my next batch. To remedy the muffins' pallor, I needed to rapidly brown their tops before the interiors dried out. While my working recipe had me baking on the middle rack at 375 degrees, I tinkered with temperatures and oven rack placement and discovered that cranking the heat to 425 degrees and moving the rack to the upper-middle position was enough to dramatically boost browning.

This final dozen was an impressive batch. Beautifully browned, tender, and filling the air with their intoxicating aroma, these muffins bore little resemblance to their sugar-slicked cousins. I didn't mind—I was pretty sweet on them already.

—RUSSELL SELANDER, *America's Test Kitchen Books*

Naturally Sweet Anise-Poppy Seed Muffins

MAKES 12 MUFFINS

You can skip grinding the Sucanat in step 1; however, the muffins will have a speckled appearance. You can substitute ½ cup plus ⅓ cup (4 ounces) coconut sugar for Sucanat, grinding it as instructed in step 1; the muffins will taste slightly sweeter and have a pronounced anise flavor. You can also substitute ⅓ cup plus ¼ cup granulated sugar (4 ounces) for Sucanat, skipping grinding in step 1; the muffins will be less sweet and lighter in color. Low-fat yogurt can be substituted for the whole-milk yogurt, but the muffins will be slightly drier.

¾ cup (4 ounces) Sucanat
8 tablespoons unsalted butter, cut into 8 pieces
1½ cups plain whole-milk yogurt
2 large eggs
1 tablespoon vanilla extract
1 tablespoon grated lemon zest
2¾ cups (11 ounces) cake flour
3 tablespoons poppy seeds
2 teaspoons baking powder
¾ teaspoon baking soda
1 teaspoon ground anise seeds
¾ teaspoon salt

1. Adjust oven rack to upper-middle position and heat oven to 425 degrees. Grease 12-cup muffin tin. Working in 3 batches, grind Sucanat in spice grinder until fine and powdery, about 1 minute.

2. Melt 6 tablespoons butter in 10-inch skillet over medium-high heat until it begins to turn golden, about 2 minutes. Continue to cook, swirling pan constantly, until butter is dark golden brown and has nutty aroma, 1 to 3 minutes. Transfer browned butter to large bowl and stir in remaining 2 tablespoons butter until melted; let cool slightly.

3. Whisk yogurt, eggs, vanilla, and lemon zest into browned butter until smooth. In large bowl, whisk ground Sucanat, flour, poppy seeds, baking powder, baking soda, anise, and salt together. Using rubber spatula, stir in yogurt mixture until combined.

4. Divide batter evenly among prepared muffin cups. Bake until golden brown and toothpick inserted in center of muffin comes out clean, 15 to 20 minutes, rotating muffin tin halfway through baking.

5. Let muffins cool in tin for 10 minutes, then transfer to wire rack and let cool for 20 minutes before serving.

NOTES FROM THE TEST KITCHEN

PORTIONING MUFFIN BATTER

For neat, evenly sized muffins, portion batter into each cup using measuring cup or ice cream scoop, then circle back and evenly distrbute remaining batter with spoon.

VEGAN CURRANT SCONES

✓ **WHY THIS RECIPE WORKS:** Light, fluffy, barely sweet British-style cream scones are made by cutting cubes of chilled butter into the dry ingredients. To translate this technique over to vegan baking, we called on soy creamer and coconut oil for a tender crumb and rich flavor. Because coconut oil doesn't have water in it (as butter does), it didn't require chilling; instead, we simply pinched room-temperature oil into pieces and pulsed them into the dry ingredients in the food processor. This technique ensured even distribution of the oil, and it coated some of the flour granules with fat for a perfectly cakey crumb.

The first challenge in turning Britain's famous cream scone vegan was right there in its name: cream. If I wanted to convert this tender, fluffy scone into a vegan-friendly treat, I couldn't simply swap in my favorite nondairy milk and hope for the best. As in many baked goods, the dairy ingredients are central to the chemistry behind these teatime specialties, so when I began my work on my new scones, I had to start from scratch.

Classic cream scones are a simple affair. After cutting cold butter into the dry ingredients, you work egg and cream into the mix to create a dough, incorporate dried currants for small bites of sweetness, and cut the dough into wedges before baking. The key to the perfect texture is to not overwork the dough.

To turn this no-fuss recipe into an equally accessible vegan version, I gathered some vegan-friendly ingredients and began experimenting. The easiest swap was the sugar. Conventional cane sugar isn't always vegan because some manufacturers process it through animal bone char to bleach it. It's impossible to know what method a given brand uses, so strict vegans stick to organic sugar, which is always produced without animal products. I wanted my scones to play by the rules, so I had no qualms about this switch.

There's no shortage of nondairy milks on the market, but I suspected that these lean milks would struggle to replicate the richness of cream. Nonetheless, I decided I would give all my options a shot, gathering everything I could find, from almond, soy, rice, coconut, and oat milks to a handful of vegan creamers.

Next came the butter. The key to the delicate crumb in these scones is an even distribution of cold butter in the dough. As the butter melts, it steams and creates delicate little air pockets throughout the scones. I investigated my replacement options, which ranged from vegetable shortening to margarine to coconut oil, and began eliminating those fats that wouldn't serve my scones well. For one, liquid fats like vegetable oil are widely used in vegan baking (as in traditional baking) to turn out ultramoist baked goods, but I needed something that I could incorporate while solid to achieve the right crumb structure. Looking back at the milks and creamers I'd picked up, I realized that none of their fat contents were even within striking distance of heavy cream. If I wanted that tender texture in my vegan scones, I'd have to make up for the lean cream replacement with plenty of saturated fat. Refined coconut oil seemed like the best bet because it is solid at room temperature but melts easily and has a neutral flavor. I still wanted to test out my alternatives, but I suspected coconut oil would be my winner.

All I had left were the eggs. A little research introduced me to the many ways of replacing eggs in baking, from aquafaba (the liquid drained from canned chickpeas that behaves a lot like egg whites) to the gluey properties of ground flaxseeds. But before adding these tests to my already long to-do list, I stopped to consider what I wanted from an egg substitute. The benefits of both ground flaxseeds and aquafaba were their binding properties, but my scones didn't need binding, they needed egg's lift and structure. Knowing this, I decided to nix the egg replacements and play with leavener amounts instead. And with that, it was finally time to start baking.

The first step in making authentic cream scones is to cut the fat into the dry ingredients so that it's evenly distributed. In typical preparations the butter is chilled, so I followed suit, chilling my various fats and pulsing the dry ingredients—flour, organic sugar, salt, and baking soda—in the food processor for even mixing. When I tried to incorporate the chilled fat into the mix, I hit my first speed bump. The coconut oil had solidified in the refrigerator, and any attempt to scoop it out was met with flaky shards of the white oil. After cutting the margarine into one batch and shortening into a second, I opted to pinch portions of room-temperature coconut oil into the third, pulsing them all to combine. While the margarine quickly turned oily and the shortening clumped unevenly, the coconut oil easily integrated into the flour mixture. Thinking back to the lean milks and creamers, I decided to add an extra tablespoon of the coconut oil for added richness, and then I moved on to the liquid.

Off the bat, I was able to eliminate the milks. All, as I suspected, were too lean, and most had other problems as well: The soy milk's flavor was noticeable among the otherwise neutral ingredients in the scone; the almond milk left the scones tasting a little salty; and the rice milk gave them a starchy aftertaste. The sweetness of oat milk and mildness of coconut milk didn't hurt the flavor, but, as with the other milks, they left the scones tasting lean. That's where the vegan creamers came in. While I didn't have high hopes for the zero-fat, stabilizer-thickened almond and coconut creamers, soy creamer seemed promising, containing the highest fat content of all the products I'd gathered. I gave all three a try, and the soy was the clear winner. While the almond creamer (again) yielded salty scones and the coconut produced a dry texture, the higher-fat soy creamer gave me a workable dough that baked into a rich yet soft crumb.

Finally, to get a good rise out of my scones, I ran a few more tests, gradually increasing the amount of baking powder. My starting measurement of ½ teaspoon yielded squat scones, but as I incrementally upped the leavener, I starting seeing results. When I reached a full tablespoon, the scones were baking up nice and tall.

With many rounds of kneading, shaping, wedge-cutting, and baking behind me, I knew I was nearly there, but I had to make one final adjustment. Though the scones were an appealing golden brown, their undersides were burned. This was an easy fix: By baking my next (and final) batch on a doubled baking sheet, I created a reliable layer of insulation against scorching.

And there they were: Tender, light, "butter"-y scones dotted with sweet currants. With their rich flavor and flaky texture, these scones were sure to stand out on any teatime spread.

—LEAH COLINS, *America's Test Kitchen Books*

Vegan Currant Scones

MAKES 8 SCONES

The dough will be quite soft and wet; dust the counter and your hands with flour. Do not overwork the dough. Bake the scones on two stacked baking sheets so the bottoms don't scorch. Using almond or coconut creamer will work, but almond creamer produces chewy, salty-tasting scones; coconut creamer produces drier, denser scones.

2 **cups (10 ounces) all-purpose flour**
3 **tablespoons organic sugar**
1 **tablespoon baking powder**
½ **teaspoon salt**
5 **tablespoons coconut oil**
½ **cup dried currants**
¾ **cup unsweetened soy creamer**

1. Adjust oven rack to middle position and heat oven to 450 degrees. Set rimmed baking sheet in second rimmed baking sheet and line with parchment paper.

2. Pulse flour, sugar, baking powder, and salt in food processor until combined, about 3 pulses. Pinch off ¼-inch pieces of oil into flour mixture and pulse until mixture resembles coarse cornmeal with some pea-size pieces of oil remaining, about 10 pulses. Transfer mixture to large bowl and stir in currants. Stir in soy creamer until dough begins to form, about 30 seconds.

3. Turn dough and any floury bits out onto floured counter and knead until rough, slightly sticky ball forms, 5 to 10 seconds. Pat dough into 8-inch round and cut into 8 wedges. Space wedges about 2 inches apart on prepared sheet. Bake until tops are light golden brown, 12 to 15 minutes, rotating sheet halfway through baking. Transfer scones to wire rack and let cool for at least 10 minutes. Serve warm or at room temperature.

VARIATIONS

Vegan Lemon-Glazed Ginger Scones

Substitute ½ cup chopped crystallized ginger for currants and add ginger to food processor with oil. Whisk 1¾ cups organic confectioners' sugar, 1 teaspoon grated lemon zest, and 3 tablespoons lemon juice in bowl until smooth. Pour glaze over cooled scones and let sit for 10 minutes before serving.

Vegan Maple-Glazed Pecan Scones

Substitute ½ cup pecans, toasted and chopped, for currants. Whisk 1¾ cups organic confectioners' sugar, 6 tablespoons maple syrup, and 1 tablespoon water in bowl until smooth. Pour glaze over cooled scones and let sit for 10 minutes before serving.

ENGLISH MUFFINS

✔ **WHY THIS RECIPE WORKS:** For the ultimate English muffin—one that's chock-full of butter-thirsty nooks and crannies—we found that we needed a high-hydration dough. Drier doughs produced muffins with a compressed, even crumb. To enhance the bubbly crumb, we incorporated a series of folds into our recipe to encourage the yeast to produce more gases and to build the structure necessary to trap them. English muffins have a distinct yeasty character, so we allowed the shaped dough to proof slowly in the refrigerator so it would develop more flavor.

It's hard to top the nooks and crannies in a good English muffin. Crisp-edged when toasted and ready to sop up everything from melted butter to a runny egg yolk, those tiny caverns are what make this humble breakfast bread so wonderful. For years I'd stuck to the packs from the supermarket, if only because every homemade version I'd tried yielded what were essentially dinner rolls that merely *looked* like English muffins; as soon as they were sliced open, the tight crumb told the real story. So when we began work on a new collection of bread recipes, I set out to unlock the secrets behind those craggy crumbs.

I started by baking my way through five existing recipes to see what the differences were and figure out what caused them. The first thing that became clear was the connection between hydration and structure. The higher the hydration (i.e. the higher the ratio of water to flour), the bigger the air pockets, meaning bigger nooks. The drier doughs baked up dense because when it came time to toast the muffins in a skillet, they needed to be pressed flat, deflating any possible air pockets. On the other hand, one recipe took its hydration too far, producing more of a crumpet that required a mold to keep its shape. With these lessons in mind, I set off to create my own dough.

I decided to use my tasters's preferred recip as my jumping-off point, but I still had a long way to go. To multiply the muffins' air pockets, I gradually increased the liquid-to-flour ratio until I had a dough that held together but was still plenty wet. Proofing the sticky dough in a greased bowl allowed the dough to expand unencumbered, and giving it a few good folds partway through helped organize the gluten strands for easier shaping later on.

My dough emerged from this proofing and folding with a cohesive structure, making it easy to portion it into individual rolls. I rolled out a dozen dough balls, rolled them in cornmeal, pressed them flat, and left them for a second rise. When I began the stovetop toasting, my soft dough balls relaxed onto the hot skillet, spreading slowly and taking on the characteristic English muffin shape as they built up a distinct crust. I flipped the muffins over, allowed the same process to repeat on the other side. Because I didn't have to press down on the dough balls as they toasted in the skillet (a common practice in many recipes), I was able to keep those precious nooks and crannies intact. From there, all I had to do was bake them through in the oven, a process that took only 10 minutes or so.

These English muffins were well on their way, with more nooks and crannies than before and a straightforward process, but I wasn't quite finished. First off, the muffins had only a scant dusting of cornmeal. Though this crunchy coating may seem superfluous, it actually facilitates an even rise by preventing the moisture-rich dough from sticking to the surface on which the rolled balls proof. I'd need to make sure I could get it to really cling next time. I also wanted more yeasty flavor, and I wondered if I could possibly pack in more air pockets. Inspired by the heady aromas and irresistible chew in artisan-style breads, I decided to follow their lead by adding a period of cold fermentation. I readied my next batch, and this time I made sure the cornmeal really stuck by spreading it over a baking sheet and arranging the dough balls right on top of it. I wanted big, open air pockets, but I wanted them to form within the confines of the classic English muffin shape, so before I slid these muffins into the fridge, I covered the balls with a sheet of lightly greased plastic and rested a second baking sheet on top. This subtle weight encouraged the dough balls to proof outward, not upward, just as I wanted. I gave my muffins 12 hours of cold fermentation and, following a second countertop

ENGLISH MUFFINS

rest to bring them back to room temperature and reinvigorate the yeast, I began the toasting and baking again, taking care not to disrupt all the hard-earned air pockets in my English muffins.

My caution and patience paid off tenfold, with muffins that outshone anything I'd ever picked up at the supermarket. These rolls were fragrant, yeasty, filled top to bottom with a delicate network of air pockets, and had a distinct and pleasant chew. Topped with any number of spreads or sandwich fixings, these English muffins were crunchy, cranny-packed perfection.

—NICOLE KONSTANTINAKOS,
America's Test Kitchen Books

English Muffins

MAKES 12 MUFFINS

Split muffins can be stored in a zipper-lock bag at room temperature for up to three days. Wrapped in aluminum foil before being placed in the bag, the muffins can be frozen for up to one month. We do not recommend mixing this dough by hand. After you brown the muffins, group the batches in different spots on the baking sheet to help you keep track of their cooking times.

3¼	cups (16¼ ounces) all-purpose flour
1	tablespoon instant or rapid-rise yeast
2	teaspoons salt
1	cup (8 ounces) whole milk, room temperature
½	cup (4 ounces) water, room temperature
2	tablespoons unsalted butter, melted
1	tablespoon sugar
6	tablespoons (1¾ ounces) cornmeal

1. Whisk flour, yeast, and salt together in bowl of stand mixer. Whisk milk, water, melted butter, and sugar in 4-cup liquid measuring cup until sugar has dissolved. Using dough hook on low speed, slowly add milk mixture to flour mixture and mix until cohesive dough starts to form and no dry flour remains, about 2 minutes, scraping down bowl as needed.

2. Increase speed to medium-low and knead until dough is smooth and elastic and clears sides of bowl but sticks to bottom, about 8 minutes. Transfer dough to lightly greased large bowl or container, cover tightly with plastic wrap, and let rise for 30 minutes.

3. Using greased bowl scraper (or your fingertips), fold dough over itself by gently lifting and folding edge of dough toward middle. Turn bowl 90 degrees and fold dough again; repeat turning bowl and folding dough 2 more times (total of 4 folds). Cover tightly with plastic and let dough rise until doubled in size, 30 minutes to 1 hour.

4. Sprinkle half of cornmeal over rimmed baking sheet. Press down on dough to deflate; transfer to well-floured counter, divide into quarters, and cut each quarter into thirds (2½ ounces each). Cover loosely with greased plastic.

5. Working with 1 piece of dough at a time (keep remaining pieces covered), form into rough ball by stretching dough around your thumbs and pinching edges together so that top is smooth. Place ball seam side down on clean counter and, using your cupped hand, drag in small circles until dough feels taut and round.

6. Arrange dough balls seam side down on prepared sheet, spaced about 2 inches apart. Cover loosely with greased plastic, then gently place second baking sheet on top.

7. Let dough balls rest for 30 minutes, then refrigerate for at least 12 hours or up to 24 hours. Remove top sheet and loosen plastic covering muffins. Let muffins sit at room temperature for 1 hour. Sprinkle muffins with remaining cornmeal and press gently to adhere.

8. Adjust oven rack to lower-middle position and heat oven to 350 degrees. Heat 12-inch skillet over medium heat for 2 minutes. Using metal spatula, carefully place 4 muffins in skillet and cook until puffed and well browned, 3 to 6 minutes per side. Do not press down on muffins.

9. Transfer muffins to clean baking sheet and bake until sides are firm and muffins register 205 to 210 degrees, about 10 minutes. Repeat with remaining muffins in 2 batches, adjusting burner temperature as needed to prevent burning.

10. Transfer muffins to wire rack and let cool for 15 minutes. Split muffins open with fork and toast before serving.

NEW JERSEY CRUMB BUNS

✔ **WHY THIS RECIPE WORKS:** For buns piled high with sweet crumb topping, we had to pay special attention to the types of flour and sugar we used in each layer. Using all-purpose flour in the cakey base created a satisfyingly chewy texture. Cake flour, which is finer and lower in protein than all-purpose flour, gave the crumb topping its signature softness, and a combination of white and brown sugars ensured that the crumb buns had the optimal flavor and texture.

I remember the disappointment I felt upon eating my first crumb cake outside my native Garden State. "Where's the topping?" I asked, eyeing the measly sprinkling of streusel over a thick layer of coffee cake. Where I grew up, we stacked a mountain of crumbs over a thin sheet of yeasted cake and called it a crumb bun.

Bringing this favorite breakfast pastry into the test kitchen took a little explaining. Strangers to New Jersey crumb buns guffawed when I told them about the traditional 3:1 ratio of topping to cake. They were certain it would be too sweet, too crumbly—a mess. Though my first batch wasn't perfect, my coworkers started to see the light. This pastry unapologetically magnifies the best part of crumb cake—the crumbs—so they need to be perfect.

The ingredients are simple: butter, sugar, and flour. But the ratios need to be just right. Too much butter and the topping bakes into a dense, sugary layer rather than craggy crumbs. Too little butter and the crumbs feel dry and sandy. Though sugar and flour both sound like straightforward ingredients, I was shocked by how big a difference the right type of each made.

Let's start with sugar. Brown sugar is actually just white sugar plus molasses, which changes the sugar's color, flavor, and moisture content. While granulated sugar worked well in my cake base, the topping was dry, pale, and lacking in complexity when I used just white sugar. Using only brown sugar added too much extra moisture, rendering my crumbs too soft. A combination of the two provided the best flavor and texture for the topping.

Now on to the flour. There are significant differences in protein content and absorbency among all-purpose (the variety most common in home kitchens), cake, pastry, and bread flours. Each of these factors matters.

When I used all-purpose flour in the topping, the crumbs were dry and tough. With so many crumbs in the topping, they needed to be soft enough to bite through without crumbling off. With its lower protein and gluten content, cake flour tends to produce more delicate pastries. Cake flour (unlike all-purpose flour) is usually bleached, generally with benzoyl peroxide. This gas reacts with the starch, making cake flour easier to hydrate for a moist final product. I gave cake flour a shot to see if it would help me produce that yielding crumb, and it worked. I revisited my cake layer to see if I could make the swap to cake flour in that part of the recipe, too.

Nope. Changing the flour in the cake produced dramatic but dead-end results. What was yeasty and satisfyingly chewy when made with all-purpose flour turned lofty and fluffy like an angel food cake. Cake flour was the answer to perfectly moist crumbs, but it decidedly did not work in the cake base. All-purpose flour was the way to go there.

The key to perfect crumb buns? Use all-purpose flour from the pantry for the cake and make a special trip to the store for a box of cake flour for the crumbs. You'll thank me later when you sink your teeth into a tender, sweet (mostly) crumb bun.

—KATIE LEAIRD, *Cook's Country*

New Jersey Crumb Buns

SERVES 12

We call for both cake and all-purpose flours in this recipe. Do not substitute all-purpose flour for the cake flour (or vice versa), or the cake will be airy and fluffy and the topping will be tough and dry. We developed this recipe using Pillsbury Softasilk bleached cake flour; the topping will be slightly drier if you use unbleached cake flour.

CAKE

- 2¼ cups (11¼ ounces) all-purpose flour
- ¾ cup milk
- ¼ cup (1¾ ounces) granulated sugar
- 1 large egg
- 2¼ teaspoons instant or rapid-rise yeast
- ¾ teaspoon salt
- 6 tablespoons unsalted butter, cut into 6 pieces and softened

NEW JERSEY CRUMB BUNS

TOPPING

- 18 tablespoons (2¼ sticks) unsalted butter, melted
- ¾ cup (5¼ ounces) granulated sugar
- ¾ cup packed (5¼ ounces) brown sugar
- 1½ teaspoons ground cinnamon
- ½ teaspoon salt
- 4 cups (16 ounces) cake flour

  Confectioners' sugar for dusting

1. FOR THE CAKE: Adjust oven rack to middle position and heat oven to 350 degrees. Grease 13 by 9-inch baking dish. In bowl of stand mixer fitted with dough hook, combine flour, milk, sugar, egg, yeast, and salt. Knead on low speed until dough comes together, about 2 minutes.

2. With mixer running, add butter 1 piece at a time, waiting until each piece is incorporated before adding next. Increase speed to medium-high and continue to knead until dough forms stretchy, web-like strands on sides of bowl, about 6 minutes longer (dough will be soft and sticky).

3. Using greased rubber spatula, transfer dough to prepared dish. Using your floured hands, press dough into even layer to edges of dish. Cover dish tightly with plastic wrap and let dough rise at room temperature until slightly puffy, about 1 hour.

4. FOR THE TOPPING: Ten minutes before dough has finished rising, whisk melted butter, granulated sugar, brown sugar, cinnamon, and salt together in bowl. Add flour and stir with rubber spatula or wooden spoon until mixture forms thick, cohesive dough; let sit for 10 minutes to allow flour to hydrate.

5. Using your fingers, break topping mixture into rough ½-inch pieces and scatter in even layer over dough in dish. (If dough has pulled away from sides of dish after rising, gently pat it back into place using your floured fingers. Be sure to scatter all crumbs even though it may seem like too-large amount.)

6. Bake until crumbs are golden brown, wooden skewer inserted into center of cake comes out with no crumbs attached, and cake portion registers about 215 degrees in center, about 35 minutes. Transfer dish to wire rack and let cake cool completely. Using spatula, transfer cake to cutting board and cut cake into 12 squares. Dust squares with confectioners' sugar and serve.

TO MAKE AHEAD: Once dough has been pressed into even layer in baking dish and dish has been wrapped tightly in plastic wrap, dough can be refrigerated for at least 4 hours (to ensure proper rising) or up to 24 hours. When ready to bake, let dough sit on counter for 10 minutes before proceeding with step 4. Increase baking time to 40 minutes.

PLETZEL

☑ **WHY THIS RECIPE WORKS:** Pletzel is an old-school deli flatbread featuring an onion and poppy seed topping. Our challenge in baking our own lay in properly handling the superhydrated dough. Kneading the dough with a stand mixer kept things tidy and efficient. After combining the flour, water, and salt, we gave the mixture a 20-minute rest so it could fully hydrate, promising a chewy texture. From there, we added the yeast and kneaded at a high speed for a full 10 minutes. After letting it rise, we pressed the dough onto a rimmed baking sheet. Rather than forcing it into the pan's corners, we spread the dough across its surface and gave it one more rest. Before baking, we gave the dough a final stretch and topped it with a mixture of sautéed onions, poppy seeds, and a pinch of salt. After around 20 minutes in a hot oven, our flatbread baked up crisp yet chewy, with an irresistible salty, buttery, oniony topping.

During its heyday in the 1950s and 1960s, Fritzel's restaurant in Chicago attracted big names: Tony Bennett, Phyllis Diller, Joe DiMaggio, and Marilyn Monroe were just some of the celebrities who ate there. And back then, eating at Fritzel's meant sharing one of its most celebrated dishes: pletzel.

This focaccia-like flatbread is not as well-known as other staples of Jewish delis and bakeries, but those who know pletzel really love it. It took some doing to find existing recipes for pletzel, but persistence paid off, and I found five, including an old recipe from Fritzel's.

The versions varied widely. One was thin and brittle; others were soft and doughy. The one my tasters liked best had a crisp exterior and a chewy, tender interior with lots of air bubbles. Its very sticky dough was tough to work with, but I decided to pursue this version.

My first fix to the recipe proved to be the best fix: Rather than kneading the wet, sticky dough, I resolved to let the stand mixer deal with it. I attached the dough hook to the stand mixer and combined flour, water, and a bit of salt. I then let it sit for 20 minutes to allow the flour to fully hydrate—a step our resident bread expert recommended to help ensure that chewy interior.

At that point, I added the yeast and a bit of sugar for sweetness and browning and set the mixer on high for about 10 minutes until the dough was glossy and began to pull away from the edges of the mixer bowl.

I turned out the dough into a large oiled bowl, covered it with plastic wrap, and set it aside to rise. After about 2 hours, it had tripled in volume. I transferred it to a well-oiled rimmed baking sheet and pressed it flat, nudging it into the corners as best I could. (This sticky task was easier to do with lightly oiled hands.)

But the dough kept springing back, so I stepped away for a moment, hoping that if I let the dough relax for a few minutes, it would be easier to cover the entire baking sheet. I was right. I let the dough rise for 30 more minutes before sliding it into a very hot (500-degree) oven. About 20 minutes later, my pletzel came out even and crisp, and the holes in its interior were exactly what I wanted.

Next: toppings. I put together another pletzel dough. While it was rising on the sheet, I gently cooked chopped onions and a bit of salt in a skillet until they were golden. I then stirred in poppy seeds and spread the mixture evenly over the risen dough before it went into the oven.

Once the pletzel was baked, I cut it into squares and called over my tasters. It was crispy on the outside and soft and chewy on the inside, with plenty of sweet, oniony topping. Although a celebrity-filled visit to Fritzel's is impossible now (it was shuttered in the early 1970s), I'd re-created a little part of it.

—ASHLEY MOORE, *Cook's Country*

Pletzel

SERVES 6 TO 8

Kneading the dough in a stand mixer may cause the mixer to wobble. To prevent this, place a towel or shelf liner under the mixer and watch it during mixing. Handle the dough with lightly oiled hands and do not flour your fingers or the dough might stick.

- 3 cups (15 ounces) all-purpose flour
- 1⅔ cups water, room temperature
  - Kosher salt
- 1½ teaspoons instant or rapid-rise yeast
- 1¼ teaspoons sugar
- 5 tablespoons olive oil
- 3 onions, chopped fine
- 2 tablespoons poppy seeds

1. Place towel or shelf liner beneath stand mixer to prevent wobbling and fit mixer with dough hook. Add flour, room-temperature water, and 2½ teaspoons salt to bowl and mix on low speed until no patches of dry flour remain, about 4 minutes, occasionally scraping sides and bottom of bowl. Turn off mixer and let dough rest for 20 minutes.

2. Sprinkle yeast and sugar over dough. Knead on low speed until fully combined, about 2 minutes, occasionally scraping sides and bottom of bowl. Increase mixer speed to high and knead until dough is glossy, smooth, and pulls away from sides of bowl, 8 to 10 minutes. (Dough will only pull away from sides while mixer is on. When mixer is off, dough will fall back to sides.)

3. Using your fingers, coat large bowl and rubber spatula with 1 tablespoon oil. Using oiled spatula, transfer dough to bowl and pour 1 tablespoon oil over top. Flip dough over once so it is well coated with oil; cover bowl tightly with plastic wrap. Let dough rise at room temperature until nearly tripled in volume and large bubbles have formed, 2 to 2½ hours.

4. Meanwhile, heat 1 tablespoon oil in 12-inch skillet over medium heat until shimmering. Add onions and 1 teaspoon salt and cook, stirring occasionally, until onions are golden brown, about 10 minutes. Remove from heat and stir in poppy seeds. Transfer to bowl; set aside. Adjust oven rack to lowest position and heat oven to 500 degrees.

5. Coat bottom and sides of rimmed baking sheet with 1 tablespoon oil. Using oiled rubber spatula, turn dough out onto prepared sheet along with any oil remaining in bowl.

6. Using your oiled fingertips, press dough out toward edges of sheet, taking care not to tear it. (Dough will not fit snugly into corners. If dough resists stretching, let it relax for 5 to 10 minutes before trying to stretch again.) Let dough rise, uncovered, at room temperature for 30 minutes. (Dough will increase but not quite double in volume.)

7. Using your oiled fingertips, press dough out toward edges of sheet once more. Using dinner fork, poke surface of dough 30 to 40 times. Brush top of dough with remaining 1 tablespoon oil and sprinkle with 1½ teaspoons salt. Distribute onion–poppy seed mixture evenly over dough, leaving ½-inch border around edge.

8. Bake until golden brown, 18 to 23 minutes, rotating sheet halfway through baking. Using metal spatula, transfer pletzel to cutting board. Slice and serve.

TO MAKE AHEAD: Once dough has been placed in oiled bowl, flipped to coat in oil, and covered in step 3, it can be refrigerated for up to 24 hours. Let dough come to room temperature, 2 to 2½ hours, before proceeding with step 4.

BOSTON BROWN BREAD

✔ **WHY THIS RECIPE WORKS:** Inspired by Fannie Farmer's classic recipe for crustless, subtly sweet brown bread, we set out to make this loaf using ingredients available in modern supermarkets. Easy-to-find whole-wheat flour, rye flour, and finely ground cornmeal in equal amounts created balanced whole-grain flavor; molasses added a hint of both sweetness and bitterness; and melted butter contributed richness to the otherwise lean loaves. A combination of baking soda and baking powder served as the leavening agent, lightening the bread's texture. Baking this bread in a can is traditional, so we followed suit, pouring the batter into two 28-ounce cans and placing the cans in a stockpot filled with 3 quarts of simmering water. The all-encompassing heat steadily baked the bread through in 2 hours.

As a born and bred New Englander, I've always had a thing for Boston brown bread. It's deeply, darkly delicious—sort of a cross between a cake and a quickbread in texture and rich with molasses, raisins, and the complex flavors (and nutrition) of whole grains. When colonists started making this unyeasted, one-bowl bread in the 18th century, most cooking was done over an open hearth—a tricky environment for bread baking. To get around this, brown bread was steamed in lidded tin pudding molds in a kettle of simmering water over an open fire, giving the loaves a distinctive shape and a smooth, crustless exterior—and keeping the whole-grain crumb remarkably moist. Yankees have always paired brown bread with baked beans for supper, but it is equally delicious toasted, with a schmear of cream cheese or butter, for breakfast or as a snack.

To create a brown bread recipe of my own, I turned to one of the best-known recipes for inspiration. It comes from *Fannie Farmer's Boston Cooking-School Cook Book* (1898) and calls for grains that were plentiful and cheap at the time: rye meal, granulated (coarse) cornmeal, and graham flour. The grains are mixed with salt and baking soda, and then molasses and buttermilk are poured in to create a thick, bubbly batter. The batter is then scooped into a buttered mold, leaving ample space for the bread to expand during cooking. Next, the mold is covered and set in a boiling-water bath until the bread is fully cooked, which takes about 4 hours since the grains require time to tenderize. Finally, the bread is slid out of the mold and allowed to cool before being sliced and served. I followed the recipe as written, except for employing the modern approach of using a coffee can in place of the pudding mold.

Farmer's recipe has stood the test of time—it was quite good—so I decided to use it as a starting point for my own recipe. I evaluated the ingredients one by one. "Rye meal" simply refers to coarsely ground rye; it has a sandy texture similar to that of grits. Most modern recipes opt for more readily available rye flour, so I followed suit. Using more finely ground, quicker-cooking rye flour helped cut down the long steaming time. For the same reason, I found it best to use finely ground cornmeal rather than coarse. Finally, the graham flour. This is just coarsely ground whole-wheat flour, so I swapped in much more readily available regular whole-wheat flour. I used equal amounts of these three components so that their flavors would get equal billing.

Farmer called for molasses as the sole sweetener in the bread, but many contemporary recipes also include milder sugars such as brown or white. However, I found that these made the bread sweeter than it really should be and masked the pleasing trace of bitterness that is essential to brown bread. Molasses alone was the way to go, and any type—except for blackstrap, which is far too intensely flavored—worked just fine.

That said, I did come across a few modern refinements that were worth implementing. Adding a second leavener (baking powder) helped give the bread a lighter texture. And mixing in fat—in the form of a few tablespoons of melted butter—gave the bread a welcome richness and softened its coarse texture.

Finally, there was the question of cooking the bread in a 1-pound coffee can. Since nowadays few people buy coffee in metal cans and even fewer own pudding molds, it seemed like a good idea to scale the recipe to fit into two 28-ounce tomato cans. BPA-free cans are now available, which alleviates any safety concerns. To prevent sticking, I greased the interiors; once the cans were loaded with batter, I wrapped their tops with greased aluminum foil.

I came across a few recipes that suggested baking the bread in a gentle oven instead of steaming it, but to prevent the tops of the loaves from getting overly dark and leathery, I had to set the oven so low that they took a very long time to cook through. Steaming on the stovetop by setting the cans in a stockpot of simmering water was faster and ensured that the loaves stayed moist inside and out. (Even though the cans are wrapped tightly and the steam never makes contact with the bread, it prevents the loaves from exceeding 212 degrees.) After 2 hours, I pulled two steamy cylinders of utterly delicious whole-grain bread from the pot, happy to carry on the tradition.

—ANDREW JANJIGIAN, *Cook's Illustrated*

Boston Brown Bread

MAKES 2 SMALL LOAVES; SERVES 6 TO 8

This recipe requires two empty 28-ounce cans. Use cans that are labeled "BPA-free." We prefer Quaker white cornmeal in this recipe, though other types will work; do not use coarse grits. Any style of molasses will work except for blackstrap. This recipe requires a 10-quart or larger stockpot that is at least 7 inches deep. Brown bread is traditionally served with baked beans but is also good toasted and buttered.

- ¾ cup (4⅛ ounces) rye flour
- ¾ cup (4⅛ ounces) whole-wheat flour
- ¾ cup (3¾ ounces) fine white cornmeal
- 1¾ teaspoons baking soda
- ½ teaspoon baking powder
- 1 teaspoon salt
- 1⅔ cups buttermilk
- ½ cup molasses
- 3 tablespoons butter, melted and cooled slightly
- ¾ cup raisins

1. Bring 3 quarts water to simmer in large stockpot over high heat. Fold two 16 by 12-inch pieces of aluminum foil in half to yield two rectangles that measure 8 by 12 inches. Spray 4-inch circle in center of each rectangle with vegetable oil spray. Spray insides of two clean 28-ounce cans with vegetable oil spray.

2. Whisk rye flour, whole-wheat flour, cornmeal, baking soda, baking powder, and salt together in large bowl. Whisk buttermilk, molasses, and melted butter together in second bowl. Stir raisins into buttermilk mixture.

Add buttermilk mixture to flour mixture and stir until combined and no dry flour remains. Evenly divide batter between cans. Wrap tops of cans tightly with prepared foil, positioning sprayed side of foil over can openings.

3. Place cans in stockpot (water should come about halfway up sides of cans). Cover pot and cook, maintaining gentle simmer, until skewer inserted in center of loaves comes out clean, about 2 hours. Check pot occasionally and add hot water as needed to maintain water level.

4. Using jar lifter, carefully transfer cans to wire rack set in rimmed baking sheet and let cool for 20 minutes. Slide loaves from cans onto rack and let cool completely, about 1 hour. Slice and serve. (Bread can be wrapped tightly in plastic wrap and stored at room temperature for up to 3 days or frozen for up to 2 weeks.)

PANETTONE

✓ **WHY THIS RECIPE WORKS:** To bake up indulgent panettone loaves at home, we needed an approachable recipe that yielded impressive results. We packed the dough with butter, eggs, and extra yolks for richness and a golden color, but the abundant fat made the bread dense and crumbly. To remedy this, we used high-protein bread flour and kneaded the dough for a full 8 minutes before incorporating softened butter, a little at a time, so the dough had a strong gluten structure to support all that fat. We stuck with the traditional flavors of golden raisins, candied orange peel, orange zest, and vanilla and almond extracts to finish. Elongated fermentation and proofing times gave the rich bread a remarkably fluffy texture and slightly tangy flavor.

When it comes to baked goods, panettone is the epitome of luxury. This stately enriched bread is a Milanese Christmastime treat that makes its way into supermarkets every December. For years I simply couldn't understand the hype—most of the loaves I'd tasted were plenty sweet, but very often they were unpalatably dry and dense. It wasn't until I got my hands on some fresh homemade panettone that I saw the light. This bread was totally indulgent, with plenty of sweet candied fruit studding the moist, fluffy bread. I could see myself giving this handsome homemade bread as a holiday gift, but when I studied the recipe, I realized why so many people prefer to pick up their panettone at the

PANETTONE

supermarket: This traditional approach took about a week to complete. After a little more research, I discovered that long, involved recipes are the standard for panettone, so I made it my mission to turn out a more streamlined panettone without sacrificing flavor or texture along the way.

I began by giving a sampling of existing recipes a shot and was met with mixed results. My loaves emerged burned, dry, overly cakey, overly sweet, and entirely too dense. After a week of baking and tasting panettone, I knew what I wanted from mine: richness, subtle sweetness, a light, fluffy texture, and an accessible technique. With that, I got to work.

The greatest challenge of baking panettone is creating a strong enough gluten network to support the weight of its abundant butter, eggs, sugar, and sweet dried fruit while maintaining a feathery texture, so I decided to tackle the structure first. Taking my cues from the traditional recipes, I began by kneading the dough in my stand mixer, first streaming a mixture of milk, sugar, and eggs into the flour, yeast, and salt and then incorporating two sticks of softened butter. As the dough began to take shape, its greasy appearance made it clear I'd overshot my mark. I cleared out my mixing bowl and restarted, this time adding the butter more slowly, a tablespoon at a time. This approach extended the kneading time to almost 20 minutes, but the dough turned out silky, elastic, and supple. Before moving on, I added a scoop of golden raisins as my placeholder mix-in to see how well the dough held them suspended in the bread.

Next, I needed to think about proofing. I didn't want this bread to take all week, but I didn't want its flavor and rise to fall short, either, so I needed to find the right balance of time commitment and standout results. After letting the dough proof in a greased, covered bowl, I gave it a good fold to build up its gluten level and let it rise again. Given that panettone is a yeasted bread, I knew that the best way to build up its flavor would be through fermentation. Yeast readily consumes sugars and leavens breads at room temperature, but chilling slows that activity, allowing new flavors to develop. Since a streamlined panettone was my end goal, I set out to keep the fermentation period as short as possible while still drawing out noticeable flavor. A 12-hour stint seemed like a good starting place.

Following my dough's time in the fridge, I set it on the counter to bring it up to room temperature and re-activate the yeast before baking. It took about an hour and a half for my ultrarich dough to proof—more than twice the time needed for your typical bread dough—but this made sense, as the abundant sugar, eggs, and fat impede the yeast's development.

Panettone is often baked and sold in a sturdy paper mold, which allows the loaf to stand tall and makes it all the easier to give out as a gift. Luckily, the classic paper molds were easy to track down in my local baking supply store. As soon as my dough was proofed and ready, I divided it in half (one loaf to give, one to keep), forming each half into a round, and transferring each into a mold seam side down for an attractive domed appearance. I let the two loaves rise one last time (for about 3 hours) and then swiftly slashed a cross into their tops. This simple step created a designated weak spot in the loaf's surface, thereby controlling where it expanded during baking.

After an hour in the oven, my loaves emerged a gorgeous golden brown, and once they had cooled, I took my first taste: rich, buttery, and sweet. I knew my recipe was on track, but I couldn't help but wonder how much more flavor I could coax out of my dough after longer fermentation. I still didn't want this bread to take days to prepare, so I readied a few more batches, upping each respective batch's fermentation time by just 4 hours. As expected, these longer-fermented loaves were far superior to my original 12-hour batch. The 16-hour panettone had that distinct tang and nuance that had been hard to distinguish in my original batch, and that flavor only got deeper and more defined in the subsequent loaves. In the end, I decided to give a range of 16 to 48 hours in my recipe.

With my proofing periods set and my dough decided on, I was ready to refine my recipe. When it comes to flavor, buttery richness is the hallmark of good panettone, but sweet, fruity accents are also important. The raisins had fared well in my bread's strong gluten network, so I was confident I could add a bit more flair for my final version. A simple orange flavor profile seemed like an easy way to bring authentic northern Italian influence to my panettone. I prepared my final batch, this time plumping the raisins in fresh orange juice, boosting the wet ingredients with orange juice and vanilla and almond extracts, and introducing plenty of zest and sweet candied orange peels at the end of kneading. These easy additions were enough to put my panettone's flavor and rich aroma right over the top.

Rising high above its mold and taking on a winning golden-brown hue, my homemade panettone was a striking Italian beauty. These were loaves that would be well worth slaving over for a week, but I was proud that, with my new recipe in hand, I wouldn't have to.

—LEAH COLINS, *America's Test Kitchen Books*

Panettone

MAKES 2 LOAVES

Because this bread is often given as a gift, our recipe makes two loaves in decorative baking paper. You can find paper panettone molds online or at kitchen supply stores. We do not recommend mixing this dough by hand. Be sure to reduce the oven temperature immediately after putting the loaves in the oven.

- 1¼ cups (6¼ ounces) golden raisins
- 1½ tablespoons grated orange zest plus ¼ cup (2 ounces) juice
- 5 cups (27½ ounces) bread flour
- 2 tablespoons instant or rapid-rise yeast
- 1½ teaspoons salt
- 2 cups (16 ounces) whole milk, room temperature
- 4 large eggs plus 3 large yolks, room temperature
- ⅔ cup (4⅔ ounces) sugar
- 2 teaspoons vanilla extract
- 1 teaspoon almond extract
- 8 tablespoons (4 ounces) unsalted butter, softened
- 1¼ cups (6 ounces) finely chopped candied orange peel

1. Microwave raisins and orange juice in covered bowl until steaming, about 1 minute. Let sit until raisins have softened, about 15 minutes. Drain raisins and reserve orange juice.

2. Whisk flour, yeast, and salt together in bowl of stand mixer. Whisk milk, eggs and yolks, sugar, vanilla, almond extract, and reserved orange juice in 4-cup liquid measuring cup until sugar has dissolved. Using dough hook on low speed, slowly add milk mixture to flour mixture and mix until cohesive dough starts to form and no dry flour remains, about 5 minutes, scraping down bowl as needed.

3. Increase speed to medium-low and knead until dough is elastic but still sticks to sides of bowl, about 8 minutes. With mixer running, add butter, 1 tablespoon at a time, and knead until butter is fully incorporated, about 4 minutes. Continue to knead until dough is satiny and elastic and very sticky, about 3 minutes. Reduce speed to low, slowly add candied orange peel, raisins, and orange zest and mix until incorporated, about 3 minutes. Transfer dough to lightly greased large bowl or container, cover tightly with plastic wrap, and let rise for 30 minutes.

4. Using greased bowl scraper (or your fingertips), fold dough over itself by gently lifting and folding edge of dough toward middle. Turn bowl 90 degrees and fold dough again; repeat turning bowl and folding dough 2 more times (total of 4 folds). Cover tightly with plastic and let dough rise for 30 minutes. Fold dough again, then cover bowl tightly with plastic and refrigerate for at least 16 hours or up to 48 hours.

5. Let dough sit at room temperature for 1½ hours. Press down on dough to deflate. Transfer dough to well-floured counter, divide in half, and cover loosely with greased plastic. Press 1 piece of dough (keep remaining piece covered) into 6-inch round. Working around circumference of dough, fold edges toward center until ball forms. Flip ball seam side down and, using your cupped hands, drag in small circles on counter until dough feels taut and round and all seams are secured on underside. Repeat with remaining piece of dough.

NOTES FROM THE TEST KITCHEN

PREVENTING LUMPS IN PANETTONE DOUGH

Stream liquid ingredients mixture slowly into dry ingredients when mixing dough. If lumps form, turn off mixer and break up lumps by pressing them against side of mixer bowl with rubber spatula.

DELI RYE BREAD

6. Place dough rounds into two 6 by 4-inch paper panettone molds, pressing dough gently into corners. Transfer to wire rack set in rimmed baking sheet, cover loosely with greased plastic, and let rise until loaves reach 2 inches above lip of molds and dough springs back minimally when poked gently with your knuckle, 3 to 4 hours.

7. Adjust oven rack to middle position and heat oven to 400 degrees. Using sharp paring knife or single-edge razor blade, make two 5-inch-long, ¼-inch-deep slashes with swift, fluid motion along top of each loaf to form cross.

8. Place baking sheet in oven and reduce oven temperature to 350 degrees. Bake until loaves are deep golden brown, about 40 minutes, rotating sheet halfway through baking. Tent loaves with aluminum foil and continue to bake until loaves register 190 to 195 degrees, 20 to 30 minutes. Let loaves cool completely on wire rack, about 3 hours, before serving.

DELI RYE BREAD

WHY THIS RECIPE WORKS: For a moist, chewy loaf of rye bread baked using mostly rye flour, we needed to create a superhydrated dough. To provide adequate structure without weighing the loaf down, we used King Arthur all-purpose flour rather than lower-protein all-purpose flour or higher-protein bread flour, mixing it in with rye flour and yeast. Caraway seeds contribute to the bread's distinct flavor, so we included them with the dry ingredients. After many rounds of testing, we determined that 13⅓ ounces of water produced a moist yet structured loaf. Molasses, dissolved in the water, lent a subtle sweetness, and a small amount of vegetable oil also helped keep the crumb tender. Creating a steamy baking environment by placing a pan filled with water in the oven promised a tender, evenly risen crust, and a cooked cornstarch wash gave it a glossy sheen.

Ask people what they think is the epitome of a deli sandwich, and I'd bet most would say pastrami on rye. I'd agree that it's one of the best uses of rye out there, but deli rye is also great for grilled cheese or even just spread with butter and sprinkled with flaky salt. But a good loaf isn't always easy to come by.

Unlike German and Scandinavian rye breads, which are dark, crumbly, and dense, American deli rye relies on the addition of wheat flour to make a loaf that is lighter in both color and texture. A great loaf should have a fine, even crumb and a tender-yet-sturdy texture that will hold up under sandwich fillings. It's usually a torpedo-shaped free-form loaf, but unlike the crust on a rustic loaf, this loaf's crust should be soft and pliable. And what about the flavor? Caraway seed's anise-like flavor is strongly associated with deli rye, but try a loaf without caraway and you'll notice that rye's flavor is actually fairly similar to that of very fresh wheat flour, although it's sweeter and lacks the bitter edge.

I tried a handful of recipes, most of which produced bread that was either too dense, dry, or crumbly, or too light on rye flavor and more like regular white or wheat bread. Some loaves were also far too small for sandwich making.

To fashion my own recipe, I combined 2 cups of bread flour, 1 cup of medium rye flour, yeast, water, and molasses in a stand mixer. I kneaded this until a loose dough formed, and then I let it sit for 20 minutes. This resting stage, known as an autolyse, helps a dough build structure. I figured I needed the insurance since the test loaves I had made were in need of more. I then added the salt and continued kneading until a smooth dough formed. I took it out, gave it a few more kneads and shaped it into a ball, and transferred it to a bowl to proof for a couple of hours, until it had doubled in size. I shaped it into a log, covered it, and allowed it to proof again until it had nearly doubled. I scored it with a sharp knife every inch or so across the top and baked it in a 375-degree oven for about an hour.

This loaf wasn't horrible, but it was a bit light on rye flavor, the slashes were too deep, and the crumb was a bit tight. In addition, the crust lacked an appealing sheen and was somewhat tough, and the loaf was too narrow.

My first change was increasing the proportion of rye flour to wheat flour. But as the percentage of rye flour increased, the density and dryness of the loaf did, too. Here's the thing about working with rye flour: It doesn't contain the proteins that exist in wheat flour that form gluten, the elastic network that gives bread structure and allows it to hold the carbon dioxide produced during fermentation. On top of that, rye does contain carbohydrates called arabinoxylans, which you don't find in wheat flour. They allow rye flour to absorb four times as much water as wheat flour. You might think this would make a loaf more moist, but in reality more water gets bound up by the flour, producing a loaf that tastes drier. This explains why German- and Scandinavian-style rye breads, made with 100 percent rye flour, are so dense and why wheat flour is key in deli rye.

For a moister loaf, the fix is obvious: Add more water. But there's a limit; you can add only so much water before the gluten is too dilute and the loaf lacks structure. After tinkering with the amounts, I hit the limit: 13⅓ ounces of water and 8¼ ounces of rye flour (at least 10 percent more than most recipes call for) with 12½ ounces of bread flour.

Now my bread was moist and had nice rye flavor, but the crumb was a bit too chewy. In many breads, this can be attributed to the formation of too much gluten. Bread flour is comparatively high in gluten, and I didn't want to change my proportion of wheat flour to rye flour, so I tried swapping an equal amount of lower-protein all-purpose flour for the bread flour. This was too far in the other direction—now the loaf didn't have enough structure. King Arthur all-purpose flour, which lands midway between most all-purpose flours and bread flours in terms of gluten, was just right. To further tenderize the loaf, I also added a little vegetable oil.

To fix the narrow width of my loaf, I reevaluated the shaping process. Instead of rolling the dough up like a carpet to form a log, which produced small tapered ends, I came up with an approach that relied on a series of folds to produce a loaf of even size from end to end.

Slashing a loaf before baking allows it to expand evenly in the oven, so the fact that the slashes remained as gouges in the finished bread meant the crumb wasn't expanding much. I looked at factors that might affect oven spring, the rapid rise in volume that yeast breads experience when they enter a hot oven. First, I added steam by pouring boiling water into a preheated pan at the bottom of the oven. The steam, which transfers heat to the loaf more quickly than dry air does, keeps the loaf's exterior soft during the initial stages of baking so that it can expand easily.

Second, I looked at the oven temperature; I decided to increase it from 375 to 450. With these changes, the slashes smoothed out considerably and the crumb opened up, giving me a less dense interior. Adding the extra oomph of a preheated baking stone was all it took to finish the job.

As for the dull, tough crust, many recipes call for brushing the loaf with an egg wash before baking. This produces an attractive sheen, but the crust will still be tough. I used an alternative approach: a cooked cornstarch wash brushed on after baking. The starch produced a good sheen, and because it was brushed on after baking, the moisture helped soften the crust.

With a top-notch deli rye at the ready, I just needed to find some worthy pastrami.

—ANDREW JANJIGIAN, *Cook's Illustrated*

Deli Rye Bread

MAKES 1 LOAF

We prefer King Arthur all-purpose flour for this recipe; if you have trouble finding it at your supermarket, you can use any brand of bread flour instead. Any grade of rye flour will work in this recipe, but for the best flavor and texture we recommend using medium or dark rye flour. For an accurate measurement of boiling water in step 9, bring a full kettle of water to a boil and then measure out the desired amount. Do not use blackstrap molasses here; its flavor is too intense.

2½   cups (12½ ounces) King Arthur all-purpose flour
1½   cups (8¼ ounces) rye flour
1   tablespoon caraway seeds
2½   teaspoons instant or rapid-rise yeast
1⅔   cups (13⅓ ounces) plus ½ cup (4 ounces) water, room temperature
1   tablespoon vegetable oil
2   teaspoons molasses
1½   teaspoons salt
4   teaspoons cornstarch

1. Whisk all-purpose flour, rye flour, caraway seeds, and yeast together in bowl of stand mixer. Whisk 1⅔ cups water, oil, and molasses in 4-cup liquid measuring cup until molasses has dissolved.

2. Fit stand mixer with dough hook; add water mixture to flour mixture and knead on low speed until cohesive dough starts to form and no dry flour remains, about 2 minutes, scraping down bowl as needed. Cover bowl tightly with plastic wrap and let dough rest for 20 minutes.

3. Add salt to dough and knead on medium-low speed until dough is smooth and elastic and clears sides of bowl, about 5 minutes.

4. Transfer dough to lightly floured counter and knead by hand to form smooth, round ball, about 30 seconds. Place dough seam side down in lightly oiled large bowl, cover tightly with plastic, and let rise until doubled in size, 1½ to 2 hours.

5. Transfer dough to lightly floured counter and gently press into 8-inch disk, then fold edges toward middle to form round. Cover loosely with plastic and let rest for 15 minutes.

6. Adjust oven racks to middle and lowest positions, place baking stone on upper rack, and heat oven to 450 degrees. Line overturned rimmed baking sheet with parchment paper and dust lightly with rye flour. Gently press and stretch dough into 12 by 9-inch oval, with short end of oval facing edge of counter. Fold top left and right edges of dough diagonally into center of oval and press gently to seal. Fold point of dough into center of oval and press seam gently to seal. Rotate dough 180 degrees and repeat folding and sealing top half of dough.

7. Fold dough in half toward you to form rough 8 by 4-inch crescent-shaped loaf. Using heel of your hand, press seam closed against counter. Roll loaf seam side down. Tuck ends under loaf to form rounded torpedo shape. Gently slide your hands underneath loaf and transfer, seam side down, to prepared sheet.

8. Spray sheet of plastic with vegetable oil spray and cover loaf loosely. Let loaf rise until increased in size by about half and dough springs back minimally when poked gently with your knuckle, 45 minutes to 1¼ hours.

9. Place empty loaf pan on bottom oven rack. Using sharp paring knife or single-edge razor blade, make six to eight 4-inch-long, ½-inch-deep slashes with swift, fluid motion across width of loaf, spacing slashes about 1 inch apart. Pour 2 cups boiling water into empty loaf pan in oven.

10. Slide parchment and loaf from sheet onto baking stone. Bake until deep golden brown and loaf registers 205 to 210 degrees, 25 to 30 minutes, rotating loaf halfway through baking. Transfer loaf to wire rack.

11. Whisk cornstarch and remaining ½ cup water in bowl until cornstarch has dissolved. Microwave, whisking frequently, until mixture is thickened, 1 to 2 minutes.

12. Brush top and sides of loaf with 3 tablespoons cornstarch mixture (you will have extra cornstarch mixture). Let cool completely, about 3 hours, before slicing and serving.

NOTES FROM THE TEST KITCHEN

SHAPING A DELI RYE LOAF

1. Once you have pressed dough into 12 by 9-inch oval, with short end facing edge of counter, fold top left and right edges of dough diagonally into center and press to seal.

2. Fold point of dough toward center and press to seal. Rotate 180 degrees and repeat folding and sealing.

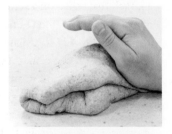

3. Fold dough in half toward you to form 8 by 4-inch crescent shape. Using heel of your hand, press seam closed.

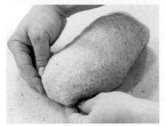

4. Roll loaf seam side down. Tuck ends under loaf to form rounded torpedo shape.

DESSERTS

CLASSIC CHEWY OATMEAL COOKIES

✓ **WHY THIS RECIPE WORKS:** Many oatmeal cookies are dry, cakey, and overly spiced. Using vegetable oil and butter in a 2:1 ratio yielded a chewy cookie with perfectly crisp edges. Browning the butter and using it to bloom the cinnamon introduced some welcome nuance, and adding an extra egg yolk also upped the richness to complement the oaty flavor. Most recipes use a stand mixer, but the melted butter made hand mixing easy and promised a dense (rather than cakey) texture. We added a classic mix-in, raisins, for chewy bursts of sweetness.

Why does the man on the Quaker oatmeal package look so smug? Maybe it's because he's the cunning perpetrator of a wildly successful cookie con. The evidence is anecdotal but persuasive: When I asked several friends to share their favorite family recipe for oatmeal cookies, many produced (often unbeknownst to them) the recipe from the Quaker Oatmeal website, Quaker's Best Oatmeal Cookies. The guy on the canister has apparently cornered the market, but do his cookies really deserve all the love?

The recipe goes like this: Use a mixer to cream the butter and sugar and then add an egg and some vanilla. Stir in some flour, leavening, salt (oddly optional in this recipe), spices (a generous amount), and old-fashioned rolled oats, and then spoon the mixture onto baking sheets. As they bake, the cookies fill the house with the heady scents of butter and cinnamon.

One bite of a cooled cookie, though, and the problems were apparent: The Quaker standby was crumbly at the edges and dry and cakey in the middle. Plus, the abundant spices overpowered the subtle flavor of the oats. I wanted a cookie with a crispy edge; a dense, chewy middle; and true oaty flavor. I was confident I could attain these goals and, in doing so, topple the oatmeal cookie kingpin. But I wasn't above using his recipe as a starting point.

I planned to make the salt mandatory instead of optional and to tone down the spices, but other than that I saw no reason to change the key ingredients in the Quaker recipe at this point—they each played a role—so I turned my attention to the ingredient proportions.

Most of those seemed OK, too. Only one, the 2½ sticks of butter, stood out as scandalously extravagant. The only cookie I know that has such a high proportion of butter to flour is shortbread, and that was definitely not the texture I was after. Instead, I placed a more reasonable 1½ sticks of softened butter in the mixer bowl. The brown sugar, granulated sugar, egg, vanilla, flour, and baking soda amounts all remained the same. But because I wanted just a hint of spice, I cut the cinnamon back to a mere ¼ teaspoon and eliminated the nutmeg altogether.

All was going well until it was time to add the oats. The mixture was simply too dry to accommodate all of them; I ended up with something that resembled crumble topping more than it did cookie dough.

I abandoned that batch and started over, keeping the butter to 1½ sticks but reducing the flour to 1 cup. This worked better: The cookies weren't as dry, and with less flour in the mix, the flavor of the oats stood out more.

Unfortunately, these cookies tasted a bit tinny. They also seemed rather lean, and the cakey texture remained. The metallic flavor, I knew, was coming from the baking soda—a full teaspoon was too much for the reduced amount of flour, especially now that there wasn't as much spice to hide behind. The excess soda might have been contributing to the cakey texture, too, but I suspected something else was at play.

The whole point of creaming butter and sugar when baking is to seed the softened butter with millions of tiny air bubbles. When the alkaline leavener reacts with acidic ingredients in the dough to produce carbon dioxide, the gas inflates the air bubbles, producing a light texture. If I wanted flatter, less cakey cookies, I probably didn't need—or want—the mixer.

But combining the butter and sugar by hand sounded like a chore. Then it occurred to me: If I wasn't whipping air into it, there was no need for the butter to be solid. Instead, I melted it. Eliminating the creaming step made the recipe easier and, along with cutting the baking soda amount in half, produced cookies that were flatter and denser in a good way. They were still a bit lean, but I didn't want to increase the butter because of the textural issues, so I'd need to enrich them in another way. And they still weren't as chewy as I wanted.

Luckily, I had some experience with making baked goods chewy, having developed our recipe for Chewy

Brownies. The key lies in the chemistry of fats. Both saturated fats (such as butter) and unsaturated fats (such as vegetable oil) consist of long chains of carbon atoms strung together with hydrogen atoms attached to them. The carbon chains in saturated fats have the maximum number of hydrogen atoms attached, so they can pack together more closely into a solid like butter. Unsaturated fats have fewer hydrogen atoms attached, so the chains pack more loosely and thus remain fluid, like vegetable oil. The right combination of loosely and tightly packed chains will produce the ideal chewy texture. When developing my brownie recipe, I learned that 3 parts unsaturated fat to 1 part saturated fat was the magic ratio.

Would the same hold true for my oatmeal cookies? With 12 tablespoons of butter (which is mostly saturated fat) and 1 egg, the fat in my recipe was currently 35 percent unsaturated and 65 percent saturated. For my next batch of cookies, I switched out 8 tablespoons of butter for ½ cup of vegetable oil. I also added an extra egg yolk for richness. Now the cookies had 71 percent unsaturated fat and 29 percent saturated, which was much closer to that 3:1 ideal.

So how were they? The texture—crispy on the edges and chewy in the middle—was at last spot-on. But with so much of the butter replaced by neutral-tasting vegetable oil, the flavor was a bit bland and boring. The recipe would need a few more tweaks.

If I had only 4 tablespoons of butter to work with, I was determined to get as much flavor out of it as I could, so I cooked it in a skillet until it was fragrant and the milk solids had turned a dark golden brown before transferring it to the mixing bowl. And rather than increasing the amount of cinnamon, I added the ¼ teaspoon to the warm browned butter to let it bloom, making its flavor rounder and more complex. Correct seasoning is every bit as important in sweets as it is in savory dishes; for my last adjustment, I bumped up the salt to ¾ teaspoon.

The three tweaks were, in combination, surprisingly effective. My cookies now had not only the right texture but also a rich, toasty flavor: buttery, sweet oats with a subtle spice background. A small handful of raisins stirred into the last batch of dough added pops of bright

flavor and reinforced the cookies' chew. Knowing that they're a controversial addition, I kept them optional in the recipe.

The Quaker guy no longer has the best recipe, so I guess I'll have to come up with another reason for his smug expression now. Maybe it's the hat.

—ANDREA GEARY, *Cook's Illustrated*

Classic Chewy Oatmeal Cookies

MAKES 20 COOKIES

Regular old-fashioned rolled oats work best in this recipe. Do not use extra-thick rolled oats, as they will bake up tough in the cookies. For cookies with just the right amount of spread and chew, we strongly recommend that you weigh your ingredients. If you omit the optional raisins, the recipe will yield 18 cookies.

1	cup (5 ounces) all-purpose flour
¾	teaspoon salt
½	teaspoon baking soda
4	tablespoons unsalted butter
¼	teaspoon ground cinnamon
¾	cup (5¼ ounces) dark brown sugar
½	cup (3½ ounces) granulated sugar
½	cup vegetable oil
1	large egg plus 1 large yolk
1	teaspoon vanilla extract
3	cups (9 ounces) old-fashioned rolled oats
½	cup raisins (optional)

1. Adjust oven rack to middle position and heat oven to 375 degrees. Line 2 rimmed baking sheets with parchment paper. Whisk flour, salt, and baking soda together in medium bowl; set aside.

2. Melt butter in 8-inch skillet over medium-high heat, swirling pan occasionally, until foaming subsides. Continue to cook, stirring and scraping bottom of pan with heat-resistant spatula, until milk solids are dark golden brown and butter has nutty aroma, 1 to 2 minutes. Immediately transfer browned butter to large heatproof bowl, scraping skillet with spatula. Stir in cinnamon.

3. Add brown sugar, granulated sugar, and oil to bowl with butter and whisk until combined. Add egg and yolk and vanilla and whisk until mixture is smooth. Using wooden spoon or spatula, stir in flour mixture until fully combined, about 1 minute. Add oats and raisins, if using, and stir until evenly distributed (mixture will be stiff).

4. Divide dough into 20 portions, each about 3 tablespoons (or use #24 cookie scoop). Arrange dough balls 2 inches apart on prepared sheets, 10 dough balls per sheet. Using your damp hand, press each ball into 2½-inch disk.

5. Bake, 1 sheet at a time, until cookie edges are set and lightly browned and centers are still soft but not wet, 8 to 10 minutes, rotating sheet halfway through baking. Let cookies cool on sheet on wire rack for 5 minutes; using wide metal spatula, transfer cookies to wire rack and let cool completely.

SOFT AND CHEWY GINGERBREAD COOKIES

✔ **WHY THIS RECIPE WORKS:** Tired of bland gingerbread cookies, we set out to bake a batch of soft, chewy cookies brimming with ginger and molasses flavors and ready for decorating. We ensured plenty of chew by incorporating a whopping 12 tablespoons of melted butter. Mixing the dough in the food processor kept things easy, allowing us to fully combine the dry ingredients before adding the butter, molasses, and milk. Rolling the dough to a ¼-inch thickness proved ideal for the texture we sought. We baked the cookies until they were just set around the edges and slightly puffed. As they cooled, the cookies settled into perfect chewiness, and a quick icing made for easy decorating.

Slide a batch of gingerbread cookies into the oven and the aromas of cinnamon, nutmeg, and cloves swirl through the air. Everyone can agree that they smell wonderful. But ask them whether they prefer thin and crisp or soft and chewy and people pick sides.

I know this because I surveyed my fellow test cooks on a recent morning: Would you rather have a crisp cookie or a soft one? While many professed a preference for crisp cookies, soft and chewy cookies won the poll. A bit of research into the history of this holiday classic confirmed that this is no newfangled twist; fans of softer cookies have been around for generations.

Many of the gingerbread recipes I found had a low ratio of fat to flour, which made the dough easy to roll out and cut but meant that once baked, the cookies were too crunchy. I needed a dough that was firm enough to hold its shape in the oven (I wanted gingerbread people, not gingerbread amoebas) but that would stay soft and chewy after the cookies cooled; to get there, I'd need more fat. After a few tests, I arrived at 12 tablespoons of butter.

While recipes often call for a stand mixer for creaming the butter into the other ingredients, I opted for an even quicker path: the food processor. What's more, rather than waiting for butter to soften, I simply melted the butter gently in the microwave and allowed it to cool for just 5 minutes before adding it to the processor with the other ingredients (including a balanced blend of ground cinnamon, ginger, and cloves). The dough came together in just seconds, and nothing was lost for the lack of a creaming step. I turned my dough out onto a lightly oiled counter for a quick knead before wrapping it and refrigerating it for an hour.

After rolling out dozens of doughs, I learned that rolling to a ¼-inch thickness was ideal for soft and chewy cookies every time. Using parchment paper kept the mess to a minimum. I cut the cookies out right away (no need for a second visit to the fridge) and baked them until they were just set around the edges and slightly puffed in the center. As they cooled, the slightly puffed cookies settled into a sublime chewiness.

No gingerbread cookie should go undecorated, so I set to experimenting with decorative icing. Basic icing made from confectioners' sugar and milk was too runny to achieve clearly defined decorating lines. Instead, I whipped egg whites and sugar into a stiffer mixture. The result was a structured frosting that was easy to apply, with a beautiful bright white gloss.

My simple soft and chewy gingerbread cookies boasted the full package: memory-sparking aroma, satisfying flavor, and festive decoration.

—KATIE LEAIRD, *Cook's Country*

SOFT AND CHEWY GINGERBREAD COOKIES

Soft and Chewy Gingerbread Cookies
MAKES ABOUT 24 COOKIES

Let the melted butter cool before adding it in step 1, or the dough will be too sticky to work with. Note that the dough needs to rest for at least an hour before rolling. Because we roll the dough between sheets of parchment paper (no flour is added), scraps can be rerolled and cut as many times as necessary. The cookies can be stored in a wide, shallow airtight container with sheet of parchment or waxed paper between each layer for up to 3 days.

    3   cups (15 ounces) all-purpose flour
    ¾   cup packed (5¼ ounces) dark brown sugar
    1   tablespoon ground cinnamon
    1   tablespoon ground ginger
    ¾   teaspoon baking soda
    ½   teaspoon ground cloves
    ½   teaspoon salt
    12 tablespoons unsalted butter, melted and cooled
    ¾   cup molasses
    2   tablespoons milk

1. Process flour, sugar, cinnamon, ginger, baking soda, cloves, and salt in food processor until combined, about 10 seconds. Add melted butter, molasses, and milk and process until soft dough forms and no streaks of flour remain, about 20 seconds, scraping down sides of bowl as needed.

2. Spray counter lightly with baking spray with flour, transfer dough to counter, and knead until dough forms cohesive ball, about 20 seconds. Divide dough in half. Form each half into 5-inch disk, wrap disks tightly in plastic wrap, and refrigerate for at least 1 hour or up to 24 hours.

3. Adjust oven racks to upper-middle and lower-middle positions and heat oven to 350 degrees. Line 2 rimmed baking sheets with parchment paper. Working with 1 disk of dough at a time, roll dough between 2 large sheets of parchment to ¼-inch thickness. (Keep second disk of dough refrigerated while rolling out first.) Peel off top parchment sheet and use 3½-inch cookie cutter to cut out cookies. Peel away scraps from around cookies and space cookies ¾ inch apart on prepared sheets. Repeat rolling and cutting steps with dough scraps. (Depending on your cookie cutter dimensions, all cookies may not fit on sheets and second round of baking may be required. If so, let sheets cool completely before proceeding.)

4. Bake until cookies are puffy and just set around edges, 9 to 11 minutes, switching and rotating sheets halfway through baking. Let cookies cool on sheets for 10 minutes, then transfer to wire rack and let cool completely before decorating and serving.

Decorating Icing
MAKES 1⅓ CUPS

This recipe makes bright white icing. For colored icing, stir 1 to 2 drops of food coloring into the icing to achieve the desired color before transferring it to a pastry bag.

    2   large egg whites
    2⅔ cups (10⅔ ounces) confectioners' sugar

1. Using stand mixer fitted with whisk attachment, whip egg whites and sugar on medium-low speed until combined, about 1 minute. Increase speed to medium-high and whip until glossy, soft peaks form, 2 to 3 minutes, scraping down bowl as needed.

2. Transfer icing to pastry bag fitted with small round pastry tip. Decorate cookies and let icing harden before serving.

COWBOY COOKIES

✔ **WHY THIS RECIPE WORKS:** Lots of takes on rustic, oversized cowboy cookies are tough and dry due to an excess of rolled oats and coconut. To make sure our cookies came out moist and chewy, we added an extra egg yolk; melted butter rather than softened butter also helped. For our mix-ins, we stirred in nutty toasted pecans, sweet shredded coconut, and plenty of chocolate chips. Baking generous ¼-cup portions ensured big, evenly sized cookies, and deliberately underbaking them and allowing the cookies to cool on the hot pan meant they turned out soft with crisp edges.

Cowboy cookies—packed with rolled oats, chocolate chips, toasted nuts, and flakes of coconut—have little to do with 10-gallon hats or gunfights at high noon. Instead they are a product of 1950s nostalgia for the American cowboy. Family recipes fondly call them hearty enough for the Western frontier.

A (home-on-the-) range of sample recipes took heartiness seriously, as my tasters and I found out. One version crammed in so much coconut that our jaws hurt from chewing; another had more chocolate than anything else, throwing the other ingredients off-balance. Sizes varied, but we agreed that larger cookies seemed heartier. I wanted big cookies with chewy interiors, crisp exteriors, and balanced "cowboy" ingredients.

I started with a standard cookie method: creaming butter and sugar together in a stand mixer, adding wet then dry ingredients, and finally folding in those cowboy add-ins. But the dough was stiff and hard to mix, and my tasters complained that the cookies were tough to chew.

Taking a closer look at the dough formula, large volumes of oats and coconut flakes introduced dry textures to the dough and absorbed what little moisture it contained, leading to tough cookies. Decreasing the add-ins would preserve moisture but would throw off the balance. Perhaps more moisture was the solution?

Increasing from one egg to two caused the cookies to spread too much. Adjusting to one egg plus one yolk worked better, but I still wasn't satisfied. I recalled some test kitchen cookie recipes that call for using melted butter and decided to give it a go. With the butter in liquid form, more moisture was readily available to the other ingredients, which became sufficiently hydrated such that I didn't need to add anything else. The resulting dough was easy to mix by hand—plus, now I didn't have to wait for the butter to soften.

Doubling down on my quest for a softer cookie, I deliberately underbaked the next batch, calling them done when I saw lightly browned edges and a hint of raw cookie dough showing through surface cracks. Thanks to a bit of carryover cooking, the cookies were perfect once they had cooled, with a soft chew and crisp exteriors.

My dough baked evenly without any fussy portioning, rolling, or flattening—simply dropping ¼-cup portions of dough onto the sheets gave me excellent, rustic results. Staggering the portions 2½ inches apart gave them enough room to spread to the proper cowboy size.

Earthiness from the oats, sweetness from the chocolate, nuttiness from the pecans, and complexity from the coconut combined for a huge hit.

—CECELIA JENKINS, *Cook's Country*

Cowboy Cookies

MAKES 16 COOKIES

We prefer old-fashioned rolled oats in this recipe, but quick or instant oats will work in a pinch. Do not use thick-cut oats. These big cookies benefit from the extra space provided by a rimless cookie sheet.

- 1¼ cups (6¼ ounces) all-purpose flour
- ¾ teaspoon baking powder
- ½ teaspoon baking soda
- ½ teaspoon salt
- 1½ cups packed (10½ ounces) light brown sugar
- 12 tablespoons unsalted butter, melted and cooled
- 1 large egg plus 1 large yolk
- 1 teaspoon vanilla extract
- 1¼ cups (3¾ ounces) old-fashioned rolled oats
- 1 cup pecans, toasted and chopped coarse
- 1 cup (3 ounces) sweetened shredded coconut
- ⅔ cup (4 ounces) semisweet chocolate chips

1. Adjust oven rack to middle position and heat oven to 350 degrees. Line 2 rimless cookie sheets with parchment paper. Whisk flour, baking powder, baking soda, and salt together in bowl.

2. Whisk sugar, melted butter, egg and yolk, and vanilla in large bowl until combined. Stir in flour mixture until no dry streaks remain. Stir in oats, pecans, coconut, and chocolate chips until fully combined (mixture will be sticky).

3. Lightly spray ¼-cup measure with vegetable oil spray. Drop level ¼-cup portions of dough onto prepared sheets, staggering 8 portions per sheet and spacing them about 2½ inches apart. Divide any remaining dough among portions.

4. Bake cookies, 1 sheet at a time, until edges are browned and set and centers are puffed with pale, raw spots, 15 to 17 minutes, rotating sheet halfway through baking. Do not overbake.

5. Let cookies cool on sheet for 5 minutes, then transfer to wire rack and let cool completely before serving. (Cookies can be stored for up to 3 days.)

TO MAKE AHEAD: Following step 3, wrap sheets tightly in plastic wrap and refrigerate for up to 2 days. Increase baking time to 16 to 18 minutes. To freeze, portion dough onto parchment-lined sheets and freeze until solid. Transfer frozen portions to zipper-lock bag and freeze for up to 2 months. Do not thaw before baking. Increase baking time to 17 to 19 minutes.

MILLIONAIRE'S SHORTBREAD

WHY THIS RECIPE WORKS: The only way we could improve millionaire's shortbread—bars that layer crunchy, buttery shortbread; a chewy, caramel-like filling; and a shiny, snappy chocolate top—was to streamline the methods behind the three distinct layers. To do this, we started by simplifying the crust, baking a quick, stir-together shortbread made with melted butter. Pressing the just-baked crust with a spatula compacted the crumb for easier slicing. Sweetened condensed milk is a key flavor component for the filling, and adding heavy cream and corn syrup ensured an even consistency; brown sugar and plenty of butter reinforced this layer's rich, caramelized flavor. Our only task for the top layer was to melt the chocolate gradually. Microwaving chopped chocolate at 50 percent power and stirring frequently kept it from breaking, and adding in grated chocolate at the end made for a smooth, firm top layer.

I'll concede that millionaire's shortbread is a corny name, but it fits this impressively rich British cookie/confectionery hybrid: a crunchy, buttery shortbread base topped with a chewy, caramel-like layer, which is in turn topped with a thin layer of shiny, snappy chocolate. It's an indulgent combination of textures and flavors, all stacked in a sleek package.

I ate a lot of it when I lived in the United Kingdom, and since it has a good shelf life (more than a week), I figured it would make an ideal holiday gift. But after giving a few recipes a try, I realized that a gift-worthy recipe wasn't going to just come to me wrapped neatly with a bow.

The shortbread base in most recipes was easy enough in terms of composition—just flour, butter, sugar, and salt—but recipes differed in terms of procedure, calling for softened butter and a stand mixer, cold butter and a food processor, or getting in there and rubbing everything together with your fingers as you would for pie dough. The caramel portion of this cookie is unique: It's based on sweetened condensed milk, which gives it a luxurious creaminess. Instructions were all simple—cook sweetened condensed milk, butter, sugar, and corn syrup in a saucepan until thickened—yet unpredictable. In some batches the butter separated out, but in other batches it didn't, and I wasn't entirely sure why. As for the chocolate, you can't just melt it any which way and expect it to reset with

its original sheen and snap. With each batch, I was left with dull, soft chocolate that was a mess as soon as I touched it. I was determined to devise strategies that delivered three perfect layers every time, and I would streamline as much as possible along the way.

Knowing that the other two layers were going to be challenging, I gave myself a break with the shortbread and turned to an approach I've used before that skips the solid butter. I whisked together 2½ cups of flour, ½ cup of sugar, and ¾ teaspoon of salt and stirred in two sticks of melted butter. I patted the dough into a foil-lined baking pan, pricked it all over with a fork to prevent pockets of steam from building up underneath, and then baked it until it was golden brown and firm. My melted butter shortcut produced a level, crunchy shortbread layer in no time flat. On to the chocolate.

It would be so handy if chocolate were like wax: You could melt it and cool it, and it would always have that same texture and appearance when it resolidified. Sadly, it's not that forgiving. Good chocolate right out of the package has a nice snap and sheen. But when you heat it past 94 degrees and leave it to resolidify, it takes on a dull, dusty appearance and soft texture. This is because the crystal structure of the cocoa butter fats in the chocolate has changed. Cocoa butter can solidify into any of six different crystal formations, but only one—beta crystals—sets up dense and shiny. For the layer of chocolate for my millionaire's shortbread, there was no settling for anything but beta.

Since heating chocolate beyond 94 degrees destroys the beta crystal structure, a chocolatier would temper the chocolate to reestablish that beta structure. It's an elaborate process of melting chocolate, cooling it, warming it, holding it at that temperature for a while, and then warming it a bit more (but not too much!). Luckily, I came up with an alternative that's much easier and more foolproof: Melt a portion of the chocolate very gently, being careful not to let it get too warm, and then stir in the remaining chocolate, which has been finely grated. These small flakes disperse throughout the melted chocolate, and their temperature remains so low that most of their beta crystals remain intact, triggering the formation of new crystals as the chocolate cools so it sets up perfectly shiny and snappy.

I melted 6 ounces of finely chopped chocolate in the microwave at 50 percent power (small pieces would melt more quickly and help minimize the chance of overheating). I stirred the chocolate every 15 seconds,

MILLIONAIRE'S SHORTBREAD

holding the bowl in the palm of my hand so I could monitor the temperature: If it felt warmer than my hand, I stirred until it cooled down before returning it to the microwave. Once it was all melted and still a bit warm, I deployed my secret weapon: 2 ounces of finely grated chocolate. Finely grating the chocolate would ensure even dispersal and mean it needed minimal, if any, additional heating to fully melt; plus, it seeded the melted chocolate with beta crystals. I stirred the grated chocolate into the bowl, heating for only 5 seconds at a time if necessary. I poured it onto the caramel (a placeholder recipe for now) and spread it into an even layer. It started to set right away—a hallmark of beta chocolate. With top and bottom squared away, I moved on to the middle: the caramel.

Recipes for the caramel layer were all about the same: Dump one can of sweetened condensed milk, some butter, brown sugar, and corn syrup (my substitute for Britain's golden syrup) into a saucepan and cook the mixture over medium heat while stirring until it turns thick and brown. Pour it over the baked shortbread, and that's it.

Except that it wasn't. My results were inconsistent. Sometimes the sauce broke; sometimes it didn't—and I couldn't figure out why. I also noticed that when I added ½ teaspoon of salt to help offset the sweetness, breaking was pretty much a given. I was baffled.

It must have been fate that just at this point in my testing, Dr. Janice Johnson, a food scientist from Cargill who specializes in salt, paid the test kitchen a visit. I told her all about my breaking filling. She was not surprised. She explained that whey proteins in the sweetened condensed milk were one of the major classes of proteins responsible for keeping the caramel mixture emulsified but that those proteins had two enemies: salt and heat. As the mixture cooked, moisture evaporated, which increased the concentration of salt. At high concentrations of salt, proteins can fall out of solution and the caramel can take on a grainy appearance. At the same time, the heat was also damaging the proteins, which had already been compromised during the processing that transforms fresh milk into sweetened condensed milk.

If too much heat was a problem, maybe all my recipe needed was more precision. After several tests, I determined that I should cook the mixture to 236 degrees—hot enough to give it the proper texture

but, most of the time, not so hot that it broke. But maddeningly, I found that I got different results when I used different brands of sweetened condensed milk, with some more prone to breaking than others.

And then it occurred to me: If the compromised whey proteins in sweetened condensed milk were the problem, why not use fresh dairy since its proteins haven't been damaged by processing? But subbing it in for the canned stuff would change the flavor profile of the filling, so I decided to try using it as a supplement. I knew from experience that milk didn't have enough fat to prevent curdling at high temperatures, so it would have to be cream. Indeed, the whey in just ½ cup of cream proved to be enough to keep my caramel intact without compromising the flavor. Finally, I knew it would work to my satisfaction every time.

From top to bottom, my version of this British classic was as perfect—and as gift-worthy—as I could have hoped.

—ANDREA GEARY, *Cook's Illustrated*

Millionaire's Shortbread

MAKES 40 COOKIES

For a caramel filling with the right texture, monitor the temperature with an instant-read thermometer. We prefer Ghirardelli 60% Cacao Bittersweet Chocolate Premium Baking Bar for this recipe. Grating a portion of the chocolate is important for getting the chocolate to set properly; the small holes on a box grater work well for this task. Stir often while melting the chocolate and don't overheat it.

CRUST

2½ cups (12½ ounces) all-purpose flour
½ cup (3½ ounces) granulated sugar
¾ teaspoon salt
16 tablespoons unsalted butter, melted

FILLING

1 (14-ounce) can sweetened condensed milk
1 cup packed (7 ounces) brown sugar
½ cup heavy cream
½ cup corn syrup
8 tablespoons unsalted butter
½ teaspoon salt

CHOCOLATE

8 ounces bittersweet chocolate (6 ounces chopped fine, 2 ounces grated)

1. FOR THE CRUST: Adjust oven rack to lower-middle position and heat oven to 350 degrees. Make foil sling for 13 by 9-inch baking pan by folding 2 long sheets of aluminum foil; first sheet should be 13 inches wide and second sheet should be 9 inches wide. Lay sheets of foil in pan perpendicular to each other, with extra foil hanging over edges of pan. Push foil into corners and up sides of pan, smoothing foil flush to pan. Combine flour, sugar, and salt in medium bowl. Add melted butter and stir with rubber spatula until flour is evenly moistened. Crumble dough evenly over bottom of prepared pan. Using your fingertips and palm of your hand, press and smooth dough into even thickness. Using fork, pierce dough at 1-inch intervals. Bake until light golden brown and firm to touch, 25 to 30 minutes. Transfer pan to wire rack. Using sturdy metal spatula, press on entire surface of warm crust to compress (this will make finished bars easier to cut). Let crust cool until it is just warm, at least 20 minutes.

2. FOR THE FILLING: Stir all ingredients together in large, heavy-bottomed saucepan. Cook over medium heat, stirring frequently, until mixture registers between 236 and 239 degrees (temperature will fluctuate), 16 to 20 minutes. Pour over crust and spread to even thickness (mixture will be very hot). Let cool completely, about 1½ hours.

3. FOR THE CHOCOLATE: Microwave chopped chocolate in bowl at 50 percent power, stirring every 15 seconds, until melted but not much warmer than body temperature (check by holding in palm of your hand), 1 to 2 minutes. Add grated chocolate and stir until smooth, returning to microwave for no more than 5 seconds at a time to finish melting if necessary. Spread chocolate evenly over surface of filling. Refrigerate shortbread until chocolate is just set, about 10 minutes.

4. Using foil overhang, lift shortbread out of pan and transfer to cutting board; discard foil. Using serrated knife and gentle sawing motion, cut shortbread in half crosswise to create two 6½ by 9-inch rectangles. Cut each rectangle in half to make four 3½ by 9-inch strips. Cut each strip crosswise into 10 equal pieces. (Shortbread can be stored at room temperature, between layers of parchment, for up to 1 week.)

HONEY LEMON SQUARES

✔ **WHY THIS RECIPE WORKS:** For lemon squares with a mouthwateringly tart, lusciously smooth curd coupled with a sturdy, buttery crust, we harnessed the subtle flavor and smooth texture of honey. A simple, honey-sweetened press-in crust made by mixing softened butter and flour to a sandy texture offered a rich, sturdy base. We simplified the curd, relying on honey's viscosity (rather than flour) to produce a smooth, velvety curd. A generous number of egg yolks enriched and emulsified the curd and produced a vibrant yellow color while plenty of lemon zest boosted the citrus flavor. Rather than risk overcooking it in the oven, we perfected the curd's texture by starting it on the stovetop and straining before pouring it over the crust and baking.

In theory, lemon squares are the perfect treat: sweet yet tart, bright yet indulgent, velvety-smooth yet appealingly crumbly. In practice, however, the ideal bar is elusive. Whether they deliver an instant sugar rush or have a gluey, uneven texture, these seemingly simple bars are easy to get wrong in terms of both flavor and texture. When I began work on a new collection of naturally sweet and low-sugar baked goods, I set my sights on squares with a brightly flavored, smooth curd and a buttery, crisp crust.

I decided to tackle the sweetness head-on. Many recipes (including the test kitchen's old standby) call for a combination of confectioners' and granulated sugars for sweetness and structure, but there's more than one way to counter tartness in baking. Determined to impart similar sweetness without the help of granulated sugar, I started to feel out my options for natural sweeteners. Some, like turbinado sugar and stevia, were just as processed as white sugar, while products like rapadura were too inconsistent across brands for them to be reliable. Date sugar, maple syrup, and barley malt have distinct flavors that I knew would distract from the lemon. Finally, I narrowed my options to Sucanat—a molasses-y natural cane sugar—and honey.

Knowing it would be this recipe's biggest challenge, I started my testing with the curd. Lemon curd is one of those confections that comes together as if by magic, transforming humble ingredients—eggs, sugar, butter, lemon zest and juice, cream, and flour—into a velvety-smooth treat with a clear, sweet-tart taste. For my first batch, I gave Sucanat a go, starting out with a

HONEY LEMON SQUARES

very traditional flour-thickened curd, whisking whole eggs and yolks, ½ cup of Sucanat, plenty of zest, and the juice of four lemons. I poured the filling over the waiting crust and baked the bars just long enough to set the filling.

This first batch made it clear how far I had to go. After keeping a watchful eye on the curd's doneness, I pulled it from the oven to find portions of the sensitive filling cracked. With that, I knew I needed to aim for a smoother, more foolproof curd. Furthermore, the color was dead wrong. Lemon squares should be a bright, sunny yellow thanks to the abundant egg yolks, but the Sucanat turned them a bleary, muddy brown hue. I was also concerned by the crust, which had baked up disappointingly pale and soggy. This shortbread-like crust needed more crunch and color, and I suspected that baking it beneath the thick layer of curd was not helping.

It was time to give honey a try. Unlike granular sweeteners, the viscous texture of this pantry staple seemed suited to the creamy-yet-sturdy texture of the curd; plus, it would also offer an understated sweetness to the crust. Furthermore, where traditional recipes need a whole cup of sugar to impart noticeable sweetness, honey is naturally sweeter and possesses more complex flavor than granulated sugar, so I could easily reduce the overall sugar while turning out an appealingly sweet, nuanced treat. I finally felt poised to crack the code on low-sugar lemon squares.

Not so fast. Whisked together with the eggs, yolks, and flour, the honey caused the flour to form clumps I simply couldn't break apart. So much for a smoother curd. I started over, and this time moved the production to the stovetop where I could more easily monitor the curd's progress. This swap meant I could eliminate the flour and really take advantage of the honey's natural viscosity. A whopping ¼ cup of zest meant plenty of lemon flavor and ⅔ cup of juice (just a little more than the amount of honey) delivered that tartness I craved. I played around with the total number of egg yolks, bumping up the number until I had the sunshine-yellow color and thick, rich body I wanted. Stirring the curd over medium-low allowed it to thicken gradually, and straining it evened out its texture.

Now that my curd was taking shape, I revised my approach to the crust. After churning out another batch of the sandy mixture (subtly sweetened with a teaspoon of honey), I took a tip from my favorite pie recipe and parbaked the base. Baking the buttery crust for 15 minutes firmed it up and gave it some appealing color, all of which seemed promising.

I poured the warm strained curd over the crisp crust and baked this batch with total confidence, giving it just 15 minutes in the oven to set up the filling. What emerged was just short of perfect. The stovetop curd was spot on, with a smooth, shiny, crack-free surface. The only flaw now resided in my prebaked crust: Where my previous batch had been fall-apart soggy, this crust was dry and crumbly. A little moisture was all it needed, so for my final trial I upped the water amount just slightly and with that I was done. Luminously yellow with just the right amount of pucker, my honey lemon squares had finally hit their sweet spot.

—TIM CHIN, *America's Test Kitchen Books*

Honey Lemon Squares

MAKES 16 BARS

To avoid air bubbles in the curd, stir in the cream with a spatula.

CRUST

- 1 cup (5 ounces) all-purpose flour
- ¼ teaspoon salt
- 6 tablespoons unsalted butter, cut into 6 pieces and softened
- 2 teaspoons water
- 1 teaspoon honey

LEMON CURD

- 2 large eggs plus 7 large yolks
- ½ cup honey
- ¼ cup grated lemon zest plus ⅔ cup juice (4 lemons)
- ⅛ teaspoon salt
- 4 tablespoons unsalted butter, cut into 4 pieces
- 3 tablespoons heavy cream

1. FOR THE CRUST: Adjust oven rack to middle position and heat oven to 350 degrees. Make foil sling for 8-inch square baking pan by folding 2 long sheets of aluminum foil so each is 8 inches wide. Lay sheets of foil in pan perpendicular to each other, with extra foil hanging over

edges of pan. Push foil into corners and up sides of pan, smoothing foil flush to pan. Grease foil.

2. Using stand mixer fitted with paddle, mix flour and salt on low speed until combined, about 30 seconds. Add butter, 1 piece at a time, and mix until only pea-size pieces remain, about 1 minute. Add water and honey and continue to mix until mixture begins to clump and resembles wet sand, about 30 seconds.

3. Transfer mixture to prepared pan and press into even layer with bottom of dry measuring cup. Bake crust until golden brown, 20 to 25 minutes, rotating pan halfway through baking.

4. FOR THE LEMON CURD: Meanwhile, whisk eggs and yolks, honey, lemon zest and juice, and salt together in medium saucepan until smooth. Cook over medium-low heat, stirring constantly with rubber spatula, until mixture thickens slightly and registers 165 degrees, about 5 to 7 minutes. Off heat, whisk in butter until melted. Strain lemon curd through fine-mesh strainer into bowl, then gently stir in cream with rubber spatula.

5. Pour warm lemon curd over hot crust. Bake until filling is shiny and opaque and center jiggles slightly when shaken, 10 to 12 minutes, rotating pan halfway through baking. Let bars cool completely in pan, about 2 hours. Using foil overhang, lift bars from pan and transfer to cutting board. Cut into squares and serve.

OLIVE OIL CAKE

WHY THIS RECIPE WORKS: We wanted our olive oil cake to have a plush crumb that was light and fine-textured, with a subtle but noticeable olive oil flavor. Whipping the sugar with whole eggs (rather than just the whites) produced a batter that was airy but sturdy enough to support all the rich olive oil. To emphasize the defining flavor, we opted for a high-quality extra-virgin olive oil and supplemented its fruitiness with just a tiny bit of lemon zest. A crackly sugar topping added a final touch of sweetness and sophistication.

New England, where I've lived for most of my life, is not known for its vast and fruitful olive groves. Maybe that's why I only recently learned about olive oil cake, which is commonplace in most traditional olive-producing regions of the world.

That said, I've made plenty of cakes with neutral-flavored vegetable oil. Though most people associate cake with butter, oil is a good choice for simple snack cakes and quick breads because it provides moisture, tenderness, and richness without calling attention to itself. It also makes the mixing process simpler (more on this in a minute). But extra-virgin olive oil, the type I kept seeing called for in recipes for olive oil cake, can be noticeably grassy, peppery, and even a little bitter. That's welcome in a salad, but I was skeptical about how it would work in cake, so I made a few versions.

I happily discovered that the slightly savory notes of olive oil can, in fact, lend appealing complexity to a cake. But there's no definitive version. Some cakes had a lot of oil and a correspondingly assertive flavor and rich, dense crumb; others included only a modest amount of oil and were light and spongy, and the flavor was so faint that they might as well have been made with vegetable oil. Still others had so many additional ingredients—apples, spices, loads of citrus—that the oil's flavor was obscured.

And that's fair enough. I suspect that such recipes originated not to showcase olive oil but because people wanted cake, they needed fat to make it, and the local olive oil was the fat they had on hand. But I have my choice of fats, so if I was going to be using extra-virgin olive oil in my cake, I wanted to be able to taste it, at least a bit. I didn't want sponge-cake austerity or dense decadence but something between the two. I wanted a cake that offered some intrigue but was at the same time simple, something I could enjoy with a cup of tea.

One of the most attractive aspects of making a cake with oil rather than butter is the way it expedites the mixing process: There's no waiting for butter to come to room temperature and then beating it with sugar before you even start to add the rest of the ingredients. With many oil-based cakes, you simply whisk the dry ingredients in one bowl, whisk the wet ingredients in another, and then combine the contents of the two bowls.

So that's where I started. The dry ingredients were all-purpose flour, baking powder, and salt, and the wet ingredients were eggs, milk, and the test kitchen's favorite supermarket olive oil, plus the sugar. The batter was ready to go into the oven in 5 minutes flat, and the cake came out just 40 minutes later.

This first attempt was easy to make but not easy to love. The crumb was dry and coarse, and I could detect the olive oil flavor only if I thought about it really, really

OLIVE OIL CAKE

hard. As for the appearance, I was okay with simplicity, but this cake looked uninvitingly plain. What I really wanted was the kind of even, fine crumb that the best butter cakes have. The problem? That texture is largely due to their being made with butter.

In a butter cake, air is whipped into the butter before it's mixed with the other ingredients. In the heat of the oven, the baking powder creates carbon dioxide, which inflates those bubbles a bit more. Those tiny bubbles are what make a butter cake fluffy and fine-textured.

But I wasn't without options for producing a similar effect in my oil cake. Although most oil cakes use the "mix wet, mix dry, and combine" method, chiffon cake is an oil cake that's mixed a bit differently. Its light and fluffy texture is achieved by whipping egg whites with some sugar to form a foam, which you then fold into the batter. Might that approach work for my olive oil cake?

I applied the chiffon method to my recipe and, at the same time, implemented a couple of ingredient adjustments: I increased the eggs from two to three for better lift and the olive oil from ½ cup to ¾ cup for more richness and moisture and a more pronounced flavor. The batter was promisingly airy and mousse-like. The cake rose impressively in the oven—but it fell when it cooled. And when I cut it open, there was a line of dense, collapsed cake in the middle.

It turned out that the batter was too airy to support all the fat; it essentially overextended itself. But I was happy with the more pronounced olive oil flavor, so I was reluctant to back down. Providing more support by switching to a tube pan, the vessel of choice for chiffon cakes, could help, but frankly I didn't want my olive oil cake to be mistaken for chiffon. Instead, I'd adjust the mixing method.

If whipped egg whites were too airy, maybe whipping yolks, which aren't as good at holding air, would be better. I did a quick test, but the cake came out dense and squat. Whipping whole eggs, I hoped, would be the solution. I put all three eggs, both whites and yolks, in the mixer bowl with the sugar and whipped the mixture for about 4 minutes, until it was pale and airy. I added the rest of the ingredients, including a tiny bit of lemon zest to accentuate the fruitiness of the olive oil. After pouring the batter into the cake pan, I sprinkled the top liberally with granulated sugar to lend some visual appeal and textural contrast.

The whipped whole eggs did indeed provide just the right amount of lift, creating a crumb that was fine but not dense and light but not spongy. The sugar on top had coalesced into an attractively crackly crust that complemented the cake's plush texture, and the lemon zest supported the olive oil flavor without overwhelming it.

And there's one more advantage to my olive oil cake: Because it's made with liquid fat instead of solid, it will keep longer than its butter-based counterparts. It can be stored at room temperature for up to three days—in the unlikely event that it doesn't get eaten right away.

—ANDREA GEARY, *Cook's Illustrated*

Olive Oil Cake

SERVES 8 TO 10

For the best flavor, use fresh, high-quality extra-virgin olive oil. Our favorite supermarket option is California Olive Ranch Everyday Extra Virgin Olive Oil. If your springform pan is prone to leaking, place a rimmed baking sheet on the oven floor to catch any drips. Leftover cake can be wrapped in plastic wrap and stored at room temperature for up to three days.

- 1¾ cups (8¾ ounces) all-purpose flour
- 1 teaspoon baking powder
- ¾ teaspoon salt
- 3 large eggs
- 1¼ cups (8¾ ounces) plus 2 tablespoons sugar
- ¼ teaspoon grated lemon zest
- ¾ cup extra-virgin olive oil
- ¾ cup milk

1. Adjust oven rack to middle position and heat oven to 350 degrees. Grease 9-inch springform pan. Whisk flour, baking powder, and salt together in bowl.

2. Using stand mixer fitted with whisk attachment, whisk eggs on medium speed until foamy, about 1 minute. Add 1¼ cups sugar and lemon zest, increase speed to high, and whip until mixture is fluffy and pale yellow, about 3 minutes. Reduce speed to medium and, with mixer running, slowly pour in oil. Mix until oil is fully incorporated, about 1 minute. Add half of flour mixture and mix on low speed until incorporated, about 1 minute, scraping down bowl as needed. Add milk and mix until combined, about 30 seconds. Add remaining flour mixture and mix until just incorporated, about 1 minute, scraping down bowl as needed.

3. Transfer batter to prepared pan; sprinkle remaining 2 tablespoons sugar over entire surface. Bake until cake is deep golden brown and toothpick inserted in center comes out with few crumbs attached, 40 to 45 minutes. Transfer pan to wire rack and let cool for 15 minutes. Remove side of pan and let cake cool completely, about 1½ hours. Cut into wedges and serve.

CARROT-HONEY LAYER CAKE

✓ **WHY THIS RECIPE WORKS:** For a naturally sweetened version of our traditional carrot cake, our goal was twofold: to keep the recipe as simple as possible, and to sweeten the cake only with honey, since its floral nuances pair well with the sweet carrots and warm spices. Vegetable oil kept the cake's key flavors in focus and also allowed us to stir the batter together by hand, keeping the recipe streamlined. Stirring in just four shredded carrots was enough to impart the vegetable's flavor and sweetness without impacting the texture. Finally, we bolstered the cake's flavor by increasing the amounts of cinnamon, nutmeg, and cloves.

When I was tasked with developing appealing desserts with natural sweeteners and less sugar, I knew exactly where to start: carrot cake. Unlike your standard yellow or chocolate cakes, this one gets a good amount of sweetness from the natural sugars in carrots. The slight vegetal taste paired with a handful of warm spices give the illusion of this being an almost virtuous dessert, but when I looked a little closer at the test kitchen's favorite recipe I learned that our carrot cake, still unfrosted, contains 49 grams of sugar per serving—that's around 4 tablespoons. The cream cheese frosting—an absolute must with any good carrot cake—clocked in at almost 10 grams, just short of another tablespoon of sugar. That's a lot more than I'd expected, but I was up for the challenge, aiming to cut out as much of the sweet stuff as possible while still turning out a tasty, stately cake.

Before I started experimenting, I set a few ground rules. First, I wanted the decreased sugar to benefit, not hurt, the overall recipe. Whether it meant exploring extra flavors or bringing out better texture, I wanted my end result to be a standout among cakes, not just a good low-sugar option. Second, I wanted the carrots'

sweetness to be easily discernible, so I needed to maximize the amount of carrot shreds I could incorporate into the batter.

The surest way to reel in a recipe's sugar content is to look beyond the old standbys—white and brown sugars. Unlike many natural sweeteners, these processed sugars contribute little in the way of flavor and you need to use a large amount of them to really impart noticeable sweetness. Some of the less processed alternatives like Sucanat, date sugar, and coconut sugar pack in plenty of sweetness and flavor in smaller doses, as do pantry standbys like honey and maple syrup, so I decided to give these options a go to see what they could do.

Other than swapping in my alternate sweeteners (and halving the total volume from the original), I followed the test kitchen's favorite recipe to the letter. My cakes were all over the map both in texture and flavor. Texture could be adjusted, so for now I focused on flavor. In traditional baking, sugar takes a backseat to the surrounding flavors (in this case, the sweet carrots and warm spices), but I wanted my natural sweeteners to bring nuanced and complementary flavor to the table.

The date sugar was an easy one to cut. Because this product is made only from ground dried dates, it introduced obvious (and distracting) date flavor. The earthy taste of Sucanat and the nutty flavor and bitter aftertaste of the coconut sugar made them easy to rule out, too.

I'd expected near identical results from the honey and maple syrup—they're both liquid sugars, after all—but that was hardly the case. While the maple syrup cake baked up pale, the honey cake took on a much darker hue. Our science editor explained that the differences came down to the syrups' natural sugars: While maple syrup is made up of mostly slow-browning sucrose, honey's higher fructose content made for rapid, more intense browning (and therefore, more flavor). With that, the honey won me over; plus, its floral flavor seemed well suited to the carrots and warm spices.

With my sweetener picked out, I started thinking about how to pack my cake with carrots. The three shredded carrots I'd been using in my tests were not quite enough to shine through the spices and honey. After running a few tests with additional carrots, I was pleased to find that four shredded carrots was enough to impart distinct sweetness—any more and the texture of the cake suffered. My tasters were put off by the slight crunch in the shreds, but a fellow test cook tipped me off that adding some baking soda to the batter would help soften the carrots during baking. I gave it a shot, and the results were spot-on, with plenty of tender carrot shreds in every slice.

Before claiming this cake a honey-sweetened victory, I needed to do a little bit of flavor and texture tweaking. To firmly establish the cake's warm spiced identity, I ran a few tests, incrementally upping the amounts of cinnamon, nutmeg, and ground cloves. Bumping up the cinnamon to 2 teaspoons brought in plenty of warmth, and just a slight increase in nutmeg and cloves kept the cake's flavors in balance without making it too intense. What really made a difference, though, was the amount of vanilla. While the spices contributed an aromatic, warming quality to the cake, the vanilla created the illusion of additional sweetness in its taste and scent. After starting with just a teaspoon of extract, I slowly added more and more, finally landing on a full tablespoon for maximum impact.

With my flavors figured out, I ran a few last tests to make sure my cake had great texture and would stand tall and proud in even layers. In addition to the baking soda, I also incrementally increased my baking powder amount. At 2 teaspoons, I had cakes that rose beautifully, with flat, even tops and a tender, moist crumb.

I was finally ready to frost my layer cake, and I decided to bring honey into the cream cheese frosting as well. The downfall of most cream cheese frostings is their toothachingly saccharine taste, so I treaded carefully as I beat honey into a mixture of cream cheese and butter. Much to my pleasure, a small amount of the sweet honey played well off the cream cheese's tang, offering a sophisticated profile; a hit of vanilla once again offered that nuanced aromatic quality.

Richly spiced and packed with sweet carrot flavor, the relative lack of sugar in this showstopping layer cake was no shortcoming; if anything, the floral, fragrant sweetness of honey was this carrot cake's greatest asset.

—SARA MAYER, *America's Test Kitchen Books*

Carrot-Honey Layer Cake

SERVES 10 TO 12

Shred the carrots on the large holes of a box grater or in a food processor fitted with the shredding disk. If using dark-colored cake pans, start checking the cakes for doneness 5 to 10 minutes earlier.

1¾ cups (8¾ ounces) all-purpose flour
2 teaspoons baking powder
1 teaspoon baking soda
2 teaspoons ground cinnamon
1 teaspoon ground nutmeg
½ teaspoon ground cloves
½ teaspoon salt
⅓ cup plus ¼ cup honey
¾ cup vegetable oil
3 large eggs
1 tablespoon vanilla extract
2⅔ cups shredded carrots (4 carrots)
1 recipe Honey Cream Cheese Frosting

1. Adjust oven rack to middle position and heat oven to 350 degrees. Grease two 9-inch round cake pans, line with parchment paper, grease parchment, and flour pans.

2. Whisk flour, baking powder, baking soda, cinnamon, nutmeg, cloves, and salt together in bowl. In large bowl, whisk honey, oil, eggs, and vanilla together until smooth. Stir in carrots. Add flour mixture and fold with rubber spatula until mixture is just combined.

3. Divide batter evenly among prepared cake pans and smooth tops. Bake until cakes are set and center is just firm to touch, 16 to 20 minutes, rotating pans halfway through baking.

4. Let cakes cool in pans for 10 minutes. Remove cakes from pans, discard parchment, and let cool completely on wire rack, about 1 hour. (Cake layers can be wrapped in plastic wrap and stored at room temperature for up to 3 days.)

5. Line edges of cake platter with 4 strips of parchment to keep platter clean and place dab of frosting in center to anchor cake. Place 1 cake layer on platter and spread 1 cup frosting evenly over top. Top with second cake layer, press lightly to adhere, then spread

1 cup frosting evenly over top. Spread remaining frosting evenly over sides of cake. To smooth frosting, run edge of offset spatula around cake sides and over top. Carefully remove parchment strips and serve.

Honey Cream Cheese Frosting

MAKES 3 CUPS

Do not substitute low-fat cream cheese here or the frosting will have a soupy consistency. If the frosting becomes too soft to work with, refrigerate it until firm.

- 12 ounces cream cheese, softened
- 8 tablespoons unsalted butter, cut into 8 pieces and softened
- 2 teaspoons vanilla extract
- ⅛ teaspoon salt
- 6 tablespoons honey

1. Using stand mixer fitted with whisk attachment, whip cream cheese, butter, vanilla, and salt on medium-high speed until smooth, 1 to 2 minutes.

2. Reduce mixer speed to medium-low, add honey, and whip until smooth, 1 to 2 minutes. Increase speed to medium-high and whip frosting until light and fluffy, 3 to 5 minutes.

NOTES FROM THE TEST KITCHEN

SHOPPING FOR HONEY

There are two distinct categories of honey: traditional, which is pressure filtered to remove pollen and create a clear appearance, and raw, which is only lightly filtered and retains much of its pollen. We prefer the taste of raw honey in Carrot-Honey Layer Cake and Honey Lemon Squares because it is much more nuanced and balanced in flavor than traditional honey. The bees' diet also affects the flavor of the honey. While bees who feed mostly on clover will produce a mild-flavored honey, bees with a more varied diet will produce a more complexly flavored honey. Our favorite product, **Nature Nate's 100% Pure Raw and Unfiltered Honey**, sources its honey from bees that feed on a blend of wildflowers, clover, Chinese tallow, and vetch; it is slightly bitter and floral, with a deep, balanced sweetness.

VEGAN DARK CHOCOLATE CUPCAKES

✓ WHY THIS RECIPE WORKS: The ultimate dark chocolate cupcake must be moist and tender with deep chocolate flavor. To bake a batch of vegan cupcakes with a light, fluffy crumb, we folded whipped aquafaba, stabilized with cream of tartar, into the batter. For deep flavor, we melted bittersweet chocolate with coconut oil and a generous ½ cup of Dutch-processed cocoa powder. The combination created cupcakes with complex dark chocolate flavor and a tender texture. A mixture of baking powder and baking soda offered effective leavening and 1 cup of organic sugar kept them just sweet enough. No cupcake should go unadorned, so we melted chocolate into coconut milk and beat the creamy mixture into a lush, mousse-like frosting.

If you ask me, rich, chocolatey treats should never be off-limits. Vegan home cooks have long been innovating and experimenting in pursuit of passable dairy- and egg-free baked goods, but I wanted better than "fine"—I wanted truly fantastic vegan chocolate cupcakes.

Before I started baking, I set a few clear goals for my cupcakes. First off, these were not going to be your everyday birthday party fare; I wanted midnight-black, superchocolatey cakes with lush, indulgent frosting to boot. To contrast the intense flavor, I wanted these miniature cakes to be beautifully light and tender. And for the frosting, I wouldn't settle for a plasticky texture or unpleasant off-flavors; I wanted an airy, whipped consistency with enough unadulterated chocolate flavor to stand up to the rich cakes.

I wanted to use an easy-to-find butter replacement for these cupcakes, so for my first test I baked one batch of chocolate cupcakes using coconut oil and another using vegetable oil. I quickly realized that vegetable oil wouldn't cut it. While the coconut oil, melted down with chocolate chips and vanilla, yielded perfectly tender cupcakes, the vegetable oil batch emerged dense and irreparably wet. After consulting with our science editor, this difference made sense. Coconut oil shares more properties with butter than vegetable oil does: It's meltable and also comprised of mostly saturated fat (vegetable oil is mostly unsaturated fat). However, while butter contains a moderate amount of water,

VEGAN DARK CHOCOLATE CUPCAKES

coconut oil is pure fat, meaning it lubricates flour and hinders gluten formation to make baked goods that turn out tender rather than chewy or bready. This was good news—by using coconut oil, my dairy-free cupcakes would naturally resemble traditional cakes at least in texture.

For my egg replacement I turned to another pantry staple: aquafaba, the starchy, protein-rich liquid in which canned chickpeas are suspended. Because aquafaba is beloved in vegan baking for its egg white–like properties, I was excited to see if it lived up to the hype. I shook up and drained a few cans of chickpeas (the shaking helps distribute the starches) and started whipping in my stand mixer. As promised, within 20 minutes the liquid began to form distinct peaks, meaning lots of cupcake-leavening air, but as I readied the rest of my ingredients, I saw my hard-earned foam starting to deflate.

I wasn't sure how important a frothy aquafaba would be to my finished product, so to compare, I readied a second batch of foam, this time taking my cues from meringue and adding a stabilizer. A teaspoon of cream of tartar added before I began whipping produced the same billowy foam, but this time it came together in around 5 minutes. That seemed promising. As I readied the batter, the foam stood tall without any weeping. I carefully folded the unstabilized and stabilized aquafaba foams into the batters and baked them off. As soon as I pulled the two tins from the oven, I had my answer: The stabilized cupcakes emerged with high domes and an open, soft crumb. The unstabilized batch was OK, but the cakes were noticeably more squat. I'd keep the cream of tartar.

Finally, the chocolate. I picked up a few bars of bittersweet chocolate (making sure they were vegan), chopped them up, and melted the chocolate along with the coconut oil. After stirring the chocolaty mixture into the flour and sugar and folding the batter into my billowy aquafaba, I baked off cupcakes that looked the part, but the chocolate bars had let me down: My cupcakes had turned unappealingly grainy. Although the bittersweet chocolate had delivered plenty of chocolate taste, the cocoa butter had formed crystals as the cakes cooled, creating a chalky texture. Adding cocoa powder, which is void of additional fat or moisture, seemed like an easy way to smooth out this situation, so I reduced the amount of bittersweet chocolate and

added some powder. My instincts were dead-on—the next batch had a silky, even texture—but my tasters thought these cupcakes were actually *too* chocolatey. I played around with proportions, finally arriving at ½ cup of Dutch-processed cocoa powder (natural cocoa powder turned my cupcakes rubbery) and 1 ounce of bittersweet chocolate. This rejiggering produced just the chocolate flavor I craved: deep and dark but still sweet and fruity.

Next, I tackled the frosting. While I'd normally defer to cream, butter, and confectioners' sugar for a smooth, lush topping, here I turned to coconut milk for my creamy substitute. Unlike the thinner variety sold in cartons, canned coconut milk is made by steeping shredded coconut in water and then pressing it to yield a creamy, coconutty liquid. For my purposes, the canned version had a hidden benefit: When left to sit, it naturally separates into two layers, with a rich, semisolid layer sitting atop the thinner liquid layer. But when I cracked open my first can, I found only a modicum of that skimmable cream. To help speed up the separation, I popped a few cans into the fridge. The next day, the milk had fully separated, leaving me plenty of easily scoopable, thickened cream to work with.

Aiming to keep the flavors consistent, I melted chopped bittersweet chocolate into the cream in the microwave, but the flavor proved far too intense. Switching over to semisweet chips was a twofold improvement, offering a slightly sweeter taste and a smoother, more stable texture thanks to the emulsifying agents in the chips. Once cooled, the mixture was as thick as cream cheese with a rich, indulgent taste, but it was definitely too dense. This was an easy fix: I whipped the mixture in a stand mixer until it took on a mousse-like texture.

I couldn't wait any longer: I spread some frosting over a cupcake, peeled off the wrapper, and took a bite. Forget vegan; this was an outstanding cupcake, period.

—ANNE WOLF, *America's Test Kitchen Books*

Vegan Dark Chocolate Cupcakes
MAKES 12 CUPCAKES

Note that not all brands of bittersweet chocolate are vegan; be sure to read the label carefully. Do not use natural cocoa powder in this recipe; it gives the cupcakes a rubbery, spongy texture. Aquafaba is the starchy liquid in canned chickpeas. We found that the aqua-faba drained from most brands of chickpeas worked well, the exception being chickpeas from Progresso. To measure the aquafaba, start by shaking an unopened can of chickpeas well. Drain the chickpeas in a fine-mesh strainer set over a bowl and reserve the beans for another use. Whisk the aquafaba to evenly distribute the starches and then measure. The cupcakes are best eaten the day they are made.

1⅓ cups (6⅔ ounces) all-purpose flour

1 cup (7 ounces) organic sugar

¾ teaspoon baking powder

¼ teaspoon baking soda

½ teaspoon salt

1 cup water

1 ounce bittersweet chocolate, chopped

½ cup (1½ ounces) Dutch-processed cocoa powder

¼ cup refined coconut oil

¾ teaspoon vanilla extract

¼ cup aquafaba

1 teaspoon cream of tartar

1 recipe Creamy Chocolate Frosting (recipe follows)

1. Adjust oven rack to middle position and heat oven to 400 degrees. Line 12-cup muffin tin with paper or foil liners. Whisk flour, sugar, baking powder, baking soda, and salt together in large bowl.

2. In separate bowl, microwave water, chocolate, cocoa, oil, and vanilla together at 50 percent power, whisking occasionally, until melted and smooth, about 2 minutes; set aside to cool slightly.

3. Meanwhile, using stand mixer fitted with whisk attachment, whip aquafaba and cream of tartar on high speed until stiff foam that clings to whisk forms, 3 to 9 minutes. Using rubber spatula, stir chocolate mixture into flour mixture until batter is thoroughly combined and smooth (batter will be thick). Stir ⅓ of whipped aqua-faba into batter to lighten, then gently fold in remaining aquafaba until no white streaks remain.

4. Portion batter evenly into prepared muffin tin. Bake cupcakes until tops are set and spring back when pressed lightly, 16 to 20 minutes, rotating muffin tin halfway through baking.

5. Let cupcakes cool in tin for 10 minutes, then transfer to wire rack to cool completely, about 1 hour. Spread frosting evenly over cupcakes and serve.

Creamy Chocolate Frosting

MAKES 2 CUPS

Not all semisweet chocolate chips are vegan, so check the ingredient list carefully. Use two cans of coconut milk to obtain the ¾ cup of cream. Note that this frost-ing is made over two days.

2 (14-ounce) cans coconut milk

1¼ cups (10 ounces) semisweet chocolate chips

⅛ teaspoon salt

1. Refrigerate unopened cans of coconut milk until 2 distinct layers form, at least 24 hours. Skim top layer of cream from each can and measure out ¾ cup cream (save any extra cream for another use and discard milky liquid).

2. Microwave chocolate, coconut cream, and salt in bowl at 50 percent power, whisking occasionally, until melted and smooth, 2 to 4 minutes; transfer to bowl of stand mixer. Place plastic wrap directly against surface of chocolate mixture and refrigerate until cooled com-pletely and texture resembles firm cream cheese, about 3 hours, stirring halfway through chilling. (If mixture has chilled for longer and is very stiff, let stand at room temperature until softened but still cool.) Using stand mixer fitted with whisk attachment, whip at high speed until fluffy, mousse-like, and soft peaks form, 2 to 4 minutes, scraping down bowl halfway through whip-ping. Serve.

GÂTEAU BRETON WITH APRICOT FILLING

✔ **WHY THIS RECIPE WORKS:** Hailing from France's Brittany coast, gâteau Breton is a simple yet stately cake with a dense yet tender crumb. We avoided incorporating too much air (thereby creating a too-fluffy texture) by creaming the butter and sugar for only 3 minutes before adding the yolks and flour. Briefly freezing a layer of the batter in the cake pan made easy work of spreading a bright homemade apricot filling over the batter, and a second stint in the freezer firmed up the apricot-topped batter so we could apply the top layer without disrupting the filling. From there, we scored the surface, brushed on an egg wash for some appealing sheen, and baked it. The understated cake emerged buttery, rich, and beautifully browned.

I first encountered gâteau Breton years ago while living in France, and I was smitten from my first bite. As its name implies, the cake hails from the Brittany region of France, which lies on the western edge of the country, abutting the Atlantic Ocean. It's a simple yet pretty cake, rich in butter, with a dense, tender crumb that falls somewhere between shortbread cookies and pound cake. In my favorite versions, the cake camouflages a thin layer of jam or fruit filling baked into its center, which delivers a vein of sweet acidity that balances the cake's richness. The cake's firm structure allows it to be cut into thin wedges for nibbling with an afternoon cup of tea, but in my experience, a portion so small is never enough.

When I tried my hand at gâteau Breton by baking five existing recipes, I quickly learned that there are plenty of ways to go wrong. One cake, made with buckwheat flour (an ancient tradition from the days when wheat flour was unavailable in Brittany), was dry enough for a colleague to liken it to "compressed sawdust." The center of another was so wet and gummy that folks were convinced it included gooey marzipan. As for the fillings, most tasted flat and were thin and runny; spreading them evenly over the sticky batter proved to be quite a challenge. I wanted a cake with a crumb to rival the very best I had enjoyed in France, along with a lively filling with a workable consistency.

Most modern recipes call for four main ingredients: all-purpose flour, salted butter, sugar, and egg yolks. (Since the test kitchen almost exclusively uses unsalted butter for baking, I would investigate later whether salted butter was worth a special purchase.) I used one of the better recipes from my first round of testing as a starting point. It was pleasantly dense but a little too wet and greasy, so I spent a few afternoons in the test kitchen, baking gâteau after gâteau, slowly increasing the amount of dry ingredients and decreasing the amount of butter until I got a cake I liked.

I also examined the technique. Most recipes call for creaming the butter and sugar before incorporating the yolks and flour, and some specify upwards of 10 minutes of creaming. But extensive creaming incorporated too much air into the batter and resulted in a light, fluffy crumb—just the opposite of what I wanted. Ultimately, I landed on creaming two sticks of butter with a little less than 1 cup of sugar in a stand mixer for only 3 minutes, adding five yolks one at a time, and finally mixing in 2 cups of flour. This produced an ultrathick batter that baked up with the trademark firm yet tender crumb that I was after.

With the cake nailed down, I dug deeper into the butter issue. Bretons insist that their local butter made with sea salt is key to this cake, so I arranged a head-to-head comparison of cake made with the test kitchen's favorite salted butter, Lurpak (a cultured butter from Denmark), and cake made with our favorite unsalted sticks, from Land O'Lakes (with some salt stirred into the batter to compensate). Not surprisingly, tasters found that the European butter delivered a slightly more complex cake, but in the end I decided that the difference wasn't enough to warrant the extra cost or trip to the market.

I did, however, want to explore other ways to add complexity. In France, liquor is often used as a flavor enhancer for this cake, so why not add some to mine? I experimented with kirsch and Calvados before finally settling on dark rum for its rich caramel notes. I also added vanilla extract for even more depth.

I'd produced a rich, flavorful cake with just the right dense texture. Now it was time to address the filling. A prune puree is traditional, and while I did end up developing a prune variation, I preferred to showcase a version with a brighter, bolder filling. I'd seen recipes featuring chocolate, date, or apricot fillings, and apricot seemed like the ideal foil to my buttery cake.

Unfortunately, store-bought apricot jam was too sweet and dull; plus, it was too thin and runny to work well as a filling. You see, when constructing this cake, you first spread half the thick batter in the bottom of

GÂTEAU BRETON WITH APRICOT FILLING

a buttered cake pan, and then you layer on the filling before finally spreading the rest of the batter on top and baking the cake. If the filling is too thin, it'll either get picked up and mixed in with the batter or leak from the sides of the cake as it bakes, creating a real mess.

I thought that reducing the jam might concentrate its flavor and give me the consistency I wanted, but ultimately I decided to craft my own filling from dried apricots so that I could achieve the exact flavor and consistency I wanted.

Too bad my first batch didn't taste very good. I had made the puree with dried Turkish apricots, and they just didn't have enough oomph. Using dried California apricots remedied this weakness in a hurry: Their concentrated sweet-tart flavor delivered a bright, fruity zing. I chopped up the apricots, tossed them into a blender with enough water to engage the blade, and whizzed them until smooth. After cooking the puree in a skillet with sugar until it thickened and darkened slightly, I squeezed in a bit of fresh lemon juice. Now I had a thick, fruity puree to highlight the rich, buttery cake.

To make the assembly of the cake foolproof, I experimented with what a fellow test cook called a "jam dam," a lip of batter at the edge of the pan designed to hold the filling in place and keep it from oozing out the sides of the cake during baking. It worked well enough in that regard but did little to keep the jam from mixing with the cake batter. Ultimately, I solved the problem with a bakery trick: quickly chilling the first layer of batter by sliding the cake pan into the freezer. Given the high concentration of butter in this cake, just 10 minutes of chilling did the trick: The batter became so firm that it didn't budge when I spooned on the apricot puree. Putting the pan back into the freezer for 10 minutes once the jam layer was on ensured that everything stayed put when the remaining batter was added.

All that was left to do was pretty up the cake with a simple egg wash and decoration. Here, I didn't deviate at all from tradition. I first brushed the cake with an egg yolk beaten with a teaspoon of water (this would give it a slight sheen) and then gently dragged the tines of a fork across the cake's surface in a crisscrossing diamond pattern. This branded my dessert as a classic gâteau Breton and was the final step in ensuring that my beautiful, buttery cake stayed true to its roots.

—STEVE DUNN, *Cook's Illustrated*

Gâteau Breton with Apricot Filling

SERVES 8

We strongly prefer the flavor of California apricots in the filling. Mediterranean (or Turkish) apricots can be used, but increase the amount of lemon juice to 2 tablespoons.

FILLING

⅔ cup water

½ cup dried California apricots, chopped

⅓ cup (2⅓ ounces) sugar

1 tablespoon lemon juice

CAKE

16 tablespoons unsalted butter, softened

¾ cup plus 2 tablespoons (6⅛ ounces) sugar

6 large egg yolks (1 lightly beaten with 1 teaspoon water)

2 tablespoons dark rum

1 teaspoon vanilla extract

2 cups (10 ounces) all-purpose flour

½ teaspoon salt

1. FOR THE FILLING: Process water and apricots in blender until uniformly pureed, about 2 minutes. Transfer puree to 10-inch nonstick skillet and stir in sugar. Set skillet over medium heat and cook, stirring frequently, until puree has darkened slightly and rubber spatula leaves distinct trail when dragged across bottom of pan, 10 to 12 minutes. Transfer filling to bowl and stir in lemon juice. Refrigerate filling until cool to touch, about 15 minutes.

2. FOR THE CAKE: Adjust oven rack to lower-middle position and heat oven to 350 degrees. Grease 9-inch round cake pan.

3. Using stand mixer fitted with paddle, beat butter on medium-high speed until smooth and lightened in color, 1 to 2 minutes. Add sugar and continue to beat until pale and fluffy, about 3 minutes longer. Add 5 egg yolks, one at a time, and beat until combined. Scrape down bowl, add rum and vanilla, and mix until incorporated, about 1 minute. Reduce speed to low, add flour and salt, and mix until flour is just incorporated, about 30 seconds. Give batter final stir by hand.

4. Spoon half of batter into bottom of prepared pan. Using small offset spatula, spread batter into even layer. Freeze for 10 minutes.

5. Spread ½ cup filling in even layer over chilled batter, leaving ¾-inch border around edge (reserve remaining filling for another use). Freeze for 10 minutes.

6. Gently spread remaining batter over filling. Using offset spatula, carefully smooth top of batter. Brush with egg yolk wash. Using tines of fork, make light scores in surface of cake, spaced about 1½ inches apart, in diamond pattern, being careful not to score all the way to sides of pan. Bake until top is golden brown and edges of cake start to pull away from sides of pan, 45 to 50 minutes. Let cake cool in pan on wire rack for 30 minutes. Run paring knife between cake and sides of pan, remove cake from pan, and let cool completely on rack, about 1 hour. Cut into wedges and serve.

VARIATION

Gâteau Breton with Prune Filling

Increase water to 1 cup, substitute 1 cup pitted prunes for apricots, and omit sugar. Bring water and prunes to simmer in small saucepan over medium heat. Reduce heat to medium-low and cook until all liquid is absorbed and prunes are very soft, 10 to 12 minutes. Remove saucepan from heat, add lemon juice, and stir with wooden spoon, pressing prunes against side of saucepan, until coarsely pureed. Transfer filling to bowl and refrigerate until cool to touch, about 15 minutes.

APPLE PANDOWDY

✔ **WHY THIS RECIPE WORKS:** Unlike traditional skillet pie, apple pandowdy's crust is gently pressed into the filling (or "dowdied") during baking so the juices flood the top and caramelize in the oven. To bake this rustic classic at home, we tossed wedges of buttery Golden Delicious apples in cinnamon and brown sugar for sweet-spiced flavor and partially cooked them before adding a cornstarch slurry to thicken the filling. Topping the apples with squares of dough allowed steam to escape during baking, preventing the apples from overcooking, and dowdying partway through baking created the dessert's signature sweet finish.

One of many old-school New England desserts with funny names (slumps, grunts, etc.), an apple pandowdy is pie or biscuit dough casually laid atop a pan of apple filling and baked. It's similar to a skillet pie, but during baking, the crust is pressed or slashed into the filling so the juices flood over the top crust and caramelize in the oven. That's right, you purposefully mess up the top of your dessert, a process called "dowdying," which leaves a dowdy-looking but eminently delicious result.

The inventor's name is lost to history, but way back in the colonial era (and even before), this counterintuitive process helped soften tough dough to make it easier to eat. The happy side effect was a dessert with layers of texture (some crisp, some soft) and an unexpected range of deep, sweet flavors.

These days, using modern kitchen equipment and more-standardized ingredients, we can easily create delicate crusts, so softening the dough is no longer an urgent goal. But I did want that caramelized top—along with perfectly cooked apples and a thick, syrupy sauce to drizzle over a side of vanilla ice cream.

Existing recipes confused me. Some called for dowdying the dough before baking and others halfway through, while still others instructed you to wait until after baking. But reading through them made it clear that I'd have to nail down my filling first. I started with Granny Smith apples, which held their shape during baking but turned unpleasantly acidic once cooked. Golden Delicious apples, however, remained sweet and buttery and just firm enough. And while many old recipes called for molasses as a sweetener, I found it far too intense. Instead, I chose brown sugar (for gentler molasses flavor) and a bit of tart apple cider and lemon juice for balance. I knew I'd have to precook the apples briefly; doing so helps set their pectin, allowing them to hold their shape while concurrently softening as they cook. Done. I was back to the dough.

Placing a round of homemade all-butter dough (to which I added just a tablespoon of sour cream for tang) over the cooked apples and pressing it into the filling raw before baking it off was a disaster—I ended up with cardboard. Dowdying the crust after it was fully baked only made it soggy. So I tried dowdying halfway through baking. This was the ticket; it first allowed the crust time to set up and then gave the flooded juices time to caramelize. I was onto something.

But my excitement was short-lived. Digging deeper, I found a mess of mushy apples. My dough, though dowdied, had resealed itself over the filling, leaving no escape for moisture and turning my filling into, essentially, applesauce. Simply slashing ventilation holes in the top wasn't enough either; there was still too much moisture.

APPLE PANDOWDY

For my next test I cut my dough into 2½-inch squares and arranged them in a rough overlapping pattern. When I opened the oven halfway through baking to do my dowdying, I felt a jolt of excitement. The partial coverage and overlapping squares of dough appeared to be promoting ventilation, allowing the apples to keep their shape and not overcook. Plus, this new setup gave the crust even more textural contrast: sticky caramelization, flaky pastry, and a few soft spots. The juices were still too thin, but a simple cornstarch slurry fixed that in my next round of testing, giving me a luxuriously syrupy sauce.

I'm always looking for shortcuts, so I decided to try the pandowdy using a store-bought pie crust. The results were totally disappointing, gummy and dull. A naturally denser product, store-bought crust turned gluey and didn't produce pandowdy's hallmark textures.

On my last day of testing, I scooped portions of pandowdy and served them with vanilla ice cream, drizzling a little extra syrup over top. I asked my tasters for feedback, but they were too busy licking their spoons to respond.

—CECELIA JENKINS, *Cook's Country*

Apple Pandowdy

SERVES 6

Disturbing the crust, or "dowdying," allows juices from the filling to rise over the crust and caramelize as the dessert continues to bake. Removing the skillet from the oven allows you to properly press down on the crust. Do not use store-bought pie crust in this recipe.

PIE DOUGH

- 3 tablespoons ice water
- 1 tablespoon sour cream
- ⅔ cup (3⅓ ounces) all-purpose flour
- 1 teaspoon granulated sugar
- ½ teaspoon salt
- 6 tablespoons unsalted butter, cut into ¼-inch pieces and frozen for 15 minutes

FILLING

- 2½ pounds Golden Delicious apples, peeled, cored, halved, and cut into ½-inch-thick wedges
- ¼ cup packed (1¾ ounces) light brown sugar
- ½ teaspoon ground cinnamon

- ¼ teaspoon salt
- 3 tablespoons unsalted butter
- ¾ cup apple cider
- 1 tablespoon cornstarch
- 2 teaspoons lemon juice

TOPPING

- 1 tablespoon granulated sugar
- ¼ teaspoon ground cinnamon
- 1 large egg, lightly beaten

Vanilla ice cream

1. FOR THE PIE DOUGH: Combine ice water and sour cream in bowl. Process flour, sugar, and salt in food processor until combined, about 3 seconds. Add butter and pulse until size of large peas, 6 to 8 pulses. Add sour cream mixture and pulse until dough forms large clumps and no dry flour remains, 3 to 6 pulses, scraping down sides of bowl as needed.

2. Form dough into 4-inch disk, wrap tightly in plastic wrap, and refrigerate for 1 hour. (Wrapped dough can be refrigerated for up to 2 days or frozen for up to 1 month. If frozen, let dough thaw completely on counter before rolling.)

3. Adjust oven rack to middle position and heat oven to 400 degrees. Let chilled dough sit on counter to soften slightly, about 5 minutes, before rolling. Roll dough into 10-inch circle on lightly floured counter. Using pizza cutter, cut dough into four 2½-inch-wide strips, then make four 2½-inch-wide perpendicular cuts to form squares. (Pieces around edges of dough will be smaller.) Transfer dough pieces to parchment paper–lined baking sheet, cover with plastic, and refrigerate until firm, at least 30 minutes.

4. FOR THE FILLING: Toss apples, sugar, cinnamon, and salt together in large bowl. Melt butter in 10-inch skillet over medium heat. Add apple mixture, cover, and cook until apples become slightly pliable and release their juice, about 10 minutes, stirring occasionally.

5. Whisk cider, cornstarch, and lemon juice in bowl until no lumps remain; add to skillet. Bring to simmer and cook, uncovered, stirring occasionally, until sauce is thickened, about 2 minutes. Off heat, press lightly on apples to form even layer.

6. FOR THE TOPPING: Combine sugar and cinnamon in small bowl. Working quickly, shingle dough pieces over filling until mostly covered, overlapping

"DOWDYING" THE CRUST

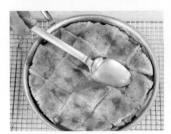

Once crust has begun to puff and brown, press down on center of crust until juices come up over top of crust. Repeat four more times before returning to oven to finish baking.

as needed. Brush dough pieces with egg and sprinkle with cinnamon sugar.

7. Bake until crust is slightly puffed and beginning to brown, about 15 minutes. Remove skillet from oven. Using back of large spoon, press down in center of crust until juices come up over top of crust. Repeat four more times around skillet. Make sure all apples are submerged and return skillet to oven. Continue to bake until crust is golden brown, about 15 minutes longer.

8. Transfer skillet to wire rack and let cool for at least 20 minutes. Serve with ice cream, drizzling extra sauce over top.

APPLE STRUDEL

✔ **WHY THIS RECIPE WORKS:** For apple strudel loaded with spiced apples sealed in flaky pastry, we started by swapping laborious handmade dough for store-bought phyllo dough. Dusting confectioners sugar between the phyllo layers helped seal the sheets together for a neater presentation. Warming the apple pieces in the microwave ensured they would hold their shape during baking. Using ultradry panko bread crumbs instead of homemade crumbs protected against a pasty texture. To avoid a compressed, tough underside, we changed the typical wrapping technique so the seam was on top instead of on the bottom. Brushing some of the apples' sweet exuded liquid on top helped seal the seam while also promising extra browning.

In the world of pastries, apple strudel seems unassuming, a marriage of flaky pastry and just-sweet-enough raisin-studded apples ideal for dessert, with afternoon coffee, or even for breakfast. No wonder it's an everyday favorite all over central Europe.

And yet making strudel, at least the traditional way, is not at all simple. To create the swirl of delicate pastry that defines it (strudel means "whirlpool" or "eddy" in German), you start by stretching a piece of dough the size of a brick until it measures well over 4 feet long and 4 feet wide and is so thin you can read a newspaper through it. You brush it with butter and then pile a mixture of chopped apples, sugar, spice, raisins, and toasted bread crumbs (to absorb exuded juice) along one edge. The sides are folded over, and then it's ever-so-carefully rolled up, transferred to a baking sheet, and baked.

The dough is such an ordeal (and requires so much counter space) that rarely does anyone other than a professional baker make strudel this way anymore. The modern approach is to swap in a stack of store-bought phyllo sheets. Yet after making a few of these "simpler" recipes, I discovered that these versions are still rife with problems. Brushing each sheet with butter (both for flavor and to make the sheets more pliable) and rolling up the strudel without ripping the pastry was tricky. Plus, the bottom crusts all came out dense and tough, while the top was a mess of flyaway sheets that flaked off as soon as I started slicing (if not before). The fillings weren't so great either. Many had collapsed, leaving a gaping void between the filling and the top of the pastry, and they all had a gummy, pasty texture and muted apple flavor. And despite the bread crumbs, sweet juice still leaked out, gluing the pastry to the pan. I wanted to come up with a phyllo-based strudel recipe that was easy to make, had a flavorful and tender apple filling that stayed put, and featured a crust that held together but was still flaky.

First, I needed a filling. I quickly settled on Golden Delicious apples since they are easy to find and hold their shape when cooked. After cutting the apples into ½-inch pieces (1¾ pounds of apples seemed about right for six servings), I tossed them with sugar, cinnamon, ground ginger, and some lemon zest and juice. Since I suspected that the bread crumbs were responsible for dulling the flavor and creating the pasty texture, I decided to leave them out. I had a parcooking technique in mind that I hoped would not only eliminate excess liquid (and thus the need for bread crumbs) but also keep the filling from collapsing.

We've found that parcooking apples briefly can set off an enzymatic reaction that causes the pectin in the fruit to set, meaning the fruit will hold its shape when it continues cooking at higher temperatures. A

APPLE STRUDEL

couple of minutes in the microwave warmed the apples just enough. They also exuded about ⅓ cup of liquid, which I drained off and reserved before stirring in the raisins. I wrapped this simple filling up in a stack of phyllo, placed it seam side down on a baking sheet, and baked it in a 375-degree oven until it was golden.

On the upside, the apples were now tender yet still held their shape—no collapsed filling. But clearly I hadn't drained off enough of the apples' juice, which had seeped through, caramelized in the hot oven, and glued the strudel to the pan.

Instead of turning to the usual freshly toasted bread crumbs to soak up the juice, I decided to reach for panko. Commercially dried panko bread crumbs are drier than homemade, which meant I could use less of them and soak up a comparable amount of liquid (we avoid regular commercial bread crumbs in the test kitchen since they are too fine and dusty). After a few tests, I found that just 1½ tablespoons of panko stirred into the parcooked apples was all my filling needed to effectively contain the juice. And best of all, the filling had a bright apple flavor—no dullness or pasty texture. It was time to deal with the pastry.

Phyllo can be intimidating to work with, but a few tips that we've come up with in the past helped make it easier out of the gate. I also made an immediate change to the strudel's assembly. Rolling the phyllo around all that filling and getting it onto the baking sheet was cumbersome and tricky. Instead, I'd divide it up and make two smaller strudels.

First, I decided to tackle the layers of tough, dense phyllo on the bottom of the strudel. Some recipes use as many as 11 sheets of phyllo, and while flakiness is a goal, I had to wonder if more was necessarily better. The weight of the filling seemed to be compressing the layers on the strudel's bottom, making them tough. Maybe using fewer sheets would give me a more delicate, tender base? Indeed, going down to seven sheets made a noticeable difference. But it wasn't perfect.

By rolling the strudels like logs and placing them seam side down, I'd created areas with overlapping layers of phyllo on the undersides of the strudels—there were 14 sheets where the edges overlapped rather than just seven. What if I put the seam on the top, where toughness wasn't an issue? For the next strudel, I placed the filling on the phyllo stack, folded the sides up over the filling, and then folded the top and bottom up and over, much like folding a letter. To seal the seam, I brushed the dough with some of the sticky apple liquid that had been released in the microwave (and while I was at it, I also brushed the liquid over the entire surface to help the strudels brown). I transferred the strudels to a baking sheet and popped them into the oven. Finally, the undersides were perfect: crisp on the exterior yet tender and easy to get a fork through. Plus, this method was much easier, with less risk of tearing since I didn't have to manipulate the strudels so much.

On to the messy top layers. To keep them from shattering everywhere, I came up with a two-pronged solution. First, I lightly "glued" the sheets together by sprinkling each one with confectioners' sugar after brushing it with butter. In the heat of the oven, the sugar melted and sealed the sheets together just enough to keep them from flying apart. And second, as soon as the strudel was out of the oven, I transferred it to a cutting board and sliced it after just a few minutes. When hot, the pastry was softer and thus less prone to shattering; once cooled, it crisped up beautifully.

At last, I had a simpler strudel that was so good, I could see myself enjoying it on a regular basis.

—LAN LAM, *Cook's Illustrated*

Apple Strudel

SERVES 6

Gala apples can be substituted for Golden Delicious. Phyllo dough is also available in larger 18 by 14-inch sheets; if using, cut them in half to make 14 by 9-inch sheets. Thaw phyllo in the refrigerator overnight or on the counter for 4 to 5 hours; don't thaw it in the microwave.

1¾	pounds Golden Delicious apples, peeled, cored, and cut into ½-inch pieces
3	tablespoons granulated sugar
½	teaspoon grated lemon zest plus 1½ teaspoons juice
¼	teaspoon ground cinnamon
¼	teaspoon ground ginger
	Salt
3	tablespoons golden raisins
1½	tablespoons panko bread crumbs
7	tablespoons unsalted butter, melted
1	tablespoon confectioners' sugar, plus extra for serving
14	(14 by 9-inch) phyllo sheets, thawed

1. Toss apples, granulated sugar, lemon zest and juice, cinnamon, ginger, and ⅛ teaspoon salt together in large bowl. Cover and microwave until apples are warm to touch, about 2 minutes, stirring once halfway through microwaving. Let apples stand, covered, for 5 minutes. Transfer apples to colander set in second large bowl and let drain, reserving liquid. Return apples to bowl; stir in raisins and panko.

2. Adjust oven rack to upper-middle position and heat oven to 375 degrees. Spray rimmed baking sheet with vegetable oil spray. Stir ⅛ teaspoon salt into melted butter.

3. Place 16½ by 12-inch sheet of parchment paper on counter with long side parallel to edge of counter. Place 1 phyllo sheet on parchment with long side parallel to edge of counter. Place 1½ teaspoons confectioners' sugar in fine-mesh strainer (rest strainer in bowl to prevent making mess). Lightly brush sheet with melted butter and dust sparingly with confectioners' sugar. Repeat with 6 more phyllo sheets, melted butter, and confectioners' sugar, stacking sheets one on top of other as you go.

4. Arrange half of apple mixture in 2½ by 10-inch rectangle 2 inches from bottom of phyllo and about 2 inches from each side. Using parchment, fold sides of phyllo over filling, then fold bottom edge of phyllo over filling. Brush folded portions of phyllo with reserved apple liquid. Fold top edge over filling, making sure top and bottom edges overlap by about 1 inch. (If they do not overlap, unfold, rearrange filling into slightly narrower strip, and refold.) Press firmly to seal. Using thin metal spatula, transfer strudel to 1 side of prepared baking sheet, facing seam toward center of sheet. Lightly brush top and sides of strudel with half of remaining apple liquid. Repeat process with remaining phyllo, melted butter, confectioners' sugar, filling, and apple liquid. Place second strudel on other side of prepared sheet, with seam facing center of sheet.

5. Bake strudels until golden brown, 27 to 35 minutes, rotating sheet halfway through baking. Using thin metal spatula, immediately transfer strudels to cutting board. Let cool for 3 minutes. Slice each strudel into thirds and let cool for at least 20 minutes. Serve warm or at room temperature, dusting with extra confectioners' sugar before serving.

NOTES FROM THE TEST KITCHEN

WRAPPING APPLE STRUDEL

1. Mound half of filling along bottom third of 7 layered phyllo sheets on parchment paper, leaving 2-inch border at bottom edge and sides of phyllo.

2. Using parchment, fold sides of phyllo over filling, then fold over bottom edge of phyllo. Brush folded portions with apple liquid.

3. Fold top edge of phyllo over mounded filling, which should overlap bottom edge by about 1 inch. Press to seal. Repeat with second strudel.

OREGON BLACKBERRY PIE

✓ WHY THIS RECIPE WORKS: The hallmark of Oregon blackberry pie is its sturdy, fruity filling. To re-create that texture at home, we turned to the clean-tasting, quick-thickening power of cornstarch. Tossing the blackberries in a mixture of sugar, cornstarch, and salt kept the focus on the fruit, and stirring in lemon juice highlighted the tart berries. Baked in a rich, buttery homemade crust with a lattice top allowed for the evaporation of excess moisture. This pie turned out flaky, sweet-tart, and showstopping.

In high summer, blackberry brambles blanket the Pacific Northwest, and a slice of blackberry pie is never far from reach. In Oregon it's known as marionberry pie, named after the native blackberry variety prized by pie makers. Cut into a good example of this seasonal staple and you'll see what sets it apart from other fruit pies: You won't get a soupy, oozy slice. Instead, the purple filling retains its shape.

But how? Aficionados I spoke with claimed that

there are no tricky tricks, no added pectin or gelatin, nothing stranger than a bit of starch. As trustworthy as my sources were, I was skeptical. Could I create a cohesive blackberry filling with tart, clean, fresh summertime flavor? Only one way to find out. I grabbed a handful of existing recipes and got to baking.

Settling on a crust was the easy part. Tasters preferred the flavor of pies with all-butter crusts to crusts that used shortening. After a few quick tests, I settled on the test kitchen's recipe for all-butter pie crust, with 3 tablespoons of sour cream added for a richer dough that was just a bit easier to roll out. Bonus: The acid in the sour cream inhibited the gluten from overdeveloping and becoming tough. And because I knew I'd need to leave open some avenues for evaporation, I chose to follow the example set by blackberry pie pros and use a lattice top.

Now for the filling. Before tackling the puzzle of a thick filling that would hold its shape, I nailed down the flavors. Heavily sweetened pies and added spices confused the blackberry flavor. After baking several pies with different ratios of flavors, I settled on ¾ cup of sugar, a bit of salt, and a good hit of lemon juice for a sweet-enough filling with clear and present blackberry flavor.

But my pies were soupy. A thickener was essential. I needed to take care here; the thickener couldn't influence the flavors, and it also had to help create a smooth, cohesive texture that held its shape without being like Jell-O.

Simply smashing some of the berries should, in theory, release more of the natural pectin found in the berries to help set the pie. But with this technique, the filling felt jammy, and besides, tasters preferred whole berries.

I tried tapioca, a favorite test kitchen thickener, but this created a gelatin-like texture. Flour turned things gluey. I landed on cornstarch, which gave me a good texture and didn't muck up the flavor. After testing amounts from 1 teaspoon to ½ cup, I learned that 5 tablespoons did the trick.

One final touch made this pie even easier: I developed a quicker, more foolproof lattice top by simply laying four horizontal strips across the pie and then four vertical strips over those. This gave the same woven effect without my having to weave the strips together. I had a beautiful, flavorful blackberry pie to be proud of.

—CECELIA JENKINS, *Cook's Country*

Oregon Blackberry Pie

SERVES 8

Be sure to rinse the berries and dry them thoroughly before using. Do not use frozen berries in this recipe. Freezing the butter for the dough for 15 minutes before processing it in step 1 is crucial to the flaky texture of this crust—do not skip this step. If working in a hot kitchen, refrigerate all the ingredients before making the dough. Note that the pie dough needs to chill for at least an hour before rolling. When brushing the lattice strips with egg wash, be sure to leave the ends of each strip unbrushed so the wash doesn't impede the crimping process.

PIE DOUGH

- ⅓ cup ice water, plus extra as needed
- 3 tablespoons sour cream
- 2½ cups (12½ ounces) all-purpose flour
- 1 tablespoon sugar
- 1 teaspoon salt
- 16 tablespoons unsalted butter, cut into ¼-inch pieces and frozen for 15 minutes

FILLING

- ¾ cup (5¼ ounces) sugar, plus 1 teaspoon for topping
- 5 tablespoons (1¼ ounces) cornstarch
- ¼ teaspoon salt
- 20 ounces (4 cups) blackberries
- 2 tablespoons lemon juice
- 2 tablespoons unsalted butter, cut into ½-inch pieces
- 1 large egg, lightly beaten

1. FOR THE PIE DOUGH: Mix ice water and sour cream in bowl. Process flour, sugar, and salt in food processor until combined, about 5 seconds. Scatter butter over top and pulse until butter is size of large peas, about 10 pulses.

2. Pour half of sour cream mixture into bowl with flour mixture and pulse until incorporated, about 3 pulses. Scrape down bowl and repeat with remaining sour cream mixture. Pinch dough with your fingers; if dough feels dry and does not hold together, sprinkle 1 to 2 tablespoons extra ice water over mixture and pulse until dough forms large clumps and no dry flour remains, 3 to 5 pulses.

3. Transfer dough to lightly floured counter. Divide dough in half and form each half into 4-inch disk. Wrap disks tightly in plastic wrap and refrigerate for

1 hour. (Wrapped dough can be refrigerated for up to 2 days or frozen for up to 1 month. If frozen, let dough thaw completely on counter before rolling.)

4. Adjust oven rack to lower-middle position and heat oven to 400 degrees. Let chilled dough sit on counter to soften slightly, about 10 minutes, before rolling. Roll 1 disk of dough into 12-inch circle on lightly floured counter. Loosely roll dough around rolling pin and gently unroll it onto 9-inch pie plate, letting excess dough hang over edge. Ease dough into plate by gently lifting edge of dough with your hand while pressing into plate bottom with your other hand.

5. Wrap dough-lined plate loosely in plastic and refrigerate until dough is firm, about 30 minutes. Roll other disk of dough into 12-inch circle on lightly floured counter, then transfer to parchment paper–lined baking sheet. Using pizza cutter, cut dough into twelve 1-inch strips. Discard 4 short end pieces, then cover remaining 8 long strips with plastic and refrigerate for 30 minutes.

6. FOR THE FILLING: Whisk sugar, cornstarch, and salt together in large bowl. Add blackberries and toss gently to coat. Add lemon juice and toss until no dry sugar mixture remains. (Blackberries will start to exude some juice.)

7. Transfer blackberry mixture to dough-lined pie plate and dot with butter. Lay 4 dough strips parallel to each other across pie, about 1 inch apart. Brush strips with egg, leaving ½ inch at ends unbrushed. Lay remaining 4 strips perpendicular to first layer of strips, about 1 inch apart.

8. Pinch edges of lattice strips and bottom crust firmly together. Trim overhang to ½ inch beyond lip of plate. Tuck overhang under itself; folded edge should be flush with edge of plate. Crimp dough evenly around edge of plate using your fingers.

NOTES FROM THE TEST KITCHEN

LAYING A (FAUX) LATTICE

Lay 4 parallel strips about 1 inch apart. Brush with egg, leaving ½ inch at ends unbrushed. Lay remaining 4 strips perpendicular to first layer, about 1 inch apart.

9. Brush lattice top and crimped edge with egg and sprinkle with remaining 1 teaspoon sugar. Set pie on parchment-lined baking sheet. Bake until golden brown and juices bubble evenly along surface, 45 to 50 minutes, rotating sheet halfway through baking. Let cool on wire rack for at least 4 hours before serving.

SOUR ORANGE PIE

✓ **WHY THIS RECIPE WORKS:** Sour orange pie is northern Florida's answer to Key lime, with a tart, custard-like filling made with the juice of wild sour oranges. Since fresh sour oranges are hard to source, we re-created their distinct taste with frozen orange juice concentrate, lemon juice, and orange and lemon zests. We mixed the juice with sweetened condensed milk for sweetness and egg yolks for structure. Slightly sweet animal crackers made a crunchy crust to contrast the filling. Chilled and topped with orange-flavored whipped cream, this pie tasted bright and refreshing.

Local cooks and writers refer to sour orange pie as northern Florida's answer to South Florida's Key lime pie: a prebaked crust and a custard-like interior made with sweetened condensed milk and the juice of wild sour oranges, which are otherwise thrown away since they are far too tart to eat straight from the branch. I imagined transforming this much-maligned citrus into a lush and fruity dessert, the tart tang balanced by sweetness and floral orange notes.

I started with a simple crust of crushed graham crackers and melted butter but later swapped out graham for animal crackers; the slightly sweeter cookies highlighted the sour citrus filling.

But the interior was more difficult—mostly because sour oranges aren't easy to come by in much of the country. I finally found some at a local Latin American grocer, but the variation from orange to orange proved too tricky to even out—they ranged in size from golf balls to softballs, in color from green to pale yellow, and in liquid content from dry to watery. Since good quality sour oranges were too hard to find, I'd have to make my sour orange pie without sour oranges.

I started playing with combinations of (sweet) orange juice, lemon juice, lime juice, and grapefruit juice. I enlisted tasters to sip samples until we found one that accurately mimicked the flavor of true sour oranges:

SOUR ORANGE PIE

a mix of orange and lemon juice. But once mixed with egg yolks for structure and sweetened condensed milk for sweetness and creaminess and baked into the pie, the combination lost nuance and was far too lemony.

I couldn't decrease the lemon because of the crucial sour punch it added, so I had to bump up the orange. Enter frozen orange juice concentrate, a bolder, more intensely flavored product. Together with lemon, it delivered a bright, complex orange flavor balanced by a faintly bitter bite from the citrus's zest. Additional orange zest in the whipped cream gave the dessert a floral essence.

I look forward to trying an authentic sour orange pie on my next visit to Florida. But in the meantime, I'll gather these ingredients at the grocery store and imagine warm Floridian afternoons while I eat this refreshing, sunny pie.

—KATIE LEAIRD, *Cook's Country*

Sour Orange Pie

SERVES 8

If sour oranges are available, use ¾ cup of strained sour orange juice in place of the lemon juice and orange juice concentrate. Minute Maid Original Frozen is our favorite orange juice concentrate. Depending on the brand, 5 ounces is between 80 and 90 animal crackers.

CRUST

- 5 ounces animal crackers
- 3 tablespoons sugar
  Pinch salt
- 4 tablespoons unsalted butter, melted

FILLING

- 1 (14-ounce) can sweetened condensed milk
- 6 tablespoons frozen orange juice concentrate, thawed
- 4 large egg yolks
- 2 teaspoons grated lemon zest plus 6 tablespoons juice (2 lemons)
- 1 teaspoon grated orange zest
  Pinch salt

WHIPPED CREAM

- ¾ cup heavy cream, chilled
- 2 tablespoons sugar
- ½ teaspoon grated orange zest

1. FOR THE CRUST: Adjust oven rack to middle position and heat oven to 325 degrees. Process crackers, sugar, and salt in food processor until finely ground, about 30 seconds. Add melted butter and pulse until combined, about 8 pulses. Transfer crumbs to 9-inch pie plate.

2. Using bottom of dry measuring cup, press crumbs firmly into bottom and up sides of pie plate. Bake crust until fragrant and beginning to brown, 12 to 14 minutes. Let cool completely, about 30 minutes.

3. FOR THE FILLING: Whisk all ingredients in bowl until fully combined. Pour filling into cooled crust.

4. Bake pie until center jiggles slightly when shaken, 15 to 17 minutes. Let cool completely. Refrigerate until fully chilled, at least 3 hours, or cover with greased plastic wrap and refrigerate for up to 24 hours.

5. FOR THE WHIPPED CREAM: Whisk cream, sugar, and orange zest in medium bowl until stiff peaks form, 2 to 4 minutes. Slice chilled pie and serve with whipped cream.

CHOCOLATE HAUPIA CREAM PIE

✓ **WHY THIS RECIPE WORKS:** Hawaii's beloved coconut pudding known as haupia is a dense, subtly sweet treat we wanted to reimagine as a pie filling. To keep things simple, we used a store-bought pie shell and focused on the pudding. We decided to prepare two distinct layers, one of plain haupia with clear coconut flavor, and the other boosted with the richness of chocolate. A combination of cornstarch, milk, and high-fat coconut milk created the perfect stable consistency and using whole milk created the richest flavor. After thickening the pudding on the stovetop, we created the chocolate layer by pouring some of the hot coconut pudding over semisweet chocolate chunks, stirring it together and pouring it into the parbaked shell. We topped it off with the remaining coconut pudding, allowed the filled pie to chill, and, for a sweet, creamy finish, topped it off by piping whipped cream stars over the entire surface.

The firm pudding made with coconut milk and customarily served in chilled cubes is known as haupia (pronounced how-PEE-ah) in Hawaii. Though it's wonderful on its own, why not put it in a pie? And for that matter, why not put it in a two-tone pie with melted chocolate added to one layer? This is not just a good idea—it's a delicious reality at Hawaiian bakeries such as Ted's, located on Oahu. I wanted to bring it home to my kitchen.

Rather than the rich, ploppable stuff you usually think of as pudding, haupia is firmer. Experiments with existing recipes gave me haupia that resembled bouncy Jell-O and was far too sweet. I wanted stable yet delicate pudding, balanced but insistent coconut flavor, and measured sweetness.

I also wanted my pie to be easy, so I decided up front to use a store-bought pie crust, which I baked until it was golden brown and flaky. I then set it aside to cool and got to work on the filling.

Haupia's key ingredient is coconut milk. To ensure a thick pudding, I knew I'd need a product with plenty of fat (our favorite is Chaokoh). I whisked a 13.5-ounce can of coconut milk together with 1 cup of water, ½ cup of sugar, and 3 tablespoons of cornstarch and cooked the lot in a saucepan over medium heat until it began to thicken, about 6 minutes.

Next, I melted 4 ounces of chopped semisweet chocolate in the microwave and stirred it together with half the pudding. I spread this chocolaty mixture into the cooled pie shell and rewhisked the remaining coconut pudding in the saucepan to smooth out any lumps that had formed while it sat. I then poured it on top of the chocolate layer, spreading it evenly with a spatula. I chilled the pie in the fridge until I was certain it had set up completely, about 4 hours.

Slicing into this first attempt, my heart sank. The knife mushed the layers together, leaving me with a droopy, sad blob that ran all over the plate—not the perfect, semifirm, two-tone slice I'd imagined. And my layers were uneven, with the chocolate layer much too thick.

To address the consistency of the pudding, I increased the amount of cornstarch to 5 tablespoons, but this gave me a too-firm filling that I could bounce a nickel off (true story; I tried). Decreasing the cornstarch to 4 tablespoons proved best for creating clean slices.

One ingredient was bugging me: water. I knew I needed the liquid to dissolve the cornstarch and achieve the consistency I sought, but I wondered:

Would a more flavorful liquid give me a better pie? To find out, I made three pies: one with water, one with milk, and one with an additional cup of coconut milk.

The pie with the extra coconut milk tasted chalky and a bit sour; the pie with water was too lean. But the pie with milk had rich, round coconut flavor. Further testing showed me that both whole milk and 2 percent low-fat milk worked fine, but skim milk was a bust.

I looked over my method for more ways to stream line it, and found that I could ditch the microwave and simply pour the hot pudding over the chopped chocolate to let its residual heat do the work. After a few more experiments, I determined that rather than dividing the pudding equally and adding chocolate to one portion, dividing it slightly unevenly and mixing the chocolate with just a cup of the hot pudding created perfectly equal layers.

NOTES FROM THE TEST KITCHEN

PIPING WHIPPED CREAM STARS

1. Whip cream and sugar to stiff peaks and transfer to pastry bag.

2. Using gentle pressure and working in concentric circles, pipe even-sized stars over top of pie.

PICKING A PIPING TIP
To finish off Chocolate Haupia Cream Pie with flair, fit a pastry bag with a medium (½-inch diameter) star pastry tip. We use a Wilton brand closed tip for stars with a sharp appearance. An open tip will also work, but it will create softer stars.

CHOCOLATE HAUPIA CREAM PIE

To finish things off, I piped sweetened whipped cream on top of the pie. I then sliced it and stood back while coworkers dove in like surfers along Waikiki Beach.

—CECELIA JENKINS, *Cook's Country*

Chocolate Haupia Cream Pie

SERVES 8 TO 10

We prefer Chaokoh or Thai Kitchen coconut milk for this recipe. Do not use "lite" coconut milk or any coconut milk that has less than 12 grams of fat and/or greater than 3 grams of sugar per ⅓-cup serving. If you do, the pudding will be too runny and sweet. While we prefer whole milk in this recipe, 2 percent low-fat milk will also work. We use a pastry bag outfitted with a star tip to decorate the pie with whipped cream. Our favorite piping set is the Wilton 20-Piece Beginning Buttercream Decorating Set.

CRUST

   1 **(9-inch) store-bought pie dough round**

FILLING

   4 **ounces semisweet chocolate, chopped**

   1 **(13.5-ounce) can unsweetened coconut milk**

   1 **cup whole milk**

  ½ **cup (3½ ounces) sugar**

  ¼ **cup (1 ounce) cornstarch**

  ⅛ **teaspoon salt**

TOPPING

   1 **cup heavy cream, chilled**

   1 **tablespoon sugar**

1. FOR THE CRUST: Adjust oven rack to lower-middle position and heat oven to 375 degrees. Roll dough into 12-inch circle on lightly floured counter. Loosely roll dough around rolling pin and gently unroll it onto 9-inch pie plate, letting excess dough hang over edge. Ease dough into plate by gently lifting edge of dough with your hand while pressing into plate bottom with your other hand.

2. Trim overhang to ½ inch beyond lip of plate. Tuck overhang under itself; folded edge should be flush with edge of plate. Crimp dough evenly around edge of plate using your fingers. Wrap dough-lined plate loosely in plastic wrap and freeze until dough is firm, about 15 minutes.

3. Line chilled pie shell with parchment paper or double layer of aluminum foil, covering edges to prevent burning, and fill with pie weights. Bake until edges are light golden brown, about 20 minutes, rotating plate halfway through baking. Remove parchment and weights and continue to bake until crust is golden brown, 7 to 11 minutes longer. Let crust cool completely in plate on wire rack before proceeding with filling, about 45 minutes. (Baked, cooled crust can be wrapped in plastic wrap and stored at room temperature for up to 24 hours.)

4. FOR THE FILLING: Once crust has cooled completely, place chocolate in medium bowl; set aside. Whisk coconut milk, milk, sugar, cornstarch, and salt in medium saucepan until no lumps of cornstarch remain. Cook over medium heat, stirring and scraping saucepan corners constantly with rubber spatula, until mixture thickens to glue-like consistency and large bubbles break surface, about 6 minutes.

5. Quickly pour 1 cup coconut pudding over chocolate in bowl and whisk until smooth. Spread chocolate pudding evenly in cooled pie shell. Using clean, dry whisk, vigorously rewhisk remaining coconut pudding in saucepan, then gently pour on top of chocolate pudding and spread into even layer with rubber spatula. Refrigerate, uncovered, until set, at least 3 hours or up to 24 hours.

6. FOR THE TOPPING: Once pie is fully chilled, use stand mixer fitted with whisk attachment to whip cream and sugar on medium-low speed until foamy, about 1 minute. Increase speed to high and whip until stiff peaks form, 1 to 3 minutes. Transfer whipped cream to pastry bag fitted with medium open or closed star tip (about ½-inch diameter). Pipe whipped cream stars onto top of pie until completely covered. Serve.

FROZEN YOGURT

✔ **WHY THIS RECIPE WORKS:** For frozen yogurt that was perfectly dense and smooth with an appealingly tart taste, we had to limit the formation of ice crystals. We used plain whole-milk yogurt as our base, straining it to eliminate excess liquid. Sweetening the yogurt with Lyle's Golden Syrup highlighted the yogurt's tang and made for a creamy texture. A little gelatin, bloomed in some of the yogurt's whey and stirred into the base, further ensured a scoopable texture. After chilling the mixture, we churned it in an ice cream maker until it had achieved an indulgent consistency.

When I set out to make frozen yogurt for the first time, I thought the task would be simple. Unlike ice cream recipes, which typically call for cooking (and then cooling) a finicky custard for a base, most of the fro yo recipes I came across required nothing more than throwing yogurt, sugar, and maybe a few flavorings into an ice cream maker and churning. But these recipes were hugely disappointing: The yogurt turned out icy and rock-hard. I realized that this was partly because frozen yogurt doesn't have the advantage of yolks or cream, both of which give ice cream proportionally more fat and less water. Fat makes ice cream taste creamier and smoother, while less water in the base means there's less of it to form ice crystals, leading to a more velvety, scoopable texture. I found a few frozen yogurt recipes that tried to improve texture by adding cream to the mix. But while these versions did turn out less icy, their tangy yogurt flavor had been muted.

For me, this was a nonstarter. I wanted my frozen yogurt to put the tartness of yogurt front and center. The challenge was to figure out how to do that and achieve a dense, creamy texture at the same time.

The obvious thing was to try to eliminate some water from the yogurt. In my initial tests, I had been using regular whole-milk yogurt (plain was a must, since I wanted to be able to control flavorings and sweetness myself). What if I switched to Greek yogurt, which has had much of the liquid whey strained out? When my first test produced an oddly crumbly texture, I switched to another brand and then another—but they all produced unappealing results.

So I considered another option: straining regular yogurt. I spooned a quart of yogurt into a fine-mesh strainer lined with cheesecloth and set over a bowl and left it overnight. By the following morning, a generous amount of whey had drained into the bowl. The fro yo I made with this yogurt was much smoother; I knew this step was a must.

The next ingredient to go under my microscope was sugar. Just as in ice cream and sorbet, sugar doesn't serve as a mere sweetener in frozen yogurt. It also affects the texture. Once dissolved, sugar depresses the freezing point of water, which means the more you use, the more water in the mix will stay in liquid form after churning. That translates not only to fewer ice crystals but also to a more scoopable product straight from the freezer. But balance would be key—I didn't want to make it so sweet that the yogurt's flavor was overshadowed. I found that I could go up to a full cup of sugar per quart before the yogurt turned too sweet.

I also knew from my ice cream testing that there were other sweeteners worth considering beyond the granulated stuff. One secret to the velvety texture of an ice cream recipe I'd developed a few years back was swapping out some of the granulated sugar for corn syrup. This sweetener contains starch chains that keep water molecules from joining up and forming large ice crystals. When I tried it in my frozen yogurt, it worked pretty well at minimizing iciness, but the yogurt's flavor seemed muted. A little research informed me why: Those starch chains trap flavor molecules. This wasn't a problem in tame vanilla ice cream, but in tart frozen yogurt, the dulling effect was clear.

My next thought was to try incorporating a source of invert sugar, which is better than granulated sugar at depressing the freezing point of water. Why? Unlike granulated sugar, which is made up of larger sucrose molecules, invert sugar is made up of two smaller molecules, glucose and fructose. Freezing-point depression is directly related to the number of molecules dissolved in the water. So a tablespoon of invert sugar provides twice as many sugar molecules and roughly twice as much freezing-point depression as a tablespoon of granulated sugar. Supermarket options for invert sugar include honey and agave syrup, but each has a distinct flavor that I didn't want in my frozen yogurt. Luckily, I knew of another option: Lyle's Golden Syrup. While only half invert sugar (the other half is sucrose), Lyle's was good enough to work magic. Just 3 tablespoons (along with ¾ cup of granulated sugar) noticeably reduced the iciness. This was impressively creamy frozen yogurt. But I suspected I could do better.

Many manufacturers add pectin, gums, or modified starches to get smoother, less icy results. These ingredients essentially trap water, which will minimize large water droplets—and thus large ice crystal formation. Pectin and gelatin seemed most promising, but the citric acid in pectin made the frozen yogurt taste almost fruity. Gelatin, however, was perfect. I needed a liquid to bloom it in, so I reserved ½ cup of whey when I drained the yogurt and microwaved the whey with the gelatin to quickly dissolve the gelatin before incorporating the mixture into my base. Just 1 teaspoon of gelatin gave me the smoothest, creamiest frozen yogurt yet.

There were just a few more details to attend to. Quickly freezing the base was key, since faster freezing, along with agitation, promotes the formation of smaller ice crystals. I refrigerated my base until it registered 40 degrees or less before churning. And as with my ice cream recipe, in addition to churning until it looked like thick soft-serve, I also made sure it registered 21 degrees (the temperature at which roughly 50 percent of the water has frozen) for the most consistent results.

My frozen yogurt took some time, but it was mostly hands-off. And best of all, it boasted a wonderfully creamy, smooth texture as well as the distinctively tangy, fresh flavor of its namesake ingredient.

—DAN SOUZA, *Cook's Illustrated*

Frozen Yogurt

MAKES ABOUT 1 QUART

This recipe requires draining the yogurt for 8 to 12 hours. We prefer the flavor and texture that Lyle's Golden Syrup lends this frozen yogurt, but if you can't find it, you can substitute light corn syrup. Any brand of whole-milk yogurt will work in this recipe. You can substitute low-fat yogurt for whole-milk yogurt, but the results will be less creamy and flavorful. If you're using a canister-style ice cream maker, be sure to freeze the empty canister at least 24 and preferably 48 hours before churning. For self-refrigerating ice cream makers, prechill the canister by running the machine for 5 to 10 minutes before pouring in the yogurt.

1   quart plain whole-milk yogurt
1   teaspoon unflavored gelatin
¾   cup sugar
3   tablespoons Lyle's Golden Syrup
⅛   teaspoon salt

1. Line colander or fine-mesh strainer with triple layer of cheesecloth and place over large bowl or measuring cup. Place yogurt in colander, cover with plastic wrap (plastic should not touch yogurt), and refrigerate until 1¼ cups whey have drained from yogurt, at least 8 hours or up to 12 hours. (If more than 1¼ cups whey drains from yogurt, simply stir extra back into yogurt.)

2. Discard ¾ cup drained whey. Sprinkle gelatin over remaining ½ cup whey in bowl and let sit until gelatin softens, about 5 minutes. Microwave until mixture is bubbling around edges and gelatin dissolves, about 30 seconds. Let cool for 5 minutes. In large bowl, whisk sugar, syrup, salt, drained yogurt, and cooled whey-gelatin mixture until sugar is completely dissolved. Cover and refrigerate (or place bowl over ice bath) until yogurt mixture registers 40 degrees or less.

3. Churn yogurt mixture in ice cream maker until mixture resembles thick soft-serve frozen yogurt and registers about 21 degrees, 25 to 35 minutes. Transfer frozen yogurt to airtight container and freeze until firm, at least 2 hours. Serve. (Frozen yogurt can be stored for up to 5 days.)

VARIATIONS

Ginger Frozen Yogurt

Stir 1 tablespoon grated fresh ginger and 1 teaspoon ground ginger into whey-gelatin mixture as soon as it is removed from microwave. After mixture has cooled for 5 minutes, strain through fine-mesh strainer, pressing on solids to extract all liquid. Proceed with recipe as directed.

Orange Frozen Yogurt

Substitute ½ cup orange juice for ½ cup whey in step 2. Stir ½ teaspoon grated orange zest into orange juice–gelatin mixture as soon as it is removed from microwave.

Strawberry Frozen Yogurt

Substitute ¾ cup strawberry puree for ½ cup whey in step 2.

TEST KITCHEN RESOURCES

Every product tested may not be listed in these pages. Please visit CooksIllustrated.com and CooksCountry.com to find complete listings and information on all products tested and reviewed.

BEST KITCHEN QUICK TIPS

EASY WAY TO CORE A JALAPEÑO

Jim Summerour of Atlanta, Ga., discovered a way to remove the seeds and ribs from a large fresh jalapeño without having to touch the chile's hot interior. He plunges his apple corer through the top (no need to trim); when he removes it, the ribs and seeds come out, too.

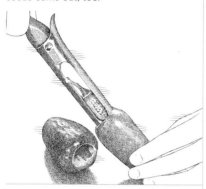

COCKTAILS IN A FAT SEPARATOR

Whenever Maddy Reed of Kamuela, Hawaii, makes a batch of cocktails for a party, she uses her fat separator for mixing and serving the drinks—it strains the ice out with no mess.

SEED-FREE CITRUS JUICING

Christina Wyman of Virginia Beach, Va., saves the netting from garlic and shallot bulbs for juicing lemons and limes. With the cut side of a citrus half placed inside the netting before squeezing, the fine-mesh weave easily keeps seeds out of her juice and doesn't impart any flavors or odors.

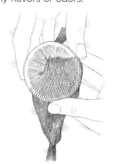
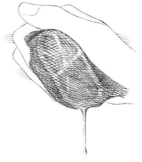

QUICK FOOD PROCESSOR CLEANING

When Marilyn Whitlock of Austin, Texas, needs to quickly rinse her food processor between tasks, she adds a couple of drops of dish soap and warm water up to the recommended liquid line, runs the machine for a few minutes, and then rinses the bowl well before moving on to the next task.

A BETTER WAY TO CHOP THROUGH BONE-IN CUTS

Some chopping jobs require both a full-powered swing and considerable precision, like cutting up bone-in chicken parts. For the cleanest cuts, Marvin Swartz of Durham, N.C., places the blade of his chef's knife or meat cleaver directly on the target and then sharply strikes the back of the knife with a rubber mallet.

SUBMERGE FOOD IN A STEAMER BASKET

When Edmund Gallizzi of St. Petersburg, Fla., wants to keep artichokes or other foods submerged in a cooking liquid, he pulls out his folding steamer basket. He removes the basket's handle, inverts the basket, and places it on top of the food. The leaves cover the surface of the food and keep it from bobbing above the liquid, ensuring even cooking.

DRY BAKING SHEETS ON A ROASTING RACK

When she runs out of space for drying baking sheets, Jennifer Clayton of Cheektowaga, N.Y., pulls out her V-shaped roasting rack. She turns it upside down, and—voilà—she can place the sheets in the slots created, while the handles keep the rack from tipping over.

WHO GETS WHICH BURGER?

When making burgers of various degrees of doneness for a crowd, Lacey Matthews of Boise, Idaho, keeps track of which finished patty goes to which guest by writing each person's initials on one cut side of the bun with ketchup or mustard from a squirt bottle. She keeps the initialed side faceup as she hands them out.

EASY PIE SHIELD

Miriam Clubok of Athens, Ohio, was inspired by our recent idea for a homemade pie shield and wanted to share her own method: She cuts out the center of a disposable pie plate and uses the rim as the shield. If the crust's edges are looking too brown, she can easily place the ring on top to protect the edge while the pie continues to bake. Plus, the pie shield can be washed and reused.

CLEANING NONSTICK PANS

Bill McDonald of Vancouver, Wash., finds that food or grease sometimes stays stuck in the nooks and crannies of his nonstick pans, especially around the handle. A clean electric toothbrush, he's discovered, is perfect for this cleaning task. The stiff bristles' circular motion acts like a buffer, removing stuck-on grime, but the bristles are still soft enough for a nonstick surface.

A BETTER WAY TO TRANSPORT ROLL-OUT COOKIES

Using a spatula to transfer cut-out cookies from the counter to the baking sheet inevitably means some shapes bend or break in transport. Lily Giordano of Arlington, Va., has devised a less frustrating approach. She rolls out the dough to the desired thickness on parchment cut to fit her baking sheets and then cuts the cookies right on the parchment, spaced according to the recipe. She peels away the scraps and transfers the parchment with the cookies to the baking sheet.

SANDWICH BREAD SWAPS IN PANADE

We often call for hearty white bread when making a panade, a paste of starch and dairy that helps keep meatballs, meatloaf, and burgers tender and moist. But when Jessica Pantzer of Brooklyn, N.Y., is out of sandwich bread, she swaps in hamburger or hot dog buns. After determining that one slice of sandwich bread weighs 1½ ounces and yields ½ cup of crumbs when coarsely ground in a food processor, it's easy to make the swap by using a volume or weight equivalent of her available alternative.

SAFELY STORING A CORKSCREW

Shaun Breidbart of Pelham, N.Y., has found that if he keeps a cork on the end of his corkscrew, he won't stab his hand when reaching into the drawer to grab it. Plus, he always has an extra cork if he needs one for an open wine bottle.

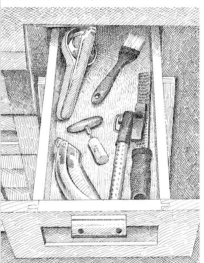

PORTION SAVVY

To divide a package of dried peas, beans, or short noodles in half without measuring or pulling out a storage container, Nancy Zinn of Clarksville, Md., lays the package flat to distribute the contents evenly. Then she pinches and twists the package in the middle and secures it with a rubber band. When she's ready to cook, she snips one corner of the bag with scissors and pours the contents into a bowl. The other half is already sealed and ready to store.

BEST KITCHEN QUICK TIPS

BASTE AWAY EXCESS WATER FROM A COFFEE MAKER

Anne Marie Draganowski of Saint Paul, Minn., occasionally adds too much water to her drip coffee maker's reservoir. Rather than precariously tip the entire machine over to empty just the right amount into the sink, she uses a turkey baster to remove the water, checking against the machine's water gauge until there is just the right amount of water left.

PORTIONING FROSTING WITH EASE

Sarah Quigley of San Francisco, Calif., likes to use a 2-tablespoon portion scoop to dollop frosting onto cupcakes. It ensures that all the cupcakes are equally frosted and that the dollops of frosting are even and easy to spread.

BAGGING WET LETTUCE

Grocery stores mist leafy greens with water to keep them hydrated, but damp heads of lettuce are tricky to get into plastic produce bags. Barbara Morrissette of Buckhannon, W. Va., puts her hand inside the bag, grabs the root end of the lettuce with her "glove," and pulls the bag over the wet lettuce.

HOT HANDLE REMINDER

When roasting foods in a skillet in the oven, Henny Wright of Dallas, Texas, hangs a potholder on the oven door so it's at the ready to cover his hand before transferring the hot skillet to the stovetop. He then leaves the potholder over the pan's handle to help him remember (and signal to others) that the handle is still hot.

SALT-AND-PEPPER GRINDER

Michael Marrone of Pittsburgh, Pa., keeps a pepper grinder filled with equal amounts of black peppercorns and coarse salt. The seasonings' relatively similar size keeps them well blended in the grinder and makes for an even sprinkling of both in a single twist. (Use a zipper-lock bag as a funnel to load the grinder.)

SQUEEGEE CLEAN

In place of a bench scraper, Stephanie Schelling, Lake Ariel, Pa., uses a clean window squeegee to corral crumbs, flour, and other messes. Its sharp edge easily slides under crumbs and scrapes them into the sink or garbage.

PARCHMENT PAPER ORIGAMI

To tame the curl of a freshly cut sheet of parchment paper, Michael LaFosse of Haverhill, Mass., folds evenly spaced, parallel creases in both the short and long directions. When unfolded, the creased grid helps to keep the paper from rolling back into a cylinder, and it also works as a guide for evenly spacing cookie dough. (The number of pleats may be adjusted for more or fewer spots depending on what is being baked.)

SPONGE DRYER

Georgette Naccarato of Kingston, Idaho, never had a use for her hair dryer's diffuser attachment until she discovered it was the perfect way to hold kitchen sponges. It keeps them tidy and allows them to dry quickly.

SPACE-SAVING SAUCE STORAGE IN THE FREEZER

Instead of using ice cube trays to store small amounts of thick sauces such as *sofritos* or pestos, Carla Krash of Narberth, Pa., uses plastic Easter eggs, which hold more and are easier to store. She fills both sides of the egg, snaps the sides together, and tucks the eggs into the freezer anywhere they fit. When she's ready to use the contents, she runs warm water over the egg to make it easy to open.

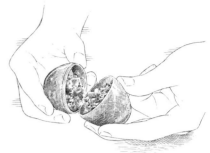

DIY GARLIC PEELER

Robert Cerniglia of Rhinebeck, N.Y., doesn't own a garlic peeler, but hacks the device by wrapping a swath of silicone shelf-liner around a clove and rolling it on his countertop. The skin comes off smoothly and easily with no need to smash the clove first.

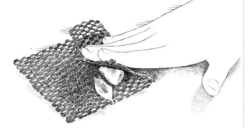

SPRITZ COOKIE–SPAETZLE PRESS

Mark Brighton of Buffalo, N.Y., found that his cookie press can also produce spaetzle when he uses the disk with the smallest holes.

SIFT YOUR CEREAL

When he gets close to the bottom of a box of cereal, David Salafia of Meriden, Conn., uses a small fine-mesh strainer to sift out the powdery crumbs, which would otherwise turn pasty in his bowl.

NO MORE WRESTLING PLASTIC WRAP

Boxes of plastic wrap are lightweight, so the roll tends to lift up out of box and make it difficult to unroll and tear cleanly. James Speed Hensinger of Westminster, Colo., adds weight to the plastic wrap tube by sliding a honing steel into the roll. The box prevents the rod from sliding out, and the steel adds resistance so he can smoothly pull off a portion of the wrap without having to fight it. This also works with parchment paper, wax paper, and aluminum foil.

A STAND-IN FOR PIE WEIGHTS

When prebaking 9-inch tart shells, instead of covering the dough with foil and weighing it down with pie weights after trimming the dough, Jaime Pedraza of Minneapolis, Minn., puts an 8- to 8½-inch-diameter pot lid on top of the foil. It's effective at preventing the pastry from puffing up as it bakes, and it is even easier to put in place and remove than weights are.

EASIER CAKE ROTATING

To rotate cakes halfway through baking, Chris Lucas of Medford, Mass., forgoes a potholder (which can accidentally touch the cake) and instead uses a large, sturdy spatula or a small pizza peel, which can easily slide under the baking pan.

HOW TO KNOW WHEN FOOD IS DONE

Don't flub a beautifully rosy steak or a perfectly chewy batch of cookies because you couldn't pinpoint the moment to stop cooking.

FOR THE BEST RESULTS, GET OUT YOUR THERMOMETER

The axiom "knowledge is power" holds especially true in the kitchen—the more you know about what's going on inside your food as it cooks, the more you can control the result. That's why we're so gung ho about using an instant-read thermometer in the kitchen, as more control means less stress and better results.

OUR FAVORITE INSTANT-READ THERMOMETERS

The **ThermoWorks Thermapen Mk4** (left, $99) and our Best Buy, the **ThermoWorks ThermoPop** (right, $29), are accurate, fast, and easy to use.

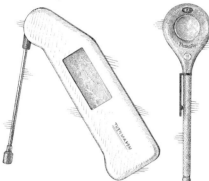

TAKE MULTIPLE READINGS

Especially with large roasts and turkeys, it's important to take the temperature in multiple places since it can vary in thicker and thinner areas, as well as near bones. Food is only done once all parts reach the target temperature.

MEAT AND POULTRY

DON'T FORGET CARRYOVER COOKING

The temperature of many proteins will continue to rise once they're taken off the heat and allowed to rest before serving, a phenomenon known as carryover cooking. This is particularly true for thick roasts cooked at high temperatures, which must be removed from the heat as much as 10 to 15 degrees below the desired doneness. We've also learned that carryover cooking is negligible in burgers, whole chickens, and whole fish; the loose grain of burgers and the hollow cavities of chicken and fish allow heat to escape, so these items should be cooked to the desired degree of doneness.

	Cook To	Serve At
BEEF/LAMB		
Rare	115°F–120°F	125°F
Medium-Rare	120°F–125°F	130°F
Medium	130°F–135°F	140°F
Medium-Well	140°F–145°F	150°F
Well-Done	150°F–155°F	160°F
GROUND BEEF		
Medium-Rare*	125°F	125°F
Medium*	130°F	130°F
Medium-Well*	140°F	140°F
Well-Done	160°F+	160°F+
PORK		
Medium	140°F–145°F	150°F
Well-Done	150°F–155°F	160°F
CHICKEN		
White Meat	160°F	160°F
Dark Meat	175°F	175°F

COOK SOME CUTS LONGER

Whereas most proteins are best cooked just to an internal temperature at which they're safe to eat, items like braised or slow-roasted dark-meat chicken, pork butt, and beef chuck often taste better when they're cooked longer. That's because these tough cuts are loaded with collagen, which breaks down into gelatin between 140 and 195 degrees and lubricates the muscle fibers, making them seem more moist and tender. It's also important to cook these cuts slowly; the longer they spend in that collagen breakdown window, the more tender the meat will be.

PINK POULTRY AND PORK CAN BE SAFE

Pink-tinted turkey and pork aren't necessarily undercooked. Often, the color is an indication that the pH of the meat is relatively high, which stabilizes the meat's pink pigment so that it doesn't break down when exposed to heat. As long as the meat registers the prescribed temperature, it's safe to eat.

*The USDA recommends cooking all ground beef to 160 degrees.

TIPS FOR TAKING MEAT'S TEMPERATURE

STEAKS AND CHOPS Hold the steak or chop with tongs and insert the thermometer through the side of the meat. This method also works for chicken parts.

BURGERS Leaving the burger in the pan (or on the grill), slide the tip of the thermometer into the top edge and push it toward the center, making sure to avoid hitting the pan (or grate).

ROASTS Insert the thermometer at an angle, pushing the probe deep into the roast and then slowly drawing it out. Look for the lowest temperature to find the center of the meat.

WHOLE POULTRY, BREAST Insert the thermometer from the neck end, holding it parallel to the bird. (Avoid hitting the bone, which can give an inaccurate reading.)

WHOLE POULTRY, THIGH Insert the thermometer at an angle away from the bone into the area between the drumstick and breast.

WHOLE STUFFED POULTRY In addition to taking the temperature of the white and dark meat, insert the thermometer into the cavity. Stuffing is safe to eat at 165 degrees.

FISH AND SHELLFISH

SALMON	Cook To
Farmed	125°F
Wild	120°F
TUNA	
Rare	110°F
Medium-Rare	125°F
OTHER	
White-Fleshed Fish	140°F
Sea Scallops	115°F
Lobster (tail)	140°F

SALMON With less fat than farmed salmon, wild salmon is more prone to drying out and overcooking, so we cook it to a lower temperature.

SWORDFISH The exterior of cooked swordfish should feel firm while the inside is just opaque but still moist.

SHRIMP Cooked shrimp should look pink, feel just firm to the touch, and be slightly translucent at the center.

MUSSELS An opened mussel is cooked, but one that remains closed might just need more cooking. Microwave it for 30 seconds; if it still doesn't open, discard it.

CLAMS Open clams are done—and overcook quickly. Remove clams as they open and keep them warm in a covered bowl while the rest finish cooking.

DISCOVERY TEMP BAKED POTATOES Baking a potato to between 205 and 212 degrees ensures that the interior will be uniformly fluffy.

BAKED GOODS AND SWEETS

We also use a thermometer to gauge the doneness of many baked goods. And when a food doesn't lend itself to temperature-taking, visual guidelines are just as helpful.

WHEN TO USE A THERMOMETER

YEAST BREADS

We have found that yeast bread can reach its recommended temperature for doneness well before the loaf is actually baked through. You should take the temperature of your bread as a backup, but stick to the recommended baking time and make sure the crust is well browned before removing the loaf from the oven and checking its temperature.

Lean (e.g., sandwich bread)	205–210°F
Enriched (e.g., brioche)	190–195°F

LOAF-PAN LOAVES Insert the thermometer from the side, just above the pan edge, and direct it at a downward angle into the center of the loaf.

FREE-FORM LOAVES Tip the loaf (cover your hand with a dish towel) and insert the probe through the bottom into the center.

CHEESECAKE

NEW YORK CHEESECAKE The velvety consistency of this style is achieved when the center registers 165 degrees.

OTHER BAKED CHEESECAKES For an all-over creamy consistency, we bake them to between 145 and 150 degrees.

CUSTARDS AND PUDDINGS

STOVETOP CUSTARDS We cook custards to a relatively low 175 degrees to prevent the egg proteins from curdling.

ICE CREAM BASES Custard bases for ice cream should be thicker than conventional custards, so we cook them to 180 degrees.

BAKED CUSTARDS Applications like flan and crème brûlée should jiggle when gently shaken and should register between 170 and 180 degrees.

CUSTARD PIE FILLINGS

Because baked custard fillings like pumpkin pie filling continue to set up as they cool, it's important to remove custard pies from the oven when they're slightly underdone. The edges of the filling should be set, while the center should jiggle slightly (but not slosh) when the pie is shaken and should register between 170 and 175 degrees.

WHEN TO USE VISUAL CUES

CAKES, MUFFINS, AND QUICK BREADS

For thin (less than ¾-inch) items
Test for springback. Gently press the center of the food; it should feel springy and resilient. If your finger leaves an impression or the center jiggles, it's not done.

For thick (at least ¾-inch) items
Use a skewer. Poke a wooden skewer or toothpick into the center; it should emerge with no more than a few crumbs attached. If you see moist batter or lots of crumbs, bake it longer.

COOKIES, BAR COOKIES, AND BROWNIES

For chewy centers, underbaking is key—but tricky to gauge. Look for these visual cues.

DROP COOKIES Cookies should hang over the edge of a metal spatula blade.

CRACKLY COOKIES Cracks should appear shiny.

STAMPED AND SLICED COOKIES Edges should be light brown and centers slightly moist.

For uniformly crisp cookies, remove the cookies when the edges are deep golden brown and crisp, and the centers yield to slight pressure.

BROWNIES Poke a wooden toothpick into the center and look for a few moist crumbs; moist batter means they're not ready. Overbaking will yield dry, chalky results with diminished flavor.

PIE CRUST

The pastry should be well browned. We bake crusts in glass pie plates, which allow us to monitor browning on the sides and bottom of the crust.

FRUIT PIES

Filling should bubble at the edges and in the vents.

THE BEST COUNTERTOP APPLIANCES

The right appliances not only make cooking easier and more enjoyable but can also help your recipes turn out better.

Too often, appliances promising convenience wind up as clutter. Decades of testing have taught us which pieces of equipment are the most useful and which models are the highest quality and most durable. Here's our guide to the best options for key appliances that can improve how you bake and cook.

FOOD PROCESSOR

CUISINART Custom 14 Food Processor ($199.99)
A food processor is essential for kneading dough, cutting butter into pastry, and grinding meat. With a powerful motor, responsive pulsing action, and sharp blades, this model effortlessly handles these tasks. It also chops, slices, and shreds neatly and with ease.

SMALL FOOD PROCESSOR

CUISINART Elite Collection 4-Cup Chopper/Grinder ($59.95)
Smaller processors can't handle doughs or large-quantity prep, but the powerful motor on this model makes it super-convenient for zipping through smaller-quantity jobs like chopping nuts, grinding bread crumbs, or dicing an onion or two.

BLENDER

VITAMIX 5200 ($449)
This impressive, powerful commercial-style blender crushes ice with ease and makes lump-free smoothies, hummus, and more. Its performance commands a steep price, but it is exceptionally durable and comes with a seven-year warranty.

BEST BUY BREVILLE The Hemisphere Control ($199.99)
If you subject your blender to heavy-duty use, we recommending saving up for a Vitamix. However, at less than half the price, the relatively powerful Breville is an excellent choice for routine use.

SLOW COOKER

KITCHENAID 6-Quart Slow Cooker with Solid Glass Lid ($99.99)
This digital cooker simmers food gently and evenly. Testers liked its cool-to-the-touch handles and intuitive-to-use control panel.

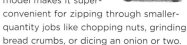

ELECTRIC CITRUS JUICER

BREVILLE Stainless Steel Juicer ($199.99)
The Breville extracts every last drop of juice with minimal effort. This attractive stainless-steel machine is easy to clean (all nonmotorized parts are dishwasher-safe) and quiet enough to use in the early morning.

BEST BUY DASH GO Dual Citrus Juicer ($19.99)
While it lacks the Breville's motorized lever, this model still performed every bit as well.

ELECTRIC KETTLE

CAPRESSO Silver H2O Electric Kettle ($55.69)
Equally handy at making a cup of tea or quickly boiling water for cooking tasks, this kettle rapidly heats water and boasts a deep, stable base. Our preference is for models with glass pitchers, which make it easy to monitor water levels, and bright indicator lights.

STAND OR HANDHELD?

If you are a regular baker, a stand mixer is imperative for mixing pizza and bread doughs, whipping cream and egg whites, and creaming butter and sugar. However, if you seldom bake, you can get by with a handheld mixer for occasional mixing, whipping, and creaming.

STAND MIXER

KITCHENAID Pro Line Series 7-Qt Bowl Lift Stand Mixer ($549.95)
Its robust motor, durability, and smart design make this mixer truly worth the investment if you do a lot of heavy-duty baking. It effortlessly handles a range of volumes of food, from small amounts of whipped cream to heavy batches of bread or pizza dough to stiff cookie dough.

BEST BUY KITCHENAID Classic Plus Series 4.5-Quart Tilt-Head Stand Mixer ($229.99)
This basic, compact machine is an excellent choice for budget-conscious bakers. We wish that its bowl had a handle and that the machine had a bowl lift, but these are small concessions given its affordable price.

HANDHELD MIXER

KITCHENAID 5-Speed Ultra Power Hand Mixer ($69.99)
A handheld mixer lacks the power of a stand mixer but works just fine for occasional light tasks. (It's also just nice to have on hand, even if you own a stand mixer. It's far easier to pull out when all you needed to do is whip ½ cup of cream.) This model is light, maneuverable, and efficient.

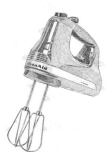

BEST BUY CUISINART PowerSelect 3-Speed Hand Mixer ($26.77)
Though it has just three speeds compared to our winner's five, this comfortable-to-hold mixer is plenty powerful for simple tasks.

FORGET TOASTERS. BUY A TOASTER OVEN.

Our advice on buying toasters and toaster ovens has changed: In 2009, we halfheartedly recommended our winning toaster oven because of the expense and said that you'd be better off buying a toaster and using your oven (unless you do a lot of small cooking projects). Today, the best two-slot toaster we can find (the MagiMix by Robot-Coupe Vision Toaster) costs a staggering $249.00, and our Best Buy, the KitchenAid 2 Slice Manual High-Lift Lever with LCD Display, can't be counted on to consistently produce evenly browned toast—and still costs $99.99. Our new recommendation? Consider skipping a toaster altogether. Instead, choose a regular or "compact" toaster oven that can perform as both a toaster and a small oven—our winners are exceptional and serve both functions well.

TOASTER OVEN

BREVILLE The Smart Oven by Breville ($249.95)
A small second oven is handy for preparing side dishes, toasting nuts and bread crumbs, or even roasting a chicken, and it helps keeps the kitchen cool in hot weather. Five quartz heating elements consistently cool and reheat, producing uniform browning and cooking.

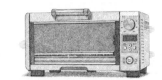

COMPACT CHOICE

BREVILLE Mini Smart Oven with Element IQ ($149.95)
This toaster oven, which is roughly 25 percent smaller than the full-size model, aced every test we threw at it, from roasting chicken breasts to baking cookies and toasting bread. It's a great choice—even if you just use it for toast.

DRIP COFFEE MAKER

TECHNIVORM Moccamaster 10-Cup Coffee Maker with Thermal Carafe ($299)
This hand-built, intuitive Dutch machine is utterly consistent, producing pot after pot of a "smooth," "velvety" brew by hitting the ideal temperature zone for the optimal length of time.

BEST BUY BONAVITA 8-Cup Coffee Maker with Thermal Carafe ($189.99)
This brewer is also an excellent choice, producing "rich," "full-flavored" coffee. Its thermal carafe kept coffee very hot for up to 3 hours.

SPICE/COFFEE GRINDER

KRUPS Fast-Touch Coffee Mill ($19.99)
This model produces an exceptionally fine, uniform grind and easily pulverizes spices of varying hardness, density, and shape. What's more, it is easy to fill and use. If you grind coffee beans regularly, we advise buying two mills and using one exclusively for coffee and one for spices.

ICE CREAM MAKER

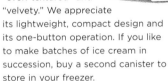

CUISINART Automatic Frozen Yogurt, Ice Cream & Sorbet Maker ($53.99)
This exceptionally affordable model churns out frozen desserts that are "even-textured" and "velvety." We appreciate its lightweight, compact design and its one-button operation. If you like to make batches of ice cream in succession, buy a second canister to store in your freezer.

ANGLING FOR A SHARPER EDGE?

We've long appreciated the thinner blade of our winning chef's knife, the Victorinox 8" Swiss Army Fibrox Pro, which boasts the finer 15-degree angle more typically found on Japanese knives. Many other European bladesmiths are now making knives with a similar ultrathin edge. But if you have a traditional Western knife with a 20-degree blade angle, our winning Trizor electric sharpener offers a great perk: It can hone a wider cutting edge to 15 degrees.

RICE COOKER

AROMA 8-Cup Digital Rice Cooker and Food Steamer ($29.92)
This inexpensive appliance makes cooking white, brown, and sushi rice convenient and entirely foolproof. Useful features include a digital timer that lets the cook know when the rice is nearly ready, a clear audio alert, and a delayed-start function.

FASTER RICE Brown rice can take up to an hour to cook. To reduce the cooking time to just 30 minutes, soak the rice (1½ cups of water per cup of rice) directly in the rice cooker pot for 6 to 24 hours in the refrigerator. When you're ready to cook, add salt, put the pot in the cooker, and turn on the heat.

HOME SELTZER MAKER

SODASTREAM Source Starter Kit ($99.95)
This countertop machine transforms tap water into sparkling water by applying light pressure to a carbonating block that allows you to choose between gentle carbonation or intense effervescence. Long-lasting CO2 canisters are convenient to exchange (at 50 percent of the price of new) in dozens of retail stores.

FOR THE MOST FIZZ, USE ICE-COLD WATER When we carbonated 32-degree water, 68-degree water, and 140-degree water, the 32-degree sample was by far the most effervescent, with small, long-lasting bubbles. That's because cold water can hold five times more carbon dioxide than warm water can.

ELECTRIC KNIFE SHARPENER

CHEF'SCHOICE Trizor XV Knife Sharpener ($149.99)
Its diamond abrasives consistently produced 15-degree edges that were sharper than those on new knives. After 10 minutes of sharpening, a severely nicked knife looked and cut like a brand-new blade.

BEST BUY CHEF'SCHOICE Diamond Sharpener For Asian Knives ($79.99)
Also fitted with diamond abrasives, this model wasn't quite as effective as its sibling. It removed nicks in the blade after 30 minutes and a tiring 223 swipes.

OUR GUIDE TO CHOCOLATE

Chocolate is notoriously fussy—even choosing the wrong brand can ruin dessert. Here's what you need to know for foolproof baking and cooking.

WHAT IS CHOCOLATE, ANYWAY?

The base of all processed chocolate is chocolate liquor, a dark paste produced from grinding the nibs extracted from dried, fermented, roasted cacao beans. In its natural state, chocolate liquor is about 55 percent cocoa butter, which gives chocolate its unique texture. The remaining 45 percent is the cocoa solids responsible for chocolate's flavor. The cocoa butter and cocoa solids in chocolate liquor may be separated and recombined in different ratios; together, they make up the cacao percentage in a processed chocolate.

SHOPPING

Brand really matters with chocolate. In tastings we found that nearly half (or even more) of the products in our lineup weren't up to par, no matter the type of chocolate. So for best results, stick with our winners.

BITTERSWEET/ SEMISWEET CHOCOLATE

WHAT IT IS Also known as dark chocolate, bittersweet and semisweet chocolates (there is no official distinction) must contain at least 35 percent cacao; the remainder is mainly sugar with a small amount of emulsifiers and flavorings.

HOW WE USE IT With its strong chocolate flavor and smooth texture, bittersweet is our go-to chocolate. We use it for most baked goods and desserts and for dipping and coating.

GOOD TO KNOW Cacao percentage matters. It affects the flavor as well as the texture of creamy desserts. For cooking and baking, we prefer 60 percent cacao. In tests, some chocolates with cacao percentages even a few points less than 60 percent (and thus a lower percentage of cacao solids) produced loose custards. Chocolates with cacao percentages higher than this (and thus with more cacao solids) turned out chalky custards.

FAVORITE Ghirardelli 60% Cacao Bittersweet Chocolate Premium Baking Bar ($2.99 for 4 oz)

SUBBING WITH UNSWEETENED In a pinch, replace 1 ounce of bittersweet chocolate with ⅔ ounce of unsweetened chocolate and 2 teaspoons of sugar, but note that texture may be affected.

MILK CHOCOLATE

WHAT IT IS With only 10 percent cacao required, milk chocolate tastes more milky than chocolaty. Milk fat, along with cocoa butter, gives it its ultracreamy texture.

HOW WE USE IT We generally like milk chocolate more for snacking than baking.

FAVORITE Dove Silky Smooth Milk Chocolate ($2.79 for 3.53 oz)

COCOA POWDER

WHAT IT IS Cocoa powder is chocolate liquor that has been pressed to remove most of the cocoa butter, leaving behind cocoa solids that are then finely ground. Dutch-processed cocoa is less acidic than natural cocoa, but their flavors are similar.

HOW WE USE IT Ounce for ounce, cocoa powder packs more chocolate flavor than any other form of chocolate. Because it is relatively low in fat, we like to use cocoa powder in applications that already contain a lot of fat, like cakes and cookies.

FAVORITE Hershey's Natural Cocoa Unsweetened ($3.49 for 8 oz)

UNSWEETENED CHOCOLATE

WHAT IT IS

Typically, unsweetened chocolate is pure chocolate liquor formed into bars.

HOW WE USE IT In recipes like brownies or cake, unsweetened chocolate's lack of sugar allows us to control more variables to achieve a desired texture.

WHY IT HAS NO SUBSTITUTE Some sources recommend subbing cocoa powder and butter or oil for unsweetened chocolate, but these fats don't have the subtle cocoa flavor or contribute the same texture as cocoa butter.

GOOD TO KNOW Because unsweetened chocolate isn't for snacking, some manufacturers don't use the best beans. But since it's also not typically refined or conched (a process that mellows harsh flavors), there's no hiding the flavor of mediocre beans. In taste tests, we had reservations about or disliked four out of nine products.

FAVORITE Hershey's Unsweetened Baking Bar ($1.99 for 4 oz)

DARK CHOCOLATE CHIPS

WHAT THEY ARE

Dark chocolate chips are bittersweet chocolate with at least 35 percent cacao—the same as dark bar chocolate—but they typically have less cocoa butter, so they're cheaper to make and will hold their shape on the production line.

HOW WE USE THEM Chocolate chips get the most use as mix-ins for cookies and brownies.

GOOD TO KNOW Most companies don't cite cacao percentages for chips. And in lab tests, we found that chips produced by such companies had far less cacao than in bar chocolate—and correspondingly weaker flavor and grainier texture.

FAVORITE Ghirardelli 60% Cacao Bittersweet Chocolate Chips ($3.50 for 11.5 oz)

With the same cacao percentage as our winning bittersweet bar, these morsels have complex chocolate flavor. They also have comparable cocoa butter, for morsels that melt appealingly in cookies.

SUB CHIPS FOR CHOPPED? Unless you use our winner, forget it. Chips have less flavor than most bar chocolates, and because they usually have less cocoa butter, most chips left behind graininess in sauces, mousses, and custards.

WHITE CHOCOLATE

WHAT IT IS

Technically not chocolate since it's made with cocoa butter, milk, sugar, emulsifiers, and flavorings but no cocoa solids, white chocolate has a milky taste and satiny texture. Some products substitute other fats for all or some of the cocoa butter; these can only be labeled "white" and not "chocolate."

HOW WE USE IT In mousses, frostings, and soufflés, it adds creaminess and subtle milky flavor.

GOOD TO KNOW Products with "fake" flavor and "chalky" texture abound. We had reservations about four out of 10 in our tasting lineup.

FAVORITE Guittard Choc-Au-Lait White Chips ($3.29 for 12 oz)

Though they're not real white chocolate since they contain palm kernel oil, we found that the refined fat helped these chips melt and solidify at higher temperatures, preventing crystals in mousse.

SEIZED CHOCOLATE

Seizing—the nearly instantaneous transformation of melted chocolate from a fluid state to a stiff, grainy one—is usually the result of a tiny amount of moisture being introduced.

PERFECTLY MELTED

SEIZED

PREVENTING SEIZING

In recipes that contain no liquid, don't let moisture get into the melted chocolate. Even a tiny amount will form a syrup with the sugar in the chocolate to which the cocoa particles will cling, creating grainy clumps. In recipes containing liquids like melted butter, liqueur, or water, always melt the chocolate along with these ingredients.

FIXING SEIZING

Surprisingly, adding liquid will return seized chocolate to a fluid state, as the liquid dissolves seized sugar and cocoa particles. Add boiling water to the chocolate, 1 teaspoon at a time, stirring vigorously after each addition until smooth. But don't use the diluted chocolate for baking; use it for chocolate sauce or hot chocolate.

STORING

Wrap open bars of chocolate tightly in plastic wrap and store them in a cool pantry. Avoid the refrigerator or freezer, as cocoa butter easily absorbs off-flavors from other foods and temperature changes can alter its crystal structure so it behaves differently in recipes.
Note: The milk solids in white and milk chocolates give them a shorter shelf life.

2 SHELF LIFE **6**

YEARS | MONTHS

UNSWEETENED AND DARK CHOCOLATE | WHITE AND MILK CHOCOLATE

WORKING WITH CHOCOLATE

FINELY CHOPPING CHOCOLATE

Finely chopping chocolate helps it melt evenly and quickly. Place the tip of a serrated knife on a cutting board and the blade on a corner of the chocolate and bear down with both hands. The serrations will break the chocolate into fine shards.

HOW TO MAKE CHOCOLATE CURLS

Chocolate curls add a professional touch to cakes, pies, and mugs of hot cocoa. Use block (not bar) chocolate—bittersweet/semisweet and white chocolate work well—that's at least 1 inch thick. Soften the chocolate slightly by microwaving it on the lowest power setting for 1 minute. (It shouldn't melt, but it should soften a little.) Run the blade of a vegetable peeler along the width of the softened chocolate, creating a curl. The longer the block, the bigger the curl.

TEMPERING MADE EASY

Good chocolate has a sheen and a satisfying snap, but if you simply melt it, chocolate cools into a soft, dull mess. That's because the cocoa butter's crystal structure has changed. Of cocoa butter's six crystal types, only beta crystals set up dense and shiny and stay that way. Chocolate with a uniform beta crystal structure is said to be "in temper." Traditional tempering requires a painstaking process of heating, cooling, and reheating. In our easier method, we melt three-quarters of the chocolate gently and then stir in the remaining portion, which has been finely grated. The flakes appear to melt, but their temperature is so low that most of the beta crystals remain intact, triggering the formation of new beta crystals as the chocolate cools.

1. Microwave 3 ounces finely chopped chocolate (decrease or increase amount here and below as needed) at 50 percent power, stirring every 15 seconds, until fully melted but not much warmer than body temperature, 1 to 2 minutes. (Stir often while melting and monitor temperature by holding bowl in palm of your hand.)

2. Add 1 ounce finely grated chocolate (use small holes of box grater) and stir until smooth, returning to microwave for no more than 5 seconds at a time if necessary.

DON'T OVERBAKE

The volatile compounds in cocoa solids that give chocolate much of its flavor are also driven away by heat. The longer chocolate is heated, the more compounds are driven off, so don't bake chocolate desserts longer than you need to. In tests, chocolate crinkle cookies baked for 2 minutes longer than the recipe calls for had a less intense flavor than cookies baked according to the recipe.

USING BLOOMED CHOCOLATE

Storing chocolate at temperatures that are either too warm or too cool will cause a white film, or bloom, to develop on the surface. In our tests, we found that bloomed chocolate was fine for baking, but when melted and used for dipping, the bloom reappeared or caused a grainy coating.

USING CACAO NIBS

We like crunchy, bitter cacao nibs best in baked goods where there aren't many other competing flavors or textures; they're also great in granola. Use ½ to ⅔ cup per loaf of quick bread, dozen muffins, or 9-cup batch of granola.

COOKING IN—AND CARING FOR—CAST IRON

Game for any recipe from seared steak to fried eggs to apple pie, a cast-iron skillet can be the most versatile piece of cookware in the kitchen.

A CHEMICAL-FREE, DURABLE, AFFORDABLE WORKHORSE

Since its inception in sixth-century BCE China, cast iron has been a favorite cookware material across the globe. Here in the United States, early settlers took advantage of its high-heat compatibility for open-fire cooking. Though it fell out of favor in the early 20th century when Teflon became widely available, it's recently regained popularity as an alternative to both traditional and nonstick cookware. Here's what it offers:

EXCEPTIONAL HEAT RETENTION Though it transfers heat very slowly compared with aluminum or stainless steel, cast iron retains heat much more effectively than these materials, making it ideal for browning, searing, and shallow-frying.

NATURALLY NONSTICK SURFACE Whereas most cookware deteriorates over time, cast iron only gets better, gradually developing a slick patina, or "seasoning," which releases food easily. A well-seasoned pan can rival and outlast the slickness of a nonstick pan—with no harmful chemicals involved.

UNBEATABLE DURABILITY AND VALUE Cast iron is virtually indestructible and easily restored if mistreated. Plus, a good skillet can be had for well under $50 and should last for generations.

FAVORITE TRADITIONAL CAST-IRON PAN
Lodge Classic Cast-Iron Skillet, 12", $33.21

THE OTHER CAST IRON: ENAMELED

Enameled cast-iron skillets are coated with a porcelain finish that makes them nonstick. They cost more than traditional cast iron (as much as eight times more), but they have certain advantages: They never have to be seasoned, their coating doesn't interact with acid, and they can be cleaned much like other pots and pans (though you should avoid abrasive cleaners). Their downside, besides their cost, is that since they lack the polymerized oil seasoning of traditional cast iron, they aren't as nonstick as a well-seasoned traditional pan.

ENAMELED FAVORITE
Le Creuset Signature 11¾" Iron Handle Skillet, $179.95

OUR FAVORITE ACCESSORIES

LIDS

Lodge 12-inch Tempered Glass Cover, $25.81
Why We Like It Lightweight, stay-cool handle; good visibility; ovensafe to 400 degrees.

RSVP Endurance Stainless-Steel Universal Lid with Glass Insert, $19.99
Why We Like It Vent to release steam, heat-resistant handle, usable with other pans.

CHAIN-MAIL SCRUBBER

Knapp Made Small Ring CM Scrubber, $19.98
Why We Like It Fine rings scour grooves with ease, won't damage pan's finish (don't use on enameled cast iron), doesn't rust.

COMMON MYTHS, BUSTED

After testing dozens of skillets, we upended these common misconceptions about cast iron.

MYTH You should never wash cast iron with soap.
REALITY A few drops of dish soap are not enough to interfere with the polymerized oil bonds that comprise the surface of a well-seasoned pan. In fact, a little soap can help rid the pan of excess greasiness.

MYTH It's bad to cook with acidic ingredients in cast iron.
REALITY It's OK to cook with acidic ingredients but keep the cooking time to 30 minutes and remove the food immediately after cooking. Longer exposure can damage the seasoning and cause trace amounts of metal to leach into the food, imparting metallic flavors.

MYTH Metal utensils will scratch the seasoning.
REALITY The seasoning on a cast-iron pan is chemically bonded to the surface, and it will not chip or scratch off. When we slashed the surface of our favorite Lodge skillet with a chef's knife and scraped it repeatedly with a metal spatula, it survived with nary a scratch.

MYTH If a cast-iron pan rusts, it's ruined.
REALITY It takes a lot to kill a cast-iron skillet. If yours does rust, the rust can easily be removed by stripping and reseasoning the pan (see "Servicing Your Skillet"). Only if the pan has literally rusted through is it time to throw it out.

MYTH Cooking fatty meat like bacon in cast iron is the best way to season it.
REALITY Fat from animal proteins will lubricate the pan's surface but won't season it. These highly saturated fats don't polymerize as well as highly unsaturated oils like sunflower, soybean, and corn. (For more information, see "The Science of Seasoning.")

THE SCIENCE OF SEASONING

When fat or cooking oil is heated for a long enough time in cast iron, its fatty acids oxidize and reorganize together (or "polymerize") into a new plastic-like layer of molecules. This layer becomes trapped within the pitted surface of the pan and bonds to the metal itself, creating the slick coating known as seasoning. Repeated exposure to hot oil continues to build on this coating, making it more slippery and durable. That's why the surface will become even more nonstick with repeated use.

WHAT DOES "WELL-SEASONED" MEAN?

A well-seasoned skillet will have a dark, semiglossy finish and won't be sticky or greasy to the touch. It won't have rust or any dull or dry patches. An easy way to test a skillet's seasoning is to heat 1 tablespoon vegetable oil in skillet over medium heat for 3 minutes, then add an egg. If your pan is well-seasoned, you won't experience any major sticking.

USE THE RIGHT OIL

The more unsaturated the oil, the more readily it will oxidize and polymerize. Flaxseed oil, which oxidizes and polymerizes faster than other vegetable oils, forms a particularly durable seasoning, but cheaper oils like sunflower and soybean work fine.

OIL	BEST	GOOD, LOWER-COST CHOICES				WORST
	Flaxseed	Sunflower	Soybean	Corn	Canola	Bacon Fat
% SATURATED	9%	10%	16%	13%	7%	39%
% MONOUNSATURATED	18%	20%	23%	28%	63%	45%
% POLYUNSATURATED	68%	66%	58%	55%	28%	11%

SERVICING YOUR SKILLET

Caring for a cast-iron skillet is like caring for a car: Service it regularly and it will last forever; neglect it, and it will need more heavy-duty repair work. These care guidelines will bring your skillet back to life, no matter what condition it's in.

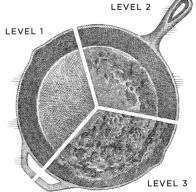

LEVEL 1
LEVEL 2
LEVEL 3

LEVEL 1: ROUTINE MAINTENANCE

1. Clean after every use While skillet is still warm, remove excess food and oil with paper towels. Rinse under hot running water, scrubbing with brush or nonabrasive scrub pad to remove traces of food. (Use small amount of soap if you like; rinse well.)

2. Lightly reseason after each cleaning Dry thoroughly (do not drip-dry) and set over medium-low heat until all traces of moisture disappear. Add ½ teaspoon of oil to pan and use paper towels to rub oil into skillet until surface looks dark and shiny and has no remaining oil residue. Let cool completely.

LEVEL 2: MINOR SERVICE

Stovetop repair (for dull, patchy skillets) Heat skillet over medium-high heat and wipe it with paper towels (held with tongs) dipped in 2 tablespoons oil until surface looks dark and semiglossy but isn't sticky or greasy. Repeat 3 to 5 times with oil-soaked towel, letting skillet cool for a few minutes after each round.

Oven repair (when stovetop repair doesn't work) Heat oven to 500 degrees. Rub 1 tablespoon (for 12-inch skillet) or 2 teaspoons (for 10-inch skillet) oil all over surface of skillet using paper towels. Using clean paper towels, thoroughly wipe out excess oil (skillet should look dry, not glistening). Place skillet upside down in oven and bake for 1 hour. Using potholders, remove skillet from oven and let cool completely.

LEVEL 3: MAJOR SERVICE

Over the lifetime of a cast-iron skillet, you'll usually just maintain or touch up its seasoning. But if the seasoning becomes very dull or damaged (seasoning flakes off) or if it badly rusts (can't be scrubbed away), you'll need to give it an overhaul by stripping and reseasoning the surface. Follow our oven repair method, repeating it six times or until the skillet has a smooth, dark black, semiglossy finish.

HACK YOUR SKILLET

Here are unexpected ways to use a cast-iron skillet.

MAKESHIFT FLAME-TAMER A cast-iron skillet makes a great flame-tamer. Place the skillet over a low flame and place your pot or saucepan in the skillet. The skillet will moderate the heat.

PANINI WITHOUT A PANINI PRESS Set cast-iron skillet over medium-high heat and place assembled sandwiches in middle. Place smaller cast-iron skillet on top of sandwiches to press. (If you have only one cast-iron pan, place sandwiches in traditional skillet and weigh them down with cast-iron skillet.) Cook until bottoms of sandwiches are golden brown; flip and repeat on other side.

IN-A-PINCH PIE PLATE A seasoned cast-iron skillet can be a handy pie plate alternative so long as your skillet is 9 or 10 inches in diameter to keep the volume and baking times consistent.

TROUBLESHOOTING

PROBLEM Lingering fishy odors
SOLUTION Bake in 400-degree oven for 10 minutes. High heat eliminates fishy-smelling compounds called trialkylamines and oxidized fatty acids.

PROBLEM Stuck-on food
SOLUTION Rub skillet with fine steel wool; wipe clean. Heat ¼ inch oil over medium-low heat for 5 minutes. Off heat, add ¼ cup of kosher salt. Using potholder to grip handle, scrub skillet with paper towels (held with tongs). Rinse with hot water; dry well. Repeat if necessary (no need to lightly reseason).

BUYING AND COOKING SALMON

High in fat and flavor, with lush meat and skin that crisps, salmon is America's most-consumed fin fish. Here's our guide to cooking it right.

A great choice for pan searing, grilling, roasting, poaching, smoking, and curing, salmon is one of the most versatile fish you can buy. If you're buying it fresh, it should look moist and shiny, not dull, and should smell of the sea rather than overtly fishy. And don't shy away from buying frozen salmon. If it's been vacuum-sealed and the label indicates that it was flash-frozen immediately after harvest, it may taste fresher than the fish behind the counter (which is often flash-frozen fish that's been thawed).

WHAT MAKES SALMON DIFFERENT?

SKIN THAT CRISPS As salmon's abundant fat renders during cooking, its skin browns and crisps as nicely as chicken skin.

MARBLED FAT Unlike most whitefish, salmon's fat is marbled throughout its flesh, making it taste rich and silky.

MOIST FLESH Salmon's thick muscle fibers can hold more water than those in whitefish, making it particularly moist.

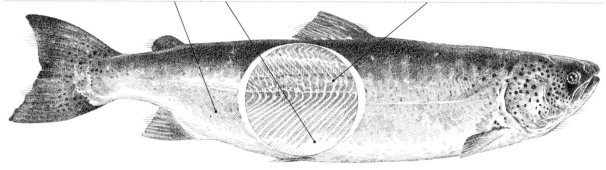

WILD

ALIAS Pacific
SPECIES Chinook (king), chum (dog or silverbrite), coho (silver), masu (cherry), pink (humpy or humpback), sockeye (red)
FLESH COLOR Deep pink due to compound called astaxanthin
TEXTURE Firm and meaty
AVAILABILITY Late spring to early fall

FARMED

ALIAS Atlantic
ORIGIN Raised on farms primarily in Norway, Scotland, Chile, and Canada
FLESH COLOR Naturally gray but dyed pale pink by synthetic astaxanthin and carotenoid pigment in feed
TEXTURE Soft and buttery
AVAILABILITY Year-round

SALMON IS FULL OF (GOOD) FAT

Salmon contains much more fat than whitefish such as cod, halibut, and flounder, but much of it is the healthy omega-3 kind. Generally speaking, farmed salmon is much fattier than wild varieties, though the amount of fat varies from species to species.

SPECIES	TYPE	FAT*
Atlantic	Farmed	13.4 g
Chinook (king)	Wild	11.7 g
Sockeye (red)	Wild	7.3 g
Masu (cherry)	Wild	7.0 g
Coho (silver)	Wild	5.6 g
Pink (humpy/humpback)	Wild	4.4 g
Chum (dog/silverbrite)	Wild	3.7 g

*Fat levels based on 100 grams of salmon

SALMON BY THE NUMBERS

353,000 Tons consumed annually in United States

70 Percentage of global market salmon that is from aquaculture

13 Percentage of fat in some farmed salmon, which rivals that of some premium ice cream

DON'T OVERCOOK WILD SALMON

We always cook farmed salmon to 125 degrees, at which point its flesh is ideally firm yet silky. However, the naturally firmer and less fatty flesh of wild salmon tastes much better cooked to 120 degrees; when cooked to 125 degrees, wild salmon tends to taste overly dry.

SHOPPING FOR SMOKED SALMON

Most supermarket smoked salmon is sold sliced and cold-smoked: It's cured to draw out moisture and then smoked between 75 and 85 degrees for 6 to 12 hours, which produces a dense, silky, translucent texture. (Hot-smoked salmon is sold by the piece and smoked between 120 and 180 degrees until cooked through and flaky; it is not widely available in stores.) We tasted five nationally available products and found that neither the variety of salmon nor the type of wood affected our preferences. What did matter were the curing method and the thickness of the slices. We preferred salmon that was cured with only salt, and we liked relatively thin, nicely tender slices. Our favorite, Spence & Co. Traditional Scottish Style Smoked Salmon ($10.99 for 4 ounces), is "silky," "delicate," and "lush."

TIPS AND TECHNIQUES

PLUCK PINBONES

Filleted fish has the backbone and ribs removed, but the thin, needle-like pinbones must be removed separately. Most fish are sold with the pinbones removed, but they are difficult to see and are sometimes missed by the fishmonger.

1. Drape fillet over inverted mixing bowl to help any pinbones protrude. Then, working from head end to tail end, locate pinbones by running your fingers along length of fillet.

2. Use tweezers to grasp tip of bone. To avoid tearing flesh, pull slowly but firmly at slight angle in direction bone is naturally pointing rather than straight up. Repeat until all pinbones are removed.

CUT YOUR OWN FILLETS

When making any salmon recipe that calls for fillets, it's important to use fillets of similar thickness so that they cook at the same rate. We find that the best way to ensure uniformity is to buy a large center-cut fillet (1½ to 2 pounds if serving four) and cut it into four equal pieces.

TUCK THE BELLY

If your salmon fillet comes with the belly portion attached, this thinner section will overcook when roasted or seared. To ensure that it cooks on pace with the rest of the fillet, trim away any chewy white membrane on the surface, flip the fillet skin side up, and gently fold the flap over. Secure the flap by horizontally inserting a toothpick through it and into the thicker portion of the fillet.

BRINE BRIEFLY

Though it may seem odd to brine something that spent its life in salted water, it's worth doing. Brining salmon helps the flesh stay moist, seasons it, and reduces the presence of albumin, a protein that can congeal into an unappealing white mass on the surface of the fish when heated. Plus, brining works a lot faster on fish than on meat because fish's shorter, looser muscle structure allows the solution to penetrate more rapidly.

Dissolve 5 tablespoons of salt in 2 quarts of water, add 6 fillets, and let them sit for 15 minutes. Dry the fish well with paper towels just before cooking it.

THE GRAY ANATOMY

The gray tissue just below salmon skin is a fatty deposit rich in omega-3 fatty acids and low in the pink pigments found in the rest of the fish. Many sources claim that it tastes fishier than the rest of the fillet and recommend removing it, but our tasters could barely detect a difference between fillets cooked with and without this portion, so we don't think it's worth doing. If you do choose to remove it, simply peel the skin off the cooked fillet and scrape it away with the back of a knife.

SKIN IT (IF YOU LIKE)

When well rendered and seared to a crisp, salmon skin can rival great roasted or fried chicken skin. But when you want skinless fillets, you can easily remove the skin before or after cooking.

BEFORE COOKING

1. Place fish skin side down. Using boning knife or chef's knife, insert blade just above skin about 1 inch from 1 end of fillet. Cut through nearest end, keeping blade just above skin.

2. Rotate fish and grab loose piece of skin. Run knife between flesh and skin, making sure knife is just above skin, until skin is completely removed.

AFTER COOKING

Gently slide thin, wide spatula between flesh and skin and use the fingers of your free hand to help separate skin. It should peel off easily and in 1 piece.

REHEAT GENTLY

Reheating salmon can make it smell even fishier, since heat oxidizes its abundant fatty acids into strong-smelling aldehydes. But reheating it gently will minimize the oxidation.

Place fillets on wire rack set in rimmed baking sheet, cover with foil (to prevent exteriors from drying out), and heat in 275-degree oven until fish registers 125 to 130 degrees, about 15 minutes for 1-inch-thick fillets (timing varies according to fillet size).

PUT IT ON ICE

Salmon can last up to twice as long if stored closer to 32 degrees, rather than at the typical home refrigerator temperature of 40 degrees. Place the fish in a zipper-lock bag on ice in a bowl (or cover it with ice packs) and place it at the back of the fridge, where it's coldest.

WHY IS SALMON STINKY?

Virtually all fish contain the compound TMAO, which transforms into a fishy-smelling compound called TMA when the fish are killed and can be detected when the fish is raw or cooked. But cooked salmon produces an even more pungent fishy odor for a different reason: Its highly unsaturated fat oxidizes when exposed to heat. To minimize fishy odor, consider choosing leaner wild salmon.

THE BEST WAYS TO CLEAN COOKWARE

If you're spending as much time cleaning your kitchen equipment as you are cooking with it, it's time for some better methods.

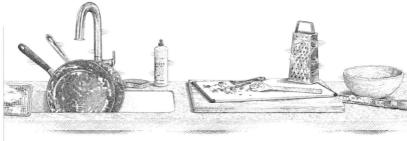

STAINLESS-STEEL, NONSTICK, AND HARD-ANODIZED ALUMINUM PANS

Everyday Messes

Boil and scrape Fill pan halfway with tap water; bring to boil, uncovered; and boil briskly for 3 minutes. Scrape skillet with spatula or spoon, pour off water, and let skillet sit briefly. Residue will start to flake off as skillet dries. Rinse well and wash.

Stubborn Messes

Sprinkle with Bar Keepers Friend cleanser Moisten stainless-steel or hard-anodized aluminum skillet with water, then sprinkle cleanser on top. Scrub with copper scrubber (stainless-steel) or nylon scrubber (hard-anodized aluminum). Rinse well and wash. (Note: We don't recommend using this cleanser on nonstick skillets. If our approach for removing everyday messes doesn't remove all stuck-on food, the skillet's nonstick coating may be worn out and it may be time for a new skillet.)

Burnt and Blackened Pan Bottoms

Apply oven cleaner Working outdoors or in well-ventilated area, place skillet upside down on newspapers. Wearing rubber gloves, spray even layer of oven cleaner on exterior of skillet only. Let sit for 20 minutes. Wipe off, rinse well, and wash.

CARBON STEEL SKILLET

Everyday and Stubborn Messes

Because the seasoning, or "patina," on carbon steel does not adhere as well as it does to cast iron, gentle cleaning is best. **Rinse and rub with oil** Wipe skillet with nonabrasive scrub pad, rinse clean, dry thoroughly on low burner, and rub with light coat of oil. If you scrub off some patina, wipe skillet with thin coat of oil and place it over high heat for about 10 minutes, until surface darkens (it will smoke; turn on exhaust fan).

BASTING BRUSHES

Salt bath

After washing the dirty brushes, rinsing them well, and shaking them dry, place the brushes, with the bristles pointing down, into a cup and fill the cup with coarse salt until the bristles are covered. The salt draws moisture out of the bristles and keeps them dry and fresh between uses.

WIRE RACK

Soak in baking sheet Most sinks aren't large enough to hold a rack when flat, so we soak it in a rimmed baking sheet. Squirt dish soap into the sheet and fill it with warm water. Invert the rack in the sheet and soak until all food particles are loosened. Scrub the rack gently in the direction in which the wires run, widthwise on top and lengthwise on underside.

GARBAGE DISPOSAL

Grind lemon pieces Toss cut-up pieces of spent lemon into the empty disposal while cold water runs; turn on disposal until lemon is ground up. You can freeze spent lemons until ready to use. Alternatively, freeze cubes of white vinegar to have at the ready.

WOODEN BOWL

Sand and stain To remove sticky residue, "refinish" the wood by rubbing its surface with sandpaper and coating with mineral oil.

CUTTING BOARDS

Lab tests determined that, if you can't use a dishwasher (which won't work for wood, bamboo, and some composite boards), scrubbing your board thoroughly with hot, soapy water is just as effective at killing harmful bacteria as using bleach or undiluted vinegar. If stains and/or odors persist, try the following tricks.

Stubborn Odors

Baking soda paste For boards made of any material, scrub board with paste of 1 tablespoon baking soda mixed with 1 teaspoon water.

Stubborn Stains on Plastic Boards

Overnight bleach bath Put 1 tablespoon bleach per quart of water in sink and immerse board dirty side up. When board rises to surface, drape clean white dish towel over top and splash towel with another ¼ cup bleach. Let soak overnight, then wash with hot, soapy water.

SPONGES

Boil for 5 minutes We microwaved, bleached, froze, and boiled sponges that had seen a month of test kitchen use; we also ran them through the dishwasher and washed them with soap and water. Lab results showed that microwaving and boiling were most effective, but since sponges can burn in a high-powered microwave, we recommend boiling them.

SINK

Sanitize with bleach Studies have found that the kitchen sink is crawling with even more bacteria than the garbage bin (the drain alone typically harbors 18,000 bacteria per square inch). Clean these areas frequently with a solution of 1 tablespoon of bleach per quart of water (bleach will also kill off some microbes in the drain).

WOODEN UTENSILS

Scrub with baking soda paste Alkaline baking soda neutralizes odor-causing acids, and since it is water-soluble, it is drawn into the wood along with the moisture in the paste. For every tablespoon of baking soda, use 1 teaspoon of water.

RASP GRATER

Wash ASAP Immediately after use, rinse the blade under warm water and then run a wet sponge along the grating surface, moving toward the handle (moving away from the handle will cause bits of sponge to get caught in the teeth). If food dries out and bonds itself to the grating surface, soak the grater before proceeding.

BOX GRATER

Grate stale bread Stale bread is hard enough to remove stuck-on food and dry enough that it won't leave behind any sticky residue of its own. Grate the bread over a plate to catch the crumbs.

FAVORITE CLEANING PRODUCTS

Method All-Purpose Natural Surface Cleaner ($3.79 for 28 oz)
Cuts grease, lifts stuck-on messes, and leaves surfaces shining.

Mrs. Meyer's Clean Day Liquid Dish Soap ($3.99 for 16 oz)
Cleans burnt-on food more than twice as fast as other soaps we tested.

Casabella Premium Water Stop Gloves ($5.49)
Slender fingers and tapered wrists fit snugly and comfortably; long sleeves cleverly dammed at end by self-folding cuff.

OXO Steel Soap Squirting Dish Brush ($11.99)
Built-in scraper tackles stubborn bits of food that its bristles—and other models—missed.

Skoy Earth Friendly Cloth ($5.99 for 4 cloths)
Easily sweeps up sauce and rinses clean; nontoxic; washer/dryer safe; can be easily sterilized in microwave.

ALKALIES AND ACIDS

In some cases, common household products can clean just as effectively as dedicated soaps, sprays, and cleaners. Use **baking soda** and **lemon** to freshen odors, **vinegar** as a surface spray, and **bleach** to sanitize.

SPLATTER CONTROL

The best way to tackle kitchen messes is to prevent them from happening in the first place.

REDUCING FLOUR SPRAY

No matter how carefully you open a new bag of flour, a cloud of fine white dust sprays the counter. To settle the flour so that it stays in the bag, slap the top of the bag before opening it.

MINIMIZING SAUTÉ SPLATTER

When browning meat on the stove, grease inevitably splatters on the stovetop and gunks up the unused burners and burner plates. To shield them, position an inverted disposable aluminum pie plate over each burner. Alternatively, use a large cookie sheet to cover more than one burner at a time.

A NO-MESS WAY TO GREASE BAKEWARE

Coating bakeware with nonstick spray inevitably means that your counter or floor will end up greasy. To prevent this, open your dishwasher door, place the vessel on the door, and spray. Any excess or overspray will be cleaned off the door the next time you run the dishwasher. Spraying over your sink or trash can works, too.

SPLASH-FREE POURING

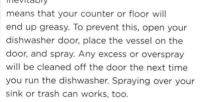

Transferring sauces, soups, or stews from one container to another can result in messy splatter, but the mess can be easily averted. Place the convex side of a large spoon under the pouring stream to deflect the liquid.

APPLIANCES

SPICE GRINDER

Most grinders can't be immersed in water. "Dry-clean" your grinder by adding several tablespoons of raw white rice. Pulverize the rice to fine powder; the powder will absorb residue and oils.

GRIND CLEAN
Dry rice absorbs residue.

BLENDER

Fill the blender jar (regular blender) or 2-cup glass measuring cup (immersion blender) halfway with hot water and add a few drops of dish soap. Blend for 30 seconds, and rinse.

BLEND CLEAN
Buzz with soap and water to clean.

MICROWAVE

Heat 2 cups of water on high power until steaming heavily but not boiling, about 2 minutes. Let sit 5 minutes. The steam will loosen dried, stuck-on food.

STEAM CLEAN
Easily wipe down walls.

WAFFLE IRON

Use a cotton swab to wipe away residue between the ridges.

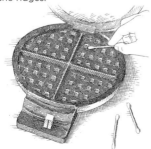

SWIPE CLEAN
Swab between ridges.

PREMIUM EXTRA-VIRGIN OLIVE OIL

We gathered oils from France, Italy, Spain, Greece, Tunisia, Portugal, and the U.S. and tasted them plain, tossed with lettuce, and drizzled over warm cannellini beans. Our first impression was that all of these oils were remarkably fresh. With lettuce and beans, we marveled at how each oil was distinct with flavors we'd never experienced in supermarket oils: "artichoke," "wet coppery soil," "watercress," and even "dark wood." In each case, they elevated the food's mundane flavors to something out of the ordinary. For that reason, we confidently recommend all of these premium oils, dividing them here by flavor profile. We have denoted the Gaea Fresh oil as a crowd-pleaser because of its ultrasmooth flavor.

MILD

MOULIN CASTELAS Castelines Classic Extra Virgin Olive Oil
PRICE: $29.95 for 16.9 oz ($1.77 per oz)
ORIGIN: France
COMMENTS: "Ultrasmooth," "mellow," and "subtle," with "just a hint" of pepper and "afterburn." Scent of "fresh grass cuttings." "Full-bodied," "rounded," and "buttery."

CASA DE SANTO AMARO Selection Extra Virgin Olive Oil
PRICE: $21.95 for 16.9 oz ($1.30 per oz)
ORIGIN: Portugal
COMMENTS: "Green, fresh scent" and "well-balanced," "buttery and silky" flavor. "Fruit intensity without too much bitterness."

MEDIUM

GAEA FRESH Extra Virgin Olive Oil CROWD PLEASER
PRICE: $18.99 for 17 oz ($1.12 per oz)
ORIGIN: Greece
COMMENTS: "Buttery," "smooth," "lemony and clean," with "sweet" olive fruitiness, aroma like "tomato stems," and a lightly "peppery" aftertaste.

COLUMELA Original Blend Extra Virgin Olive Oil
PRICE: $19.99 for 17 oz ($1.18 per oz)
ORIGIN: Spain
COMMENTS: "Fruity and sweet"-smelling, with notes of "apricot and peach" as well as "dark wood." "Peppery flavors" like "arugula."

MEDIUM-ROBUST

GIANFRANCO BECCHINA OLIO VERDE Extra Virgin Olive Oil
PRICE: $34.95 for 16.9 oz ($2.07 per oz)
ORIGIN: Italy
COMMENTS: "Smells like fresh-cut green grass" or "artichokes," with a taste of "butter on the front, pepper on the back." "Lively heat sneaks up on you."

MEDIUM-ROBUST *(continued)*

CASTILLO DE CANENA Family Reserve Picual Extra Virgin Olive Oil
PRICE: $27.95 for 16.8 oz ($1.66 per oz)
ORIGIN: Spain
COMMENTS: "Intensely fragrant" and "grassy and green" like a "bouquet of fresh flowers" with a "spicy and savory" scent. "Rich and complex, with a bite at the end."

SCIABICA'S ARBOSANA Fall Harvest California Extra Virgin Olive Oil
PRICE: $16.00 for 16.9 oz ($0.95 per oz)
ORIGIN: USA (California)
COMMENTS: "Lush," "rich and gently bitter," "ripe," "vegetal," and "robustly spicy" with a "lingering" "peppery" aftertaste.

ROBUST

FRESCOBALDI LAUDEMIO Extra Virgin Olive Oil
PRICE: $35.95 for 16.9 oz ($2.13 per oz)
ORIGIN: Italy
COMMENTS: "Superpeppery" with a "clean finish." "Wasabi-like heat." "Mouth-coating body—the EVOO equivalent of fatty butter."

MCEVOY RANCH Certified Organic Traditional Blend Extra Virgin Olive Oil
PRICE: $27.00 for 12.7 oz ($2.13 per oz)
ORIGIN: USA (California)
COMMENTS: Aroma that's "deceptively innocuous." "Complex and bold." Remarkable for its "bracing bitterness" and "peppery wallop."

LES MOULINS MAHJOUB Organic Extra Virgin Olive Oil
PRICE: $33.00 for 33.8 oz ($0.98 per oz)
ORIGIN: Tunisia
COMMENTS: A powerhouse: "Front notes are fresh and butter-like, but the finish is pungent." "Bold but bitter" with "a good kick at the end."

APPLE CIDER VINEGAR

We use apple cider vinegar—a natural byproduct of apple cider—for a comparatively mellow, slightly sweet kick of acidity in glazes, slaws, and sauces. Our previous winner is hard to find in the United States, so we sought out a more widely available option, rounding up six American-made cider vinegars to sample plain, cooked into a pan sauce, stirred into coleslaw, and mixed into a barbecue sauce. Every vinegar we tried worked fine, but tasters zeroed in on some characteristics that separate vinegar that's "fine" from one that's really good. Cider will convert naturally to vinegar with time, but manufacturers typically speed up the process by adding a "mother," or bacteria from an established vinegar. Once the alcohol is converted to acid, the vinegar is either filtered to remove sediment of leftover mother or bottled unfiltered. In the plain tasting, testers could identify the unfiltered vinegars by their darker, hazier appearance, and they thought the unfiltered vinegars were slightly more complex—fruity, floral, and appley. These nuances were still prominent when we tasted the vinegars in a pan sauce. The lines between filtered and unfiltered blurred when we tried the vinegars in barbecue sauce and slaw, punchy foods with lots of competing flavors. There tasters wanted a bright, bold kick of tartness and preferred products they perceived as more acidic, but more acidity wasn't always a good thing. One product's tang overwhelmed the mellow pan sauce with its harsher tartness. Products with moderate acidity worked well in every recipe we tried, lending a lively bite to edgier dishes without washing out the mellower ones. Our favorite was a well-rounded, versatile vinegar that worked well across the board. Fortunately, it's also the one you're most likely to encounter at the supermarket. Vinegars are listed in order of preference.

RECOMMENDED

HEINZ Filtered Apple Cider Vinegar
PRICE: $2.79 for 16 fl oz ($0.17 per fl oz)
STYLE: Filtered
ACIDITY: 5.1%
COMMENTS: With just the right amount of acidity, this familiar supermarket vinegar was "sharp" and "punchy," with a subtle "floral" fruitiness. "I'd let this enliven my barbecue any day," said one taster.

WHITE HOUSE Apple Cider Vinegar
PRICE: $1.59 for 16 fl oz ($0.10 per fl oz)
STYLE: Filtered
ACIDITY: 5.3%
COMMENTS: With a "bright" punch of acidity and just a hint of sugar, this filtered vinegar had a "juicy," "almost drinkable" sweetness and "vibrant" notes of "green apple." It was also the cheapest vinegar in the bunch.

BRAGG Organic Apple Cider Vinegar
PRICE: $3.99 for 16 fl oz ($0.25 per fl oz)
STYLE: Unfiltered
ACIDITY: 5.1%
COMMENTS: This unfiltered vinegar emerged at the top of the pack in pan sauce, where its "boozy," "zesty" apple flavor lent a complex "zing." While these "slightly funky" notes were lost in slaw and barbecue sauce, most tasters appreciated this product's "lively" acidity and "sweet apple finish."

RECOMMENDED *(continued)*

SPECTRUM NATURALS Organic Unpasteurized Apple Cider Vinegar Filtered
PRICE: $3.99 for 16 fl oz ($0.25 per fl oz)
STYLE: Filtered
ACIDITY: 5.0%
COMMENTS: This "very pale" vinegar had a "mellow" flavor. Though tasters thought this product was "clean" and "bright," some lamented that it "lacked complexity." Still, it worked decently in every recipe we tried.

SPECTRUM NATURALS Organic Unpasteurized Apple Cider Vinegar Unfiltered
PRICE: $3.49 for 16 fl oz ($0.22 per fl oz)
STYLE: Unfiltered
ACIDITY: 5.0%
COMMENTS: When sampled plain and in pan sauce, this unfiltered vinegar had delicate hints of "melon" and "sweet apple." These nuances were much subtler in punchy recipes like slaw and barbecue sauce. This vinegar won't ruin your recipes, but there are better choices.

EDEN Organic Apple Cider Vinegar
PRICE: $3.59 for 16 fl oz ($0.22 per fl oz)
STYLE: Unfiltered
ACIDITY: 5.2%
COMMENTS: This unfiltered vinegar had plenty of acidity but no sweetness to balance it out. While its "bold" tartness was deemed "bright" in barbecue sauce, tasters found it a tiny bit "harsh" in pan sauce. Tasters were also mixed about its "boozy," "fermented" notes.

SOY SAUCE

Soy sauce is among the world's oldest foods, and in the test kitchen we harness its savory impact in everything from stir-fry to vegetable soup. However, not every bottle delivers the flavor and nuance that good soy sauce should, so we rounded up top-selling products (including tamari, soy sauce's wheat-free relative) to find one that excelled as both a condiment and a staple cooking ingredient. After trying them plain and in teriyaki sauce, our tasters reported that they could both taste and smell distinct differences among the samples. Some boasted a sweet-savory aroma while others were void of complexity. As for the tamaris, two were intolerably salty while one balanced salt and sweet better than many of the soy sauces. After doing some investigating, we found that our top-ranking sauces were all made the old-fashioned way: by fermenting or "brewing" boiled soybeans and roasted wheat with a mold, creating a coveted mixture called *koji*, for anywhere from a few months to 2 years. (The lower-ranking bottles undergo more rapid processing and rely on doctored colors and flavors to imitate the competition.) You won't go wrong as long as you buy a soy sauce that's labeled "fermented" or "brewed," but we still recommend Kikkoman above the rest. Soy sauces are listed in order of preference.

RECOMMENDED

KIKKOMAN Soy Sauce
PRICE: $2.79 for 10 oz ($0.28 per oz)
STYLE: Fermented
TIME TO PRODUCE: 6 to 8 months
COMMENTS: Thanks to its relatively long fermentation time, our favorite soy sauce came across as "rich," "well-balanced," and "complex," with notes of "caramel," and a level of saltiness that was "just right."

LEE KUM KEE Table Top Premium Soy Sauce
PRICE: $3.49 for 5.1 oz ($0.68 per oz)
STYLE: Fermented
TIME TO PRODUCE: Not available
COMMENTS: The "dark and earthy" flavor of this product may have been bolstered by its added sugar and nucleotides that magnify the umami impact. Tasters found it "sweet, rich," "buttery," and "complex" in teriyaki.

KIKKOMAN Gluten-Free Tamari Soy Sauce
PRICE: $3.99 for 10 oz ($0.40 per oz)
STYLE: Fermented
TIME TO PRODUCE: 6 to 8 months
COMMENTS: The only tamari we liked, this makes a good, "classic"-tasting soy substitute in cooked applications, though tasters still found it too salty when sampled straight.

OHSAWA Organic Nama Shoyu
PRICE: $9.99 for 10 oz ($1.00 per oz)
STYLE: Fermented, unpasteurized
TIME TO PRODUCE: 2 years
COMMENTS: Despite its long fermentation time, this sauce came across as subtle in the plain tasting. Cooked in teriyaki sauce, it won praise for its "buttery, savory, sweet" flavors.

LEE KUM KEE Panda Brand Premium Soy Sauce
PRICE: $7.50 for 16.9 oz ($0.44 per oz)
STYLE: Fermented
TIME TO PRODUCE: Not available
COMMENTS: This product tasted "aggressively salty" straight from the bottle. Once cooked with the teriyaki ingredients, it took on a "savory caramel" flavor we enjoyed.

RECOMMENDED WITH RESERVATIONS

YAMASA Soy Sauce
PRICE: $2.49 for 10 oz ($0.25 per oz)
STYLE: Fermented
TIME TO PRODUCE: 6 months
COMMENTS: This soy sauce boasted a "big umami aroma" but actually tasted "mild" and "not terribly complex." Even cooked in chicken teriyaki, it tasted "shallow" and slightly out of balance.

LA CHOY Soy Sauce
PRICE: $2.59 for 10 oz ($0.26 per oz)
STYLE: Hydrolyzed
TIME TO PRODUCE: "A few days"
COMMENTS: Some appreciated this sauce's "deep, dark" flavor, while others rejected its "supersalty," "cheap takeout soy" profile. It fared better in cooked sauce, though even there it met criticism for tasting "fake."

CRYSTAL Soy Sauce
PRICE: $2.53 for 12 oz ($0.21 per oz)
STYLE: Hydrolyzed
TIME TO PRODUCE: Not available
COMMENTS: This soy sauce tasted unacceptably "harsh" and "salty" straight from the bottle, though it was passable as a cooking ingredient. Corn syrup lent it plenty of sweetness, which tasters liked in the teriyaki sauce.

NOT RECOMMENDED

SAN-J TAMARI Gluten Free Soy Sauce
PRICE: $2.99 for 10 oz ($0.30 per oz)
STYLE: Fermented
TIME TO PRODUCE: 4 to 6 months
COMMENTS: This tamari tasted "quite salty" and even "fishy" in both the plain and teriyaki tastings. In general, tasters found it "overpowering" and plagued by off-flavors.

WAN JA SHAN Organic Tamari Gluten-Free
PRICE: $3.99 for 10 oz ($0.40 per oz)
STYLE: Fermented
TIME TO PRODUCE: 4 to 6 months
COMMENTS: "Salt bomb" was a common complaint about this tamari, which lacked balance despite the addition of cane juice to compensate for the lack of wheat.

CINNAMON

Whether it's swirled into oatmeal, baked into pies, or added to savory dishes, cinnamon is a familiar staple spice. However, with exotic (and expensive) options hailing from Vietnam and Indonesia popping up in the spice aisle, we wondered if it was time to branch out. We rounded up eight cinnamons—half Vietnamese, half Indonesian—and sampled them sprinkled on chilled rice pudding and baked into cinnamon rolls and on pita chips. When we tasted them raw in rice pudding, we noticed the cinnamons' varying heat. Some were pretty spicy (a few bordering on too intense), while others were more tempered with hints of sweetness. The Vietnamese cinnamons all fell on the spicier end of the spectrum, while the Indonesian cinnamons were milder. After doing some research, we learned that this variation makes sense: While Indonesian cinnamon typically comes from the bark of trees that are less than 10 years old, Vietnamese cinnamon is often harvested from trees between 20 and 25 years old. When tasted in baked applications, the heat was undetectable; because the spicy compound known as cinnamaldehyde steams off in the oven, the cinnamons all tasted virtually the same when baked. If you like a big, spicy flavor and use cinnamon frequently in unheated applications, spring for our spicy favorite; but if you use it only for baking, stick with the cheaper brands. Cinnamons are listed in order of preference.

RECOMMENDED

MORTON & BASSETT SPICES
Ground Cinnamon `MOST VERSATILE`
PRICE: $5.99 for 2.2 oz ($2.72 per oz)
ORIGIN: Indonesia   STYLE: Mild and sweet
COMMENTS: In the rice pudding tasting, this Indonesian cinnamon struck "the perfect balance of sweet and spicy." Its flavor dramatically mellowed when baked into cinnamon rolls and on pita chips.

PENZEYS Vietnamese Cinnamon
Ground `SPICY FAVORITE`
PRICE: $6.95 for 1.7 oz ($4.09 per oz)
ORIGIN: Vietnam   STYLE: Spicy
COMMENTS: With the highest percentage of volatile oils in the bunch, this Vietnamese cinnamon boasted a "bold" heat that didn't overpower its "woodsier" flavors in rice pudding. But it lost heat in baked applications.

MCCORMICK Ground Cinnamon
PRICE: $2.99 for 2.37 oz ($1.26 per oz)
ORIGIN: Indonesia   STYLE: Mild and sweet
COMMENTS: Mixed into rice pudding, this product fit the Indonesian cinnamon flavor profile: "balanced" and "not too spicy," with a "woodsy," "cedar-like" finish. In baked goods, its heat faded and it became fairly indistinguishable from any other cinnamon.

SIMPLY ORGANIC Ground Cinnamon
PRICE: $4.49 for 2.45 oz ($1.83 per oz)
ORIGIN: Vietnam   STYLE: Spicy
COMMENTS: Tasters felt the burn from this Vietnamese cinnamon, which was "spicy" and "peppery" like "Red Hots candy" in rice pudding. In baked goods, it was indistinguishable from other cinnamons.

RECOMMENDED (continued)

FRONTIER CO-OP ORGANIC
Ground Cinnamon
PRICE: $3.69 for 1.92 oz ($1.92 per oz)
ORIGIN: Indonesia   STYLE: Mild and sweet
COMMENTS: When swirled into rice pudding, this Indonesian cinnamon was pleasantly "perfume-y," with heat that was "subtle" and gave way to a "sweet," "fruity" aftertaste. Its heat and distinctive flavors faded in baked goods.

MCCORMICK GOURMET ORGANIC
Saigon Cinnamon
PRICE: $4.19 for 1.25 oz ($3.35 per oz)
ORIGIN: Vietnam   STYLE: Spicy
COMMENTS: In rice pudding, most found this cinnamon "vibrant," with "pleasant intensity," though a few deemed it a little too intense. In baked goods, it was indistinguishable from other cinnamons.

SPICE ISLANDS Saigon Cinnamon
PRICE: $6.49 for 1.9 oz ($3.42 per oz)
ORIGIN: Vietnam   STYLE: Spicy
COMMENTS: This Vietnamese cinnamon was "intensely flavored," with a strong "zing" of heat that reminded tasters of "cinnamon candy" in rice pudding. A few found this product "a little too hot," but its heat faded almost entirely in baked goods, where it tasted similar to the rest.

RECOMMENDED WITH RESERVATIONS

BADIA Cinnamon Powder
PRICE: $1.79 for 2 oz ($0.90 per oz)
ORIGIN: Indonesia   STYLE: Mild and sweet
COMMENTS: The only product with soybean oil added during processing, this cinnamon received low marks for its "sour," "musty" aftertaste. However, these off-notes mostly disappeared when we baked with it.

GRUYÈRE

Gruyère has been made in the eponymous alpine region of Switzerland for more than 900 years and is widely considered one of the great cheeses of the world. Good versions taste deeply nutty with sweet, fruity tang, nice salinity, and a good bit of earthy funk. As its stateside popularity has grown, so, too, has its availability in our supermarkets. To find our favorite Gruyère, we picked up eight nationally available cheeses—five Swiss imports bearing the *appellation d'origine protegée* (AOP) seal, meaning they were made according to strict government-mandated rules, and three domestic facsimiles. Tasted plain and baked in spinach and cheese squares, most of the Swiss-made cheeses tasted "more intense" and "complex" than the American-made ones. Two of the three domestic cheeses lacked the characteristic notes of authentic Gruyère. Those differences might be linked to aging. AOP standards dictate that Gruyère must be aged at least five months; our top cheeses were aged for even longer—between nine and 14 months. Among the winners was one of the domestic Gruyère-style cheeses, whose relatively lengthy nine-month aging period helped give it complex flavor despite the use of pasteurized milk. Cheeses are listed in order of preference.

RECOMMENDED

1655 Le Gruyère
PRICE: $19.99 per lb ($1.25 per oz)
MILK: Raw   AGE: 12–14 months
ORIGIN: Switzerland   AOP: Yes
COMMENTS: Our winner was aged the longest, between 12 and 14 months. Tasters praised its "excellent crystalline structure"; "dense," "fudgy" texture; and "deeply aged, caramel-like," "grassy" flavor that still shone when baked with spinach and onions.

MIFROMA Le Gruyère Cavern Reserve
PRICE: $19.99 per lb ($1.25 per oz)
MILK: Raw   AGE: 9–11 months
ORIGIN: Switzerland   AOP: Yes
COMMENTS: This long-aged Swiss import tasted "nutty," "toasty," and complex—tasters picked up on fruity "pineapple" tang and a "savory onion quality." It boasted a dense, "creamy" texture that was strewn with pleasantly crystalline bites.

EMMI ROTH Grand Cru Surchoix
PRICE: $18.99 per lb ($1.19 per oz)
MILK: Pasteurized   AGE: At least 9 months
ORIGIN: USA   AOP: No
COMMENTS: Despite being made with pasteurized milk, this domestic cheese boasted "caramelized" sweetness; notes of mushroom, onion, and "fruity red wine"; and a "buttery" texture that was loaded with crunchy tyrosine crystals.

EMMI Le Gruyère AOP Kalbatch
PRICE: $23.99 per lb ($1.50 per oz)
MILK: Raw   AGE: 12 months
ORIGIN: Switzerland   AOP: Yes
COMMENTS: "Would be a showstopper on a cheese plate," one taster remarked about this particularly "funky," "fruity," "nutty," "barnyard-y" sample. Several others noted a pleasant fermented quality—like "sour apple juice" or a "deep, lingering muskiness."

RECOMMENDED (*continued*)

GRAND SUISSE Le Gruyère
PRICE: $19.00 per lb ($1.19 per oz)
MILK: Raw   AGE: 5 months
ORIGIN: Switzerland   AOP: Yes
COMMENTS: Aged just five months, this "waxy" Swiss Gruyère tasted noticeably leaner and "milder" than the older samples. It was "tangy, but flat," "semi-sharp," and "tastes young." That said, it still delivered "pleasant nuttiness" and "mellow tang."

EMMI Le Gruyère AOP
PRICE: $15.44 per lb ($0.97 per oz)
MILK: Raw   AGE: 5–6 months
ORIGIN: Switzerland   AOP: Yes
COMMENTS: "Gruyère for beginners" is how one taster described this young, "buttery," "nutty" import. Compared to the denser, more crystalline structure of our favorites, it was "smooth, soft, and creamy," though texture wasn't an issue in cooked applications.

RECOMMENDED WITH RESERVATIONS

BOAR'S HEAD Blanc Grue Gruyère Cheese
PRICE: $16.58 per lb ($1.04 per oz)
MILK: Pasteurized
AGE: No standard timeframe
ORIGIN: USA   AOP: No
COMMENTS: "Not offensive, but no sparkle." "Waxy" and "bendy." "Innocuous." These comments were all good indications that this domestic facsimile was aged for far less time than other favorite cheeses. However, it melted evenly on crostini and its flavor was "mild but pleasant" with subtle nutty, sweet notes.

EMMI ROTH Grand Cru Original
PRICE: $14.99 per lb ($0.94 per oz)
MILK: Pasteurized   AGE: 4 months
ORIGIN: USA   AOP: No
COMMENTS: Several tasters compared this young cheese to deli Swiss—even called it a "faker"—citing its "mild" (albeit "pleasant") flavor and "rubbery" texture.

SUPERMARKET PARMESAN

Known for its fruity, nutty, savory notes and its crystalline crunch, real Parmigiano-Reggiano is considered the king of cheeses, but we wanted to determine how its imitators, called Parmesan in supermarkets, stacked up. To find out, we evaluated five domestic Parmesans and two certified Parmigiano-Reggianos from Italy, tasting them plain and cooked in polenta. All of the cheeses fared well in our polenta tasting, but when sampled plain, there was no comparison: Most of the domestic products tasted rubbery and bland while the Parmigiano-Reggiano was complex and nutty. The differences came down to three factors: True Parmigiano-Reggianos are made with raw milk, the cows eat at least 75 percent local grasses, and the cheeses are aged for at least 12 months. It made sense, then, that our favorite domestic was the only one that mimicked those guidelines. Though the milk was pasteurized, it came from cows with a varied diet and the cheese was aged for 20 months. Nothing we tasted topped the real thing, but finding a standout domestic Parmesan was a pleasant surprise. Cheeses are listed in order of preference.

RECOMMENDED

BOAR'S HEAD Parmigiano-Reggiano
PRICE: $19.99 per lb ($1.25 per oz)
ORIGIN: Italy AGE: 24 months
COW DIET: Local grass MILK: Raw
COMMENTS: This "robust" Parmigiano-Reggiano was the most aged in our lineup. It earned raves from tasters, who pronounced it "intensely flavorful," "strong," and "nutty." "Piquant," with notes of fruit and umami, it was "very dry" with a delightfully crystalline texture. In a word: "Delicious!"

IL VILLAGGIO Parmigiano-Reggiano 18 Month
PRICE: $19.99 per lb ($1.25 per oz)
ORIGIN: Italy AGE: 18 months
COW DIET: Local grass MILK: Raw
COMMENTS: Tasters found this Parmigiano-Reggiano to be "more assertive" than its domestic counterparts, with an "authentic tang and nuttiness." It was "robust" and "pungent," with "a little funk" that spoke of both "tropical fruits" and "savory mushrooms." It was "dry and crumbly," with a "nice crystal structure."

SARVECCHIO Parmesan
PRICE: $17.99 per lb ($1.12 per oz)
ORIGIN: USA AGE: At least 20 months
COW DIET: Alfalfa hay, grass hay, corn silage, soybeans MILK: Pasteurized
COMMENTS: This was the best domestic Parmesan we sampled, likely because it's aged twice as long as the four other American cheeses in our lineup. Tasters called it "nutty" and "pleasant," with a "sweet start" and hints of "caramel" and "butterscotch." The structure was "crumbly," though "slightly waxy," with "a little crystal crunch."

RECOMMENDED WITH RESERVATIONS

DIGIORNO Natural Cheese Wedge Parmesan
PRICE: $11.49 per lb ($0.72 per oz)
ORIGIN: USA AGE: 10 months
COW DIET: Corn, alfalfa, soybeans
MILK: Pasteurized
COMMENTS: Tasters picked up on savory, umami notes in this cheese, "like chicken stock." But it was muted, and in polenta it provided no "clear central cheesy note." Others compared it to gouda, cheddar, or Swiss cheese. Its "creamy," "gummy" texture was "too soft."

STELLA Parmesan Cheese
PRICE: $10.99 per lb ($0.69 per oz)
ORIGIN: USA AGE: At least 10 months
COW DIET: Proprietary MILK: Proprietary
COMMENTS: This cheese was "slightly nutty," "briny," "milky," and "meaty" but "overall bland." In polenta, where it melted readily, it didn't foster any complaints about texture, but tasters noted that it was "soft" and "waxy" when eaten plain. "No crystalline crunch! Disappointing!"

SARGENTO Hard Grating Parmesan
PRICE: $5.38 per lb ($0.34 per oz)
ORIGIN: USA AGE: At least 6 months
COW DIET: Unknown MILK: Pasteurized
COMMENTS: This little wedge had a hint of Gruyère-like nuttiness but was otherwise "quite mild," so much so that tasters "hardly knew there was cheese" in the polenta made with 2 cups of it. It was inoffensive but more cheddar-like, "moist" and "creamy," without the "crystalline snap."

BELGIOIOSO Parmesan
PRICE: $9.99 per lb ($0.62 per oz)
ORIGIN: USA AGE: At least 10 months
COW DIET: Grass and grains MILK: Raw
COMMENTS: "Impostor!" declared one taster sampling this younger cheese. It didn't taste bad, but it was denser and softer than a Parmesan should be. Tasters compared it to gouda, cheddar, and mozzarella. It was "mild" "with no real tang."

BLOCK MOZZARELLA

Unlike milky, soft fresh mozzarella, which is packed in brine, block mozzarella is an American product, sometimes called "pizza cheese." This variety has a lower moisture content, higher acidity, more longevity, and the ability to grate and melt beautifully. To find the best block for cooking, we gathered a mix of whole milk and part-skim products and tasted them plain and on pizza. (We also included our winning shredded mozzarella by Polly-O.) While all of the cheeses shredded easily and melted well, our tasters preferred the fuller, more dairy-rich flavor of whole-milk cheeses. Our top-ranked cheeses were rich, pleasantly tangy, and dry enough to shred and melt well, but had enough moisture to give them a soft, smooth texture (even when melted) approaching that of fresh mozzarella. Cheeses are listed in order of preference.

RECOMMENDED

POLLY-O
Whole Milk Mozzarella Cheese
PRICE: $5.99 for 16 oz ($0.37 per oz)
MOISTURE: 53%
COMMENTS: This brand was remarkably "soft" and "milky," with a "creaminess" and "hint of salt" that drew comparisons to fresh mozzarella. On pizza, its "rich" flavor "held up against the tomato sauce," and it melted into stretchy sheets that were "elastic, but not gooey" and "adhered well" to the pizza.

GALBANI Whole Milk Mozzarella
PRICE: $4.99 for 16 oz ($0.31 per oz)
MOISTURE: 52%
COMMENTS: "Classic pizza parlor cheese," said one taster about this whole milk mozzarella, which was "tangy," "moist," and "tender." When melted, it was "chewy" and "creamy," with "a little bit of pull" that tasters loved. Though many detected a "nutty" sharpness in this cheese, a few tasters thought it had a slightly "dull" flavor.

BOAR'S HEAD Whole Milk Low Moisture Mozzarella Cheese
PRICE: $6.99 for 16 oz ($0.43 per oz)
MOISTURE: 45%
COMMENTS: This mozzarella is sliced in fresh blocks from the deli counter and tastes "nutty" and "milky," with a "slight tang." It melted down "glossy" and "stretchy" on pizza, with evenly browned pockets that were "buttery," but "not greasy."

POLLY-O Low Moisture Whole Milk Shredded Mozzarella
PRICE: $2.98 for 8 oz ($0.37 per oz)
MOISTURE: 46%
COMMENTS: Our favorite shredded mozzarella performed admirably alongside the block mozzarellas on pizza, where tasters noted it was "nutty" and "creamy," with a "bit of stretch." Most tasters detected a "powdery" chalkiness from their coating of cellulose powder (used to keep strands separated) when sampled plain, so we'd choose a different product for snacking and salads.

RECOMMENDED (continued)

GALBANI Part Skim Mozzarella
PRICE: $4.99 for 16 oz ($0.31 per oz)
MOISTURE: 53%
COMMENTS: Many remarked that this part-skim mozzarella was "springy" and "firm," if not a bit "rubbery" when eaten plain. It melted well on pizza, where it produced "thick" and "chewy" strands that were still "buttery" and "moist." Most described its flavor as "mild" and "light," with a "slight tang."

POLLY-O Part Skim Mozzarella Cheese
PRICE: $5.99 for 16 oz ($0.37 per oz)
MOISTURE: 53%
COMMENTS: Though tasters liked the punch of this "tangy" part-skim cheese, a few remarked that its "squeaky" texture was reminiscent of "string cheese" when tasted plain. It retained its "hearty," "milky" flavor on pizza and its texture mellowed out to a "smooth," "stretchy" sheet when melted.

RECOMMENDED WITH RESERVATIONS

ORGANIC VALLEY Low Moisture Mozzarella, Part Skim
PRICE: $4.99 for 8 oz ($0.62 per oz)
MOISTURE: 45%
COMMENTS: Though some tasters liked this organic cultured cheese's "funkier" sharpness, many were thrown by its "yellow" color and "cheddar-y" flavor. Though still faintly yellow when melted on pizza, its "sharper" notes were mellowed by the sauce, and tasters liked its "fresh dairy flavor." A few remarked that the pizza was "a bit greasy."

CRUSHED TOMATOES

Crushed tomatoes are a convenient way to bring tomato flavor to dishes year round, but there's no regulation of the term "crushed." We tasted tomatoes plain as well as in a simple pasta sauce in search of a favorite and we discovered just how varied the textures and flavors of crushed tomatoes could be. In both instances, our tasters preferred a chunkier product, with distinct firm-tender bites of tomatoes. Tomatoes with a watery or stringy consistency fell to the bottom of our ranking, and we were quick to rule out cans labeled "unpeeled," as the remaining skins were plasticky and unpleasant. Lab analysis of the pH (a measure of acidity) and Brix (a measure of sweetness) pointed out that the cans our tasters praised for fresh, bright flavor were also the products with the most acidity and sweetness. Products without salt or citric acid (often added to boost fresh flavor) fell to the bottom for their dull, bland flavor, and the two samples containing basil were polarizing—most tasters liked it, but some felt that it "overwhelmed" the tomato flavor. Any of our top five products would make a fine base for sauce or soup and save you the trouble of crushing whole tomatoes. Crushed tomatoes are listed in order of preference.

RECOMMENDED

SMT Crushed Tomatoes
PRICE: $3.50 for 28 oz ($0.13 per oz)
PH: 4.2 BRIX: 9.0
COMMENTS: Our favorite tasted "very bright and sweet" with "full tomato flavor"—no surprise, given its high levels of sweetness and acidity. Added diced tomatoes, though nontraditional in crushed products, contributed a hearty texture that impressed our panel.

RED PACK Crushed Tomatoes in Puree (also sold as Red Gold Crushed Tomatoes)
PRICE: $1.50 for 28 oz ($0.05 per oz)
PH: 4.2 BRIX: 9.3
COMMENTS: With the right balance of sweetness and acidity, this brand was praised for its "complex, tomatoey flavor." The pieces were crushed to a slightly smaller size, but they still made a "good building block" for pasta sauce.

PASTENE Kitchen Ready Chunky Style Ground Peeled Tomatoes
PRICE: $1.99 for 28 oz ($0.07 per oz)
PH: 4.1 BRIX: 8.9
COMMENTS: Besides praising its "sweet tomato flavor," tasters appreciated this sample's relatively large pieces, which helped make a hearty sauce.

CENTO Organic Chunky Style Crushed Tomatoes
PRICE: $4.69 for 28 oz ($0.17 per oz)
PH: 4.3 BRIX: 7.1
COMMENTS: These firm yet tender crushed tomatoes tasted pleasantly "fresh." Although some tasters thought that the basil flavor was a bit strong in the plain tasting, many thought it was a welcome addition in sauce. The fairly large pieces of tomato lent the sauce a "chunky" texture that tasters liked.

RECOMMENDED (continued)

CONTADINA Crushed Roma Tomatoes
PRICE: $2.49 for 28 oz ($0.09 per oz)
PH: 4.2 BRIX: 8.5
COMMENTS: With "bright," "fruity" flavor and meaty (½-inch) pieces, these tomatoes would have had it all, except for one flaw: The skins tended to peel away from the fruit in the plain tasting and were unpleasantly tough.

RECOMMENDED WITH RESERVATIONS

MUIR GLEN Crushed Tomatoes with Basil
PRICE: $2.99 for 28 oz ($0.11 per oz)
PH: 4.0 BRIX: 8.5
COMMENTS: Large, chunky tomato pieces appealed to tasters, particularly in pasta sauce. But while the ample sweetness, acidity, and salt should have highlighted the fruit's bright taste, the dried basil flavor was so overwhelming that panelists compared this product to pizza sauce.

HUNT'S Crushed Tomatoes
PRICE: $2.19 for 28 oz ($0.08 per oz)
PH: 4.1 BRIX: 9.3
COMMENTS: These tomatoes are crushed fairly small, so the resulting sauce was pretty thin, but it still coated pasta well. Several tasters noticed a slight "metallic" taste.

NOT RECOMMENDED

BIONATURAE Organic Crushed Tomatoes
PRICE: $3.69 for 28.2 oz ($0.13 per oz)
PH: 4.5 BRIX: 5.3
COMMENTS: Without citric acid or added salt and with the lowest sweetness level by far, it was no wonder we found these tomatoes "bland" and "dull." Even onions and garlic weren't enough to save them when cooked in tomato sauce. Plus, the small pieces of tomato practically disappeared when cooked, resulting in a "watery" sauce.

SUPERMARKET BARBECUE SAUCE

Americans love barbecue sauce, and while everyone has a favorite regional style, supermarket sauces are typically modeled after Kansas City's thick, sweet, and tangy tomato-based version. To find our top pick, we rounded up seven top-selling brands and tasted each plain, stirred into pulled pork, and as a dip for chicken fingers. Sweetness had a big impact on our tasters' preferences; their top picks all list a sweetener as a primary ingredient. However, while the sauces with the most sugars scored well, neither one was our winner, as the true "sweet spot" was a slightly lower sugar level. Our winner contained about 30 percent less sugar than the runner-up, and our tasters thought it was just right. We also learned that our tasters liked sauces with a pronounced tomato flavor among the smoke, spice, and tang, and when it came to consistency, those with middle-of-the-road "ketchup-y" thickness came out on top. Our winning product was delicious and versatile, neither too thick nor too thin. Barbecue sauces are listed in order of preference.

RECOMMENDED

BULL'S-EYE Original BBQ Sauce
PRICE: $2.59 for 18 oz ($0.14 per oz)
SUGARS: 11 g
COMMENTS: This "all-purpose" product won tasters over with its "balanced sweetness," "tomato-y" flavor, "subtle smoke," and "nice tang," all "without any of the flavors overwhelming each other." This "straightforward" barbecue sauce was "immediately pleasing to the palate," and "not as gloppy" as some others.

HEINZ BBQ Sauce Classic Sweet & Thick
PRICE: $2.79 for 21.4 oz ($0.13 per oz)
SUGARS: 16 g
COMMENTS: Though some tasters found this product "a tad too sweet," others enjoyed this "bold" barbecue sauce's "very sweet" and "peppery" flavor combo, as well as the "bit of tang" and "nice, smoky aftertaste." This "viscous" product's "smooth" texture and "addictive flavor" led one taster to declare, "The more I eat, the more I like it."

SWEET BABY RAY'S Barbecue Sauce
PRICE: $2.69 for 18 oz ($0.15 per oz)
SUGARS: 16 g
COMMENTS: Pleasantly "sugary" and "robust," this product's "instant hit of flavor" and "tangy bite" added up to "pretty perfect" flavor for some tasters, even though it seemed "super sweet" to others. This product's "ketchup-y" texture made it an "excellent barbecue sauce for dipping," while the "good spiciness" lent a "touch of heat."

RECOMMENDED WITH RESERVATIONS

KC MASTERPIECE Original Barbecue Sauce
PRICE: $1.69 for 18 oz ($0.09 per oz)
SUGARS: 12 g
COMMENTS: Most tasters enjoyed this product's "pleasantly smoky" and "super sweet" flavor, while its "good cling" and "thick" texture further won over tasters. A few tasters took issue with the sauce's "unassuming" taste, saying the flavor was "too weak" and "needed a little more of a kick."

KRAFT Original Barbecue Sauce & Dip
PRICE: $1.99 for 18 oz ($0.11 per oz)
SUGARS: 13 g
COMMENTS: This "candy-like" sauce's "unique flavor" reminded tasters of "pumpkin spiced barbecue" and "roasted fruit." Even though this "very sweet" product was overwhelming for some, and the "almost plum-y" flavor "may not be mainstream enough," the sauce was lauded for its "nice heat" and "hint of smoke."

JACK DANIEL'S Barbecue Sauce, Original No. 7 Recipe
PRICE: $2.99 for 19 oz ($0.16 per oz)
SUGARS: 9 g
COMMENTS: "It tastes exactly like a campfire," noted one taster, describing this product's "woodsy" and "liquid smoke" flavor. The "deep and smoky" sauce was "delicious," "pure BBQ flavor" to some, but others found it "artificial" and thought this "meaty and savory" sauce "could use a pinch more sweetness."

NOT RECOMMENDED

STUBB'S Original Legendary Bar-B-Q Sauce
PRICE: $4.49 for 18 oz ($0.25 per oz)
SUGARS: 4 g
COMMENTS: Tasters likened this Texas (not Kansas City)-style product to "spicy, watery ketchup" that "was not sweet at all." The "tart" and "sour" flavor reminded one taster of "old tomato puree," while others took issue with the "metallic aftertaste" and "very thin" texture.

SPIRAL-SLICED HAM

Salty-sweet spiral-sliced ham is precooked, sliced for easy carving, and feeds a crowd, but with so many products on the market, which one should you buy? To answer this, we selected seven widely available varieties and sampled them plain and in sandwiches. None of the hams were awful, but some were definitely better than others. Lower-ranked hams were one-trick ponies, with smokiness, saltiness, or sweetness overwhelming the other flavors and unpleasantly dry, chewy, or spongy texture. The variables distinguishing each product were many, from brining time and the seasoning therein to "massaging" time (when the brined hams are tumbled and rolled to tenderize the meat) to smoking time (and most of the details were proprietary). In the end, we approved of all the hams, but our winner stood out for its tender, juicy meat and perfectly balanced flavors. Hams are listed in order of preference.

RECOMMENDED

JOHNSTON COUNTY Spiral-Sliced Smoked Ham
PRICE: $64.95
SALT: 940 mg   SUGAR: 2 g
AVAILABILITY: In stores and online ($34.15 shipping fee)
COMMENTS: Our winning ham scored highly for flavor and texture. Tasters noted its "nice smokiness" and said it had "just enough sweetness." This ham was "tender and moist" with the "classic ham flavor" tasters wanted.

BURGER'S SMOKEHOUSE Spiral-Sliced City Ham
PRICE: $66.50
SALT: 870 mg   SUGAR: 0 g
AVAILABILITY: Online (free shipping)
COMMENTS: This ham appealed to tasters who preferred "porky" hams with a "very smoky flavor" that was assertive but not over the top. This product was balanced, with a texture that was "moist" and "tender."

APPLEWOOD FARMS Spiral-Sliced Ham
PRICE: $45.00
SALT: 910 mg   SUGAR: 2 g
AVAILABILITY: Online ($19.95 shipping fee)
COMMENTS: The flavors in this mellow, "pleasantly hammy," crowd-pleasing ham were nicely balanced. This ham appealed to those who preferred flavors more mellow than the bold "smoky sweetness" of the top two products.

RECOMMENDED WITH RESERVATIONS

COOK'S Spiral Sliced Hickory Smoked Ham
PRICE: $24.40
SALT: 830 mg   SUGAR: 2 g
AVAILABILITY: In stores
COMMENTS: This one nailed that "classic" spiral-sliced ham flavor. Tasters were impressed by its combination of "smoky sweet" and "hammy, meaty" flavors. But it was downgraded slightly for a texture described as a bit "spongy."

CARANDO Hickory Smoked Spiral Sliced Ham
PRICE: $24.50
SALT: 850 mg   SUGAR: 5 g
AVAILABILITY: In stores
COMMENTS: Tasters liked the "distinctly porky" and "mildly sweet and smoky" flavor of this ham. But their enthusiasm was tempered by a slightly "dry" and "chewy" texture.

HONEYBAKED Ham
PRICE: $75.95
SALT: 1,230 mg   SUGAR: 4 g
AVAILABILITY: In stores and online ($9.95 to $39.95 shipping fee)
COMMENTS: The original spiral-sliced ham, HoneyBaked strongly divided our tasters. Some found its sweet "honey" and "maple" flavors "delicious." Others found it "oddly sweet," verging on "candied," and overly salty (it has the most salt of any ham we tasted).

HICKORY FARMS Spiral-Sliced HoneyGold Ham
PRICE: $75.00
SALT: 750 mg   SUGAR: 4 g
AVAILABILITY: Online ($10 shipping fee)
COMMENTS: Tasters enjoyed this ham's "smoky," "meaty" flavor and "firm," "hearty" texture in sandwiches but found it "tough" and "leathery" when served plain. More than one taster noticed a faint "burnt" flavor.

100 PERCENT WHOLE-WHEAT BREAD

Whole-wheat bread boasts a flavor and nutrient profile far more robust than that of white bread, but not all loaves live up to their name. "Whole wheat" isn't a term strictly regulated by the U.S. Food and Drug Administration, but "100 percent whole wheat" is, so when we set out to find which bread is best, we stuck with that designation. After tasting the breads plain, in ham and cheese sandwiches, and as buttered toast, we found all acceptable, but we had a clear preference for those with cleaner, deeper flavors. We also liked a touch of sugar: Our top two breads had 3.5 grams of sugar per serving, enough to balance out the savory toasty, nutty flavors. Breads with minor off-flavors from stabilizers, emulsifiers, and preservatives (or even from the wheat itself) were passable; what made a really good bread stand out was its texture. We favored moist, springy, chewy breads that were hearty and dense enough to stand up to deli meats and butter. This distinction was easy to spot, too: The bottom five breads had square slices and airy crumbs while the top two featured wide, rectangular slices and dense crumbs. Breads are listed in order of preference.

RECOMMENDED

ARNOLD'S Whole Grains 100% Whole Wheat Bread
PRICE: $4.49 per 24 oz loaf ($0.19 per oz)
SUGAR: 3.5 g per 50 g serving
COMMENTS: Our winner swept all three taste tests with its "hint of sweetness," "mild nuttiness," and "clean wheat flavor" which had "none of the bitterness" of typical bakery aisle bread. It was "tender and chewy" but not "too soft." Both crumb and crust were speckled with crunchy flecks of bulgur that were "substantial and pleasing."

PEPPERIDGE FARM Farmhouse 100% Whole Wheat Bread
PRICE: $3.99 per 24 oz loaf ($0.17 per oz)
SUGAR: 3.5 g per 50 g serving
COMMENTS: Like the winner, the runner up "actually tastes of wheat." It was praised for its "slightly sweet" and "mild nutty" notes as well as its "dense," "cakey," but "tender" crumb. Our only quibble was with the aftertaste, described as "very wheaty" by charitable tasters and "slightly bitter" by more critical palates.

RECOMMENDED WITH RESERVATIONS

NATURE'S OWN 100% Whole Wheat Bread
PRICE: $3.29 per 20 oz loaf ($0.16 per oz)
SUGAR: 1.8 g per 50 g serving
COMMENTS: Tasters enjoyed this brand's "light wheaty sweetness," mild "nutty flavor," and "classic sandwich bread" texture. Though some perceived a faintly "sour" aftertaste, our main gripe was with its "open," "airy" crumb that "wimped out with butter" and compressed "to nothing" under the modest heft of thinly sliced ham and cheese.

RECOMMENDED WITH RESERVATIONS (continued)

WONDER 100% Whole Wheat Bread
PRICE: $2.99 per 16 oz loaf ($0.19 per oz)
SUGAR: 0 g per 50 g serving
COMMENTS: Tasters deemed this brand a "standard wheat sandwich bread" with "a nice sweetness" and wheat flavor that was "just assertive enough." But some noticed a "weird," "slightly sour" aftertaste. And many disapproved of the "spongy," "overly airy" texture that "collapsed from the weight of the sandwich" and seemed "mushy."

NATURE'S HARVEST Stone Ground 100% Whole Wheat Bread
PRICE: $3.99 per 20 oz loaf ($0.20 per oz)
SUGAR: 0 g per 50 g serving
COMMENTS: Tasters liked this brand's "wheaty but mild" taste and "nice earthy notes." However, the texture was "thin," "flimsy," and "distressingly easy to squish." It "didn't stand up to the butter" and slumped under the weight of the sandwich. But the cracked wheat topping imparted a "slightly nutty" flavor that some tasters found pleasing.

SARA LEE 100% Whole Wheat Bread
PRICE: $3.99 per 20 oz loaf ($0.20 per oz)
SUGAR: 1.9 g per 50 g serving
COMMENTS: Served plain, this brand had "almost no taste" and collapsed into a "dense wad" when chewed. It was also a bit "flimsy" for sandwiches. However, tasters enjoyed this bread toasted and buttered, describing it as "a good piece of toast" with a "nice crumb" that "stands up to the butter."

MARTIN'S 100% Whole Wheat Potato Bread
PRICE: $3.69 per 20 oz loaf ($0.18 per oz)
SUGAR: 4.3 g per 50 g serving
COMMENTS: Although this bread includes reconstituted potato, it's still 100% whole wheat since it contains no white flour. Potato bread enthusiasts praised its "fluffy," "cottony" texture and "slightly sweet" flavor. But tasters expecting more conventional whole wheat bread found its "jaundiced" hue "very off-putting" and the flavor "not wheaty at all."

BAGGED POPCORN

Microwave popcorn sales have dipped of late, but bagged popcorn is on the rise, so we rounded up seven top-selling brands to see if we could pick a favorite. Most manufacturers offer multiple flavors, but we stuck with basic salt-and-oil varieties, sampling the popcorns side by side in a blind tasting. Tasters noted clear differences between samples: Some were toasty, nutty, and slightly sweet, while others tasted bland, flat, or even a bit burnt. Examining ingredient labels, we saw no trend in type or amount of oil or type of popcorn (all labels just listed "popcorn"), but the salt was another story. Products with too little salt were deemed "muted," while those with too much lacked nuanced toasted-corn flavor. We preferred those with moderate levels of sodium (about 110 milligrams per 1-ounce serving), which allowed the popcorn's subtleties to shine. Tasters cared about texture and showed a clear preference for certain samples, so we took a closer look at each individual piece. All popcorn pops the same way: As kernels are heated, the water inside them steams, building up pressure and causing starch in the kernels to gelatinize. Once enough pressure builds up, the foamy starch bursts through the tough outer layer of the kernels and solidifies as it hits the air—that's the whitish, billowy part of popped kernels. As we scrutinized the popcorn pieces, we discovered that top-ranked popcorns contained more than 50 percent unilateral pieces—the pieces resembling little octopuses, with dense, round bodies and appendages extending from the bodies on one side—while the lowest-ranked sample had a paltry 4 percent. Tasters perceived products with a high percentage of unilateral pieces to be crunchier and more substantial, while those with fewer unilateral pieces were "spongy." In the end, tasters deemed our winning popcorn, made up of half unilateral pieces, crisp and substantial, with a balanced, fresh flavor. Popcorns are listed in order of preference.

RECOMMENDED

CAPE COD Sea Salt Popcorn
PRICE: $3.15 for 4.4 oz ($0.72 per oz)
SODIUM: 110 mg
PERCENTAGE UNILATERAL PIECES: 50%
COMMENTS: This popcorn won tasters over with its "nutty," "toasty" corn flavor and "well-calibrated salt." Its "hearty," "puffy" kernels were "crisp" and "crunchy" up front, with a tender interior that "almost melted" in tasters' mouths as they ate. "This is pretty ideal popcorn," summarized one taster.

SMARTFOOD DELIGHT
Sea Salt Popcorn
PRICE: $3.99 for 5.5 oz ($0.73 per oz)
SODIUM: 115 mg
PERCENTAGE UNILATERAL PIECES: 63%
COMMENTS: Tasters loved this familiar popcorn's "round," "bubbly," "cartoon-y fluffy" pieces, which were "plump" and "meaty," with "good crunch." It also had a nice subtle saltiness and a "toasty" flavor. "Reminds me of the movies," said one taster.

KETTLE Sea Salt Popcorn
PRICE: $3.29 for 3 oz ($1.10 per oz)
SODIUM: 240 mg
PERCENTAGE UNILATERAL PIECES: 38%
COMMENTS: Though many tasters liked this product's "toasty" notes and "crisp" exterior, some thought the popcorn tasted "slightly burnt." Still, most loved these "airy," "fluffy" kernels, which had a subtly "sweet corn flavor."

RECOMMENDED (continued)

POPCORN INDIANA Sea Salt Popcorn
PRICE: $3.79 for 4.75 oz ($0.80 per oz)
SODIUM: 220 mg
PERCENTAGE UNILATERAL PIECES: 18%
COMMENTS: With a "natural sweetness" and "toasty," almost "buttery" notes, this product was deemed similar to "movie popcorn." Unfortunately, some tasters were disappointed with the "less substantial" shape and size of the kernels, which were "soft" and "lacked crunch."

RECOMMENDED WITH RESERVATIONS

BOOMCHICKAPOP Sea Salt Popcorn
PRICE: $3.09 for 4.8 oz ($0.64 per oz)
SODIUM: 90 mg
PERCENTAGE UNILATERAL PIECES: 34%
COMMENTS: With less salt than most other products, this popcorn was "inoffensive" and "mild," if not "a little bland." Though some tasters did pick up on subtle "toasty," "corn-y" notes in these kernels, many were distracted by their "rubbery," "cardboard-y" texture.

SKINNYPOP Popcorn Original
PRICE: $3.79 for 4.4 oz ($0.86 per oz)
SODIUM: 75 mg
PERCENTAGE UNILATERAL PIECES: 4%
COMMENTS: These smaller, angular pieces lacked structure and shape, compressing between tasters' teeth like "spongy," "stale" bits of "Styrofoam." Flavor was "muted" from lack of salt, though a few salt-conscious tasters appreciated the "purity" of this "mild" popcorn.

NONSTICK SKILLETS

Nonstick skillets are great at cooking those delicate foods that stick, like eggs or fish, or when preparing stir-fries. Hoping to find our ideal model—one that's easy to handle, durable, has great release, and cooks food evenly with appropriate browning—we fried dozens of eggs and intentionally broke every rule we could think of. We cut food in the skillets with knives, used metal spatulas and abrasive sponges, stacked the skillets, repeatedly shocked them in cold water, and washed them in a dishwasher. We even banged them on a concrete ledge to simulate years of rough handling. What did we learn? First of all, size, shape, and design matter. Smaller pans were a bust: Their narrow cooking surfaces saw food riding up the sides and anything we sautéed was crowded and browned poorly. Heavy pans and hot handles were major negatives; we preferred lightweight pans with stay-cool, grippy handles and low, flared sides. As for the nonstick coatings, pans with raised patterns (ostensibly for durability and better heat transfer) weren't very nonstick, mangling fried eggs. Top performers had at least three layers of smooth nonstick coating. In the end, we only found two pans we could recommend. Our winner boasts a broad, smooth, flat surface that cooked and released food perfectly, and its darker finish promoted beautiful browning. Products are listed in order of preference.

HIGHLY RECOMMENDED	PERFORMANCE		TESTERS' COMMENTS
OXO Good Grips Non-Stick 12-Inch Open Frypan MODEL: CW000957-003 PRICE: $39.99 LAYERS OF NONSTICK COATING: 3 DIAMETER: 12.25 in USABLE SURFACE AREA: 9.75 in	NONSTICK ABILITY FOOD QUALITY MANEUVERABILITY CAPACITY DURABILITY	★★★ ★★★ ★★★ ★★★ ★★½	This pan came slick and stayed that way throughout testing. It cooked and released food perfectly, thanks to its darker finish and excellent nonstick coating. Its gently flared sides and lightweight design made it easy to load, unload, and move. Its grippy, stay-cool handle was flawless and its cooking surface was vast.

RECOMMENDED			
T-FAL Professional Non-Stick Fry Pan MODEL: E9380884 PRICE: $32.02 LAYERS OF NONSTICK COATING: 5 DIAMETER: 12.4 in USABLE SURFACE AREA: 9.5 in	NONSTICK ABILITY FOOD QUALITY MANEUVERABILITY CAPACITY DURABILITY	★★★ ★★½ ★★★ ★★★ ★★	Thanks to five layers of nonstick coating, our old winner emerged from our slicing tests virtually unmarked. It cooked and released food well, was light and comfortable, and had flared sides for easy access. Unfortunately, its surface domed slightly, so oil and egg yolks pooled around the edges. It also dented during abuse testing.

NOT RECOMMENDED			
ZWILLING Madura Plus 11" Nonstick Fry Pan MODEL: 66299-286 PRICE: $59.99 LAYERS OF NONSTICK COATING: 3 DIAMETER: 11.5 in USABLE SURFACE AREA: 8.25 in	NONSTICK ABILITY FOOD QUALITY MANEUVERABILITY CAPACITY DURABILITY	★★½ ★★½ ★★½ ★★ ★★	This pan's nonstick surface was good (not great) at browning and release. It was lightweight with nice flared sides, but it was too small: Standard fish fillets rode up its sides, and stir-fried broccoli became mushy because it was overcrowded during cooking. Its handle was comfortable but became loose during abuse testing.
FARBERWARE High Performance Stainless Steel 12-inch Nonstick Skillet MODEL: 77227 PRICE: $32.99 LAYERS OF NONSTICK COATING: 2 DIAMETER: 12 in USABLE SURFACE AREA: 10 in	NONSTICK ABILITY FOOD QUALITY MANEUVERABILITY CAPACITY DURABILITY	★★ ★★½ ★½ ★★★ ★★½	With the fewest layers (two) of coating of the skillets in our testing and a raised polka-dot pattern that hindered its nonstick abilities, this pan really let us down. Worse, this skillet was heavy, with an uncomfortable handle and awkward straight sides.
CUISINART Chef's Classic Non-Stick Stainless 12" Skillet MODEL: 722-30HNS PRICE: $52.95 LAYERS OF NONSTICK COATING: 3 DIAMETER: 12.4 in USABLE SURFACE AREA: 9.5 in	NONSTICK ABILITY FOOD QUALITY MANEUVERABILITY CAPACITY DURABILITY	★★ ★★ ★★ ★★★ ★★	This sturdy-feeling pan wasn't very nonstick. It tended to overcook food around its perimeter, thanks to a small disk bottom underneath and low bulging sides, which allowed the burner's flame more direct access to the food around the exterior. It was also quite heavy, and its handle dug into our hands and got very hot.
CIRCULON Symmetry 11-inch Open Skillet MODEL: 82894 PRICE: $37.31 LAYERS OF NONSTICK COATING: 3 DIAMETER: 11 in USABLE SURFACE AREA: 8.75 in	NONSTICK ABILITY FOOD QUALITY MANEUVERABILITY CAPACITY DURABILITY	★½ ★★ ★★ ★★ ★★½	This pan was sticky, small, and imprinted with a bull's-eye pattern for durability. Its finish was resistant to scratching, but eggs clung to it, fish fillets laid up its sides, and the broccoli in the stir-fry was mushy, thanks to overcrowding. Its steep sides made accessing food awkward, and its angular handle hurt our palms over time.

INEXPENSIVE DUTCH OVENS

A Dutch oven just might be the most versatile pot around, moving seamlessly from stove to oven and ideal for braising meat; cooking soups, stews, and sauces; frying; and even baking bread. After years of using them daily in the test kitchen, we've determined that we like round Dutch ovens that hold a minimum of 6 quarts. We also favor heavy pots made of enameled cast iron, which conduct and retain heat well and are easy to clean. Le Creuset makes our favorite model, but at nearly $350, its stellar performance comes with a steep pricetag. So we sought a great Dutch oven for under $125. Of the products we gathered, all the pots cooked food acceptably, but certain traits set the best apart. First, material: Light aluminum pots were prone to scorching and dented easily. Big, comfortable handles were a must for these heavy pots, and enameled pots with a light interior made it easy to monitor browning. Our testing also bore out a preference for pots with shorter sides, as tall sides made it awkward to add food to hot oil in a safe, splash-free manner. But what really made a difference was shape, and broad bases with straight sides were best. Our winner performed like a champ in all of our tests, and at $121.94, it was a great value. Products are listed in order of preference.

HIGHLY RECOMMENDED

		PERFORMANCE	TESTERS' COMMENTS

CUISINART 7 Qt Round Covered Casserole
MODEL: CUI CI670-30CR   PRICE: $121.94
MATERIAL: Enameled cast iron
CAPACITY: 7 qt   WEIGHT: 16.8 lb
USABLE COOKING SURFACE: 10 in

COOKING ★★★
CAPACITY ★★★
EASE OF USE ★★½
DURABILITY ★★½

With a design similar to the Le Creuset pot—low, straight sides and a broad, off-white cooking surface—it allowed us to easily move food, sear in fewer batches, and monitor browning. It's heavier and has smaller handles, but it's a great alternative.

RECOMMENDED

COOKING WITH CALPHALON Enamel Cast Iron Red 7-Qt Dutch Oven with Cover
MODEL: 1835758   PRICE: $111.30
MATERIAL: Enameled cast iron
CAPACITY: 7 qt   WEIGHT: 15.45 lb
USABLE COOKING SURFACE: 9.5 in

COOKING ★★½
CAPACITY ★★★
EASE OF USE ★★½
DURABILITY ★★½

This pot had comfortable handles and a generous cooking surface. Its interior was black, which made it slightly harder to monitor browning, and because dark colors conduct heat faster, it tended to cook faster, too (its bread was a bit dark on the bottom, though still acceptable). It also chipped very slightly during abuse testing.

LODGE ENAMEL 7.5 Quart Dutch Oven
MODEL: EC7D43   PRICE: $84.99
MATERIAL: Enameled cast iron
CAPACITY: 7.5 qt   WEIGHT: 18.15 lb
USABLE COOKING SURFACE: 8.5 in

COOKING ★★★
CAPACITY ★★
EASE OF USE ★★
DURABILITY ★★½

This pot cooked food well with nice low sides, making it easy to safely move food in and out of it. It had comfortable handles and an off-white interior, but it was the heaviest in the lineup and had a small usable cooking surface.

RECOMMENDED WITH RESERVATIONS

TRAMONTINA 6.5 Qt Covered Round Dutch Oven
MODEL: 80131/076DS   PRICE: $69.96
MATERIAL: Enameled cast iron
CAPACITY: 6.5 qt   WEIGHT: 13.45 lb
USABLE COOKING SURFACE: 8.4 in

COOKING ★★★
CAPACITY ★★½
EASE OF USE ★
DURABILITY ★★½

With a light interior and comfortable handles, this pot turned out good food. Unfortunately, its shape was challenging to use: Its sides were quite tall so we had to add food at a more extreme angle, and it also had a narrower mouth. Its cooking surface was smaller, too.

LODGE ENAMEL 6 Quart Dutch Oven
MODEL: EC6D38   PRICE: $60.99
MATERIAL: Enameled cast iron
CAPACITY: 6 qt   WEIGHT: 13.85 lb
USABLE COOKING SURFACE: 7.5 in

COOKING ★★★
CAPACITY ★★
EASE OF USE ★
DURABILITY ★★½

Despite its nice handles, low sides, and a light interior, this pot's rounded sides curved in at the base and robbed some of its flat cooking surface.

IMUSA Cast Aluminum Caldero with Natural Finish
MODEL: GAU-80506W   PRICE: $24.29
MATERIAL: Cast aluminum
CAPACITY: 6.9 qt   WEIGHT: 3.7 lb
USABLE COOKING SURFACE: 8.5 in

COOKING ★★½
CAPACITY ★★★
EASE OF USE ★★
DURABILITY ★

This pot stained and dented, its knob became loose, its handles were small, and it ran hot. That said, it made good food and was ridiculously cheap. Bottom line: This is a workable pot, but be prepared to replace it.

NOT RECOMMENDED

NORDIC WARE ProCast Traditions 6.5 Qt Dutch Oven
MODEL: 21624   PRICE: $60.00
MATERIAL: Cast aluminum
CAPACITY: 6.5 qt   WEIGHT: 5.95 lb
USABLE COOKING SURFACE: 8 in

COOKING ★★½
CAPACITY ★★
EASE OF USE ★★★
DURABILITY ★

This pot was tall, narrow, and hard to get food in and out of. Its dark interior made it hard to monitor browning and its narrow base was limiting. A ridge around its rim made it hard to clip on a thermometer, something we often use with Dutch ovens while frying. Lastly, its soft aluminum dented readily during abuse testing.

RIMMED BAKING SHEETS

Rimmed baking sheets are true workhorses, used for obvious tasks like baking cookies or roasting root vegetables as well as for baking chicken or fish, toasting nuts, and baking jelly roll cakes. Slipping a wire rack inside makes these pans even more versatile—it's our go-to setup for roasting and broiling meats, holding breaded foods before and after frying, and drizzling chocolate over desserts. To find the best rimmed baking sheet on the market, we selected eight standard-size models and fired up our ovens. We examined how evenly foods browned across the surface of the pan and how cleanly they released all while keeping an eye on warping and how comfortable each pan felt when loaded with heavy foods. Luckily, all of our pans fared well with baking, roasting, and broiling, but some pans made it harder to achieve good results. From irregularly sized cooking surfaces to too-low sides that made for dangerous spills, they weren't all perfect. Tests taught us that we prefer models with straight, smooth sides of 1 inch or more. In our preheating tests, every pan warped at least a little, but only one pan's warping impeded its cooking. In the end, we were able to recommend nearly all of the baking sheets we tested. Most were good for both baking and roasting and cooked food uniformly. The two that jumped ahead of the pack had perfectly sized cooking surfaces and straight, tall sides that contained food and offered a good grip. Products are listed in order of preference.

HIGHLY RECOMMENDED		PERFORMANCE	TESTERS' COMMENTS
NORDIC WARE Baker's Half Sheet **MODEL:** 43100 **PRICE:** $14.97 **COOKING SURFACE:** 16½ x 11½ in **MATERIAL:** Aluminum		BAKING ★★★ ROASTING ★★★ WARPING ★★½ HANDLING ★★★ RACK COMPATIBILITY ★★★	Everything prepared in this sturdy, warp-resistant sheet cooked appropriately and evenly. Best of all, our new favorite is a few bucks cheaper than our old winner.
VOLLRATH Wear-Ever Heavy Duty Sheet Pan (13 gauge) **MODEL:** 5314 **PRICE:** $20.99 **COOKING SURFACE:** 16½ x 11½ in **MATERIAL:** Aluminum alloy	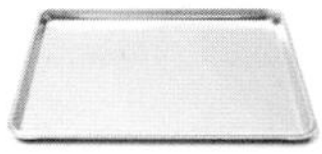	BAKING ★★★ ROASTING ★★★ WARPING ★★½ HANDLING ★★★ RACK COMPATIBILITY ★★★	Our old favorite performed flawlessly when baking cookies and cakes. It did warp slightly when roasting, but the food still came out well. It resisted scratching and snugly fit wire racks.
RECOMMENDED			
CHICAGO METALLIC Traditional Large Jelly Roll Pan **MODEL:** 49813 **PRICE:** $15.51 **COOKING SURFACE:** 16½ x 11½ in **MATERIAL:** Aluminized steel		BAKING ★★★ ROASTING ★★★ WARPING ★★ HANDLING ★★★ RACK COMPATIBILITY ★★★	This aluminum-coated steel sheet matched the performance of the all-aluminum pans. It didn't warp noticeably more than most other sheets, but it rested unevenly at the end of testing, making a popping noise when we pressed against it.
NORDIC WARE Prism Half Sheet Baking Pan **MODEL:** 43170 **PRICE:** $17.95 **COOKING SURFACE:** 16½ x 11½ in **MATERIAL:** Aluminum		BAKING ★★★ ROASTING ★★★ WARPING ★★ HANDLING ★★★ RACK COMPATIBILITY ★★★	This sheet has a ridged pattern on the cooking surface (ostensibly for increased strength and easy release) that left a houndstooth pattern on the undersides of the cake and parsnips. It held a wire cooling rack as snugly as our top models did.
NORPRO Heavy Gauge Aluminum Jelly Roll Pan **MODEL:** 3271 **PRICE:** $17.36 **COOKING SURFACE:** 16½ x 11½ in **MATERIAL:** Aluminum	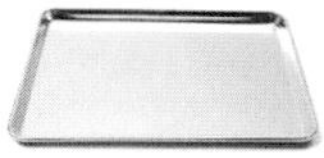	BAKING ★★★ ROASTING ★★★ WARPING ★★ HANDLING ★★★ RACK COMPATIBILITY ★★½	This sheet cooked and browned foods evenly in both baking and roasting tests. It was less warp-resistant than our favorites, especially when we roasted chicken thighs. A wire cooling rack fit fairly well and left behind minimal marks.
CHICAGO METALLIC StayFlat NSF Half-Size Sheet Pan **MODEL:** 30850 **PRICE:** $7.43 **COOKING SURFACE:** 16¾ x 11¾ in **MATERIAL:** Aluminum	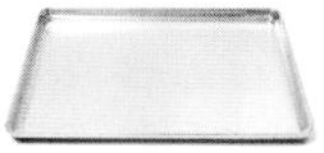	BAKING ★★★ ROASTING ★★★ WARPING ★★ HANDLING ★★★ RACK COMPATIBILITY ★★	This bargain-priced sheet felt exceptionally strong and sturdy. It did twist slightly in our chicken thigh test. The sides have a unique ridged shape that imprinted on the edges of the cake, but most testers didn't mind.
ISLAND WARE Baker's Half Sheet Pan **MODEL:** Half Sheet Pan **PRICE:** $20.99 **COOKING SURFACE:** 15¾ x 11½ in **MATERIAL:** Aluminum		BAKING ★★★ ROASTING ★★½ WARPING ★½ HANDLING ★½ RACK COMPATIBILITY ★★★	Although this sheet cooked parsnips, chicken, and cookies well, it warped awkwardly, and its low, flared sides gave us pause. Chicken fat almost spilled out of it, and our cake had odd beveled edges.
NOT RECOMMENDED			
FAT DADDIO'S ProSeries Jelly Roll Pan **MODEL:** JRP-12181 **PRICE:** $23.69 **COOKING SURFACE:** 18 x 12 in **MATERIAL:** Aluminum		BAKING ★★ ROASTING ★½ WARPING ★ HANDLING ★★ RACK COMPATIBILITY ★	This sheet was the longest in our lineup; it made a jelly roll cake that was too thin, and a wire rack slid around. It browned foods almost too well, and we had to watch them carefully so they didn't burn. It warped dramatically.

MUFFIN PANS

Gold-colored pans have dominated our recent bakeware testings, beating out darker and lighter pans in each category by turning out perfectly browned baked goods. We wondered if the trend would continue with muffin pans, so we gathered 12-cup models in a range of finishes and evaluated each on durability, release, handling, and browning. In general, lighter pans produced lighter-colored baked goods and darker pans made darker-colored baked goods. The gold pans produced muffins with just the right amount of browning, sporting crusts that were browned and flavorful but still tender. Pan color also affected the shape of the baked goods. Dark pans conduct heat faster, so the sides of baked goods set faster, leaving the rest of the batter to rise upwards, sometimes into oddly conical or bulbous shapes. Lighter and medium-colored pans made more consistent, appealingly shaped baked goods thanks to a slower, more controlled rise. The shape of the pans was also important. We only included pans that had some sort of handle or extended rim, because without a spot to grab, maneuvering a hot muffin tin proved challenging. Pans with handles seemed promising, but the handles were mostly too small—we repeatedly dented muffins with our oven mitts. Oversized rims were a much better option. The pan with the biggest rim was downright luxurious to move around and it had a gold nonstick finish that made perfectly browned baked goods. Products are listed in order of preference.

HIGHLY RECOMMENDED

OXO Good Grips Non-Stick 12-Cup Muffin Pan
MODEL: 11160500
PRICE: $24.99
FINISH: Gold

PERFORMANCE
RELEASE ★★★
BROWNING ★★★
FOOD SHAPE ★★★
HANDLING ★★★

TESTERS' COMMENTS
This pan perfectly released baked goods and was a dream to hold and turn. It has an oversized rim running all the way around it, so there was always a secure place to grasp. Its gold finish created the most appealing baked goods: evenly, lightly browned and elegantly shaped.

RECOMMENDED

WILLIAMS-SONOMA Goldtouch Nonstick Muffin Pan, 12-Well
MODEL: 13-1984111
PRICE: $29.95
FINISH: Gold

RELEASE ★★★
BROWNING ★★½
FOOD SHAPE ★★½
HANDLING ★★½

This pan released baked goods flawlessly. Its rim had a nice rolled edge but it wasn't as broad as our winner's. Its gold finish produced mostly even browning, though muffins in the exterior cups tended to darken faster than center ones.

ANOLON Advanced Bronze Bakeware 12-Cup Muffin Pan
MODEL: 57036
PRICE: $19.94
FINISH: Bronze

RELEASE ★★★
BROWNING ★★★
FOOD SHAPE ★★½
HANDLING ★★

The ridge around this pan's rim made it hard to hold; it dug into our hands if we didn't hold it right. It did have small silicone handles that worked fairly well, but we had to be a bit more precise about where we gripped. Baked goods released perfectly and were mostly consistent.

RECOMMENDED WITH RESERVATIONS

WILTON Professional Results Non-Stick 12-Cup Muffin Pan
MODEL: 2105-2245
PRICE: $13.59
FINISH: Dark

RELEASE ★★★
BROWNING ★★
FOOD SHAPE ★★½
HANDLING ★★

The dark finish on this pan made for slightly conical muffins but its baked goods were acceptable, if slightly inconsistent in color. Its indented handles worked well, but it didn't have anywhere on the sides or corners to grab to rotate the pan, so we had to reach well into the oven every time.

NOT RECOMMENDED

FARBERWARE BAKEWARE 12-Cup Muffin Pan
MODEL: 52106
PRICE: $10.30
FINISH: Medium

RELEASE ★★★
BROWNING ★½
FOOD SHAPE ★★
HANDLING ★★

This gray pan released its contents well but baked them unevenly from muffin to muffin in the same tray: While cupcakes trended pale, muffins trended dark. Its narrow rim didn't leave room to rotate it easily, and its rim was too small.

ANOLON Advanced Bakeware 12-Cup Muffin Pan
MODEL: 54710, gray
PRICE: $26.99
FINISH: Dark

RELEASE ★★★
BROWNING ★½
FOOD SHAPE ★★
HANDLING ★★

Baked goods made in this pan released well but were overbrowned. Its darker finish made the sides set faster, creating slightly conical muffins and bubble-headed cupcakes. While it had sufficient silicone handles, its rim was neither comfortable nor secure to maneuver.

CIRCULON Nonstick Bakeware 12-Cup Muffin Pan
MODEL: 51137, gray
PRICE: $14.98
FINISH: Dark

RELEASE ★★★
BROWNING ★½
FOOD SHAPE ★★
HANDLING ★★

This pan released baked goods well but they were a bit too dark; its darker finish is likely to blame. It also had very small handles and our oven mitts squished into the muffins. Its narrow side rims forced us to reach into the oven to rotate.

SERRATED KNIVES

If slicing bread feels like sawing through lumber, it's probably your knife's fault. When we put nine 10-inch knives through a series of tests to find one capable of handling all our usual tasks, we were shocked by how bad some of the knives were. The point of using a serrated blade instead of a straight-edge blade is the former's ability to bite into foods, slicing with less friction for a clean cut. Much to our dismay, we witnessed brand-new blades making a royal mess of tender yellow cakes, loaves of rustic bread, towering BLT sandwiches, and ripe tomatoes. When we took a closer look, we noticed that knives with rounded serrations struggled while those with the classic serration style of pointed tips were much more successful. The best knives had broad, deep, pointed serrations and fewer of them. When a user pushes down on a serrated knife, the force exerted is divided among the serrations, so the fewer the serrations, the more power each serration gets. Likewise, deeper serrations with pointier tips were better at biting into food than rounded or shallow serrations. And when it came to blade width, we found that narrower blades excelled while those sharpened to 20 degrees or more felt dull. The knives' handles also affected their rankings: Testers felt more secure using knives with grippy handles. Products are listed in order of preference.

HIGHLY RECOMMENDED	PERFORMANCE		TESTERS' COMMENTS
MERCER Culinary Millennia **10" Wide Bread Knife** MODEL: M23210 PRICE: $22.10 BLADE ANGLE: 16° NUMBER OF SERRATIONS: 29 AVERAGE SERRATION WIDTH: 7.73 mm AVERAGE SERRATION DEPTH: 1.81 mm	CUTTING COMFORT EDGE RETENTION	★★★ ★★★ ★★★	With the fewest, widest, and deepest serrations, this knife was a "standout." Its sharp points bit into everything from the crustiest bread to the squishiest tomato, producing crisp, clean slices. "Perfect, no crumbs, really easy," said one tester. A stellar blade coupled with a grippy, comfortable handle earned this knife the top spot.
RECOMMENDED			
MIYABI Kaizen 9.5" Bread Knife MODEL: 34186-233 PRICE: $169.99 BLADE ANGLE: 9.5 to 12° NUMBER OF SERRATIONS: 33 AVERAGE SERRATION WIDTH: 6.67 mm AVERAGE SERRATION DEPTH: 0.99 mm	CUTTING COMFORT EDGE RETENTION	★★½ ★★½ ★★★	This blade was supersharp, with broad serrations that showed only the slightest bit of hesitation on crusty loaves. It was perfectly balanced, and testers liked that the handle allowed for multiple comfortable grip options; a few complained that its straight, smooth design didn't feel as secure.
WÜSTHOF Classic 10-Inch **Serrated Bread Knife** MODEL: 4151-7 PRICE: $123.00 BLADE ANGLE: 14° NUMBER OF SERRATIONS: 36 AVERAGE SERRATION WIDTH: 6.15 mm AVERAGE SERRATION DEPTH: 1.24 mm	CUTTING COMFORT EDGE RETENTION	★★½ ★★½ ★★½	Our previous winner turned in an admirable performance. It was a shade less sharp than our top knives, but it still did well. A minority of testers complained about its handle's smooth, square sides, but most approved. Its edge showed minor damage after testing.
VICTORINOX Swiss Army Fibrox Pro 10¼" **Curved Bread Knife with Serrated Edge** MODEL: 40547 PRICE: $39.48 BLADE ANGLE: 18° NUMBER OF SERRATIONS: 41 AVERAGE SERRATION WIDTH: 5.86 mm AVERAGE SERRATION DEPTH: 1.15 mm	CUTTING COMFORT EDGE RETENTION	★★ ★★★ ★★	This knife, our former Best Buy, was reasonably sharp but had some trouble biting into crusty loaves. "It takes a little more elbow grease," said one tester. Others noted less bite and more bread "squish" over time. It had a great grippy, ergonomic handle.
DEXTER-RUSSELL 10" Sofgrip **Scalloped Bread Slicer** MODEL: SG147-10SC PRICE: $25.34 BLADE ANGLE: 20° NUMBER OF SERRATIONS: 56 AVERAGE SERRATION WIDTH: 4.05 mm AVERAGE SERRATION DEPTH: 1.22 mm	CUTTING COMFORT EDGE RETENTION	★★ ★★ ★★★	This lightweight knife did the trick but required "a bit more work" to get through crustier loaves. Some found its handle comfortable, but others felt that a protruding knob at the bottom blocked them from being able to choke up for more control. "I'm either too far back or too far forward," said one tester.
NOT RECOMMENDED			
MESSERMEISTER Four Season 10 Inch **Scalloped Baker's Bread Knife** MODEL: 5033-10 PRICE: $34.40 BLADE ANGLE: 20° NUMBER OF SERRATIONS: 36 AVERAGE SERRATION WIDTH: 6.60 mm AVERAGE SERRATION DEPTH: 0.99 mm	CUTTING COMFORT EDGE RETENTION	★½ ★½ ★★	This blade felt excessively dull, thanks to a wider edge and shallower serrations. "You really have to drive through," said one tester. Its handle was "really uncomfortable," partly because it was too thin and smooth and partly because the blade was so dull. This led one tester to remark, "I had to grip so hard I killed my hand on the top edge."

PARING KNIVES

A good paring knife is a small but mighty addition to any knife collection. We use this diminutive tool for tasks where control is paramount, like peeling or poking things without stabbing too widely or deeply. To find the best paring knife, we tested eight models, and while all the knives we tested were at least decent, our favorite came as a surprise. This knife looks cheap (and for under $10, it is): light and small with a plastic handle and none of the heft, snazzy looks, or authoritative air some of the other knives have. What separated this blade from the pack? The slight, no-frills plastic handle was comfortable and lightweight, important because paring knives are often used "in the air," off of a cutting board. We also liked its blade, which was not only sharp, but felt particularly smooth in use. All of the knives were sharp out of the box and only one knife had a notably dull, rounded tip, a nonstarter for this tool. Flexibility was paramount, allowing the blade to worm its way into tight spaces or conform to curves for cleaner cuts. Knives with stiffer blades were harder to turn, taking off more fruit with their peels. Products are listed in order of preference.

HIGHLY RECOMMENDED

VICTORINOX Swiss Army Fibrox Pro 3¼" Spear Point Paring Knife
MODEL: 47600 or 40600
PRICE: $9.47
WEIGHT: 17.52 grams
USABLE BLADE LENGTH: 3.25 inches

PERFORMANCE	
COMFORT	★★½
SHARPNESS	★★★
AGILITY	★★★

TESTERS' COMMENTS: This knife was "super adept;" its sharp, flexible blade nimbly hugged curves, so we could surgically remove peels or cores without plunging too deeply. It was the lightest knife we tested with a slim handle that felt like an extension of our hands.

RECOMMENDED

WÜSTHOF Classic 3½" Paring Knife
MODEL: 4066-7/09
PRICE: $39.99
WEIGHT: 61.98 grams
USABLE BLADE LENGTH: 3.25 inches

PERFORMANCE	
COMFORT	★★★
SHARPNESS	★★½
AGILITY	★★½

TESTERS' COMMENTS: This knife had a comfortable handle, but it felt less sharp and agile for certain tasks. For nuanced jobs, like sliding between the skin and flesh of fruit, its thick spine and rigid blade made it feel a bit "like a bulldozer."

ZWILLING J.A. HENCKELS Four Star 3" Paring Knife
MODEL: 31070-083
PRICE: $49.95
WEIGHT: 44.79 grams
USABLE BLADE LENGTH: 3 inches

PERFORMANCE	
COMFORT	★★½
SHARPNESS	★★★
AGILITY	★★½

TESTERS' COMMENTS: This "razor-sharp" little knife earned praise for its edge, which remained keen throughout testing. It was more rigid, so it was less adept at hugging curves and removed slightly fatter peels. It also had the shortest blade in our lineup, so testers struggled to cleanly quarter whole apples.

RECOMMENDED WITH RESERVATIONS

OXO Good Grips Pro 3.5" Paring Knife
MODEL: 11191100
PRICE: $11.46
WEIGHT: 69.25 grams
USABLE BLADE LENGTH: 3.5 inches

PERFORMANCE	
COMFORT	★★½
SHARPNESS	★★★
AGILITY	★★½

TESTERS' COMMENTS: This long, heavy knife crunched through apples with confidence and ease but felt "a little remote" on more delicate assignments. The weight also tired our hands eventually and it wasn't flexible, so it struggled on turns.

KITCHENAID Professional 3½" Paring Knife
MODEL: KFTR3PRWM
PRICE: $44.84
WEIGHT: 74.01 grams
USABLE BLADE LENGTH: 3.4 inches

PERFORMANCE	
COMFORT	★★½
SHARPNESS	★★★
AGILITY	★★

TESTERS' COMMENTS: This knife's blade was strong and sharp, so it made straight cuts extremely well. However, we felt its stiff, thick blade "trailing" around curves and its weight tired our hands after a while.

MERCER CULINARY Millennia 3" Slim Paring Knife
MODEL: M23900P
PRICE: $8.76
WEIGHT: 28.16 grams
USABLE BLADE LENGTH: 3.25 inches

PERFORMANCE	
COMFORT	★★½
SHARPNESS	★★
AGILITY	★★½

TESTERS' COMMENTS: This little knife looked just like our winner, but its edge didn't last. Its handle was also slightly bigger and some testers complained that it didn't sit as comfortably in their palms.

DEXTER RUSSELL Sani-Safe 3¼" Cooks Style Paring Knife
MODEL: 15303 S104
PRICE: $9.20
WEIGHT: 31.44 grams
USABLE BLADE LENGTH: 3.25 inches

PERFORMANCE	
COMFORT	★★½
SHARPNESS	★★★
AGILITY	★★½

TESTERS' COMMENTS: This looked like an oyster knife, and its tip wasn't very sharp, so it couldn't core strawberries as deftly as others. The rest of its blade was reasonably sharp but its fat white handle felt cumbersome for some.

SHUN SORA Paring Knife
MODEL: VB0700
PRICE: $31.95
WEIGHT: 58.36 grams
USABLE BLADE LENGTH: 3.5 inches

PERFORMANCE	
COMFORT	★★½
SHARPNESS	★★★
AGILITY	★★

TESTERS' COMMENTS: This long, skinny knife was very sharp but its handle was too long. Broad at the end and tapered as it approached the blade, it had a weird momentum, like our hands were always sliding towards the blade. It was on the heavier side, too.

DRY MEASURING CUPS

Success in baking starts with careful measuring, and dry measuring cups are often the most practical option. Our preferred measuring method for dry ingredients like flour and sugar is the "dip and sweep": We scoop a heaping cupful and then level it off with the back of a knife. With this in mind, we sought out models with handles flush with the rims of the cups for seamless sweeping. However, when we compared the swept cups' measurements to their weights, three sets were off by as much as 6 percent, sending them tumbling in the rankings. Among the more accurate sets, measurement markings proved important: Some sets' markings were large and well-placed on the handles while others had tiny or hidden markings. Markings printed in ink came off with very little scrubbing, so our preference was for etched-on markings. To test the cups' durability, we repeatedly scooped up wet, heavy sand to simulate years of hard use. Most plastic cups flexed with the motion and went right back into place, but a few smaller cups bent permanently. Many of the stainless-steel handles bent when we used great force; others bent immediately, with very gentle scooping. The most durable sets, including the winner, have shorter handles that are part of the cup mold (rather than riveted on) and didn't bend or flex at all. In the end our winner stood out for its durable stainless steel construction, accuracy, ease of use, and handles perfectly flush with the cup's rim. Products are listed in order of preference.

HIGHLY RECOMMENDED		PERFORMANCE		TESTERS' COMMENTS
OXO Good Grips Stainless Steel Measuring Cups MODEL: 11132000 PRICE: $19.99 NUMBER OF CUPS: 4 MATERIAL: Stainless Steel		ACCURACY DURABILITY EASE OF USE	★★★ ★★★ ★★½	Accurate and extremely durable, this set snaps together for compact storage. The handles are seamless with the cups themselves, making them easy to level off.
NORPRO Grip-EZ Set of 6 Measuring Cups MODEL: 3018 PRICE: $6.87 NUMBER OF CUPS: 6 MATERIAL: Plastic		ACCURACY DURABILITY EASE OF USE	★★★ ★★★ ★★	This set had a high degree of accuracy in every size, and it was the most durable plastic set we tested. Long handles flush with the rims aided scooping and sweeping.

RECOMMENDED				
OXO Good Grips 6-Piece Plastic Measuring Cups MODEL: 11110901 PRICE: $7.99 NUMBER OF CUPS: 6 MATERIAL: Plastic		ACCURACY DURABILITY EASE OF USE	★★★ ★★½ ★★	This accurate six-cup set's matte plastic finish gave the handles a good, tacky grip, but some testers found the handles too short. A few cups tipped over when empty.
NORPRO Grip-EZ Set of 5 Stainless Steel Measuring Cups MODEL: 3067 PRICE: $27.88 NUMBER OF CUPS: 5 MATERIAL: Stainless Steel		ACCURACY DURABILITY EASE OF USE	★★★ ★★ ★★½	This accurate, shovel-shaped set felt cup-heavy and unbalanced to some, but plastic tabs on the handles made them easy to hold. The handles bent a bit when we scooped wet sand.
AMCO Houseworks Professional Performance 4-Piece Measuring Cup Set MODEL: 864 PRICE: $15.99 NUMBER OF CUPS: 4 MATERIAL: Stainless Steel		ACCURACY DURABILITY EASE OF USE	★★½ ★★ ★★★	Our previous winner, still solid, was surpassed by sets that were slightly more accurate and more durable. The handles bent quickly when we scooped wet sand (but they easily bent back).
RSVP Endurance Measuring Cup Set MODEL: DMC-10 PRICE: $36.95 NUMBER OF CUPS: 7 MATERIAL: Stainless Steel		ACCURACY DURABILITY EASE OF USE	★★★ ★★ ★★	This set of seven cups was very accurate. But the handles bent immediately when the cups were dragged through wet sand, and the thin handles dug into some testers' hands.

RECOMMENDED WITH RESERVATIONS				
PREPWORKS by Progressive 6 Piece Measuring Cup Set MODEL: BA-3518 PRICE: $5.99 NUMBER OF CUPS: 6 MATERIAL: Plastic		ACCURACY DURABILITY EASE OF USE	★★★ ★★½ ★	The handles were slippery and too short for most testers, but this set was reasonably durable and very accurate. The handle on the smallest cup bent when scooping sand.
MIU France Stainless Steel Set of 7 Measuring Cups MODEL: 91688 PRICE: $37.28 NUMBER OF CUPS: 7 MATERIAL: Stainless Steel		ACCURACY DURABILITY EASE OF USE	★★★ ★★ ★	This accurate seven-cup set has long, uncomfortable, heavy handles that bent when scooping sand and made some cups tip over when empty.

SILICONE SPATULAS

Whether we're baking or cooking, scrambling or sautéing, flipping or folding, a heatproof silicone spatula is among our go-to tools. Nine years ago, we gave top honors to a model ubiquitous in restaurant kitchens, but it can feel unwieldy at home. So we rounded up 10 smaller spatulas from the dizzying array available and subjected each to a slew of evaluations. When it came to comfort, the best models felt like a natural extension of our hands, deftly scraping and thoroughly mixing. Others failed to reach into the edges of saucepans or left pockets of unmixed food. Some left streaks of batter on the sides of bowls. Upon closer inspection, we determined that models with small heads moved less food with each pass, so it took more work to mix cookie dough, but larger heads weren't necessarily better. While they did excel at folding, in general we found that midsize heads (roughly 4 by 2½ inches) were fast and effective at almost every task. The shape of the head proved hugely important, too. Models with sharply angled top edges lacked breadth, so we struggled to empty measuring cups and efficiently stir scrambled eggs. Those with handles inserted into the head were tricky to clean, often catching bits of food or trapping water. Thickness and rigidity also mattered: One chubby, stiff-headed model skidded over bowl sides, cut wide swaths through food, and threatened to deflate whipped cream and egg whites. The best options had a fairly straight top edge with one gently curved corner and textured silicone handles. Products are listed in order of preference.

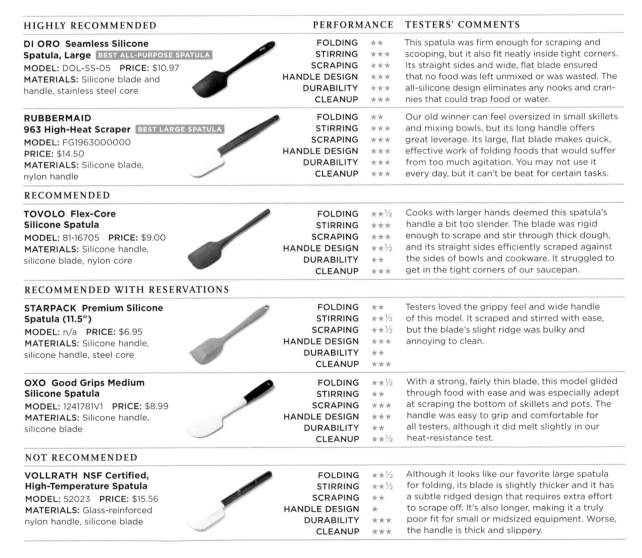

HIGHLY RECOMMENDED	PERFORMANCE		TESTERS' COMMENTS
DI ORO Seamless Silicone Spatula, Large `BEST ALL-PURPOSE SPATULA` MODEL: DOL-SS-05 PRICE: $10.97 MATERIALS: Silicone blade and handle, stainless steel core	FOLDING STIRRING SCRAPING HANDLE DESIGN DURABILITY CLEANUP	★★ ★★★ ★★★ ★★★ ★★★ ★★★	This spatula was firm enough for scraping and scooping, but it also fit neatly inside tight corners. Its straight sides and wide, flat blade ensured that no food was left unmixed or was wasted. The all-silicone design eliminates any nooks and crannies that could trap food or water.
RUBBERMAID 963 High-Heat Scraper `BEST LARGE SPATULA` MODEL: FG1963000000 PRICE: $14.50 MATERIALS: Silicone blade, nylon handle	FOLDING STIRRING SCRAPING HANDLE DESIGN DURABILITY CLEANUP	★★ ★★★ ★★★ ★★★ ★★★ ★★★	Our old winner can feel oversized in small skillets and mixing bowls, but its long handle offers great leverage. Its large, flat blade makes quick, effective work of folding foods that would suffer from too much agitation. You may not use it every day, but it can't be beat for certain tasks.

RECOMMENDED			
TOVOLO Flex-Core Silicone Spatula MODEL: 81-16705 PRICE: $9.00 MATERIALS: Silicone handle, silicone blade, nylon core	FOLDING STIRRING SCRAPING HANDLE DESIGN DURABILITY CLEANUP	★★½ ★★★ ★★★ ★★½ ★★ ★★★	Cooks with larger hands deemed this spatula's handle a bit too slender. The blade was rigid enough to scrape and stir through thick dough, and its straight sides efficiently scraped against the sides of bowls and cookware. It struggled to get in the tight corners of our saucepan.

RECOMMENDED WITH RESERVATIONS			
STARPACK Premium Silicone Spatula (11.5") MODEL: n/a PRICE: $6.95 MATERIALS: Silicone handle, silicone handle, steel core	FOLDING STIRRING SCRAPING HANDLE DESIGN DURABILITY CLEANUP	★★ ★★½ ★★½ ★★★ ★★ ★★★	Testers loved the grippy feel and wide handle of this model. It scraped and stirred with ease, but the blade's slight ridge was bulky and annoying to clean.
OXO Good Grips Medium Silicone Spatula MODEL: 1241781V1 PRICE: $8.99 MATERIALS: Silicone handle, silicone blade	FOLDING STIRRING SCRAPING HANDLE DESIGN DURABILITY CLEANUP	★★½ ★★ ★★★ ★★★ ★★ ★★½	With a strong, fairly thin blade, this model glided through food with ease and was especially adept at scraping the bottom of skillets and pots. The handle was easy to grip and comfortable for all testers, although it did melt slightly in our heat-resistance test.

NOT RECOMMENDED			
VOLLRATH NSF Certified, High-Temperature Spatula MODEL: 52023 PRICE: $15.56 MATERIALS: Glass-reinforced nylon handle, silicone blade	FOLDING STIRRING SCRAPING HANDLE DESIGN DURABILITY CLEANUP	★★½ ★★½ ★★ ★ ★★★ ★★★	Although it looks like our favorite large spatula for folding, its blade is slightly thicker and it has a subtle ridged design that requires extra effort to scrape off. It's also longer, making it a truly poor fit for small or midsized equipment. Worse, the handle is thick and slippery.

IMMERSION BLENDERS

Immersion blenders are great for pureeing and small blending jobs such as making mayonnaise, salad dressing, or whipped cream. These handheld blenders' wand shape ends in an umbrella-like hood that covers the blade, protecting the user and circulating the food for even, efficient blending. We brought a handful of models into the kitchen, and off the bat the weak contenders made themselves known: One blender's chopping wand fell off miduse and another model's wand didn't detach, making it challenging to clean. Some models offer flashy features such as "turbo" buttons and up to 15 blending speeds. To better understand how blade speed correlates with performance, we used a tachometer to measure the blade speed of each model at various settings. Unfortunately for these fully loaded models, our measurements of blade speed showed that faster blades don't necessarily make for better blending. The 15-speed Breville sounded impressive, but we found that speeds one to 13 varied very little, and it wasn't until speeds 14 and 15 that we started to see some differences. We concluded that two speeds were plenty: one low and one high, ranging between 10,000 RPM on the low end and 14,000 RPM on the high end. Some brands touted high wattage (a measure of how much electricity a motor draws), but more watts didn't equal better blending. What did make a difference? Blade, guard, and wand design. Sharp blades with guards designed to maximize food movement into the path of the blades were very important. Shorter, lighter blenders cloaked in grippy rubber were the easiest to hold and move. We preferred buttons over dials because buttons right on the grip let us hop back and forth between speeds with one hand and less fuss. Regarding accessories, we liked whisks and blending cups, which minimize splatter; we found anything else extraneous. Our winner is comfortable, secure, easy to use, and has two well-calibrated speeds. Products are listed in order of preference.

HIGHLY RECOMMENDED

BRAUN Multiquick 5
MODEL: MQ505   PRICE: $59.99
DETACHABLE WAND: Yes   SPEEDS: 2
ACCESSORIES: Whisk, blending cup

PERFORMANCE		TESTERS' COMMENTS
BLENDING	★★½	This blender's two speeds were well calibrated and all we needed to bounce from task to task with ease. It was easy to maneuver, light and slim with a grippy body.
COMFORT	★★★	
HANDLING	★★★	
SPLATTER	★★★	
DURABILITY	★★★	

RECOMMENDED

KITCHENAID 3-Speed Hand Blender
MODEL: KHB2351OB   PRICE: $59.99
DETACHABLE WAND: Yes   SPEEDS: 3
ACCESSORIES: Whisk, blending cup, chopper attachment, carrying bag

PERFORMANCE		TESTERS' COMMENTS
BLENDING	★★½	This model is a decent choice but was a bit slower and slightly more complicated to use than our favorite, thanks to a speed dial that required two hands. But it made good food, and testers liked its secure rubber grip and maneuverable body.
COMFORT	★★★	
HANDLING	★★½	
SPLATTER	★★★	
DURABILITY	★★★	

RECOMMENDED WITH RESERVATIONS

BREVILLE The Control Grip
MODEL: BSB510XL   PRICE: $99.99
DETACHABLE WAND: Yes   SPEEDS: 15
ACCESSORIES: Whisk, blending cup, chopping bowl

PERFORMANCE		TESTERS' COMMENTS
BLENDING	★★★	This big blender pureed very well. It had a trigger grip that was tiring after a while, but what really gave us pause was its 15-speed control dial that required two hands. The first 13 speeds were superfluous; only 14 and 15 got us somewhere.
COMFORT	★★½	
HANDLING	★★½	
SPLATTER	★★★	
DURABILITY	★★½	

ELECTROLUX Expressionist Immersion Blender
MODEL: ELHB08B8PS   PRICE: $99.99
DETACHABLE WAND: Yes   SPEEDS: 2
ACCESSORIES: Whisk, blending cup, chopping bowl, storage lid

PERFORMANCE		TESTERS' COMMENTS
BLENDING	★★	This blender was slim and easy to grab, but its smooth plastic body was heavy and slippery, and the hard plastic surrounding its buttons dug into our fingers. It was powerful and had well-calibrated speeds, but its guard hindered emulsification.
COMFORT	★★	
HANDLING	★★★	
SPLATTER	★★★	
DURABILITY	★★★	

DUALIT Kitchen Essentials Immersion Hand Blender with Accessories Kit
MODEL: 88880   PRICE: $129.99
DETACHABLE WAND: Yes
SPEEDS: 3, plus turbo button
ACCESSORIES: Whisk, blending cup, chopping bowl

PERFORMANCE		TESTERS' COMMENTS
BLENDING	★★★	This chrome blender was excellent at pureeing and its six-pronged blade zoomed through food. But it was bulky, slick, and had confusing controls: In addition to a nonessential turbo button, the speeds on its dial weren't labeled, so we had to figure out the setting by touch before every use.
COMFORT	★★	
HANDLING	★★	
SPLATTER	★★★	
DURABILITY	★★★	

NOT RECOMMENDED

KALORIK Combination Mixer with Mixing Cup/Chopper and Whisk
MODEL: CMM 39732 W   PRICE: $49.99
DETACHABLE WAND: Yes   SPEEDS: 2
ACCESSORIES: Whisk, chopping bowl

PERFORMANCE		TESTERS' COMMENTS
BLENDING	★½	This fat blender spread our hands too wide, and the casing around its button hurt our fingers. It did well with smooth things such as cream and mayonnaise, but when we added nuts, leafy greens, or fruit, it left whole pieces unblended.
COMFORT	★½	
HANDLING	★★★	
SPLATTER	★★★	
DURABILITY	★★½	

DIGITAL SCALES

A digital scale is a kitchen game changer, essential to accurately measure dry ingredients or portion out food by weight. Our longtime favorite costs nearly $50, so we tested out new (and less expensive) models for accuracy with an eye to design, stability, and ease of cleaning. The good news: All of the scales were acceptably accurate. Unfortunately, some the scales were either so unintuitive to operate or so hard to read that we can't recommend them. When it came to screen visibility, only the OXO truly excelled: Unlike the competition, its display bar can be pulled out 4 inches from the platform, ensuring that the screen is visible under even the biggest, bulkiest items. Lightweight scales with feet frequently teetered back and forth or slid around on the counter, while squat scales with smooth bottoms stayed put more reliably. To test each scale's ease of cleanup, we let mustard, tomato paste, and oil stains sit for 36 hours before washing them by hand. Scales with removable platforms for easy scrubbing won us over, while those models that trapped water and food residue fell to the bottom of the pack. By the end of testing, we'd found three scales that impressed us with accuracy; intuitive design; responsive, clearly labeled buttons positioned on an easily visible control panel; and slim frames that were easy to slip into a drawer or cabinet. Our original winner is still your best bet, but its runners up will not let you down. Products are listed in order of preference.

HIGHLY RECOMMENDED	PERFORMANCE		TESTERS' COMMENTS
OXO Good Grips 11 lb Food Scale with Pull Out Display MODEL: 1130800 PRICE: $49.95 MAXIMUM WEIGHT: 11 lb UNITS: Pounds/ounces, kilograms/grams	ACCURACY EASE OF USE LEGIBILITY DURABILITY CLEANUP	★★★ ★★★ ★★★ ★★★ ★★★	This scale has it all: consistent accuracy; a clear display that pulls out from the frame; clearly labeled, accessible buttons; a removable platform; and a sturdy, slim body that stores easily. It's a pricier package but worth the investment.
POLDER Easy Read Digital Kitchen Scale MODEL: KSC-310-28 PRICE: $27.98 MAXIMUM WEIGHT: 11 lb UNITS: Pounds/ounces, kilograms/grams	ACCURACY EASE OF USE LEGIBILITY DURABILITY CLEANUP	★★★ ★★★ ★★★ ★★★ ★★½	Like the OXO, this model is accurate, intuitive, and easy to read, thanks to its offset digital screen. Our only complaint is that the platform isn't removable, so we had to wash it slowly and carefully to avoid getting the interior mechanism wet.
OZERI Pronto Digital Multifunction Kitchen and Food Scale BEST BUY MODEL: ZK14 PRICE: $11.79 MAXIMUM WEIGHT: 11 lb UNITS: Ounces, pounds/ounces, grams	ACCURACY EASE OF USE LEGIBILITY DURABILITY CLEANUP	★★★ ★★½ ★★★ ★★★ ★★½	Though its frame feels flimsier than those of our top performers and it lacks a removable platform, this inexpensive scale is impressive. It's accurate and easy to use, with a bright screen that's visible even when weighing large items.
RECOMMENDED			
SALTER Aquatronic Glass Electronic Kitchen Scale MODEL: 3003BDSS PRICE: $36.23 MAXIMUM WEIGHT: 11 lb UNITS: Pounds/ounces, kilograms/grams	ACCURACY EASE OF USE LEGIBILITY DURABILITY CLEANUP	★★½ ★★★ ★★★ ★★ ★★½	Its accuracy consistently fluctuated a few grams—enough to set this scale apart from the top performers. Clearly marked buttons were easily accessible, and the display was crisp. Water became trapped under the glass platform.
RECOMMENDED WITH RESERVATIONS			
ESCALI Alimento Digital Scale MODEL: 136DK PRICE: $67.27 MAXIMUM WEIGHT: 13 lb UNITS: Ounces, pounds/ounces, grams	ACCURACY EASE OF USE LEGIBILITY DURABILITY CLEANUP	★★½ ★★★ ★½ ★★★ ★★★	The perks of this scale include spot-on accuracy, clearly marked buttons, a bright backlight, and a removable platform for easy cleanup. It's bulky but lightweight, making it a challenge to store and hold steady, and taller testers found the sharp angle of its screen difficult to read from above.
NOT RECOMMENDED			
ESCALI Arti Glass Kitchen Scale MODEL: 157 PRICE: $32.38 MAXIMUM WEIGHT: 15 lb UNITS: Ounces, pounds/ounces, grams	ACCURACY EASE OF USE LEGIBILITY DURABILITY CLEANUP	★★★ ★ ★★ ★★★ ★★★	Sleek, slim, and sturdy, this scale looks easy to use, but its buttons proved overly sensitive—we accidentally activated the power button while cleaning and the screen fluttered each time we touched the scale, so were often unsure if we were pressing the right buttons.
AMERICAN WEIGH EDGE-5K Digital Kitchen Scale MODEL: EDGE-5K PRICE: $18.34 MAXIMUM WEIGHT: 11 lb UNITS: Pounds/ounces, grams	ACCURACY EASE OF USE LEGIBILITY DURABILITY CLEANUP	★★★ ★ ★★ ★★★ ★★★	Poorly designed buttons are what brought down this accurate scale. Because they are set in the platform, they were hidden when we weighed in a large mixing bowl. What's more, the tare and on/off functions were combined into one obscurely labeled button that confused users.

SLOW COOKERS

Here in the test kitchen, we've been putting slow cookers through the wringer for years. Though new models are always popping up on the market, we always defer to those slow cookers that are intuitive to use, have clear glass lids (so we can keep an eye on the food's progress), and bring the food to a safe cooking temperature quickly. Most slow cookers (including our hands-down favorite) can be programmed to cook for a desired amount of time before switching to a "keep warm" setting, making them convenient for busy home cooks. Six-quart models with roomy, heavy stoneware crocks are expert at cooking gently and efficiently, producing tender, juicy (not overcooked) food. Our top pick is a real upgrade from old-school models in that its built-in internal sensor monitors and adjusts the cooking temperature automatically, ensuring uniform cooking. Products are listed in order of preference.

HIGHLY RECOMMENDED		PERFORMANCE		TESTERS' COMMENTS

KITCHENAID 6-Quart Slow Cooker with Solid Glass Lid
MODEL: KSC6223SS PRICE: $99.99
CROCK MATERIAL: Ceramic stoneware
CROCK AND LID DISHWASHER-SAFE?: Yes
FEATURES: 24-hour cooking time display; warm, low, medium, high settings; keeps warm for 4 hours after cooking

COOKING ★★★
EASE OF USE ★★★
CLEANUP ★★★

This model's straightforward control panel made it simple to set and monitor progress. The roomy crock cooked gently and evenly and never boiled, so food emerged tender and juicy. Its broad, grippy, protruding handles stayed cool. Thick insulation kept heat directed toward the crock, and a built-in internal sensor kept the temperature below boiling.

CUISINART 6-Quart 3-in-1 Cook Central
MODEL: MSC-600 PRICE: $148.71
CROCK MATERIAL: Nonstick aluminum
CROCK AND LID DISHWASHER-SAFE?: Yes
FEATURES: Low, high, simmer, and warm settings; brown/sauté and steam functions; metal rack for steaming; keeps warm for 24 hours after cooking

COOKING ★★★
EASE OF USE ★★½
CLEANUP ★★★

We loved the lightweight crock and stay-cool plastic handles. The crock sits directly over a built-in hot plate, so it ran a little hot and fast but it cooked evenly. Its brown/sauté function saves using a skillet, though it took longer and food steamed a little due to the crock's high sides. A great choice if you hate to lift heavy crocks.

RECOMMENDED

NINJA 3-in-1 Cooking System
MODEL: MC750 PRICE: $99.99
CROCK MATERIAL: Nonstick aluminum
CROCK AND LID DISHWASHER-SAFE?: Yes
FEATURES: Ability to brown and sauté in crock; low, high, buffet (warm) settings; keeps warm for 12 hours after cooking

COOKING ★★★
EASE OF USE ★★
CLEANUP ★★★

This model's thin, rectangular metal pot cooks fast but evenly. It has both a built-in hot plate and a belt-like heating element for different cooking functions. The cooker was easy to set, but its controls are a little complicated. Its bare metal handles got very hot, and its brown/sauté function is slower at browning food than the Cuisinart.

RECOMMENDED WITH RESERVATIONS

CROCK-POT 6-Quart Slow Cooker with Stovetop-Safe Cooking Pot
MODEL: SCCPVI600-S PRICE: $56.80
CROCK MATERIAL: Cast aluminum with ceramic nonstick coating (PTFE- and PFOA-free)
CROCK AND LID DISHWASHER-SAFE?: Yes
FEATURES: Warm, low, high settings; 20-hour countdown timer

COOKING ★★★
EASE OF USE ★★
CLEANUP ★★

The metal crock on this cooker gets very hot, so it runs slightly fast, though it cooked evenly. The crock can be used on the stovetop for browning and searing. Its metal handles became quite hot, the slick ceramic coating still felt greasy after hand-washing (frequent dishwashing is not recommended), and its lid slipped into the pot when jostled. Some found the controls confusing.

NOT RECOMMENDED

HAMILTON BEACH Stay or Go 6-Quart Programmable Slow Cooker
MODEL: 33467 PRICE: $39.99
CROCK MATERIAL: Ceramic stoneware
CROCK AND LID DISHWASHER-SAFE?: Yes
FEATURES: Lid latches down for travel with gasket to prevent leaks; warm, low, high settings

COOKING ★★★
EASE OF USE ★½
CLEANUP ★★

We liked the lid latch and spill-preventing rubber gasket, as well as the simple controls and low price. Food cooked acceptably, although its temperature climbed to boiling (or barely below) on both high and low. It lost major points because we couldn't set odd-numbered cooking times, and it didn't have a countdown timer.

CROCK-POT Smart Wifi-Enabled WeMo 6-Quart Slow Cooker
MODEL: SCCPWM600-V1 PRICE: $127.49
CROCK MATERIAL: Ceramic stoneware
CROCK AND LID DISHWASHER-SAFE?: Yes
FEATURES: Warm, low, high settings; can adjust settings using WeMo app

COOKING ★★
EASE OF USE ★½
CLEANUP ★★★

This cooker is slow. Its wattage is comparatively weak, and its housing contains insulation—good for preventing hot spots, but it made this cooker poky. Food was good, though pot roast didn't turn fully tender within our time frame. The wifi-enabled functioning was annoying, and the app left us guessing whether we'd inadvertently turned the pot off.

FIRE EXTINGUISHERS

It's wise to keep a fire extinguisher within easy reach of your stove, but it's hard to pick one out when you can't practice with them. To find out which model is up for the job, we bought eight home fire extinguishers and drove to a firefighter training facility to test them on cooking-related fires. Extinguishers with an "ABC" rating can tackle (A) cloth, wood, paper; (B) flammable liquids and gases such as grease and gasoline; and (C) electrical fires; "BC" extinguishers cover the latter two categories. For our testing, we tried both types, sticking with the smallest size since you want something most people can easily lift. We also tried two aerosol-style sprays; a fire-smothering blanket; and one "automatic" extinguishing system. After testing out each extinguisher's effectiveness on both grease and cloth fires, taking into account how intuitive it was to use and how quickly it put out the fires, we were disappointed that we had only one product we could wholeheartedly recommend. Our winner was fast and thorough, and its design was simple and obvious with a basic trigger and nozzle and easy-to-read pressure gauge. While it created a cloud of fumes (like many other models) and left residue that was hard to clean up, we can live with that. Products are listed in order of preference.

HIGHLY RECOMMENDED		PERFORMANCE		TESTERS' COMMENTS
KIDDE ABC Multipurpose Home Fire Extinguisher MODEL: FA110 PRICE: $25.99 TYPE: ABC GREASE FIRE: 2 seconds TOWEL FIRE: 2 seconds		EASE OF USE PERFORMANCE CLEANUP	★★★ ★★★ ★½	Fast and very effective, this extinguisher really works. The fire went out right away with its powerful spray on both the grease fire and the burning towel, but each time it left a big cloud of fumes, and greenish foam on the burner and pan that took some effort to wipe off.
RECOMMENDED WITH RESERVATIONS				
FIRST ALERT Tundra Fire Extinguishing Spray MODEL: AF400 PRICE: $23.88 TYPE: Aerosol spray GREASE FIRE: 2 seconds TOWEL FIRE: 3 seconds		EASE OF USE PERFORMANCE CLEANUP	★★★ ★★ ★★	This aerosol spray quickly put out the grease fire, but then we saw a flare-up after we thought it was out. The same happened with the burning towel. A small cloud of fumes went away quickly, and handling the lightweight canister is simple. Residue gunked up our stove.
AMREX 2.5 lb ABC Dry Chemical Fire Extinguisher MODEL: B417 PRICE: $41.13 TYPE: ABC GREASE FIRE: 2 seconds TOWEL FIRE: 5 seconds		EASE OF USE PERFORMANCE CLEANUP	★★★ ★★½ ★	It quickly and thoroughly put out the grease fire, but it also emitted a cloud of chemical fumes that really smelled. The powerful spray knocked the towel right off the stovetop. Residue stuck to the pan and burner and was difficult to wipe off.
FIREAWAY Fire Blanket MODEL: 3x3 Small PRICE: $30.00 TYPE: Blanket GREASE FIRE: 11 seconds TOWEL FIRE: 1 minute, 22 seconds		EASE OF USE PERFORMANCE CLEANUP	★½ ★★ ★★★	Smothering fires with a blanket is scary, but it works. You don't really know if it's out without lifting the blanket to check, which lets in air that can restart the fire. Cleanup was a snap: Nearly unscorched, the blanket was ready to use again.
NOT RECOMMENDED				
KIDDE RESSP Kitchen Fire Extinguisher MODEL: RESSP PRICE: $24.49 TYPE: BC GREASE FIRE: 26.36 seconds TOWEL FIRE: 13.45 seconds		EASE OF USE PERFORMANCE CLEANUP	★★ ★★ ★★	A brief struggle to figure out the trigger wasted some time, but once it was going, it was very effective on the grease fire and easy to control. It didn't work well on the towel, which reignited seconds after we thought it was out. We had to spray it three times to get the job done.
FIRST ALERT Kitchen Fire Extinguisher UL Rated 5-B:C MODEL: KFE2S5 PRICE: $24.49 TYPE: BC GREASE FIRE: 4 seconds TOWEL FIRE: 5 seconds		EASE OF USE PERFORMANCE CLEANUP	★½ ★ ★★★	Though its cap slowed us down, it was fast, with a well-controlled spray, and didn't leave a cloud of fumes. However, when we grabbed a fresh copy of this model, it would not spray. The brand-new extinguisher had lost pressure and was useless—a fatal flaw.
STOVETOP FIRESTOP Rangehood MODEL: 679-3D PRICE: $56.95 for two canisters (need both over a stove) TYPE: Automatic GREASE FIRE: N/A TOWEL FIRE: N/A		EASE OF USE PERFORMANCE CLEANUP	★★ N/A ★	Even set 27 inches above a grease fire (closer than the lowest distance recommended), this product did not activate. We only heard a pop after 3 minutes 15 inches above the flames. The dish towel test was also a fail.

CONVERSIONS & EQUIVALENTS

Some say cooking is a science and an art. We would say that geography has a hand in it, too. Flour milled in the United Kingdom and elsewhere will feel and taste different from flour milled in the United States. So, while we cannot promise that the loaf of bread you bake in Canada or England will taste the same as a loaf baked in the States, we can offer guidelines for converting weights and measures. We also recommend that you rely on your instincts when making our recipes. Refer to the visual cues provided. If the bread dough hasn't "come together in a ball," as described, you may need to add more flour—even if the recipe doesn't tell you so. You be the judge.

The recipes in this book were developed using standard U.S. measures following U.S. government guidelines. The charts below offer equivalents for U.S., metric, and imperial (U.K.) measures. All conversions are approximate and have been rounded up or down to the nearest whole number. For example:

1 teaspoon = 4.929 milliliters, rounded up to 5 milliliters
1 ounce = 28.349 grams, rounded down to 28 grams

VOLUME CONVERSIONS

U.S.	METRIC
1 teaspoon	5 milliliters
2 teaspoons	10 milliliters
1 tablespoon	15 milliliters
2 tablespoons	30 milliliters
¼ cup	59 milliliters
⅓ cup	79 milliliters
½ cup	118 milliliters
¾ cup	177 milliliters
1 cup	237 milliliters
1¼ cups	296 milliliters
1½ cups	355 milliliters
2 cups	473 milliliters
2½ cups	591 milliliters
3 cups	710 milliliters
4 cups (1 quart)	0.946 liter
1.06 quarts	1 liter
4 quarts (1 gallon)	3.8 liters

WEIGHT CONVERSIONS

OUNCES	GRAMS
½	14
¾	21
1	28
1½	43
2	57
2½	71
3	85
3½	99
4	113
4½	128
5	142
6	170
7	198
8	227
9	255
10	283
12	340
16 (1 pound)	454

CONVERSIONS FOR INGREDIENTS COMMONLY USED IN BAKING

Baking is an exacting science. Because measuring by weight is far more accurate than measuring by volume, and thus more likely to achieve reliable results, in our recipes we provide ounce measures in addition to cup measures for many ingredients. Refer to the chart below to convert these measures into grams.

INGREDIENT	OUNCES	GRAMS
Flour		
1 cup all-purpose flour*	5	142
1 cup cake flour	4	113
1 cup whole-wheat flour	5½	156
Sugar		
1 cup granulated (white) sugar	7	198
1 cup packed brown sugar (light or dark)	7	198
1 cup confectioners' sugar	4	113
Cocoa Powder		
1 cup cocoa powder	3	85
Butter†		
4 tablespoons (½ stick, or ¼ cup)	2	57
8 tablespoons (1 stick, or ½ cup)	4	113
16 tablespoons (2 sticks, or 1 cup)	8	227

* U.S. all-purpose flour, the most frequently used flour in this book, does not contain leaveners, as some European flours do. These leavened flours are called self-rising or self-raising. If you are using self-rising flour, take this into consideration before adding leavening to a recipe.

† In the United States, butter is sold both salted and unsalted. We generally recommend unsalted butter. If you are using salted butter, take this into consideration before adding salt to a recipe.

OVEN TEMPERATURES

FAHRENHEIT	CELSIUS	GAS MARK (imperial)
225	105	¼
250	120	½
275	135	1
300	150	2
325	165	3
350	180	4
375	190	5
400	200	6
425	220	7
450	230	8
475	245	9

CONVERTING TEMPERATURES FROM AN INSTANT-READ THERMOMETER

We include doneness temperatures in many of our recipes, such as those for poultry, meat, and bread. We recommend an instant-read thermometer for the job. Refer to the table above to convert Fahrenheit degrees to Celsius. Or, for temperatures not represented in the chart, use this simple formula:

Subtract 32 degrees from the Fahrenheit reading, then divide the result by 1.8 to find the Celsius reading.

EXAMPLE:

"Roast chicken until thighs register 175 degrees." To convert:

175° F − 32 = 143°
143° ÷ 1.8 = 79.44°C, rounded down to 79°C

INDEX

Note: Page references in *italics* indicate photographs.

M

Main dishes

Arroz con Pollo (Rice with Chicken), 157–60, *158*

Asian-Style Turkey Meatballs, 172

Beef Tenderloin with Smoky Potatoes and Persillade Relish, 130–31

Boneless Rib Roast with Yorkshire Pudding and Jus, 131–34, *133*

Cheese and Tomato Lasagna, 91–94, *93*

Chicken Mole Poblano, 162–65, *163*

Classic Chicken Curry, *44*, 45–46

Cod in Saffron Broth with Chorizo and Potatoes, 176–78, *177*

Crispy Skillet Turkey Burgers, 103

Crumb-Crusted Pork Tenderloin, *140*, 141–42

Double-Crust Chicken Pot Pie, 112–14

Easier Roast Turkey and Gravy, 173–76

Eastern North Carolina Fish Stew, 41–42, *43*

Everyday Pad Thai, *88*, 89–91

Farro Bowls with Tofu, Mushrooms, and Spinach, 107–9

Fettuccine with Butter and Cheese, 82–83

Grilled Boneless Short Ribs with Argentine-Style Pepper Sauce, 125–27, *126*

Grilled Citrus Chicken, 152–54, *153*

Grilled Frozen Steaks, 123–24

Grilled Frozen Steaks with Arugula and Parmesan, 124

Grilled Pizza, 94–99, *96*

Grilled Spice-Rubbed Chicken Drumsticks, 165–68, *166*

Hawaiian-Style Fried Chicken, 156–57

Italian-Style Turkey Meatballs, 169–70, *171*

Meatballs and Marinara, 120–22, *121*

Moroccan-Style Turkey Meatballs, 172–73

One-Pan Mediterranean Shrimp, 179

Paella on the Grill, *180*, 181–83

Panang Beef Curry, 46–49, *48*

Pan-Seared Thick-Cut Boneless Pork Chops, 136–39, *137*

Pasta with Sausage Ragu, 83–84

Pomegranate-Braised Beef Short Ribs with Prunes and Sesame, 128–29

Porchetta, 146–49, *147*

Pub-Style Steak and Ale Pie, 114–17, *115*

Rack of Pork with Potatoes and Asparagus, 144–46

Main dishes *(cont.)*

Skillet Spanakopita, 109–12, *110*

Smoked Pork Loin with Dried-Fruit Chutney, 142–44

Southern-Style Smothered Pork Chops, 135–36

Sticky Chicken, 160–62

Stovetop-Roasted Chicken

with Lemon-Caper Sauce, 155

with Lemon-Cornichon Sauce, 155

with Lemon-Herb Sauce, 154–55

with Lemon–Sun-Dried Tomato Sauce, 155

Transylvania Goulash, 39–41, *40*

Turkish Pide, 99–102, *100*

Weeknight Tagliatelle with Bolognese Sauce, 84–87, *85*

Maple-Glazed Pecan Scones, Vegan, 201

Marinara Sauce, 120–22, *121*

Measuring cups, dry, ratings of, 296

Meat

doneness temperatures, 266

taking temperature of, 266

see also Beef; Pork

Meatballs

and Marinara, 120–22, *121*

Turkey, Asian-Style, 172

Turkey, Italian-Style, 169–70, *171*

Turkey, Moroccan-Style, 172–73

Mexican-Style Pickled Vegetables (Escabeche), 107

Microwaves, cleaning, 277

Millionaire's Shortbread, 226–29, *227*

Mint

Grapefruit-Avocado Salad, 54

Kohlrabi, Radicchio, and Apple Slaw, 57

Persillade, 139

Skillet Spanakopita, 109–12, *110*

Miso-Ginger Sauce, 109

Modern Cauliflower Gratin, 66–70, *68*

Mole Poblano, Chicken, 162–65, *163*

Moroccan-Style Turkey Meatballs, 172–73

Mozzarella

block, taste tests on, 284

Grilled Pizza, 94–99, *96*

Sticks, 9–10

Muffin pans, ratings of, 293